The Cumulated Indexes to the Public Papers of the Presidents of the United States

JOHN F. KENNEDY
1961 — 1963

kto press

A U.S. Division of Kraus-Thomson Organization Ltd.
Millwood, New York
1977

First Printing
Printed in the United States of America

Library of Congress Cataloging in Publication Data
Main entry under title:

The Cumulated indexes to the public papers of the Presidents of the United States, John F. Kennedy, 1961-1963.

1. United States—Politics and government—1961-1963—Addresses, essays, lectures—Indexes. I. KTO Press.
J82.D9 1977   016.973922   77-4328
ISBN 0-527-20752-7

PREFACE

The Cumulated Indexes to the Public Papers of the Presidents of the United States provide, for the first time, full access to the papers of each presidential administration published in the government series, the *Public Papers of the Presidents.* The *Public Papers* offer a unique and remarkable view of the American presidents and of American history. The character of a president, the individuals with whom a president interacts, the historical events that are shaped by a president and that, in turn, shape his presidency, are all to be found within the pages of the *Public Papers.*

A resolution passed by the United States Congress on July 17, 1894, provided that a compilation of "all the annual, special, and veto messages, proclamations, and inaugural addresses" of all the presidents from 1789 to 1894 be printed. The publication was to be prepared by James D. Richardson, a representative from Tennessee, under the direction of the Joint Committee on Printing, of which Richardson was a member. The official set was issued in two series of ten volumes each. A joint resolution of May 2, 1896, provided for the distribution of the set to members of Congress, with the remainder to be delivered to the compiler, James Richardson. An act passed about a year later provided that the plates for *A Compilation of the Messages and Papers of the Presidents* be delivered to Richardson "without cost to him." Representative Richardson then made arrangements for the commercial publication of the set. Several other compilations of presidential papers were commercially published in the first half of the nineteenth century; these usually contained only selected documents.

The Richardson edition of the *Messages and Papers,* however, was the only set authorized by Congress and published by the government until 1957, when the official publication of the public messages and statements of the presidents, the *Public Papers of the Presidents of the United States,* was initiated based on a recommendation made by the National Historical Publications Commission (now the National Historical Publications and Records Commission). The Commission

suggested that public presidential papers be compiled on a yearly basis and issued in a uniform, systematic publication similar to the *United States Supreme Court Reports* and the *Congressional Record*. An official series thus began in which presidential writings and statements of a public nature could be made promptly available. These presidential volumes are compiled by the Office of the Federal Register of the General Services Administration's National Archives and Record Service.

As might be expected, the "public papers" vary greatly in importance and content; some contain important policy statements while others are routine messages. They include, in chronological order, texts of such documents as the president's messages to Congress, public addresses, transcripts of news conferences and speeches, public letters, messages to heads of state, remarks to informal groups, etc. Executive orders, proclamations, and similar documents that are required by law to be published in the *Federal Register* and *Code of Federal Regulations* are not reprinted, but are listed by number and subject in an appendix in each volume.

The *Public Papers of the Presidents* are kept in print, and are available from the Superintendent of Documents, United States Government Printing Office. The *Papers* of each year are published in single volumes. with each volume containing an index for that calendar year. *The Cumulated Indexes to the Public Papers of the Presidents* combines and integrates the separate indexes for a president's administration into one alphabetical listing.

References to all of the volumes of a president's public papers can thus be found by consulting this one-volume cumulated index. *See* and *see also* references have been added and minor editorial changes have been made in the process of cumulating the separate indexes.

References in *The Cumulated Indexes to the Public Papers of the Presidents* are to item numbers. Individual volumes are identified in the *Index* by year, as are the actual volumes of the *Papers*. The year identifying the volume in which a paper is located appears in boldface type. When page references are used, they are clearly noted in the entry.

Other volumes in the set of *The Cumulated Indexes to the Public Papers of the Presidents* include Richard M. Nixon, 1969-1974; Lyndon B. Johnson, 1963-1969; Dwight D. Eisenhower, 1953-1961; and Harry S. Truman, 1945-1953. Forthcoming volumes will index the papers of Herbert C. Hoover and Gerald R. Ford, as well as those of future presidents when their administrations are completed.

KTO PRESS

JOHN F. KENNEDY: 1961-1963

Abboud, Ibrahim, **1961:** 108
  Visit of, **1961:** 402, 404, 411
Abdi Aden Mohamed, 1962: 523n.
Abdirascid Ali Scermarche (Prime Minister of
    Somali), **1962:** 551 [17]
  Visit of, **1962:** 522, 523, 526
Abdullahi Issa Mohamud, **1962:** 523n.
Abel, Col. Rudolf I., **1962:** 50 [1]
Abilene, Kans, **1962:** 546 [7]; **1963:** 207
Abrams, Manuel, **1961:** 123n.
Abu Simbel temples, preservation, **1961:** 108
Academy of Motion Picture Arts and Sciences,
    1962: 161n.
Academy of Sciences, National, **1963:** 144 [6], 252,
    430
Acapulco, Mexico, **1962:** 189
Accelerator,linear election, **1961:** 94
Accident, bread-cutting, the President's, **1963:**
    169 [16]
Accident prevention
  Coal mines, **1963:** 155
  Industrial, **1963:** 119
  Traffic, **1963:** 125
Accidents, traffic, **1961:** 58, 332; **1962:** 11, 93
    (p. 237)
Accra, Ghana, **1961:** 125n.
Acheson, Dean, **1961:** 480; **1962:** 234, 507; **1963:**
    160
  NATO advisory group, **1961:** 25 [2, 17]
  News conference remarks on, **1961:** 25 [2, 17],
    258 [5, 21]
Achilles, Theodore, **1961:** 318 [15]
Acoma Indians, **1962:** 340 [22]
Acreage allotments, 1962: 25
  Agricultural, **1963:** 202 [12]
Act of Bogota, **1961:** 11, 78, 81, 122, 208, 313, 510;
    1962: 86; **1963:** 163, 323
  News conference remarks, **1961:** 35 [2], 119 [20],
    171 [3]
Action Committee for United State of Europe,
    President (Jean Monnet), **1963:** 32

Ad Hoc Committee on Federal Office Space, re-
    port, **1962:** 221
Adair, Repr. E. Ross, **1962:** 75 [22]
Adams, Abigail, **1963:** 2, 245
Adams, Avery C., **1961:** 254n.
Adams, Charles Francis, **1961:** 397; **1963:** 239
Adams, Sir Grantley, **1961:** 36
Adams, John, **1961:** 162, 217, 397, 520; **1962:** 170,
    184, 252, 270, 274n., 349; **1963:** 2, 46, 192,
    226, 228, 279, 312, 322, 385
Adams, John Quincy, **1961:** 162, 212, 397, 418,
    448 [9]; **1962:** 178, 252, 352 [21], 399;
    1963: 2, 245
Adams, Dr. Raymond, **1961:** 14
Adams, Thomas Boylston, **1961:** 397; **1963:** 245
Adams family, **1961:** 397; **1963:** 2
*Adams Papers: Diary and Autobiography of John
    Adams,* publication, **1961:** 397
Adams Papers, review of, **1963:** 2
**Addis Ababa, Ethiopia, Conference of African
    States, 1961:** 188; **1963:** 200, 228, 260 [20],
    304, 394, 397
Addonizio, Hugh J., **1962:** 450
Addresses or remarks, Congressional election cam-
    paign.
  See Election campaign, Congressional, addresses
    or remarks.
Addresses or remarks on commemorative or
    dedicatory occasions
  Adenauer, Konrad, 86th birthday, **1962:** 2
  Aerospace Medical Health Center, dedication,
    1963: 472
  Air service, scheduled 50th anniversary, **1963:**
    464
  Alliance for Progress, first anniversary, **1962:** 86
  Alliance for Progress, second anniversary, **1963:**
    326
  American University, commencement, **1963:** 232
  Amherst College, **1963:** 439, 440
  Area Redevelopment Act, first anniversary,
    1962: 165
  Atlantic Charter, 20th anniversary, **1961:** 321

Addresses or remarks — *continued*
Bataan Day, **1962:** 131
Birthday salute to the President, **1962:** 201
Boston College centennial, **1963:** 136
Chamber of Commerce of the United States, 50th anniversary, **1962:** 162
Children's Bureau, 50th anniversary, **1962:** 132
China, 50th anniversary of Revolution, **1961:** 412
Coast Guard, 171st anniversary, **1961:** 311
Colombo Plan, 10th anniversary, **1961:** 266
Columbus Day, **1962:** 450; **1963:** 410
Committee for Economic Development, 20th anniversary, **1963:** 175
Delaware-Maryland Turnpike, dedication, **1963:** 461
Delta Sigma Theta sorority, 50th anniversary, **1963:** 10
DiSalle, Gov. Michael V., birthday dinner, **1962:** 3
Dulles International Airport, dedication, **1962:** 512
Earhart, Amelia, commemorative stamp, **1963:** 315
East Coast Memorial to Missing at Sea, dedication, **1963:** 203
Emancipation Proclamation, centennial, **1962:** 399; **1963:** 153
Fermi, Enrico, nuclear experiment, 20th anniversary, **1962:** 524
First State workmen's compensation law, 50th anniversary, **1961:** 339
First unemployment insurance payment 25th anniversary, **1961:** 323
Flaming Gorge Dam, dedication, **1963:** 386
Florida Chamber of Commerce, **1963:** 465
Foreign Affairs magazine, 40th anniversary, **1962:** 387
Fulbright exchange program 15th anniversary, **1961:** 307
Greers Ferry Dam, dedication, **1963:** 400
Hayden, Sen. Carl, 50th anniversary as Member of Congress, **1961:** 476
Inaugural, first anniversary, **1962:** 15
Inaugural, second anniversary, **1963:** 24
Independence Day address, **1962:** 278
Independence Day celebration, American colony, Mexico City, **1962:** 270
Indonesia, anniversary of independence, **1962:** 334
Inter-American Defense Board, 20th anniversary, **1962:** 117
Inter-Faith Chapel, U.S. Merchant Marine Academy, dedication, **1961:** 156
International Christian Leadership, Inc., dedication breakfast, **1961:** 26

Addresses or remarks — *continued*
International Joint Commission, U.S. and Canada, 50th anniversary, **1962:** 123
Italian unification, centennial, **1961:** 84
Labor Department, 50th anniversary dinner, **1963:** 85
Land-Grant Colleges and State Universities, Association of, centennial, **1961:** 462
Life magazine, 25th anniversary, **1961:** 64
Magnuson, Sen. Warren G., 25th anniversary as Member of Congress, **1961:** 474
Marshall plan, 15th anniversary, **1963:** 124
Massachusetts General Hospital, 150th anniversary, **1961:** 14
Mormon Tabernacle, Salt Lake City, **1963:** 385
National Academy of Sciences, anniversary convocation, **1963:** 430
National Wildlife Federation, dedication of new building, **1961:** 65
NATO Naval Headquarters at Norfolk, 10th anniversary, **1962:** 135
New Dockside Terminal, New Orleans, dedication, **1962:** 170
Nigeria, First anniversary of independence, **1961:** 394
Norris, George W., 100th birthday, **1961:** 278
Northern Great Lakes Region Land and People Conference, **1963:** 378
Oahe Dam, Pierre, S. Dak., dedication, **1962:** 335
O'Hare International Airport, dedication, **1963:** 109
Paderewski, Ignace Jan, dedication of grave marker, **1963:** 173
Penn Station South Urban Renewal Project, New York City, dedication, **1962:** 200
Pinchot Institute for Conservation Studies, **1963:** 376
Presidential prayer breakfast, **1963:** 52
President's 44th birthday, **1961:** 209, 212
Puerto Rico, 10th anniversary of Commonwealth, **1962:** 305
Pulaski, Casimir, anniversary of death, **1962:** 460, 461
Red Cross, centennial year, **1963:** 83
Robert Frost Library, ground-breaking, **1963:** 440
Roosevelt, Mrs. Franklin D., commemorative stamp, **1963:** 408
Saline water conversion plant, dedication, **1961:** 248
San Diego State College, commencement, **1963:** 226
Soviet revolution, anniversary, **1961:** 453
Synchrotron, Brookhaven National Laboratory, dedication, **1961:** 361

Addresses or remarks — *continued*
  Tennessee Valley Authority, 30th anniversary, **1963:** 193
  Thomas, Repr. Albert, testimonial dinner, **1963:** 474
  Transcontinental Telegraph Centennial, **1961:** 433
  Truman, Harry S., President, 77th birthday, **1961:** 179
  Truman Doctrine, 15th anniversary, **1962:** 78, 79
  Turkish independence, 40th anniversary, **1963:** 443
  Union of African and Malagasy States, first anniversary, **1962:** 368
  United Negro Colleges Development Campaign, **1963:** 355
  University of California, 94th anniversary, **1962:** 109
  University of Maine, **1963:** 426
  University of North Dakota, **1963:** 379
  University of Washington, 100th anniversary, **1961:** 473
  University of Wyoming, **1963:** 381
  U.S. Naval Academy, **1963:** 321
  USIA transmitter, Greenville, N.C., dedication, **1963:** 55
  Vanderbilt University, 90th anniversary, **1963:** 192
  V-E Day, 17th anniversary, **1962:** 175
  Venezuelan independence, **1961:** 272
  Viet-Nam, 6th anniversary, **1961:** 435
  West Virginia centennial, **1963:** 195, 249
  Whiskeytown dam and reservoir, dedication, **1963:** 389
  White House Conference on Exports, **1963:** 361
  White House mantelpiece, dedication, **1962:** 274
  Wilson, Woodrow, birthday, **1961:** 520
Addresses or remarks to foreign or international groups
  African conference on development of education, **1961:** 188
  African national economic conference, **1961:** 107
  Allied students at Army Guided Missile School, **1962:** 371
  American Field Service students, **1961:** 282; **1963:** 308
  Argentine War College, staff and students, **1963:** 84
  Association for International Exchange of Students in Economics and Commerce, **1963:** 128
  Baptist World Alliance, **1961:** 18
  Brazilian students, **1963:** 319, 335
  Central American President's Conference, **1963:** 99
  Experiment in International Living, **1962:** 363
  Foreign military officers, **1963:** 183, 335
  Foreign students, remarks, **1961:** 181

Addresses or remarks — *continued*
  Foreign students in D.C. colleges, **1963:** 171
  Free University of Berlin, **1963:** 271
  French Institute of High Studies for National Defense, **1963:** 112
  Fulbright exchange teachers, **1962:** 341
  Fulbright scholars and teachers, **1963:** 140, 332
  Incontro Club, Italy, **1963:** 191
  Inter-American Archival Seminar, **1961:** 432
  Inter-American Press Association, **1963:** 468
  Inter-American Symposium, **1962:** 513
  International Association of Machinists, **1963:** 162
  International Bank for Reconstruction and Development, **1962:** 392
  International Christian Leadership, Inc., **1961:** 26
  International Congress on Medical Librarianship, **1963:** 247
  International Federation of Catholic Universities, **1963:** 342
  International Monetary Fund, **1962:** 392
  International Monetary Fund, meeting, **1963:** 391
  International Peace Corps Secretariat, **1963:** 176
  Irish Parliament, **1963:** 278
  Junior Red Cross, **1962:** 351
  Latin American agricultural leaders, **1963:** 404
  Latin American air forces, visiting Chiefs of Staff, **1963:** 168
  League of United Latin American Citizens, **1963:** 473
  National Conference on International Economic and Social Development, **1961:** 244
  NATO Defense Institute students, **1963:** 303
  Nobel Prize winners in Western Hemisphere, **1962:** 161
  North Atlantic Treaty Organization, **1961:** 34, 115, 220
  Organization of American States, **1961:** 122
  Pan American Highway Congress, **1963:** 164
  Paulskirche, Frankfort, **1963:** 266
  Poznan Boy's and Men's Choir, **1963:** 93
  SHAPE, **1961:** 221
  United Nations, women delegates, **1961:** 501
  United Nations General Assembly, **1961:** 387; **1963:** 366
  Universal Postal Union delegates, **1963:** 453
  University of Costa Rica, **1963:** 105
  U.S.-Japan Cultural Conference, **1963:** 424
  World Food Congress, **1963:** 217
  World Food Forum, **1962:** 197
  World Youth Forum, **1963:** 90
  Young Australian League, **1963:** 216
Addresses or remarks to national groups
  Advertising Council, **1962:** 74; **1963:** 94
  AFL-CIO convention, **1961:** 499
  AFL-CIO constitutional convention, **1963:** 462

Addresses or remarks, national — *continued*
  Air Force Association, **1962:** 398
  Amalgamated Meat Cutters and Butcher
      Workmen of North America, **1963:** 187
  American Association for the United Nations,
      1962: 82
  American Bankers Association, **1963:** 77
  American Committee on Italian Migration, **1963:**
      235
  American Field Service students, **1963:** 308
  American Foreign Service Association, **1962:** 275
  American Heritage Foundation, **1962:** 350
  American Legion, **1962:** 70
  American Newspaper Publishers Association,
      1961: 153
  American Society of Newspaper Editors, **1961:**
      138; **1963:** 134
  American Veterans of World War II, **1962:** 343
  Anti-Defamation League, B'nai B'rith, **1963:** 46
  Association of American Editorial Cartoonists,
      1963: 172
  Big Brothers of America, **1961:** 234
  Boys Nation delegates, **1963:** 312
  Brookings Institution, **1962:** 230
  Business Committee for Tax Reduction in 1963,
      1963: 351
  Campaign Conference for Democratic Women,
      1962: 205
  Catholic Youth Organization convention, **1963:**
      463
  Chamber of Commerce of the United States,
      1962: 162
  Citizens Committee for International Develop-
      ment, **1961:** 277
  Citizens Committee for Tax Reduction and Re-
      vision in 1963, **1963:** 177
  Committee for Economic Development, **1963:**
      175
  Committee on Political Education AFL-CIO,
      1963: 362
  Conference on Peaceful Uses of Space, **1961:** 206
  Conservation organizations, leaders, **1963:** 196
  Consumers' Advisory Council, **1962:** 296
  Democratic National Committee, **1961:** 3, 209
  Eleanor Roosevelt Cancer Foundation dinner,
      1961: 215
  Girls Nation delegates, **1963:** 322
  Indians, tribal representatives, **1962:** 331
  National Advisory Committee on Manpower
      Development and Training, **1962:** 412
  National Association of Broadcasters, **1961:** 178
  National Association of Home Builders, **1962:**
      545
  National Association of Manufacturers, **1961:**
      497
  National Association for Retarded Children,
      1963: 435

Addresses or remarks, national — *continued*
  National Conference of Christians and Jews,
      1961: 479
  National Conference on Cooperatives, **1963:** 149
  National Conference on Milk and Nutrition,
      1962: 19
  National Conference of State Legislative
      Leaders, **1963:** 368
  National Congress of American Indians, **1963:**
      86
  National Council of Senior Citizens, **1962:** 217;
      1963: 138
  National Education Association, **1961:** 255
  National Football Foundation, **1961:** 496
  National 4-H Club, **1961:** 67
  National High School Symphony Orchestra,
      1962: 322
  National Industrial Conference Board, **1961:** 33
  National Trust for Historic Preservation, **1963:**
      425
  Operation Crossroads Africa, **1962:** 254
  Senate Youth Program participants, **1963:** 48
  State and National Education Associations,
      officers, **1963:** 469
  United Automobile Workers of America, **1962:**
      174
  United Negro Colleges Development Campaign
      leaders, **1963:** 355
  United States attorneys, **1962:** 443
  United States Conference of Mayors, **1963:** 230
  United Steelworkers of America, **1961:** 274; **1962:**
      385
  United Steelworkers Union, **1963:** 466
  Young Democrats, **1963:** 146
    Convention, **1961:** 498
  Young Presidents' Conference, **1963:** 436
Addresses or remarks at presentation ceremonies
  AAA lifesaving awards, School Safety Partol,
      1962: 182
  Air Force unit awards, **1962:** 520
  American Legion's Distinguished Service Medal,
      acceptance, **1962:** 70
  Award of merit, National Association for Re-
      tarded Children, **1963:** 435
  B'nai B'rith award, acceptance, **1963:** 46
  Collier Trophy, Adm. William F. Raborn, Jr.,
      1961: 243
  Collier Trophy, first U.S. astronauts, **1963:** 406
  Collier Trophy, X-15 pilots, **1962:** 294
  Congressional award, Robert Frost, **1962:** 110
  Distinguished Federal Civilian Service Awards,
      1962: 323; **1963:** 238
  Distinguished Service Medal
    Anderson, Adm. George W., Jr., **1963:** 318
    Burke, Adm. Arleigh A., **1961:** 303
    Decker, Gen. George H., **1962:** 416
    Dennison, Adm. Robert L., **1963:** 147
    Lemnitzer, Gen. Lyman L., **1962:** 422

Addresses or remarks, presentation — *continued*
　Norstad, Gen. Lauris, **1963:** 8
　O'Donnell, Gen. Emmett, **1963:** 345
　White, Gen. Thomas D., **1961:** 260
Dr. Thomas A. Dooley III Medal, **1962:** 228
"E" awards for exports promotion, **1962:** 113
Enrico Fermi Award, Hans Bethe, **1961:** 493
Enrico Fermi Award, Edward Teller, **1962:** 530
Flag of Cuban Invasion Brigade, acceptance,
　1962: 556
Flight safety plaque, Strategic Air Command,
　1962: 535
Football Hall of Fame Award, acceptance, **1961:**
　496
Harmon Trophies, **1962:** 475
Harmon Trophy, test pilots of X-15 rocket plane,
　1961: 486
Honorary degrees, acceptance, **1961:** 162, 418;
　1962: 234; **1963:** 221, 226, 232, 271, 379,
　426, 439
Honorary U.S. citizenship, Sir Winston
　Churchill, **1963:** 126
Hubbard Medal, Mt. Everest Expedition, 1963:
　296
International stamps, acceptance, **1963:** 453
Joseph P. Kennedy, Jr., Foundation awards,
　1962: 534
Medal of Freedom, Paul Henri Spaak, **1961:** 47
Merchant Marine Achievement Award, Solon B.
　Turman, **1961:** 459
NASA Distinguished Service Medal
　Maj. L. Gordon Cooper, **1963:** 199
　Dr. Robert R. Gilruth and Col. John H.
　　Glenn, Jr., **1962:** 61
　Comdr. Alan B. Shepard, Jr., **1961:** 177
National Geographic Society Medal, Capt.
　Jacques-Yves Cousteau, **1961:** 134
National Medal of Science, Theodore von
　Karman, **1963:** 68
National Security Medal, Allen W. Dulles, **1961:**
　485
Navy unit citations, **1962:** 521
Officer's dirk, Black Watch, acceptance, **1963:**
　457
Painting of battle of Bunker Hill, acceptance,
　1962: 407
Parvin Foundation Awards, **1961:** 487
Presidential certificates, Capitol Page School
　graduates, **1962:** 236
Presidential merit citation, Florence Harriman,
　1963: 133
President's Cup Regatta trophy, Charles
　Thompson, Sr., **1961:** 317
Protestant Council of the City of New York,
　Family of Man Award, acceptance, **1963:**
　455

Addresses or remarks, presentation — *continued*
　Rockefeller Public Service Awards, **1961:** 490;
　　1962: 533
　Sacred Torah, acceptance, **1961:** 463
　Seal of President's Committee on Employment
　　of the Handicapped, acceptance, **1963:**
　　452
　Teacher of the Year award, Marjorie L. French,
　　1962: 188
　Thomas Nast cartoons, acceptance, **1963:** 172
　West Virginia flag, acceptance, **1963:** 195
　White House guide book, acceptance, **1962:** 262
　Woodrow Wilson's typewriter, presentation to
　　White House, **1962:** 36
　Young American Medals, **1962:** 231
Adenauer, Konrad, **1961:** 231, 482n.; **1962:** 551
　[20]; **1963:** 35 [17], 65 [17], 253-255, 257-
　259, 260 [1, 12], 261, 262, 267, 269-271,
　273, 285, 413
　Joint statement with, **1962:** 508
　Messages, **1962:** 2, 511
　News conferences remarks on, **1961:** 62 [1], 318
　　[7], 334 [23], 455 [6, 15], 488 [6, 11, 18];
　　1962: 59 [5], 179 [5], 198 [14], 210 [7], 340
　　[7]
　Visits of, **1961:** 120, 480, 481; **1962:** 506-508
Adler, Richard, **1962:** 201n.
Administrative Conference of the United States,
　1961: 121
Administrative Conference, U.S., report, **1963:** 17
Administrative Procedure Act, **1961:** 121
Adoula, Cyrille (Congo Prime Minister), **1961:** 499,
　519; **1963:** 28
　News conference remarks on, **1962:** 8 [19], 302
　　[11], 316 [7], 340 [14]
　Visit of, **1962:** 35
Adrian, Mich., aluminum extrusion plant, **1961:**
　83 [25], 171 [4]
Adult illiteracy in U.S., **1962:** 37
Advanced Research Projects Agency, **1961:** 417n.
Advent, communications satellite, **1961:** 99
Advertising Council, **1962:** 74, 75 [10], 291;
　1963: 94, 325, 358
Advisers, Government, **1963:** 31
Advisers, Presidential, **1963:** 169 [10]
Advisory Commission on Educational Exchange,
　U.S., **1961:** 57
Advisory Commission on Intergovernmental Re-
　lations, **1963:** 368
Advisory Commission on Narcotic and Drug
　Abuse, report, **1963:** 121
Advisory Committee on Government Organiza-
　tion, President's, **1961:** 29
Advisory Committee on Labor-Management
　Policy, Presidential, **1961:** 33, 40; **1963:**
　30 (p. 67), 206, 299

Advisory Committee on Management, President's,
        1961: 29
Advisory Committee of the National Cultural
        Center, 1961: 467
Advisory committee on nuclear testing, 1961: 8 [7]
Advisory Council on the Arts, President's, 1963:
        240, 246
Advisory Group for Aeronautical Research and
        Development, NATO, 1963: 68, 165
Advisory Panel on Federal Salary Systems, 1963:
        44, 148
Advisory Panel on Federal Salary Systems, Chair-
        man (Clarence B. Randall), letter, 1963:
        44
Advisory Panel on Federal Salary Systems, report,
        1962: 55
Advisory Policy Board, Area Redevelopment Ad-
        ministration, 1963: 127
Adzhubei, Aleksei, 1962: 27 [1, 4, 26], 115 [25]
    Interview with President Kennedy, 1961: 483, 488
        [4, 7]
    Meeting with Pope John, 1963: 107 [10]
Adzhubei, Mrs. Aleksei, 1962: 27 [1]
Aeronautic Association, National, 1962: 294; 1963:
        406
Aeronautical Research and Development, NATO,
        Advisory Group, 1963: 68, 165
Aeronautics and Space Act, amendment, 1961: 147
Aeronautics and space activities, report, 1962:
        26
Aeronautics and Space Council, National, 1961:
        147
Aerospace industry, 1962: 372
    Employment, 1962: 373
    Information on, availability, 1962: 410 [8]
    Labor disputes, 1962: 244, 298, 369, 376, 378
        [20], 390, 410 [6]; 1963: 39
    News conference remarks, 1962: 152 [18], 378
        [20], 410 [6, 8]
    Telegram to union and management officials,
        1962: 298
Aerospace medical center, 1963: 472
Aerospace Men of the Year, 1962: 398
Aerospace Workers, United, 1962: 390
Aeschylus, 1962: 527
Afghanistan
    Assistance, 1963: 344n.
    Detection stations, nuclear tests, proposed,
        1963: 27
    Economic and social development, 1963: 347
    King Mohammed Zaher, visit of, 1963: 343, 344,
        347
AFL-CIO, 1961: 169, 499; 1962: 47, 203, 247, 279
        [3], 324, 405; 1963: 39, 75 [11, 14], 77,
        85, 162, 174, 268, 362
    Cancer fund campaign, 1961: 414
    Convention, remarks, 1963: 462

Africa, 1961: 11, 34, 57, 72, 73, 135, 146, 155, 165,
        167, 173, 205, 220, 450, 476, 487, 515;
        1962: 7 (p. 12), 35, 70, 74, 77, 84, 85, 103,
        104, 207, 212, 216, 284, 400, 441, 444, 449,
        453, 523, 539, 541, 549 [10], 550, 551 [17];
        1963: 12 (p. 15), 13, 28, 115, 116, 258, 266,
        271, 277, 308, 366, 378, 382, 383, 426, 455,
        476
    See also specific countries.
    Assistance, 1962: 254, 314, 549 [10]; 1963: 12
        (p. 17), 124, 338, 342
    Assistance and development, 1961: 139 [4]
    Chiefs of State, meeting, 1962: 368; 1963: 200,
        228, 260 [20], 304, 394, 397
    Communism in, 1961: 499; 1963: 14, 112, 118, 478
    Economic commission for, 1961: 188
    Economic conferences of African nations, 1961:
        107, 175, 304, 430
    Economic growth, 1961: 222; 1962: 170
    Economic and social development, 1963: 12 (p.
        17), 219, 302
    Exchange teachers from, 1962: 341
    Exports to Europe, 1962: 144
    Food from Communist China, 1961: 8 [25]
    Independence movement, 1962: 206; 1963: 200,
        300, 302, 394, 416
    Joint statements, 1962: 87, 105
    Joint statement with President Bourguiba on,
        1961: 173
    Joint statement with President Nkrumah on,
        1961: 74
    Labor movement, 1963: 268
    Military assistance and defense support, 1963:
        464
    Mission of G. Mennen Williams, 1961: 62 [17]
    News conference remarks on, 1961: 8 [25], 35
        [1, 13, 16], 62 [17], 139 [4], 222; 1962:
        75 [21], 352 [11, 20], 515 [15]; 1963: 35
        [17], 120 [16], 260 [18, 20], 459 [6]
    Operation Crossroads Africa, 1962: 254
    Peace Corps in, 1963: 74, 294
    Peace Corps projects, 1962: 325
    Students from, 1963: 140, 171
    Visit of Chester Bowles, 1961: 291 [15]
    Visit to, question of, 1963: 260 [20]
    Visits by U.S. officials, 1962: 75 [21]
    Whites, rights of, 1963: 366
African Freedom Day, 1961: 125
African and Malagasy Organization for Economic
        Cooperation, 1961: 107n.
African and Malagasy States, conferences, 1961:
        107, 175, 304, 430
African and Malagasy States, Union of, 1962: 105,
        212
    Conference, 1962: 368
African States, Independent, Conference of (1958),
        1961: 125n.

African Unity, Organization of, **1963**: 304, 397n.,
398
Aged persons.
See Older persons.
Agency for International Development (AID).
See International Development Agency.
Aging, President's Council on, **1962**: 193n., 245
[11]; **1963**: 74, 92
Agricultural Act of 1961, **1961**: 300, 316; **1963**: 407
Agricultural Acts, amendments, **1961**: 85
Agricultural Commission, EEC, **1963**: 152
Agricultural commodities, **1963**: 45
See also specific commodities.
Balance of trade, **1961**: 497, 499
Consumption, **1963**: 202 [15]
Exports, **1961**: 23, 85, 127
Farmer Advisory committees, proposed, **1961**:
85
Imports and exports, **1961**: 7 (p. 14), 8 [22], 22,
25, 144, 185; **1963**: 21 (p. 35), 30 (p. 65),
45, 75 [17], 118, 202 [18], 259, 407
Joint statement with President of EEC, **1961**: 189
Marketing programs, **1963**: 169 [13], 197, 201,
202 [2, 12, 15, 18]
Prices, **1962**: 25; **1963**: 12 (p. 14), 21 (p. 32),
189, 202 [2, 12, 15]
Research, **1963**: 30 (p. 69), 110
Shipping, rate regulation, **1962**: 129
Agricultural conservation program, **1961**: 39
**Agricultural Enabling Amendments Act of 1961,
1961**: 85
Agricultural marketing programs, **1961**: 85
Agricultural productivity, **1961**: 436
U.S.-Canada, **1961**: 192
U.S. vs. Communist countries, **1961**: 316
Agricultural research, **1961**: 85
Agricultural Sciences, Inter-American Institute of,
1963: 430
Agricultural surpluses, **1961**: 9, 39, 85, 102, 113, 127,
482; **1962**: 7 (pp. 7, 14), 13 (p. 30), 25, 127,
197, 199, 205, 280, 293, 328, 413, 549;
1963: 12 (pp. 14, 17), 21 (pp. 35, 36), 45,
118, 175, 189, 197, 217, 445, 455, 458, 465
Campaign remarks, **1962**: 395, 414, 440, 456
Food for peace.
See also Food for peace program.
For needy in U.S., **1961**: 11, 17, 85, 94; **1962**:
318, 380, 395, 414
News conference remarks, **1961**: 8 [2, 25], 71 [7];
1962: 8 [11], 75 [4], 107 [10], 115 [20],
198 [11], 210 [2], 245 [9], 259 [8]; **1963**:
89 [11], 202 [2, 12, 15, 18], 448 [14], 459
[13]
Overseas relief, **1961**: 85, 94
Price supports.
See main heading.
Purchases by Soviet Union, **1963**: 405 [1, 15, 17],
407, 448 [12]
World, **1961**: 192

Agricultural Trade Development and Assistance,
Act, **1961**: 6, 127; **1963**: 306
Agricultural workers, Mexican, **1961**: 400
Agriculture, **1961**: 17, 83 [19], 94; **1962**: 3, 7 (p. 7),
13, (p. 28), 69, 74, 186, 234, 459; **1963**: 21
(p. 35), 30 (p. 58), 77, 105, 136, 177, 192,
217, 291, 404, 422, 445, 451, 468
See also Farm; *specific programs.*
Acreage allotments, **1963**: 202 [12]
Automation, **1963**: 202 [15]
Campaign remarks, **1962**: 394-396, 437, 439, 440,
456, 458, 481
Communist countries, **1962**: 74, 127; **1963**: 271
Credit agreement, U.S.-Mexico, **1962**: 268
Effect of automation on, **1961**: 139 [8]
Message to Congress, **1961**: 85; **1962**: 25; **1963**:
45
Mexican workers in U.S., **1962**: 345
News conference remarks, **1962**: 8 [11, 22], 89
[18], 107 [10], 115 [20], 198 [11, 12], 245
[9], 410, [2,3]; **1963**: 202 [2, 5, 12, 15], 405
[1]
Pakistan, **1962**: 404
Production, **1962**: 8 [11], 25, 107 [10], 127, 190,
197, 250, 440; **1963**: 1963: 21 (pp. 35, 36),
45, 110, 201, 202 [2, 12, 15], 217
Research, **1963**: 30 (p. 69), 110
Soil bank, **1963**: 202 [12]
State stabilization and conservation committees,
1962: 127
Task force report, **1961**: 15 [27]
Agriculture, Department of, **1961**: 17, 90, 94;
1962: 23, 25, 69, 93 (pp. 236, 240), 185,
197, 425, 487; **1963**: 21 (pp. 36, 42), 47,
54 [4], 82, 197, 238, 405 [1], 407
Cotton price study, **1962**: 365, 410 [9]
Estes (Billie Sol) case, **1962**: 198 [1, 17], 210
[6, 12, 18]
Farm housing loan authority, **1961**: 76
Food stamp program, **1962**: 318
Grain, sale of, **1961**: 83 [19]
News conference remarks, **1962**: 27 [7], 198 [1,
17], 210 [6, 12, 18], 352 [24], 410 [9]
Raw cotton costs, study, **1961**: 161
Rural renewal functions, **1962**: 25, 93 (p. 238)
Sugar from Dominican Republic, purchases,
1961: 517
Vocational education program, study, **1961**: 46
Agriculture Extension Service, **1962**: 93 (p. 238)
Agriculture, labor, and industry, meeting of
leaders, 8 [18]
Agriculture, Secretary of (Orville L. Freeman),
1961: 23, 39, 49, 85, 339, 478; **1962**: 15n.,
19n., 127, 128, 307, 365, 439, 440, 495;
1963: 33, 37, 45, 49, 62, 74, 130, 141, 149,
197, 217, 238n., 376-378
Letters, **1963**: 47
Memorandum, **1963**: 62

Agriculture, Secretary — *continued*
   News conference remarks on, **1961:** 15 [27, 28];
      1962: 8 [6, 11], 115 [20], 198 [1, 17], 210
      [6]; **1963:** 169 [13], 202 [15, 18]
   President's support for, **1962:** 198 [1]
   Report, **1962:** 307n.
   School lunch program, study, **1961:** 17
Agudelo Villa, Hernando, **1962:** 86n.
Aguero, Luis Conte, **1961:** 183
Ahidjo, Ahmandou, **1962:** 368n.
   Visit of, **1962:** 84, 85, 87
AID.
   See International Development, Agency for.
Aiken, Frank, **1963:** 277, 416
Aiken, Sen. George D., **1962:** 107 [5]
Air carriers, labor dispute settlement, **1961:** 50
Air Force, **1961:** 83 [25], 99; **1962:** 172, 173, 287,
      326, 395, 398, 423, 512; **1963:** 21 (p. 32),
      68, 147, 168, 227, 263, 312, 345, 396, 441,
      476
   Briefing of RB-47 fliers, **1961:** 15 [7]
   Civilian scientists and technicians, hiring of,
      1961: 83 [15]
   Increase in forces, proposed, **1961:** 99, 302
   Increase in strength, **1962:** 7 (p. 10), 13 (p. 29),
      343; **1963:** 120 [11]
   Missile base program, **1961:** 62 [18]
   News conference remarks, **1962:** 59 [13], 378 [14];
      1963: 89 [9], 120 [1, 11]
   Reserve units, **1963:** 82, 248
      Release from active duty, **1962:** 140, 309
   Secret documents, press publication of, **1963:**
      120 [1]
   Tampa fuel annex, **1963:** 465.
Air Force, Department of the, **1962:** 407
Air Force, Royal Canadian, **1963:** 476
Air Force, Secretary of the (Eugene M. Zuckert),
      1962: 172, 294, 309, 398; **1963:** 120 [1],
      221, 345, 472
Air Force Academy, U.S., **1962:** 226; **1963:** 221-
      223, 321
Air Force Association, **1962:** 398; **1963:** 356 [17]
Air forces, Latin American, **1963:** 168
Air National Guard, **1961:** 302
Air Navigation, **1962:** 93 (p. 237); **1963:** 186
Air pollution, **1962:** 7 (p. 7), 65, 93 (p. 237), 190;
      1963: 53, 248, 366, 472, 478
Air pollution Act, **1962:** 65
Air pollution control, **1961:** 49
Air power, U.S., **1961:** 99, 302
Air routes, **1963:** 461
Air traffic control, **1962:** 93 (p. 236)
Air transport agreement, U.S.-Soviet Union, **1963:**
      448 [20]
Air Transport Association, International, **1963:** 186
Aircraft
   See also Aircraft, military; Aviation.
   C-130 shot down by Soviets, **1961:** 8 [30]

Aircraft — *continued*
   C-141A jet transport, **1963:** 330
   Cuban attacks on U.S. vessels, **1963:** 75 [3, 5, 8,
      20]
   Hijacking incidents, **1961:** 312, 318 [16, 22]
   In Berlin air corridor, **1962:** 59 [8, 13], 89 [12]
   Industry, **1962:** 152 [18], 174, 247
   Supersonic civil transport, **1963:** 21 (p. 37), 29,
      221, 242
   U-2, **1962:** 50 [1], 59 [10], 75 [6], 378 [2]
   U-2 incident, **1961:** 8 [4, 30]
   U.S. violation of Soviet territory, **1962:** 493
   X-15 rocket plane, **1962:** 294
Aircraft, military, **1961:** 11, 99, 302, 415 [7];
      1962: 13 (p. 29), 172, 173, 375; **1963:** 221
   See also Aircraft; Aviation.
   Airlifts, **1963:** 144 [5], 445, 448 [3], 462, 476, 477
   Bombers, **1961:** 99, 302, 415 [7]; **1962:** 7 (p. 10),
      140, 456, 557; **1963:** 35 [12], 168, 477
      B-26, **1963:** 35 [2]
      B-36, **1963:** 476
      B-47, **1962:** 551 [13]; **1963:** 35 [20]
      B-52, **1962:** 75 [20], 551 [13]; **1963:** 35 [20]
      B-58, **1963:** 475, 476
      B-70, **1962:** 75 [20], 89 [15], 107 [20], 551 [13];
         1963: 35 [20]
      British, **1962:** 554
      Soviet, in Cuba.
         See Cuba.
   Contracts for, **1962:** 50 [14]
   C-141A jet transport, **1963:** 330
   Chinese, Indian defense against, **1963:** 75 [10]
   Escorts for Berlin corridor, **1962:** 59 [13]
   Fighters, **1962:** 140; **1963:** 21 (p. 32), 478
      TFX, **1963:** 107 [4, 19, 23], 120 [7], 169 [5],
         328 [20], 448 [23], 475, 476
   Industry, labor dispute, **1963:** 39
   Procurement decisions, **1963:** 169 [20]
   RB-47, **1962:** 50 [23]
      See also main heading RB-47 fliers.
   Reconnaissance, **1963:** 21 (p. 32)
   Soviet
      In Cuba.
         See Cuba.
      Purchase by India, **1962:** 245 [3, 9], 316 [14]
      Technicians, German, in Egypt, **1963:** 120 [10]
      Versus missiles, **1962:** 551 [14]
      X-15 rocket, **1961:** 486
Aircraft, nuclear-powered, **1961:** 99
Airlines, **1962:** 93 (p. 237), 129
   International, regulation, **1963:** 186
   Labor disputes, **1962:** 204, 245 [1], 253, 256, 516;
      1963: 298
   Ticket and waybill taxes, **1962:** 13 (p. 34), 129,
      229 [1]
   U.S.-Canada, **1963:** 179
Airlines Pilots Association, **1961:** 50; **1962:** 204,
      245 [1], 516

Airport Act, Federal, extension, **1961:** 141, 374
Airports, **1962:** 129
  Dulles International Airport, dedication, **1962:**
      512
  Federal aid, **1961:** 94, 141; **1962:** 7 (p. 7), 190,
      195, 395; **1963:** 135
  Houston International Airport, **1963:** 474
  O'Hare International Airport, dedication, **1963:**
      109
Airspace and Naval Reservation, Guam, **1962:** 342
Akalovsky, Alex, **1961:** 483n.
Alabama, **1962:** 170, 171, 378 [22]
  Gov. George C. Wallace, **1963:** 108, 169 [4], 182,
      193, 194, 202 [1], 234, 236, 243, 305 [25],
      350
  Integration at University of Alabama, **1963:** 169,
      [4], 202 [1], 234, 236, 237, 243
  National Guard, **1963:** 181, 234, 236n., 237, 243,
      350n.
  News conference remarks, **1963:** 144 [13], 356
      [22]
  School integration, **1963:** 350
Alameda Air Force Base, **1962:** 276
Alaska, **1961:** 441; **1963:** 229, 248ftn. (p. 486),
      381, 464
  Airports, Federal aid, **1961:** 141
  Education of Indian children, **1961:** 94
  Electronics trainees, **1962:** 317
  Gov. William A. Egan, **1961:** 298
  Mount McKinley Italian Expedition, **1961:** 305
Albania, **1961:** 222 [13]
Albany, Ga., civil rights dispute, **1962:** 316 [8]
Albert, Repr. Carl, **1961:** 441; **1962:** 107 [19],
      205, 397; **1963:** 202 [12]
Albert, Prince, **1963:** 80
Albuquerque, N. Mex., **1962:** 538, 539n.
Alcoholic beverages, tax, **1961:** 136
Alemann, Roberto I., **1961:** 202; **1963:** 84
Alert capacity, defense, **1961:** 99
Alessandri Rodriquez, Jorge (President of Chile),
      1962: 546 [16, 20]
  Visit of, **1962:** 542-544
Alexander, Herbert E., **1961:** 403
Alexander the Great, **1961:** 279; **1963:** 344
Alger, Repr. Bruce, **1962:** 27 [26]
Algeria, **1962:** 109. 226
  Ben Bella, Ahmed, **1962:** 464-466
  Cease-fire in, **1962:** 59 [6], 97, 107 [13]
  Independence, **1962:** 277, 465, 466
  Khemisti, Mohammed, **1962:** 465n.
  News conference remarks, **1962:** 8 [13], 59 [6], 75
      [15], 107 [13]
Algerian crises
  Communist intervention, question of, **1961:** 222
      [1]
  French-Algerian rebel peace talks, **1961:** 62 [12],
      222 [1]
  French generals' revolt, **1961:** 222 [10]

Algerian crises — *continued*
  Joint statement with President Bourguiba, **1961:**
      173
  Message to General de Gaulle, **1961:** 140
  News conference remarks, **1961:** 62 [12], 222 [1,
      10]
Alien enemy property, World War II disposition,
      1963: 89 [12]
Aliquippa, Pa., **1962:** 451
Ali Sheikh Mohamed, **1962:** 523n.
Allagash River, **1963:** 301
Allegheny River, Kinzua Dam project, **1961:** 71
      [15], 320
Allen, Ivan, Jr., **1962:** 412n.
Allen, William M., **1962:** 376n.
Alliance for Progress, **1961:** 1, 11, 78, 81, 95, 122,
      184, 208, 210, 275, 276, 285, 301, 313, 376,
      389, 466, 497, 507, 509, 512, 513, 515, 517;
      1962: 7 (p. 12), 13 (p. 29), 15 17, 54, 74,
      77, 83, 124, 125n., 170, 265, 268, 269, 273,
      275, 346, 389, 418, 513, 528, 542-544, 549
      [6, 10], 551 [21], 556; **1963:** 12 (pp. 17, 18),
      14, 21 (p. 35), 45, 73, 98, 99, 103-105, 146,
      164, 217, 228, 319, 323, 338, 361, 362, 383,
      404n., 428, 432, 455, 464, 466, 468, 473,
      476
  California-Chile project, **1963:** 61
  Campaign remarks, **1962:** 432, 452, 455, 456, 499
  Charter, **1962:** 86
  Commerce Committee, remarks, **1962:** 177
  Cuban subversion, defense measures, **1963:** 144
      [8, 17]
  First anniversary, address, **1962:** 86
  Funds for technical assistance projects, **1961:** 491
  Highway projects, **1963:** 164
  Inter-American Conference of Labor Ministers,
      1963: 163
  Joint statements, **1962:** 126, 160, 303, 529
  Letter to President Frondizi, **1961:** 149
  Letter to President Goulart, **1962:** 146
  News conference remarks, **1961:** 119 [20], 171 [3],
      291 [3], 318 [11]; **1962:** 27 [2, 15], 75
      [22], 89 [4, 17], 115 [5], 179 [8], 229 [5],
      245 [12], 279 [1], 316 [21, 23], 378 [4], 546
      [18, 20, 22]; **1963:** 107 [1, 7, 22], 120
      [12], 134 [1], 144 [8, 17], 320 [14], 328 [1],
      405 [7], 459 [6, 14, 22]
  Panel of experts, selection, **1961:** 491
  Punta del Este conference.
    See main heading, Punta del Este conference.
  Second anniversary, **1963:** 326
  Self-help and reform by beneficiaries, **1963:** 118
Allied Forces, Southern Europe, **1963:** 292
Allot, Sen. Gordon, **1961:** 476n.; **1962:** 336
Almond, J. Linday, **1962:** 340 [28]
Alphand, Herve, **1961:** 134n., 219n.; **1963:** 112
Alphand, Mme. Herve, **1961:** 134

Aluminum
Industry, **1962:** 378 [20], 410 [6]
Stockpiles, **1962:** 27 [3]
Aluminum plants
Extrusion plant, Adrian, Mich., 83 [25], 171 [4]
Washington, State of, 474
Alvarez, Luis W., **1961:** 342
AMA. *See* American Medical Association.
Amalgamated Clothing Workers, **1962:** 198 [15]
Amalgamated Meat Cutters and Butcher Workmen
of North LAmerica, **1963:** 187
Amarillo, Tex., **1963:** 478
Amateur Athletic Union, **1962:** 546 [2]; **1963:** 7
Ambassadors, U.S., **1962:** 546 [9]; **1963:** 19, 88, 98,
102, 103, 105, 126, 133, 215, 223, 256, 272,
280
See also specific countries.
Funds for, **1962:** 316 [12]
In less-developed nations, **1963:** 118
News conference remarks on, **1963:** 89 [14], 120
[16], 144 [4]
New slate of, comment on, **1961:** 15 [38]
Percentage of Negroes, **1962:** 340 [11]
American Airlines, **1961:** 50
American Association for the United Nations,
1962: 82; **1963:** 101
American Automobile Association, **1962:** 182
American Bankers Association, **1963:** 77, 89 [2]
American Bar Association, **1961:** 28; **1962:** 115 [13],
119; **1963:** 459 [23]
American Battle Monuments Commission,
Chairman (Gen. Jacob L. Devers), **1963:**
203
American Broadcasting Co., **1962:** 551n.
American Cancer Foundation, **1961:** 215n.
American Committee on Italian Migration, **1963:**
235
American Council on Education, **1961:** 144
American Editorial Cartoonists, Association of,
remarks, **1963:** 172
American Federation of Musicians, **1961:** 330
American Field Service, remarks to students, **1961:**
282; **1962:** 284; **1963:** 308
American Foreign Service Association, **1962:** 275
American Freedom From Hunger Foundation,
letter to president of, **1963:** 33
American Hebrew Congregations, Union of,
1961: 463
American Heritage Foundation, **1962:** 350
American Historical Review, **1963:** 2n.
American Indians, National Congress of, **1963:** 86
American Institute of Cooperation, **1963:** 149n.
American Legion, **1961:** 459; **1962:** 70; **1963:**
312, 356 [16]
American Library Association, **1961:** 144; **1963:** 43
American Medical Association, **1962:** 174, 202, 210,
[4], 222, 229 [13], 279 [24]

American Newspaper Publishers Association, **1961:**
153
"American Pageant of the Arts," **1962:** 527n.
American Radio Association, **1961:** 270
American Relief Administration, **1963:** 407
American Republics, **1961:** 1, 12, 25 [23], 78, 81,
139 [1]; **1962:** 263, 265, 273, 303, 486;
1963: 21 (p. 35), 65 [10], 73
See also Inter-American; Latin America; Organi-
zation of American States; *specific coun-
tries.*
International Union of the, **1961:** 122
American Republics, International Union of the,
1961: 122
American Revolution, **1961:** 78, 212, 217, 218, 397;
1962: 199, 264, 265, 523, 542; **1963:** 5, 26,
112, 114, 227, 259, 266, 271, 278, 294, 361,
420n.
American Samoa, **1962:** 196
American Society of Newspaper Editors, **1961:** 138;
1963: 134
American States, Organization of.
See Organization of American States.
American University, commencement address,
1963: 232, 253n., 260 [2, 11, 18]
American Veterans of World War II, **1962:** 343
America's Cup competition, **1962:** 383
America's Cup, yacht racing, **1963:** 216n.
Amherst College, **1963:** 439, 440
Amistad Dam and Reservoir Project, **1962:** 273
Amsterdam, **1961:** 8 [6]
AMVETS.
See American Veterans of World War II.
Anderson, Sen. Clinton P., **1961:** 474, 476n.; **1962:**
69, 202, 216, 279 [2], 292, 536-538; **1963:**
41, 196, 459 [12], 460
Medical care bill.
See King-Anderson medical care bill.
Anderson, Adm. George W., Jr., **1961:** 303; **1962:**
75 [20], 287, 423; **1963:** 225, 312
Distinguished Service Medal, **1963:** 318
News conference remarks on, **1963:** 169 [5], 356
[24]
Anderson, Gov. John, Jr., **1963:** 108
Anderson, Hurst R., **1963:** 232
Anderson, Jack, **1963:** 120 [20]
Anderson, Marian, **1961:** 482; **1962:** 527n.; **1963:**
901
Anderson, Maj. Rudolf, Jr., **1962:** 520; **1963:** 12
(p. 19)
Anderson, Robert, **1963:** 118
Anderson Robert B., **1962:** 549ftn. (p. 887); **1963:**
351
Andreotti, Giulio, **1963:** 291, 293
Andrew Jackson, U.S.S., **1963:** 203
Andrews, Willard D., **1962:** 270n.
Anfuso, Repr. Victor L., **1961:** 62 [24], 84, 239
Angara River project, Siberia, **1962:** 335

Angola, **1963:** 455

Annapolis, Md., remarks at U.S. Naval Academy, **1961:** 232

Annis, Dr. Edward R., **1962:** 222, 229 [13]

Annual Conference of National Organizations, **1963:** 101

Annual manpower report, **1963:** 30 (p. 70), 92

Anslinger, Harry J., **1962:** 411

Antarctic exploration, **1963:** 426, 430

Antarctic Treaty, **1961:** 253; **1962:** 107 [7]

Antarctica, Conference in 1959, **1961:** 253

Antarctica, joint statement with Prime Minister Holyoake on, **1961:** 66

Anti-Defamation League, B'nai B'rith, **1963:** 46

Antietam, battle of, **1961:** 461

Antitrust laws, **1961:** 455 [17]; **1962:** 33, 93 (p. 241), 129, 162

Anti-poll tax amendment, proposed, **1963:** 82

Antonini, Luigi, **1962:** 200

Antony, Mark, **1961:** 222 [13]

ANZUS, **1961:** 51, 66; **1962:** 251

Apollo project, **1961:** 415 [7]; **1962:** 13 (p. 30), 378 [14]

Apollo spacecraft, **1963:** 21 (p. 34), 328 [19]

Apostle Islands, **1963:** 377

Appalachian Governors' conference, **1961:** 176

Appalachian Regional Commission, Federal, proposed, **1961:** 176n.

Appalachian region
  See also Area redevelopment.
  Economic development, remarks at meeting on, **1963:** 127
  News conference remarks, **1963:** 305 [18]

Appropriations
  Armed forces, **1961:** 302
  Foreign assistance, **1961:** 343
  Inter-American cooperation and reconstruction in Chile, **1961:** 208

Approval of acts of Congress.
  See Legislation, statements, etc., upon approval.

Aquarium in Washington, D.C., **1962:** 546 [24]

Aquinas, St. Thomas, **1963:** 254

Arab countries, **1962:** 515 [15]

Arango, A. Guillermo, **1962:** 238n.

Archeological research, **1961:** 108

Archimedes, **1963:** 366

Architects, Pan American Congress of, **1963:** 412

Archival Seminar, inter-American, **1961:** 432

Archivist of the United States (Wayne C. Grover), **1962:** 260

Arctic, navigation beneath ice cap, **1962:** 323, 451

Area redevelopment, **1961:** 7, 17, 44, 94; **1962:** 25, 111, 165, 174, 190, 328, 340 [2], 391; **1963:** 21 (p. 36), 92, 149, 228, 248, 363, 423, 445, 458, 478
  Appalachian region, **1963:** 127

Area redevelopment — *continued*
  Bill, defeat of, statement, **1963:** 241
  Campaign remarks, **1962:** 395, 396, 414, 431, 436, 438, 446, 452, 453, 455, 458, 481, 483
  National Capital Region, **1962:** 525; **1963:** 22, 208
  Southern Illinois, **1962:** 58
  Task force, report, **1961:** 7, 35 [15]

Area Redevelopment Act, **1961:** 17, 85, 136, 155

Area Redevelopment Act of 1961, **1962:** 16 (pp. 44, 45), 111, 165, 396, 453, 455, 458, 483; **1963:** 30 (p. 70), 74, 92, 113, 127, 378, 462
  Approved, **1961:** 158

Area Redevelopment Administration, **1961:** 176; **1962:** 25, 58, 307, 380

Area Redevelopment Administrator (William L. Batt, Jr.), **1962:** 58n., 165; **1963:** 127

Arends, Repr. Leslie C., **1963:** 89 [9]

Arezzo, Italy, music contest, **1962:** 352 [3], 361

Argentina, **1961:** 202; **1962:** 27 [6], 115 [5]
  Alemann, Roberto T., **1963:** 84
  Assistance, **1963:** 35 [19]
  Assistance and development, **1961:** 202, 389
  Food for peace mission, **1961:** 15ftn. (p. 39)
  Frondizi, Arturo, **1961:** 149, 389
  Nationalization of American oil companies, **1963:** 459 [13]
  News conference remarks, **1963:** 35 [19], 120 [12], 459 [13]
  Tax reforms, **1963:** 118
  War College, **1963:** 84

Arias, Gilberto, **1962:** 238

Aristotle, **1963:** 136, 192, 416n.

Arizona, **1961:** 476; **1963:** 113
  Education of Indian children, **1961:** 94
  Gov. Paul Fannin, **1961:** 475n., 476n.; **1963:** 108

Arkansas, **1962:** 170, 361
  Gov. Orval E. Faubus, **1961:** 440; **1963:** 108, 400, 401

Arkansas River basin, **1963:** 401

Arkansas River Basin development, **1962:** 332

Arkansas River, navigation, **1961:** 440

Arlington National Cemetery, **1961:** 461; **1963:** 173

Armed forces, British, **1963:** 154

Armed forces, U.S.; **1961:** 60, 205, 448, 447; **1962:** 13 (p. 28), 232, 310 [3], 423, 485, 486, 497; **1963:** 89 [5], 112, 147, 154, 174, 183, 194, 221, 232, 251, 325, 406, 441, 445, 478

See also Military personnel.
  Appropriations, **1961:** 302
  Big Lift, **1963:** 448 [3], 447
  Casualties in, **1963:** 159, 169 [20]
  Civilian scientists and technicians, hiring, **1961:** 83 [15]
  Conventional forces, **1961:** 62 [6, 29, 30], 92 [15], 415 [7], 455 [4], 488 [10]; **1962:** 7 (p. 10), 13 (p. 28), 140, 226, 346, 549; **1963:** 12 (p. 18), 21 (p. 33), 169 [20]
  Cuban exiles in, **1963:** 134 [1]

Armed Forces — *continued*
Desegregation, **1963:** 82, 251
Enlistments, extension of, **1962:** 486n.
Equal opportunity in, **1962:** 257
In Europe, **1961:** 192, 483; **1962:** 7 (p. 10), 198 [6],
  259 [6, 14], 295, 309, 422, 537, 549 [9],
  557; **1963:** 8, 37 [17], 65 [3, 13, 15, 17, 19],
  260 [13], 448 [1], 478
In France, **1963:** 448 [1]
In Germany, **1962:** 259 [6, 14], 439; **1963:** 65 [13],
  144 [9], 266a, 272, 448 [1, 28]
In Korea, **1962:** 549 [9]; **1963:** 12 (p. 19)
In Morocco, withdrawal, **1963:** 116
In Thailand, **1962:** 192, 198 [4, 17], 210 [3, 11],
  250
In Viet-Nam, **1962:** 8 [5], 40 [4], 89 [7], 139 [16],
  439, 546 [14]; **1963:** 12 (p. 19), 202 [10],
  356 [5], 459 [21]
  Question of, **1961:** 171 [7], 415 [10]
In West Berlin, **1961:** 334 [11]
Increase in strength, **1961:** 99, 302; **1962:** 140,
  343, 346, 378 [19], 395, 432, 456, 473, 549
Induction of teachers, **1961:** 455 [20]
Medal of Honor winners, remarks at reception
  for, **1963:** 159
Mobilization, partial, question of, **1961:** 258 [5]
Modernization, **1963:** 306
Morale, **1961:** 15 [2]
News conference remarks, **1961:** 15 [2], 62 [6, 29,
  30], 83 [15], 92 [15], 171 [7], 258 [5], 334
  [11], 415 [7, 10]; **1962:** 8 [5], 40 [4], 89
  [7], 139 [5, 16], 198 [4, 6, 17], 210 [3, 11],
  245 [15], 259 [6, 14], 316 [19], 378 [19],
  410 [12], 546 [14]
Nuclear forces, **1962:** 140, 346
Overseas, **1961:** 99, 497, 499, 521; **1962:**
  316 [19], 410 [12], 521, 549 [2, 9], 550;
  1963: 134 [3], 194, 221, 227, 256, 263, 292,
  321, 385, 396, 399
Physical fitness, **1961:** 348
Procurement for overseas forces, **1962:** 23
Reduction, **1963:** 319, 448 [3]
Rejection of physically and mentally unfit, **1961:**
  496
Reserves.
  See Reserve forces.
Riot training, **1963:** 181
Space program, **1963:** 68
Space program, role in, **1962:** 245 [15]
Strength, increase in, **1963:** 21 (p. 33), 120 [11]
Use at University of Mississippi, **1962:** 551 [10]
Use in Alabama civil disturbances, question of,
  1963: 182, 202 [1]
USIA news broadcasts to, **1963:** 144 [9]
Armed Forces Radio Service, **1963:** 144 [9]
Armenia, C-130 plane shot down, **1961:** 8 [30]

Armistice Day, **1961:** 461
Arms, Cuban, in Central America, **1963:** 107 [1]
Arms Control and Disarmament Act, **1961:** 408
Arms Control and Disarmament Agency, U.S.,
  1961: 205, 365, 388
  See United States Arms Control and Dis-
    armament Agency.
Arms inspection and control, **1961:** 1, 11, 62 [19],
  115, 483; **1962:** 29, 71
  See also Disarmament.
Arms race, **1961:** 519; **1962:** 40 [11], 290, 348, 352
  [7], 494, 518; **1963:** 58, 169 [2], 232, 262,
  271, 290, 291, 426, 448 [18]
Armstrong, Hamilton Fish, **1962:** 387
Army, **1961:** 99, 205, 488 [10]; **1962:** 287, 326, 407,
  456; **1963:** 21 (p. 33), 147, 227, 263, 312,
  325, 396, 445, 447, 448 [1]
  Corps of Engineers, **1963:** 21 (pp. 36, 42), 127,
    192, 301
  Cuban invasion veterans, enlistment, **1963:** 120
    [5]
  Department of the, **1962:** 9, 69, 407
  Reserve units, release from active duty, **1962:**
    140, 309
  First Armored Division, **1962:** 519, 521
  Guided Missile School, **1962:** 371
  Increase in strength, **1961:** 99, 302; **1962:** 7
    (p. 10), 13 (p. 28), 140, 343, 378 [19], 432
  Modernization of divisional structure, **1961:** 205
  Reserves, integration and equal opportunity in,
    1963: 82, 248
  Reserve units, release from active duty, **1962:**
    140, 309
  Secretary of the (Elvis J. Stahr, Jr.), **1961:** 49, 104
    419n.; **1962:** 128, 152 [3], 216, 226
  Secretary of the (Cyrus R. Vance), **1962:** 309, 323n.
    335, 416; **1963:** 173
  Strength, increase in, **1963:** 21 (p. 33), 120 [11]
Army-Navy football game, **1963:** 445
Arnold, Gen. Henry H., **1963:** 221
Arosemena Monroy, Carlos, **1962:** 302 [9]
  Visit of, **1962:** 299, 300, 303
Arosemena Monroy, Señora, **1962:** 299, 300
Arouna, Njoya, **1962:** 85n.
Arromanches, France, **1963:** 5
Art centers, **1961:** 268
Articles by the President
  "The Arts in America," **1962:** 552
  "Physical Fitness," **1963:** 325
  "The Vigor We Need," **1962:** 291
Arts, Federal aid, **1962:** 37; **1963:** 240, 246
Arts, Federal Advisory Council on the, proposed,
  1962: 37
Arts, President's Advisory Council, report, **1963:**
  240, 246
Ashby, J.L., **1961:** 254n.
Ashland, Wis., **1963:** 377

Asia, South Asia, and Southeast Asia. **1961:** 387, 435, 476, 515; **1962:** 74, 77, 99, 173, 216, 284, 389, 400, 449, 541, 549 [10], 550; **1963:** 171, 183, 266, 271, 277, 285, 308, 311, 325, 330, 334, 340, 382, 383, 385, 390, 426, 455, 477, 478
See also specific countries.
Assistance, **1962:** 314; **1963:** 12 (pp. 15, 17, 19), 72, 89 [20], 124, 328 [1], 338, 342
Campaign remarks, **1962:** 453, 456, 461
Colombo Plan, **1961:** 266
Communism in, **1963:** 14, 89 [20], 112, 118, 144 [2, 3, 5, 16], 316, 340, 349, 447
Communist aggression, **1962:** 210 [11], 531
Communist expansion, **1961:** 11, 38, 171 [15], 138, 302
Communists in, **1961:** 499
Detection stations, nuclear tests, proposed, **1963:** 27
Economic growth, **1961:** 22; **1962:** 170
Economic and social development, **1963:** 219
Exchange students, **1963:** 140
Exchange teacher from, **1962:** 341
Exports to Europe, **1962:** 144
Foreign Service officers in, **1963:** 120 [16]
French TV and radio interview re, **1961:** 214
Independence movement, **1963:** 394n.
Joint statements, **1962:** 160, 251, 312
Joint statements with foreign leaders re, **1961:** 112, 252, 283, 456
Labor movement, **1963:** 268
Mansfield Committee, visit to, **1963:** 89 [20]
Military assistance and defense support. **1963:** 107, [5], 202 [10], 349, 464
News conference remarks, **1961:** 35 [16], 92 [1, 6] 171 [2, 14, 15], 222, 415 [1]; **1962:** 8 [9], 75 [13, 16, 19, 21], 107 [17], 139 [1], 198 [4], 210 [11], 245 [4, 8]; **1963:** 35 [17], 65 [19], 89 [20], 107 [5], 120 [16], 144 [3, 16], 260 [18], 305 [9], 320 [3], 328 [1], 405 [18], 448 [3]
Peace Corps in, **1963:** 74, 294
SEATO.
See Southeast Asia Treaty Organization.
Social and economic development, **1963:** 219
UNESCO meeting of education ministers, **1962:** 122
U.S. forces in, **1963:** 448 [3]
U.S. information broadcasts, **1961:** 205
Visit of Chester Bowles, **1961:** 291 [15]
Visit of Robert F. Kennedy, **1962:** 75, [16, 21], 243 [1]
Visit of Vice President Johnson, **1961:** 116, 339 [22], 171 [2], 203, 205; **1962:** 339
Visit to, question of, **1963:** 305 [9]
Aspinall, Repr. Wayne N., **1962:** 69, 216, 336; **1963:** 37, 41, 169 [3], 198

Associacão dos Ex-Combatentes do Brasil, **1962:** 175
Associacão Universitaria Inter-Americana, **1962:** 310n.
Associated Research Councils, **1963:** 140n.
Association of American Editorial Cartoonists, **1963:** 172
Association of American Indian Affairs, **1961:** 371; **1963:** 113
Association of Broadcasters, National, **1962:** 49, 515 [7]
Association of the Bar of the City of New York, **1961:** 152
Association for International Exchange of Students in Economics and Commerce, **1963:** 128
Association of Land-Grant Colleges and State Universities, centennial, **1961:** 462
Association for Retarded Children, National, **1962:** 534
Association for the United Nations, American, **1962:** 82
Assumption College, **1961:** 219
Astin, Allen V., **1962:** 187n.
Astronauts.
See also Manned space flights; Space research and exploration.
Soviet, **1961:** 117, 118, 119 [5]; **1962:** 340 [5, 8]; **1963:** 366, 448 [18]
Gagarin, Maj, Yuri, **1961:** 117n., 171 [13], 178, 318 [17]; **1962:** 59 [2]
Titov, Maj. Gherman, **1962:** 59 [2], 68
United States, **1963:** 366
Carpenter, Lt. Comdr. Malcolm Scott, **1962:** 213, 223; **1963:** 199
Collier Trophy, presentation to, **1963:** 406
Cooper, Maj. L. Gordon, **1963:** 190, 199, 202 [4]
Glenn, Lt. Col. John H., Jr., **1962:** 50 [19], 56, 57, 59 [1, 3], 60, 61, 63, 68, 77, 171, 323, 373; **1963:** 199
Grissom, Capt. Virgil, **1961:** 296; **1962:** 61
Physical Fitness, **1963:** 325, 472
Schirra, Comdr. Walter, **1962:** 426, 427, 435, 463
Shepard, Comdr. Allan B., Jr., 170, 171 [13], 177, 178, 205; **1962:** 61, 63, 171, 323; **1963:** 199
Aswan Dam, **1961:** 108; **1963:** 459 [13]
Athens, NATO conference, **1962:** 160, 179 [16], 198 [14]
Atherton, Robert, **1963:** 319a note
Athletes, U.S., **1962:** 546 [2]
Athletic Union, Amateur, **1962:** 546 [2]
Atlanta, Ga., **1961:** 352
Civil rights in, **1963:** 82, 230
Integration of high schools, **1961:** 334 [1]
Mayor Ivan Allen, Jr., **1962:** 412n.
Mayor William B. Hartsfield, **1961:** 334 [1]

Atlantic Alliance, **1962:** 278, 284, 295, 506-508, 557; **1963:** 12 (p. 15), 32, 35 [1, 24], 54[3, 8], 65 [3, 6, 9, 13, 17], 112, 132, 150, 156, 232, 253, 255, 257, 261, 262, 266, 285, 288, 289, 291, 293, 303, 319a., 373

Atlantic Charter, 20th anniversary, message, **1961:** 321

Atlantic City, N.J., **1962:** 385

Atlantic Community, **1961:** 34, 120, 189, 212; **1962:** 3, 7 (p. 10), 15, 16 (p. 46), 22, 86, 109, 160, 183, 199; **1963:** 15, 32, 54 [3, 8], 65 [8], 77 [4], 126, 132, 179, 253, 254, 258, 266, 288, 289-291

News conference remarks, **1962:** 107 [3], 198 [3, 16], 210 [7], 259 [9], 279 [4, 5, 6, 8]

Atomic blackmail, Soviet, **1961:** 340

Atomic bomb, **1961:** 387

See also Nuclear weapons; Nuclear weapons tests.

Atomic energy, **1961:** 83 [23], 222 [3]; **1962:** 163, 289, 514; **1963:** 21 (p. 39), 77, 193, 319a, 448 [15], 459 [6]

Fermi, Enrico, experiment, **1962:** 524

Industry, regulation, **1961:** 83 [23]

McMahon Act on control of, **1961:** 222 [3]

Peaceful uses, **1962:** 100, 289, 335, 382, 408

Atomic Energy Act, **1963:** 320 [15]

Atomic Energy Agency, International, **1963:** 430

Atomic Energy Commission, **1961:** 15 [8], 49, 83 [23], 99; **1962:** 71, 163, 530; **1963:** 21 (p. 42), 30 (p. 69), 40, 328 [4], 439

Atomic industry, regulation, **1961:** 83 [23]

Authorization bill, approval, **1962:** 408

Chairman (Glen T. Seaborg), **1961:** 262, 355, 361, 390n.; **1962:** 100, 109, 163, 356n., 530n.; **1963:** 328 [4], 354, 448 [15]

Civilian nuclear power, study, **1962:** 100

Hanford, Wash., reactor, **1962:** 289

New members, oath-of-office ceremony, **1962:** 356

News conference remarks, **1962:** 89 [4], 352 [11]

Power projects, **1961:** 278

Reactor program, reduction in funds, **1961:** 488 [8]

Atomic Energy Community, European, **1961:** 481

Atomic energy for mutual defense, U.S.-French agreement, **1961:** 355

Atomic energy for peaceful uses, **1961:** 17, 387, 474

Industrial development, safety standards, **1961:** 25 [18]

Nuclear power projects, **1961:** 49

Project Plowshare, **1961:** 349n.

Uranium-235 available for. **1961:** 390

Atomic weapons.

See Nuclear weapons.

Attorney General (Robert F. Kennedy), **1961:** 28, 48, 136; **1962:** 15, 21, 115ftn. (p. 273), 158, 201, 206, 218, 220, 231, 384, 411, 497; **1963:** 6, 49, 76n., 91, 130, 141, 170, 248, 311, 348, 407n., 423n.

Injunction in longshoremen's strike, **1962:** 428

Injunction in maritime strike, **1961:** 269, 270

Investigation of stock exchange racketeering, **1962:** 20 [24]

Letters, **1961:** 182, 269; **1962:** 247; **1963:** 39

News conference remarks on, **1961:** 15 [26], 291 [10], 415 [14]; **1962:** 20 [4, 24], 50 [11], 59 [15], 75 [16, 21], 107 [12], 139 [3], 316 [8], 546 [2]; **1963:** 35 [2], 305 [25], 320 [6]

Opinion on employment of women in Federal Service, **1962:** 304

Opinion on Presidential inability clause of Constitution, **1961:** 319

Report, **1962:** 316 [8]

Resignation from Metropolitan Club, **1961:** 415 [14]

Visit to Asia, **1962:** 75 [16, 21], 243 [1]

Attorneys, U.S., **1962:** 443

Atwood, Rollin, **1961:** 318 [15]

Auburn-Folsom South project, **1962:** 69

Auchincloss, Bayard, **1961:** 35 [10]

Audubon Society, **1963:** 196

Augusta, Ga., **1962:** 527n.

Austin, Adm. Bernard L., **1961:** 392

Austin, Tex., remarks prepared for delivery at **1963:** 478

Australia, **1963:** 171, 278, 297, 308, 476

Air defense assistance, Indian request for, **1963:** 75 [10]

Ambassador Howard Beale, **1962:** 88, 383

America's Cup competition, **1962:** 383

McEwen, John, **1962:** 88

Menzies, Robert G., **1961:** 51; **1962:** 251

Visit of, **1963:** 297

Trade with Soviet Union, **1963:** 407, 459 [19]

Wheat sales to Communist bloc, **1963:** 405 [1]

Young Australian League, remarks, **1963:** 216

Austria, **1961:** 212, 483

Ambassador Wilfried Platzer, **1962:** 168n.

Gorbach, Alfons, **1962:** 168, 169

Kreisky, Bruno, **1962:** 168n., 169

Raab, Julius, **1961:** 109

Schärf, Adolf, **1961:** 224, 226

State Treaty, **1962:** 168n., 308, 323

Steiner, Ludwig, **1962:** 168n.

Visit to, **1961:** 224, 225, 226

Austrian Trade Union Federation, **1962:** 12

Automation, **1961:** 23, 25 [25], 136, 139 [8], 171 [6], 211; **1962:** 7 (p. 6), 50 [3], 89 [5], 164, 174, 234, 549; **1963:** 77, 94, 110, 134 [3], 188, 202 [15], 226, 228, 230, 244, 248, 310, 340, 351, 363, 379, 385, 389, 436, 445, 448 [7], 466

Automation — *continued*
Presidential Commission on, **1963:** 310
Report, **1962:** 6
Automobile
Design and equipment changes, **1962:** 93 (p. 237)
Industry, **1962:** 174, 378 [20], 410 [6]; **1963:** 110, 134 [3]
Labor dispute, **1961:** 334 [12], 350
Production, **1961:** 415 [20]
Sales, **1962:** 229 [16], 302 [7], 436
Tax, **1961:** 136
Automobile, Aerospace and Agriculture Implement Workers of America, United, **1963:** 39
Automobile Association, American, **1962:** 182
Automobile Show, National, **1962:** 378 [10]
Automobile Workers of America, United, **1962:** 174, 179 [9], 298
Aviation, **1961:** 121; **1962:** 129; **1963:** 21 (p. 31), 68, 221, 238, 242, 476
See also Aircraft; Aircraft, military.
Civil Aviation, **1962:** 93 (p. 237), 129; **1963:** 29, 30 (p. 67), 179, 186, 221, 242, 464
Federal aid, **1963:** 221
Fuel tax, **1961:** 58, 136; **1962:** 13 (p. 34), 129
Harmon Trophies, presentation, **1962:** 475
Progress, **1963:** 225, 472
Women in, **1963:** 315
Awards and citations
AAA lifesaving awards, School Safety Patrol, **1962:** 182
Air Force unit awards, **1962:** 520
American Legion's Distinguished Service Medal, acceptance, **1962:** 70
Award of Merit, National Council of Senior Citizens, acceptance, **1963:** 138
B'nai B'rith award, acceptance, **1963:** 46
Collier Trophy, first U.S. astronauts, **1963:** 406
Collier Trophy, Adm. William F. Raborn, Jr., **1961:** 243
Collier Trophy, X-15 pilots, **1962:** 294
Congressional award, Robert Frost, **1962:** 110
Congressional Gold Medal, Bob Hope, **1963:** 353
Distinguished Federal Civilian Service Awards, **1962:** 323; **1963:** 238
Distinguished Service Medal
Anderson, Adm. George W., Jr., **1963:** 318
Burke, Adm. Arleigh A., **1961:** 303
Decker, Gen. George H., **1962:** 416
Dennison, Adm. Robert L., **1963:** 147
Lemnitzer, Gen. Lyman L., **1962:** 422
Norstad, Gen. Lauris, **1963:** 345
White, Gen. Thomas D., **1961:** 260
Dr. Thomas A. Dooley III Medal, **1962:** 228
"E" flag award, export expansion program, **1961:** 495; **1962:** 113
Enrico Fermi Award, Hans Bethe, **1961:** 493
Enrico Fermi Award, Edward Teller, **1962:** 530

Flight safety plaque, Strategic Air Command, **1962:** 535
Football Hall of Fame Award, acceptance, **1961:** 496
Harmon Trophies, **1962:** 475
Harmon Trophy, test pilots of X-15 rocket plane, **1961:** 486
Honorary degrees, acceptance, **1961:** 162, 418; **1962:** 234
Honorary U.S. citizenship, Sir Winston Churchill, **1963:** 126
Hubbard Medal, Mt. Everest Expedition, **1963:** 296
Joseph P. Kennedy, Jr., Foundation awards, **1962:** 534
Medal of Freedom, Paul Henri Spaak, **1961:** 47
Merchant Marine Achievement Award, Solon B. Turman, **1961:** 459
NASA Distinguished Service Medal, **1962:** 61
Comdr. Alan B. Shepard, Jr., **1961:** 177
NASA Distinguished Service Award, Maj. L. Gordon Cooper, **1963:** 199
National Association for Retarded Children, award of merit, **1963:** 435
National Geographic Society Medal, Capt. Jacques-Yves Cousteau, **1961:** 134
National Medal of Science, Theodore von Karman, **1963:** 68
National Security Medal, Allen W. Dulles, **1961:** 485
Navy unit citations, **1962:** 521
Parvin Foundation Awards, **1961:** 487
President's Cup Regatta trophy, Charles Thompson, Sr., **1961:** 317
Presidential certificates, Capitol Page School graduates, **1962:** 236
Presidential Citation of Merit, Mrs. Florence Harriman, **1963:** 133
Presidential Medal of Freedom, presentations by President Johnson, **1963:** 899
Posthumous award to President Kennedy, **1963:** 903
Protestant Council of the City of New York, Family of Man Award, acceptance, **1963:** 455
Rockefeller Public Service Awards, **1961:** 490; **1962:** 533
Sacred Torah, acceptance, **1961:** 463
Teacher of the Year award, Marjorie L. French, **1962:** 188
Young American Medals, **1962:** 231
Axis powers, **1961:** 372, 512
Aycock, William B., **1961:** 418
Ayub Khan, Mohammed, visit of, **1961:** 279, 280, 283, 291 [14]; **1962:** 402- 404, 554; **1963:** 356 [25]

Azikiwe, Nnamdi, **1961:** 188, 394
Azores, U.S. air bases, **1962:** 20 [10]
Azores, U.S. air rights, **1961:** 15 [29]

B-26 bomber, **1963:** 35 [2]
B-36 bomber, **1963:** 476
B-47 bomber, **1962:** 551 [13]; **1963:** 35 [20]
B-52 bomber, **1962:** 75 [20], 551 [13]; **1963:** 35 [20]
B-58 bomber, **1963:** 475, 476
B-70 bomber, **1962:** 75 [20], 89 [15], 107 [20], 551[13];
     1963: 35 [20]
Babcock, Gov. Tim M., **1963:** 382, 383
Bacon, Charles.L., 70n.
Bacon, Francis, **1961:** 153, 155; **1963:** 226
Bacopulos, Rev. George J., **1963:** 203n.
Bad Godesberg, Germany, visit to, **1963:** 256, 261
Bad River, **1963:** 377
Bahamas, visit to, **1962:** 553, 554
Bahia University, **1962:** 310n.
Bailey, Col. Charles J., **1962:** 287n.
Bailey, Repr. Cleveland M., **1962:** 414
Bailey, John M. (Chairman, Democratic National
     Committee), 3, 8 [20], 209, 498; **1962:** 15,
     229 [6], 233n., 346n.; **1963:** 24, 151, 204, 459,
     [15]
Bailey, Maj. Lawrence R., **1962:** 349
Baker, Robert C., **1963:** 351
Baker, Robert G, **1963:** 459 [16]
Baker, William O., **1961:** 168n.
Balaguer, Joaquin, **1961:** 517
Balance of payments,: **1961:** 11, 17, 23, 33, 41, 53, 82,
     90, 94, 99, 120, 136, 171 [6], 205, 354, 366,
     436, 437, 495, 497, 499; **1962:** 7 (pp. 13, 14)
     13 (p. 27), 14, 16 (p. 43), 22, 31, 74, 83, 108,
     162, 170, 185, 194, 199, 234, 250, 328, 392,
     395, 549, 551 [22]; **1963:** 12 (pp. 15, 16), 15,
     16, 21 (pp. 27, 29, 37, 39, 41), 30 (pp. 57-
     59, 61, 64, 65), 34, 45, 80, 94, 131, 175,
     179, 228, 306, 310, 351, 361, 381, 387, 391,
     407, 422, 436, 455, 465
   Effect of foreign aid on, **1963:** 118, 134 [3]
   Latin American, **1963:** 54 [10]
   Letters, **1962:** 114, 280
   Message to Congress, **1963:** 306
   News conference remarks, **1962:** 8 [4], 59 [12, 17]
     75 [10], 115 [2, 23], 139 [1], 152 [17], 259
     [14], 279 [12], 302 [6], 316 [19], 340 [25],
     410 [1]; **1963:** 54 [10], 65 [2, 17], 75 [19],
     77 [4], 89 [11], 305 [2, 12], 328 [23], 405 [1,
     14], 459 [19]
   Report, **1962:** 114
   Review committee on Statistics, **1963:** 143
   United Kingdom, **1963:** 228
Balance of power, **1963:** 319a
Balchen, Col. Bernt, **1961:** 486; **1962:** 475
Balderston, C. Canby, **1963:** 54 [1]
Balewa, Abubakar Tafawa, **1961:** 304; **1963:** 331
Balkan States, **1961:** 135

Ball, George W., **1961:** 91; **1962:** 8 [15], 168n.,
     180n., 248, 410 [3], 419, 554; **1963:** 32n.,
     76n., 126, 156, 169 [10], 238, 356 [25] and
     p. 899
Ballet Folklorico of Mexico, **1962:** 406
Ballistic Missile Early Warning System, **1961:** 99;
     1962: 198 [9]
Baltimore, Md., **1962:** 446
Bamboo Curtain, **1963:** 379
Bancroft, George, **1963:** 140
Banda, Hastings K., **1961:** 181
Bangalore, India, **1963:** 361
Bangkok, **1972:** 287; **1963:** 361
   SEATO Council of Ministers meeting, **1961:** 38,
     92 [1], 97
   U.S. foreign trade center, **1961:** 23
Bank for International Settlement, **1962:** 234, 279
     [19]
Bankhead-Jones Farm Tenant Act, amendment
     proposed, **1962:** 25
Banking Act of 1935, **1962:** 151
Banks, regulations, **1962:** 16 (pp. 55, 57)
Baptists, **1961:** 26
Baptist World Alliance, **1961:** 18, 26
Barall, Milton, **1961:** 285, 517
Bar Association, American, **1962:** 115 [13], 119
Barbara Anne, **1961:** 25 [10]
Barbiturates, control of, **1962:** 411
Barclay, Rev. John, **1961:** 1n.
Barghoorn, Frederick C., **1963:** 459 [2, 8, 19, 24]
Baring, Repr. Walter S., **1963:** 169 [10]
Barkan, Alexander, **1963:** 362
Barley prices, **1962:** 25
Barnett, Gov. Ross, **1962:** 420n., 445; **1963:** 305 [25]
Barr, Joseph M., **1962:** 452n.
Barr, Dr. Murray L., **1962:** 534n.
Barret, Repr. William A., **1963:** 445
Barron, Gov. William W., **1962:** 414; **1963:** 195,
     249
Barry, Commodore John, **1963:** 276, 278
Barry, Joseph, **1961:** 222 [10]
Bartlett, Sen. E. L., **1961:** 476n.
Baruch, Bernard M., **1963:** 126, 316
Baruch (Bernard) plan for internationalization of
     atom, **1961:** 387
Barwick, Garfield, **1962:** 383n.
Baseball, **1961:** 496; **1962:** 452
Basel, Switzerland, **1962:** 234, 279 [19]
Bases, military, **1961:** 23, 99, 119 [18], 436
Bases, U.S. abroad, **1962:** 139 [5], 402
   Azores, **1962:** 20 [10]
   Dhahran, Saudi Arabia, **1962:** 50 [12]
   Europe, **1963:** 65 [13]
   Guantanamo Bay, Cuba, **1963:** 202 [8]
   Guantanamo, Cuba, naval base, **1962:** 107 [14, 21]
     378 [1], 485, 515 [7]
   Italy, **1963:** 35 [18]

Bases, U.S. abroad — *continued*
  Morocco, evacuation, **1963:** 115, 116
  Okinawa, **1962:** 75 [16]
  Ryukyu Islands, **1962:** 99
  Turkey, **1963:** 35 [18]
  United Kingdom, **1962:** 316 [6]
Basic research, **1961:** 11, 94
Basilone, John, **1963:** 109
Bass, Repr. Ross, **1963:** 192
Bastogne, battle of, **1961:** 302
Bataan Day message, **1962:** 131
Batista y Zaldivan, Fulgencio, **1961:** 132
Batt, William, **1961:** 158; **1962:** 58n., 165; **1963:** 127
Battle Act, **1961:** 318 [20]; **1963:** 407
Baughman, J. Stanley, **1962:** 323, 533n.
Bay of Biscay, **1963:** 348
Bayh, Birch, **1962:** 456
Beale, Howard, **1961:** 51; **1962:** 88, 383
Beale, Lady, **1962:** 383
Beam, Jacob D., **1962:** 50 [4]
Beatrix, Crown Princess, visit of, **1963:** 132
Beaumont, Tex., **1963:** 75 [20]
Beauvais, Carl, **1963:** 390
Beck, Martin M. **1963:** 406
Beethoven album, gift to President, **1963:** 255n.
Behman, Mohammad, **1962:** 339n.
Beirne, Mrs. Francis F., **1961:** 280
Beirne, Joseph A., **1962:** 47, 412n.
Bekesy, George von, **1962:** 161n.
Belafonte, Harry, **1962:** 201, 527n.
Belgium, **1962:** 115 [23], 410 [5], 551 [22]
  Brussels, **1961:** 21
  Constitution, **1961:** 418
  Contribution to peace in Congo, **1963:** 28
  Lefevre, Theo, **1961:** 174
  Prince Albert, visit of, **1963:** 80
  U.S. Ambassador Douglas MacArthur II, **1961:** 174
Belgrade conference of nonaligned nations, **1961:** 334 [4], 359, 363, 364, 365, 387
Bell, David E., **1962:** 163, 221, 373; **1963:** 118, 169 [10], 306, 338
  See also Budget. Bureau of the, Director.
Bell, Elliot, **1961:** 40n.
Bell, Judge Griffin B., **1962:** 420
Bell Telephone Laboratories, **1962:** 398
Bellino, Carmine S., **1963:** 410n.
Bellmon, Gov. Henry, **1963:** 108
Belt, Guillermo, **1963:** 89 [16]
Beltran, Pedro, **1963:** 468
Bemis, Samuel F., **1963:** 2
Ben Bella, Ahmed, visit of, **1962:** 464-466
Benet, Stephen Vincent, **1963:** 389
Bengal, India, **1961:** 1961: 26
Benitez, Jaime, **1961:** 487n.
Benny, Jack, **1962:** 201
Benson, Ezra Taft, **1961:** 8 [10]; **1963:** 478
  Campaign remarks on, **1962:** 439, 440, 456, 481, 483

Benson, Ezra Taft — *continued*
  News conference remarks on, **1962:** 115 [20], 198 [11, 12], 245 [9], 340 [2]
Benton, Thomas Hart, **1963:** 381
Benton, William Hart, **1962:** 349
Berckemeyer, Fernando, **1961:** 373n.; **1962:** 383
Berckemeyer, Señora, **1962:** 383
Berea College, **1963:** 137
Berger, Samuel D., **1963:** 120 [16]
Bergin, Edward, **1962:** 474
Berkeley, Calif., **1962:** 109
Berle, Adolf A., Jr., **1961:** 15 [34], 25 [23, 24], 258 [17], 276
Berlin, **1961:** 41, 231, 304, 436, 473; **1962:** 7 (p. 13), 70, 74, 77, 171, 186, 212, 250, 278, 295, 309, 395, 396, 407, 456, 485, 498, 521, 549 [9], 551 [19]; **1963:** 8, 12 (pp. 11, 15, 16, 19), 14, 105, 134 [1], 194, 221, 227, 232, 237, 253n., 255, 261, 271, 278, 290, 291, 295, 306, 312, 316, 366, 390, 407, 426, 465 [1], 476-478
  Air corridor, **1962:** 59 [8, 13], 89 [12]
  Allied commitment in, **1963:** 260 [4]
  Appointment of Gen. Lucius Clay as President's personal representative, **1961:** 334 [3]
  Autobahn to, international control, proposed, **1961:** 483, 488 [7]
  Communist-built wall dividing city, **1961:** 415, [18], 515
  Crisis.
    See Berlin crisis.
  Discussions with Gen. Lucius Clay, **1962:** 145
  Free University of, address, **1963:** 271
  Joint statements on, **1962:** 419, 508, 554
  Joint statements with foreign leaders re, **1961:** 120, 223, 230, 242, 309, 411, 456
  Mansfield committee, visit to, **1963:** 89 [20]
  Mayor Willy Brandt, **1962:** 139 [8]; **1963:** 267-271, 273
  Mission of Belgrade conference representatives re, **1961:** 364, 365
  News conference remarks, **1961:** 15 [31], 222, [5], 291 [1], 318 [4], 334 [3, 5, 11, 21], 415 [18]; **1962:** 8 [2, 16], 27 [4, 23], 40 [14, 19], 50 [24], 59 [5, 8, 13, 16], 75 [13, 19], 89 [12], 107 [4, 17, 18], 115 [7], 139 [1, 5, 8], 152 [16, 19], 179 [5, 8, 16], 198 [3], 210 [9], 245 [4], 259 [6, 14], 279 [5, 20], 302 [2, 13], 340 [3, 9], 352 [6, 9, 14, 15], 378 [3]; **1963:** 65 [7, 13], 75 [18], 89 [7, 20], 107 [3, 7], 260 [1, 4, 16], 320 [4], 405 [18], 448 [1], 459 [19]
  Prohibitive zone, Communist, **1963:** 260 [4]
  Reunification, **1963:** 271
  Statements, **1962:** 4, 145
  U.S. forces in West Berlin, increase in, **1961:** 334 [11]

Berlin — *continued*
  U.S. rights, **1963:** 459 [19]
    In West Berlin, four-power agreement, **1961:** 483
    Visit of Vice President Johnson, **1961:** 325; **1962:** 339
    Visit to, **1963:** 267-273
    Wall dividing city, **1962:** 8 [16], 77, 357; **1963:** 12 (p. 18), 193, 267, 269, 270, 278
    Western access to, **1963:** 426, 459 [19]
  Berlin, East, **1961:** 509, 515
  Berlin crisis, **1961:** 329, 355, 387, 481, 496, 519
  Broadcast, **1961:** 302
  News conference remarks, **1961:** 258 [2, 5, 18], 291 [1, 6, 7, 11, 17, 19], 318 [4, 13, 23], 334 [2, 3, 5, 11, 13, 17, 19, 21, 22, 23, 25], 415 [3, 5, 13, 18, 22], 455 [6, 10], 488 [4, 6, 7, 10, 11]
  Soviet aide memoire, **1961:** 225n., 291 [1, 11, 17 19], 292, 318 [4]
  Bermuda, **1961:** 518, 591; **1962:** 70, 157n., 553
    Gov. Julian Gascoigne, **1961:** 518n.
  Bermuda, underwater nuclear test detection system, **1963:** 202 [8]
  Bernhard, Prince, visit of, **1963:** 132
  Bernstein, Edward M., **1963:** 143
  Bernstein, Leonard, **1962:** 527n.
  Berwanger, Jay, **1961:** 496
  Best, Rev. Earl V., **1963:** 203n.
  Betancourt, Romulo, **1961:** 272, 507, 509-511; **1963:** 71-73, 89 [19]
  Betancourt, Señora, **1963:** 71, 72
  Betayne, Jean-Faustin, **1962:** 85n.
  Bethe, Hans, **1961:** 493; **1962:** 107 [16]
  Bethlehem Steel Corp., **1962:** 139 [4], 233, 410 [6]
  Bethmann-Hollweg, Theobald von, **1963:** 426
  Bethune, Mary, **1962:** 27 [11]
  Bible, Sen. Alan, **1961:** 476n.; **1963:** 389, 390
  Bicycles, tariff classification, **1962:** 484
  Biddle, George, **1962:** 552
  Bidwell, Arthur J., **1963:** 368
  Biemiller, Andrew J., **1963:** 362
  Big Brothers of America, **1961:** 234
  Big Cedar, Okla., **1961:** 441
  Big Lift Operation, **1963:** 448 [3], 447
  Bigart, Homer, **1963:** 455
  Bikini Island, **1962:** 342
  Bilateral Agreement of Cooperation, U.S. Iran, (1959), **1962:** 147
  Billboards along highways, control, **1961:** 58
  Bill of Rights, **1963:** 26, 59
  Billings, Mont., **1963:** 382
  Bingham, Jonathan B., **1961:** 358n.; **1963:** 359n.
  Biological research, **1961:** 49
  Birch Grove, England, **1963:** 285
  Birch (John) Society, **1961:** 139 [14]; **1962:** 40 [13], 546 [22]

Birmingham, Ala., **1961:** 197
  Civil rights issue in, **1963:** 228, 230, 248
    News conference remarks, **1963:** 169 [1, 4, 14, 19], 202 [20]
    Radio and television remarks, **1963:** 181, 237
    Statements, **1963:** 350, 360, 365, 372
    Telegram to Governor Wallace, **1963:** 182
  Mayor Albert Boutwell, **1963:** 365, 372
Biron, Robert H., **1962:** 298n.
Birthday, the President's, **1961:** 209, 212
Birthday salute to the President, **1962:** 201
Bishop, Barry C., **1963:** 158n., 296
Bismarck, Prince, Otto von, **1961:** 418; **1962:** 109 250, 284; **1963:** 192, 257, 271, 334, 379
Bizerte, **1961:** 304
Black, Eugene R., **1961:** 119 [2], 244, 273; **1962:** 20 [3], 27 [12], 50 [10], 392, 549 [10]; **1963:** 118, 242n., 338, 391
Black Watch (Royal Highland Regiment), **1963:** 457
Blaik, Col. Earl, **1963:** 365, 372
Blaisdell, Neil S., **1963:** 229, 230
Blakley, Sen. William, **1961:** 119 [12, 22]
Blatnik, Repr. John A., **1962:** 439, 440; **1963:** 378
Blind persons, Federal aid, **1962:** 28, 328
Blindness, National Institute of Neurological Diseases and, **1963:** 435
Bliss, Anthony A., **1961:** 330n.
Block, Joseph L., **1961:** 40n., 354n; **1963:** 299
Blough, Roger M., **1961:** 254; **1962:** 139 [4, 7], 203 234; **1963:** 448 [16]
Blue Cross, **1962:** 279 [2]
  Medical insurance, **1963:** 74
Blum, Robert, **1961:** 119 [2]
Blumenthal, W. Michael, **1962:** 418
BMEWS.
  See Ballistic Missile Early Warning System.
B'nai B'rith, Anti-Defamation League of, **1963:** 46
Board of Foreign Scholarships, **1961:** 57
Boards of Federal Executives, regional, **1961:** 465
Boca Chica Naval Air Station Fla., **1962:** 521
Bockelmann, Werner, **1963:** 264-266
Boeing Airplane Company, **1961:** 281n.; **1962:** 376; **1963:** 39
Bogata, **1963:** 118, 163, 323, 361, 455
  Act of, **1961:** 11, 35 [2], 78, 81, 119 [20], 171 [3], 208, 313, 510; **1962:** 86; **1963:** 163, 323
  Visit to, **1961:** 512-516
Boggs, Rep. Hale, **1962:** 170, 171, 179 [4], 205
Boggs, Mrs. Hale, **1961:** 234
Boggs, Sen. J. Caleb, **1963:** 89ftn. (p. 243)
Bohemia, **1961:** 463n.
Bohlen, Charles E., **1961:** 25 [13], 218, 325; **1963:** 160
Bohr, Niels, death of, **1962:** 514
Bohr, Mrs. Niels, **1962:** 514
Bokaro, India, steel mill at, **1963:** 169 [17]

Boland, Repr. Edward P., **1962:** 170; **1963:** 277
Bolívar, Simón, **1961:** 78, 272, 509, 510, 515; **1962:** 86, 270, 556; **1963:** 72, 73, 99
Bolivia, **1961:** 258 [17]; **1962:** 216; **1963:** 294, 428, 431
  Assistance, **1963:** 118, 431n.
  Assistance and development, **1961:** 184, 409
  COMIBOL mining operation, **1961:** 184, 409; **1963:** 432
  Economic and social development, **1963:** 432
  Paz Estenssoro, Victor, **1961:** 184, 275, 409; **1963:** 428-432, 448 [2]
  Revolution, **1961:** 275
  Soviet aid, **1961:** 244
  Tax reforms, **1963:** 118
  U.S. Ambassador Ben S. Stephansky, **1961:** 275
  U.S. economic mission, **1961:** 71 [6]
  Yacimientos Petroliseros Fiscales Bolivianos, **1961:** 184
Bolivian National Planning Commission, **1961:** 184
Bolshikov, Georgi, **1961:** 483n.
Bolton, Repr. Frances P., **1961:** 280; **1963:** 35 [8]
Bombers, **1961:** 99, 302, 415 [7]
  See also Aircraft, military.
Bombings in Birmingham, Ala., **1963:** 181, 360, 365
Bombs.
  See also Nuclear weapons; Nuclear weapons tests; Weapons.
  Atomic, **1961:** 387
  Hydrogen, **1962:** 179 [13]
    Soviet, **1961:** 426, 442, 446
  Neutron, **1961:** 318 [18]
Bonaparte, Napoleon, **1961:** 291 [5]; **1962:** 551 [22]
Bonds, Federal
  Highway, question of, **1961:** 58
  Savings bonds, **1961:** 75; **1962:** 14; **1963:** 94, 325
  United Nations.
    See main heading.
Bonham, Tex., **1961:** 476
Bonin Island, **1961:** 252
Bonn, Germany, **1961:** 481; **1962:** 254; **1963:** 253, 256, 478
  Visit to, **1963:** 255, 257-260, 262
Bonneville Power Administration, **1962:** 289; **1963:** 21 (p. 42)
Books, publication and distribution, **1963:** 118, 137
Books, publication and distribution abroad, **1961:** 92 [14]
Books, sale of, **1962:** 552
Boris Gudonov, **1961:** 387
Boston, Mass., **1961:** 143, 155, 422; **1962:** 156n., 202, 265, 439, 450; **1963:** 223, 230, 239, 248, 254, 264, 275, 280, 368, 387, 423, 461, 463
  Mayor John F. Collins, **1961:** 212
  President's birthday dinner, **1961:** 212
  Role of President's grandparents in city government, **1961:** 219

Boston, Mass. — *continued*
  Youth orchestra, **1962:** 150
Boston College, **1963:** 136
Boston Tea Party (1773), **1962:** 199
Boswell, Pa., **1962:** 329
Bougainville, battle of, **1962:** 198 [1]
Bourguiba, Habib, visit of, **1961:** 164, 165, 171 [15], 172, 172
Boutin, Bernard L. (General Services Administrator), **1962:** 221, 260; **1963:** 26, 62, 207
Boutwell, Albert, **1963:** 365, 372
Bowers, Claude, **1963:** 445
Bowles, Chester, **1961:** 502; **1962:** 234; **1963:** 160, 169 [10]
  News conference remarks on, **1961:** 139 [7], 291 [15], 488 [9]
  Visit to Africa and Asia, **1961:** 291 [15]
Boycotts, economic, **1961:** 71 [20]
Boy Scouts, **1963:** 195, 305 [19]
Boyd, Alan S. (Chairman, Civil Aeronautics Board), **1963:** 29, 186
Boyd, Julian P., **1961:** 397; **1963:** 245
Boyne, Battle of the, **1963:** 278
Boys Nation, **1963:** 312, 322
Bradbury, Norris E., **1962:** 537; **1963:** 328 [2], 334
Brademas, Repr. John, **1962:** 456
Bradford, Saxton A., **1961:** 57n.
Bradford, William, **1961:** 375, 491; **1962:** 373
Bradley, Gen. Omar N., **1961:** 215; **1962:** 416, 422; **1963:** 44n.
Brandeis, Louis D., **1963:** 353, 459 [23]
Brandeis University, **1962:** 156n.
Brandt, Willy, **1962:** 139 [8]; **1963:** 267-271, 273
Brandy, gift to President, **1963:** 266a
Brannin, Ralph S., **1962:** 182n.
Brasília, Brazil, **1962:** 500
Bratsk, Siberia, **1962:** 335
Brazeau, Theodore, **1961:** 339
Brazil, **1961:** 81, 122, 483; **1962:** 549 [6, 10], 551 [17]
  Ambassador Roberto de Oliveira Campos, **1962:** 310; **1963:** 335
  Assistance, and development, **1961:** 102, 285; **1962:** 126, 146, 177, 210 [14]
  Dantas, San Tiago, **1962:** 146n.
  Debt refinancing, **1961:** 258 [17]
  Escola Superior de Guerra, **1962:** 496
  Food for peace mission, **1961:** 15ftn. (p. 39)
  Franco Montoro, Andre, **1962:** 54
  Goulart, João, **1962:** 75 [22], 115 [14], 124-126, 139 [14], 146, 177, 490
  Kubitschek de Oliveira, Juscelino, **1961:** 13
  News conference remarks, **1961:** 62 [11], 119 [20], 258 [17], 334 [18]; **1962:** 27 [6], 75 [9, 22], 210 [14], 515 [15], 546 [18, 20]
  Northeast development, **1961:** 285; **1962:** 126, 146, 499; **1963:** 118
  Nuclear weapons ban proposal, **1962:** 515 [15]

Brazil — *continued*
  Nuclear-free zone in Latin America, proposal for, **1963:** 432
  Quadros, Janio da Silva, **1961:** 12, 105, 285
  Recorded greetings to Brazilian people, **1961:** 105
  Students from, **1962:** 310, 496; **1963:** 319, 335
  Tax reforms, **1963:** 118
  U.S. investments, **1962:** 126
    Expropriation of U.S. property, **1962:** 75 [22], 549 [4]
  Veterans Association, message to, **1962:** 175
  Visit to, postponement, **1962:** 490
  World War II participation, **1962:** 496
Brazilian Military Institute of Engineering, **1963:** 335
Brazilian National War College, **1963:** 335
Brazos River Basin, **1962:** 313
Breathitt, Edward T., **1963:** 458
Breckenridge, Tex., boys choir, **1962:** 150
Brentano, Heinrich von, **1961:** 25 [19], 41, 62 [23, 26], 120
Bretton Woods agreements, **1963:** 306, 391
Bretton Woods Agreements Act, **1962:** 31
Brevard Music Camp, North Carolina, **1961:** 327n.
Brewster, Daniel, **1962:** 446
Brewster, Sen. and Mrs. Daniel B., **1963:** 461
Brezhnev, Leonid, **1961:** 2, 271, 453, 483, 522; **1963:** 1
Brick and tile industry, **1961:** 391
Bridgeport, Conn., **1962:** 472
Bridges, Sen. Styles, **1961:** 318 [20]
Briley, Beverly, **1963:** 192
Brinkley, David, **1963:** 349
Briscoe, Robert, **1962:** 233
Bristol Bay, **1963:** 352
British Broadcasting Company, interview with correspondent of, **1961:** 229
British Columbia, **1963:** 179
British Commonwealth, **1961:** 36; **1962:** 160, 251; **1963:** 126, 202 [3]
British Guiana, **1961:** 483; **1963:** 328 [10]
British Honduras, **1962:** 325
British Honduras, Peace Corps projects in, **1963:** 294
British West Indies, **1961:** 36
Broadcasters, National Association of, **1961:** 178; **1962:** 49, 515 [7]
Broadcasting, international, censorship of, **1962:** 352 [23]
Broadcasting System, National Emergency, **1961:** 154
Broadcasts.
  See Interviews of the President; Messages to the American people.
Bronk, Detlev W., **1961:** 110, 145; **1963:** 430
Brody, Ralph M., **1962:** 337, 338
Brookings Institution, **1962:** 245 [17]
  Balance of payments, **1963:** 305 [12]
  Public Policy Conference, **1962:** 230

Brooklyn, N.Y., **1962:** 201
Brooks, Repr. Jack, **163:**, 245
Brooks, Phillips, **1963:** 52
Brooks, Sidney, **1963:** 472
Brooks, Wayne T., **1963:** 206
Brooks Air Force Base, School of Aerospace Medicine, **1963:** 472
Brooksher, Robert R., Jr., **1961:** 440n.
Brophy, Thomas D., **1962:** 350
Brosio, Manlio, **1961:** 84n.
Brown, Gov. Edmund G., **1961:** 477; **1962:** 89 [19], 109, 218, 279 [26], 337, 338, 352 [25], 411; **1963:** 61, 226, 389
Brown, Mrs. Edmund G., **1962:** 279 [26]
Brown, Harold, **1963:** 202 [22], 334
Brown, Hugh B., **1963:** 385
Brown, Judge John R., **1962:** 420
Brown, Wayne, **1962:** 182n.
Brown, Weir M., **1961:** 123n.
Brown, Winthrop G., **1961:** 15 [15]; **1963:** 238
Broyhill, Repr. Joel T., **1962:** 378 [5]
Bruce, David K. E., **1961:** 228; **1962:** 419; **1963:** 126
Brunswick, Maine, **1962:** 326
Brussels, Belgium, **1961:** 21; **1962:** 22, 160
Bryan, George, **1963:** 387
Bryan, William Jennings, **1962:** 203, 250
Bryant, Gov. Farris, **1961:** 499; **1962:** 77; **1963:** 108, 465-468
Buchanan, Mary, **1963:** 319a note
Buck, Raymond, **1963:** 475, 476
Buckley, Repr. Charles A., **1962:** 111, 229 [23]
Buckley, William F., Jr., **1962:** 234
Budapest, Hungary, **1961:** 138
Buddhists in Viet-Nam, **1963:** 305 [10], 340, 349
Budget, **1961:** 17, 25 [25], 436; **1962:** 16 (p. 44), 203, 210 [13, 16], 234, 245 [6, 7], 279 [19], 328, 547, 549; **1963:** 12 (p. 12), 30 (pp. 60, 61, 63, 64, 66), 34, 77 [1], 89 [7], 107 [9], 188, 363, 407, 456, 459 [6], 465
  Fiscal 1959, **1963:** 94
  Fiscal 1961, **1961:** 25 [4]; **1962:** 13 (p. 35)
  Fiscal 1962, **1961:** 11, 17, 49, 205, 436; **1962:** 7 (p. 7), 13 (p. 35)
    Message to Congress, **1961:** 94
    New conference remarks, **1961:** 8 [27], 15 [20, 25], 25 [4], 62 [25], 92 [18]
  Fiscal 1963, **1961:** 302, 415 [19], 436, 497; **1962:** 7 (p. 7), 14, 16 (p. 47), 26, 83; **1963:** 50, 134 [4], 175 [4], 305 [2], 329, 351
    Message to Congress, **1962:** 13
    News conference remarks, **1962:** 198 [12], 229 [1, 16]
  Fiscal 1964, **1962:** 115 [16], 259 [8], 549; **1963:** 43, 47, 50, 53, 94, 118, 134, 148, 208, 329, 349, 351
    District of Columbia, **1963:** 22, 56

Budget — *continued*
   Messages to Congress, **1963:** 21, 22
   News conference remarks, **1963:** 65 [2], 89 [5],
      120 [11, 21], 169 [20], 175 [4]
   Fiscal 1965, **1963:** 127, 351
Budget, Bureau of the, **1961:** 15 [25], 94, 104, 130;
      1962: 13, (p. 38), 65, 129, 209, 279 [14],
      448, 476; **1963:** 30 (p. 67), 120 [6], 198, 305
      [2], 388
   Bulletin on commercial-industrial activities of
      Government, **1961:** 314
   Circular on management and operating con-
      tracts, **1961:** 314
   Government foreign economic functions, **1961:**
      207
   Overseas spending by Federal agencies, analysis,
      1961: 23
Budget, Bureau of the, Director (David E. Bell),
      1961: 5, 19, 23, 35 [10], 49, 318 [14]; **1962:**
      163, 221, 373
   Government scientific and technical contracts,
      review of, **1961:** 314
   Public works appraisal, **1961:** 17
Budget, Bureau of the, Director (Kermit Gordon),
      1963: 4, 29, 30 (p. 68), 62, 148, 306, 371
   Letter, **1963:** 143
   Memorandum, **1963:** 62
   News conference remarks on, **1963:** 144 [14]
Buenos Aires, **1961:** 122; **1963:** 103
Buffalo, N.Y., **1962:** 461
Bülow, Prince Bernard von, **1963:** 426
Bunche, Ralph J., **1963:** 169 [10], 367 and p. 902
Bundy, McGeorge, **1961:** 42; **1962:** 74, 234
Bunker, Ellsworth, **1961:** 244; **1962:** 139 [10], 210 [22],
      251, 316 [7]; **1963:** p. 902
Bunker Hill battle, painting, acceptance, **1962:** 407
Bunn, Rev. Edward B., **1963:** 136
Burauen, Theo, **1963:** 254
Burdick, Sen. Quentin N., **1963:** 379
Burke, Adm. Arleigh A., **1961:** 15 [8], 25 [22], 35 [7],
      232, 303; **1962:** 20 [2, 14], 50 [23], 423
Burke, Edmund, **1961:** 192
Burke, Repr. Frank W., **1962:** 457, 458
Burleson, Repr. Omar, **1961:** 358n.; **1962:** 150
Burma, **1961:** 231, 387, 501; **1962:** 245 [8]
  U Nu, **1961:** 367
  U.S. Ambassador John S. Everton, **1961:** 367
Burnette, Robert, **1962:** 331
Burns, Arthur F., **1961:** 40n.; **1962:** 27 [27]; **1963:** 94
Burns, Haydon, **1962:** 190n.
Burns, John A., **1962:** 196; **1963:** 229, 230
Burns, Lt. Gen. Robert W., **1962:** 117n.
Burns Creek project, **1962:** 69
Burrill, Rt. Rev. Gerald F., **1963:** 110
Burrows, William Ward, **1962:** 287
Burton-Hill hospital construction bill, **1961:** 46
Burton, Sir Richard, **1962:** 523
Burton, Robert, **1962:** 392

Burundi, Kingdom of, **1963:** 471
  King Mwami Mwambutsa, **1962:** 266
  Muhirwa, Andre, **1962:** 415
Bus tickets, tax on, **1962:** 229 [1]
Business, U.S., **1961:** 11, 33, 81, 455 [17]; **1962:** 14,
      16 (p. 44), 22, 93 (p. 242), 170, 199, 201,
      203, 230, 234, 280, 285, 286, 328, 395, 473;
      1963: 21 (p. 26), 30 (pp. 59, 62, 65), 34,
      103, 145, 175, 188, 230, 306, 351, 361, 363,
      423, 478
See also Small business.
Capital gains on sale of depreciable property,
      1961: 136
Civil rights responsiblilties, **1963:** 230
Conflict of interests, **1961:** 25 [21]
Education, support of, **1963:** 465
Ethical standards, **1962:** 10
Foreign aid participation, **1963:** 118
Foreign investments and operations, **1963:** 224,
      319
Manpower needs, **1963:** 92
News conference remarks, **1962:** 115 [16], 245 [7],
      259 [16], 279 [3, 15], 410 [1, 2, 7, 12]; **1963:**
      107 [9], 305 [2, 20]
Relations with Government, **1962:** 162, 279 [15],
      410 [2, 7, 12]; **1963:** 77, 94, 128
Tax reduction committee, **1963:** 145, 169 [15],
      351
White House conference on minority groups,
      1963: 210
Business Advisory Committee, **1962:** 203
Business Advisory Group, **1962:** 194
Business Committee for Tax Reduction in 1963,
      1963: 145, 169 [15], 351
Business Editors and Publishers, White House
      Conference of, **1962:** 410
Business Ethics Advisory Council, **1962:** 10
Business system, **1961:** 497
Business Week magazine, **1963:** 94
Businessmen, comment on, **1962:** 179 [10]
Busyhead, Dennis, **1962:** 331
Butcher Workmen of North America, Amal-
      gamated Meat Cutters and, **1963:** 187
Butter, consumption and stockpiling, **1963:** 45
Butter, price supports, **1962:** 115 [20]
Butterfield, Lyman H., **1961:** 397; **1963:** 2, 245
Buy American policy, **1961:** 497; **1962:** 410 [12]
  Lumber products, **1962:** 307
Byrd, Sen. Harry Flood, **1962:** 98, 340 [16], 449,
      459; **1963:** 434
Byrd, Sen. Robert C., **1962:** 414; **1963:** 232, 249
Byrne, Repr. James A., **1963:** 445

C-130 plane shot down in Armenia in 1958, **1961:** 8
      [30]
Cabell, Gen. C., **1961:** 485
Cabinet Committee on Economic Growth, **1963:** 30
      (p. 68)

Cabot, John M., **1962:** 245 [9]
Cadett Thomas, **1961:** 222 [8]
Caesar, Julius, **1961:** 222 [13]
Cain, Dr. James C., **1961:** 203
Cain, Walker O., **1962:** 274n.
Cairns, Joseph V., **1963:** 206
Calhoun, John C., **1962:** 234, 349; **1963:** 2, 334, 381
California, **1961:** 62 [18], 441; **1962:** 77, 109, 337,
      338, 444, 495; **1963:** 21 (p. 36), 226, 248ftn.
      (p. 486), 294, 308, 325, 381, 382, 389, 390,
      465
   Alliance for Progress participation, **1963:** 61, 118
   Central Valley reclamation, **1963:** 41
   Construction industry labor dispute, **1962:** 179
      [7], 302 [15]
   Defense contracts, **1963:** 107 [19]
   Democratic State committeewomen, **1963:** 228
   Gov. Edmund G. Brown, **1961:** 477; **1962:** 89
      [19], 109, 218, 279 [26], 337, 338, 352 [25],
      411; **1963:** 226, 389
   Gubernatorial election, **1962:** 115 [6], 229 [20],
      279 [26], 352 [25]
   Lead smelting industry in, **1963:** 202 [13]
   Mortgage interest rates, **1961:** 62 [4]
   News conference remarks, **1962:** 89 [19], 115 [6],
      179 [7], 229 [20], 279 [26], 302 [15], 352
      [25]; **1963:** 107 [19], 202 [13, 21], 320 [6],
      405 [6]
   Power transmission lines, Upper Colorado and
      Trinity projects, **1961:** 360
California Institute of Technology, **1961:** 460n.;
      1963: 477
Callas, Maria, **1962:** 201
Calvin, Melvin, **1962:** 161n.
Cambodia, **1961:** 92 [6], 205, 231, 387; **1962:** 184;
      1963: 349, 455
   Assistance, **1963:** 89 [20], 459 [1]
   Communist threat to, **1963:** 144 [16]
   News conference remarks, **1962:** 50 [9], 107 [15],
      210 [11], 245 [8], 352 [16]
   Prince Norodom Sihanouk, **1962:** 352 [16]; **1963:**
      459 [1]
Cambridge, Mass., **1963:** 426
Cambridge, Mass., storage of President's papers,
      1962: 546 [7]
Cambridge, Md., civil rights issue in, **1963:** 248,
      305 [20]
Cambridge University, **1963:** 426
Cameroon, Ahmadou Alidjo, **1962:** 84, 85, 87,
      368n.
Camp David (Maryland), **1961:** 25 [10]
Campaign Conference for Democratic Women,
      1962: 205
Campaign Costs, President's Commission on, **1962:**
      219; **1963:** 151
   Report, **1962:** 152 [4]
Campbell, Jack M., **1962:** 536; **1963:** 222

Campbell, Joseph, **1963:** 151
Campidoglio, Italy, visit to, **1963:** 288
Campobello Island, **1963:** 180
Campos, Roberto de Oliveira, **1962:** 310; **1963:** 335
Canada, **1961:** 33, 123, 133, 220; **1962:** 22, 326, 402,
      443, 449, 458, 495, 506, 541, 549 [7]; **1963:**
      8, 30 (pp. 59, 64, 65), 77, 100, 136, 150,
      162, 164, 171, 232, 266, 288, 303n., 308,
      311, 428
   Air defense assistance to India, **1963:** 75 [10]
   Assistance, **1963:** 169 [17]
   Columbia River Basin development, treaty with
      U.S., **1961:** 49, 83 [2]
   Diefenbaker, John G., **1961:** 25 [1], 45, 190, 192,
      193, 273, 298; **1962:** 477; **1963:** 54 [8]
   Fisheries dispute with Japan, **1963:** 352
   Great Lakes Maritime issue with, **1963:** 411
   Heeney, Arnold, **1961:** 45
   International Joint Commission, **1962:** 123
   Lumber imports from, **1962:** 307
   Meetings between members of U.S. and
      Canadian legislatures, **1961:** 45
   Mutual defense communications system, **1961:**
      298
   News conference remarks, **1962:** 27 [12], 198
      [16], 410 [5]; **1963:** 54 [8], 75 [10], 89
      [11], 144 [1], 169 [6, 17], 260 [1], 328 [23],
      405 [15], 459 [19]
   Passamaquoddy Tidal Power Project, **1961:** 197
   Pearson, Lester B., **1963:** 144 [1], 169 [6], 178-
      180, 411
   Royal Canadian Air Force, **1963:** 476
   Trade with Soviet Union, **1963:** 407, 459 [19]
   Trade with U.S., **1963:** 179
   U.S. Ambassador Livingston Merchant, **1961:**
      45, 191, 490
   U.S.-Canada Committee on Trade and
      Economc Affairs, **1961:** 45
   Vanier, George P., **1961:** 190
   Visit to, **1961:** 190-193
Canadian River Project Texas, **1963:** 474, 478
Canal Zone, **1963:** 311
   See also Panama Canal.
Canas, Antonio José, **1963:** 99
Cancellare, Frank, **1962:** 158
Cancer, **1962:** 65; **1963:** 74, 202 [17], 316
   And cigarette smoking, **1962:** 210 [17]
   Eleanor Roosevelt Foundation, **1961:** 215, 414
   President's conference on, **1961:** 83 [4]
Candidates for public office, **1961:** 119 [12, 22],
      447, 448, 477
   Connecticut, **1962:** 472-474
   Equal broadcast time requirements, **1962:** 279
      [13]
   Illinois, **1962:** 481-483
   Indiana, **1962:** 456

Candidates for public office — *continued*
Kentucky, **1962:** 431, 457, 458
Maryland, **1962:** 446
Michigan, **1962:** 433, 436-438
Minnesota, **1962:** 439, 440
New Jersey, **1962:** 450
New York, **1962:** 460, 461
Ohio, **1962:** 396, 432, 480
Pennsylvania, **1962:** 394, 395, 451-455
West Virginia, **1962:** 414
Cannelton decision, **1961:** 391
Cannon, Repr. Clarence, **1962:** 320
Cannon, Sen. Howard W., **1962:** 340 [5], 398; **1963:** 390
Canoyer, Helen G., **1962:** 296n.
Canyonlands National Park, **1962:** 69
Cape Canaveral, Fla., **1962:** 56, 61n., 77, 370, 373, 375, 378 [1]; **1963:** 156, 199, 464, 465, 467, 472
Cape Cod, Mass., **1963:** 266, 376
Cape Cod National Seashore Park, **1961:** 49, 315; **1962:** 69, 75 [23], 216, 336, 337, 377, 417, 459; **1963:** 379, 387
Capehart, Sen. Homer E., **1962:** 352 [14]
Capital, free flow of, **1961:** 33, 136, 488 [17]; **1962:** 22
Capital gains on sale of depreciable business property, **1961:** 136; **1962:** 13 (p. 33), 16 (p. 57)
Capital improvement programs, **1962:** 7 (p. 6), 16 (p. 52), 53, 165, 174; **1963:** 21 (p. 37), 30 (p. 66)
Depressed areas, **1962:** 111
District of Columbia, **1963:** 56
Virgin Islands, **1962:** 130
Capital investment, Federal, **1962:** 13 (pp. 36, 37)
Capitalism, **1961:** 497
Capitol building, **1962:** 221n., 552
Capitol Page School, **1962:** 236
Caples, William G., **1962:** 412n.
Caplin, Mortimer M., **1961:** 157; **1962:** 340 [13]
Capps, Ethel, **1963:** 137n.
Caracas, visit to (1961), **1961:** 507-511; **1963:** 71, 73
Caramanlis, Constantine, **1961:** 457
Visit to, **1961:** 128, 135
Caramanlis, Mrs. Constantine, **1961:** 128
Carbon County, Pa., **1962:** 328
Cardona, José Miro, **1963:** 134 [1]
Cardozo, Benjamin, **1962:** 393n.
CARE.
See Cooperative for American Remittances to Europe.
Caribbean Sea, **1962:** 384, 419
Carlson, Sen. Frank, **1961:** 26n.; **1962:** 68; **1963:** 52, 356 [18]
Carmichael, Leonard C., **1963:** 238n.
Carnegie Endowment for International Peace, **1962:** 13 (p. 38)

Carnegie Institute of Technology, **1961:** 460n.
Carpenter, Lt. Comdr. Malcolm Scott, **1962:** 213, 223; **1963:** 199, 406
Carpenter, Mrs. Malcolm Scott, **1962:** 223
Carpenters and Joiners of America, United Brotherhood of, **1962:** 247
Carpeting, tariffs on, **1962:** 98, 115 [23], 245 [16]
Carpets, import duties, **1963:** 9
Carr, James K., **1962:** 337; **1963:** 389n.
Carr, Lawrence W., **1963:** 389
Carr, Waggoner, **1963:** 476
Carr, William G., **1963:** 469
Carriers, rate regulation, **1962:** 129
Carrillo Flores, Antonio, **1962:** 265n., 269n., 270n., 406
Carroll, Diahann, **1962:** 201
Carroll, Sen. John A., **1962:** 336
Carroll, Lt. Gen. Joseph F., **1963:** 54 [5]
Carroll, Thomas H., 2d, **1961:** 162n.
Carson, Rachel, *Silent Spring*, **1962:** 352 [24]
Carter, John Mack, **1963:** 319a note
Carter, Oliver, **1963:** 389
Cartoonists, Editorial, American Association of, **1963:** 172
Carvel, Gov. Elbert N., **1963:** 108, 461
Carver, John A., **1962:** 495n.; **1963:** 113
Casablanca, **1963:** 115, 116
Casals, Pablo, **1961:** 431, 464; **1962:** 527n.; **1963:** p. 901
Casardi, Alberico, **1961:** 106
Cascade Mountains, **1963:** 47
Case, Sen. Clifford P., **1962:** 450; **1963:** 107 [19]
Case Institute of Technology, **1961:** 460n.
Casey, Repr. Bob, **1962:** 378 [22]; **1963:** 474
Casper, Sir John, **1963:** 203
Cassin, Riccardo, **1961:** 305
Cassino, Italy, Polish cemetery at, **1962:** 461
Cassiopeia A, constellation, **1962:** 155
Castro, Fidel, **1961:** 132, 138, 201, 483; **1962:** 250, 276, 396, 414n., 459, 551 [2], 556; **1963:** 14, 54 [7, 10], 65 [12], 72, 75 [18], 118, 120 [5], 134 [1], 144 [8], 356 [16, 23], 448 [19], 465 [1], 468, 478
Anti-Castro movement, **1961:** 119 [4, 20]
Communist affiliation, **1961:** 119 [6]
Interference in Brazilian affairs, **1961:** 334 [18]
News conference remarks on, **1961:** 15 [14], 25, [24], 119 [4, 6, 20], 139 [7], 171 [17], 258 [6], 334 [18, 26], 488 [1]; **1962:** 115 [11], 139 [12], 259 [11, 21], 378 [1], 515 [4]
Castroism, **1961:** 322
Casualty losses, tax deduction, **1963:** 34
Cathedral of Czestochowa, **1962:** 461
Catholics, **1961:** 26
Catholic Church, Second Vatican Council, **1962:** 430
Catholic Universities, Federation of, **1963:** 342
Catholic Youth Organization, **1963:** 463

Catledge, Turner, **1961:** 138
Catoctin Mountains, **1961:** 25 [10]
Cattle, **1963:** 197, 217
Catton, Bruce, **1961:** 461
Caulfield, Genevieve, **1963:** p. 901
Cavour, Camillo di, **1961:** 84
CCC.
    See Commodity Credit Corporation.
CED.
    See Committee for Economic Development.
Celebrezze, Anthony J.
    See Health, Education, and Welfare, Secretary of
        (Anthony J. Celebrezze).
Celler, Repr. Emanuel, **1961:** 25 [27], 119 [11], 152;
        1962: 139 [9]; **1963:** 139, 444
Censorship
    Defense and State Departments, **1962:** 50 [23]
    International broadcasting, **1962:** 352 [23]
Census Bureau, **1962:** 448; **1963:** 134
    Director (Richard M. Scammon), **1963:** 117n.,
        167
Census of 1960, **1961:** 25 [27]
Census of Transportation, proposed, **1962:** 129
CENTO.
    See Central Treaty Organization.
Central African Republic, **1962:** 85
    Letter to President Dacko, **1961:** 167
Central American Joint Planning Mission, **1963:** 99
Central American Presidents' Conference San
        José, **1963:** 89 [10], 97-100, 102-106, 107
        [1, 7, 17, 22], 118, 120 [12], 134 [1]
Central banks, foreign, **1961:** 497
Central Intelligence Agency, **1961:** 222 [10]; **1962:**
        27 [13], 50 [7], 75 [6], 107 [6], 275, 276,
        515 [19]; **1963:** 89 [3, 9], 405 [2, 12, 16],
        448 [19]
    Director (John A. McCone), **1961:** 489, 497;
        1962: 27 [13], 109; **1963:** 54 [5], 89 [9], 144
        [12], 349, 354, 405 [2, 12]
Central Treaty Organization, **1961:** 279, 476; **1962:**
        157, 340 [20]; **1963:** 378, 390, 464
Central Valley, Calif., reclamation, **1963:** 41
Century of Negro Progress Exposition, **1963:** 153
Ceylon, **1963:** 77
Ceylon, William Gopallawa, **1962:** 106
C.G. Hokanson Co., **1962:** 113n.
Chaban-Delmas, Jacques, **1961:** 219n.
Chamber of Commerce, Boston, **1963:** 239
Chamber of Commerce, Junior, **1962:** 47
Chamber of Commerce of the United States,
        1962: 113, 162, 174, 179 [7], 243, 279 [3];
        1963: 65 [17], 202 [13]
Chamber music, Vermont, **1961:** 327
Chamizal Zone controversy, U.S-Mexico, **1962:**
        279 [21]; **1963:** 89 [13], 307
    Agreement, **1963:** 432

Champion, George, **1963:** 455
Chandler, A.B., **1963:** 120 [13]
Chantilly, Va., **1962:** 512
Chapel Hill, N.C., **1961:** 418n.
Chapman, Oscar L., **1962:** 362
Charitable contributions, tax deduction, **1963:** 34
Charleston, W. Va., **1963:** 249
Charlotte, Grand Duchess, **1963:** 150, 152, 154,
        156, 157
Charlotte, N.C., **1961:** 416
Chase, John, **1963:** 172
Chatterjee, D.N., **1961:** 363n.
Chauncey, Tom, **1961:** 476
Chavez, Sen. Dennis, **1962:** 111
Chayes, Abram, **1961:** 273n.
Chelf, Repr. Frank, **1961:** 25 [27]; **1962:** 431, 458
Chen Cheng, visit of, **1961:** 306, 309
Chennault, Claire, **1963:** 472
Chenoweth, Repr. J. Edgar, **1962:** 336
Cherokee Indians, **1961:** 16
Cherry Point, N.C., **1962:** 149
Cheyenne, Wyo., Mayor Bill Nation, **1963:** 380
Chiang Kai-shek, **1961:** 412; **1962:** 115 [17, 21],
        184, 259 [13]; **1963:** 202 [16]
Chiari, Roberto, **1961:** 469; **1962:** 245 [14]; **1963:**
        99, 100, 102, 106
    Visit of, **1962:** 235, 238, 242
Chicago Association of Commerce and Industry,
        1962: 113n.
Chicago and North Western Railway Co., **1962:**
        378 [7], 386
Chicago, Ill., **1961:** 155; **1962:** 331, 340 [10],
        482, 483, 527n., 545; **1963:** 35 [9], 110,
        230, 232, 255
    Century of Negro Progress Exposition, **1963:** 153
    Mayor Richard J. Daley, **1961:** 155, 454n.; **1962:**
        482, 483; **1963:** 109, 110
    O'Hare International Airport, **1963:** 109, 110
    White House Regional Conference, **1961:** 454
Chichibu Gakuen (Japan), **1961:** 444
Chicken exports, **1963:** 75 [17], 259
Chidester, Larry D., **1962:** 152 [3]
Chief Justice of the United States (Earl Warren),
        1961: 1, 4, 10; **1962:** 20 [16], 68n., 158,
        211, 512, 527; **1963:** 52, 157, 260 [3], 416,
        and pp. 899, 900
Chiefs of Staff, Joint.
    See Joint Chiefs of Staff.
Child health center, proposed, **1961:** 25 [3], 27
Child Health and Human Development, National
        Institute of, **1962:** 65, 470; **1963:** 53, 74,
        447
Child Health and Human Development, National
        Institute of, proposed, **1961:** 27, 289, 290
"Child Is Waiting," **1962:** 534n.
Child labor, abolition of, **1963:** 85
Child Labor Act, **1962:** 236

Children
  See also Youth.
  Aid for children of unemployed workers, **1961:**
    11, 17, 22, 35 [3]; **1962:** 132, 288, 328, 414,
    446, 456; **1963:** 162, 462
  Corporal punishment in schools, **1963:** 202 [6]
  Crippled, research, **1961:** 289
  Cuban refugees, **1961:** 19
  Day care centers, **1963:** 233
  Dependent, aid for, **1962:** 132, 174, 395; **1963:**
    175 [4]
  Handicapped, concert for, **1961:** 327
  Health and welfare, **1962:** 16 (p. 43), 19, 28, 37,
    65, 132, 291, 306, 395, 470; **1963:** 22, 50,
    53, 64, 187, 217, 316, 369, 434, 435
    Handicapped, **1963:** 43, 447
  Health program, **1961:** 25 [3], 27, 289
  Indian and Eskimos, education, **1961:** 71 [5], 94
  Latin American, **1962:** 279 [1]; **1963:** 326
  Mental health, **1963:** 43, 51, 174, 228, 230, 305
    [19]
  Mental retardation, **1961:** 14, 25 [3], 413, 415 [2];
    1962: 3, 37, 65, 132, 396, 480, 534
  Mortality, **1963:** 64
  Negro children killed in bombing, **1963:** 360, 365
  Of deceased policemen and firemen, annuities,
    1961: 383
  Physical fitness, **1961:** 14, 48
  Support of, tax deduction for, **1963:** 34
Children's Bureau, **1961:** 27, 289; **1962:** 65, 132;
  1963: 50
Childs, Marquis, **1962:** 245 [7]
Chile, **1962:** 250, 544, 546 [20], 549 [6]; **1963:**
  77, 171, 432
  Alessandri Rodriguez, Jorge, **1962:** 542-544, 546
    [16, 20]
  Ambassador Walter Müller, **1962:** 542n.
  Assistance, **1963:** 61, 118
  Martínez Sotomayor, Carlos, **1962:** 543n.
  Reconstruction, U.S. assistance, **1961:** 81, 94, 208
  Tax reforms, **1963:** 118
Chimpanzee space flight, **1961:** 488 [10]
China, Communist, **1961:** 11, 139 [8], 155, 192, 205,
  509, 515; **1962:** 7 (p. 11), 74, 243 [6], 250,
  531, 549 [10], 551 [15, 17, 19]; **1963:** 79,
  105, 290, 316, 349, 382
  Admission to United Nations, question of, **1961:**
    119 [7, 8], 222 [12], 309
  Admission of U.S. correspondents, refusal, **1961:**
    71 [21]
  Agreement on Laos, **1963:** 144 [5]
  Books, worldwide distribution, **1961:** 92 [14]
  Exposition of food, **1961:** 8 [25]
  Ideological differences with Soviet Union, **1961:**
    62 [20]
  Invasion of India, **1962:** 500, 515 [3, 5, 20], 551,
    [20], 554; **1963:** 12 (p. 16), 21 (p. 34), 107
    [14], 118, 214, 219, 285, 320 [3], 459 [3]

China, Communist — *continued*
  Joint statement with Prime Minister Holyoake
    on, **1961:** 66
  Joint statement with Vice President Chen on,
    1961: 309
  Mao Tse-tung, **1962:** 184
  Negotiations on release of U.S. citizens, **1961:**
    15 [32, 33], 71 [21], 415 [6]
  News conference remarks, **1961:** 8 [25], 15 [24,
    32], 25 [7], 62 [20], 71 [18, 21], 92 [6, 14],
    119 [7, 8], 139 [8], 222 [1, 4, 6, 12, 13], 415
    [6], 455 [12]; **1962:** 50 [4, 16], 59 [15],
    89 [14], 179 [16], 210 [2, 5], 245 [10], 259
    [1, 7], 515 [3, 18, 20]; **1963:** 35 [3], 54 [7],
    107 [14], 144 [3, 5], 260 [9], 305 [13, 17],
    320 [2, 3, 11], 328 [1], 356 [19], 459 [3]
  Nuclear test ban treaty, question of signing, **1963:**
    35 [3]
  Nuclear weapons, **1963:** 260 [9], 320 [11]
  Pakistan alliance with, question of, **1963:** 356
    [25]
  Relations with Soviet Union, **1962:** 515 [18], 551
    [20]; **1963:** 12 (p. 17), 305 [13, 17], 319a,
    459 [3]
  Relations with West, **1961:** 222 [12]
  Rift with Soviet Union, **1961:** 62 [20], 455 [12]
  Trade with, **1961:** 71 [18]
  U.S. food for, question of, **1961:** 8 [25]; **1962:** 89
    [14], 210 [2], 243 [6]
  U.S. trade with, **1963:** 459 [3]
China, Republic of, **1961:** 477, 483, 509; **1962:** 70,
  531, 549 [10]; **1963:** 477
  See also Formosa.
  Assistance, **1961:** 309; **1963:** 72n., 118
  Chen Cheng, **1961:** 306, 309
  Chiang Kai-shek, **1961:** 412; **1962:** 115 [17, 21],
    184, 259 [13]; **1963:** 202 [16]
  Communist takeover in 1949, **1961:** 488 [20]
  Invasion of Communist China, question of, **1963:**
    202 [16]
  News conference remarks, **1962:** 259 [1, 5, 13],
    352 [11], 378 [2]
  Shen Chang-Huan, **1961:** 306, 309
  U-2 aircraft, U.S. exports to, **1962:** 378 [2]
  U.N. membership, **1961:** 119 [7], 309
  Yeh, George K.C., **1961:** 306, 309
Chlorine barge in Mississippi River, **1962:** 445
Choate School, **1963:** 160
Choi, Duk Shin, **1961:** 468
Choir, Poznan Boys' and Men's, **1963:** 93
Chopin, Frederic, **1963:** 173
Christian Democratic Union, German, **1963:** 265
Christian Leadership, Inc., International, **1961:**
  26; **1962:** 68n.; **1963:** 52n.
Christiana Securities Corp., **1962:** 33
Christians and Jews, National Conference of, **1961:**
  479
Christmas Carol, Charles Dickens, **1963:** 465

Christmas Island, use for U.S. nuclear tests, **1962:**
    40 [7, 21], 41, 50 [2]
Christmas plans, the President's, **1962:** 515 [9]
Christmas Tree, National Community, **1962:** 550
Chronic unemployment, areas of.
    See Depressed areas.
Chronically ill, **1961:** 406
Chrysler Corp., **1963:** 77
Chukotskiy Peninsula, **1962:** 493
Church, Sen. Frank, **1963:** 356 [18]
Church, Repr. Marguerite Stitt, **1961:** 358n.
Churches, Negro, bombing of, **1963:** 360, 365
Churches, Negro, burning of, **1962:** 378 [6]
Churches, World Council of, **1961:** 35 [11]; **1962:**
    68; **1963:** 136
Churchill, Randolph, **1963:** 126
Churchill, Winston, **1961:** 11, 178, 222 [11], 321,
    397, 404, 473; **1962:** 179 [5], 180, 201, 243,
    300, 343, 363; **1963:** 90, 215, 387, 463
    Honorary U.S. citizenship, **1963:** 35 [8], 126
    News conference remarks on, **1963:** 35 [8], 65
        [12]
    State of, proposed, **1963:** 169 [7]
Churchill, Lady, **1963:** 126n.
CIA.
    See Central Intelligence Agency.
Cigarettes, effect on health, **1962:** 210 [17], 229 [18];
    1963: 202 [17]
Cigarette tax, **1961:** 136
Cincinnati, Ohio, **1961:** 463n.; **1962:** 432
Cisneros, Manuel, **1963:** 468
Citations.
    See Awards and citations.
Citizens' Committee on Free World Security, **1963:**
    118
Citizens Committee for International Develop-
    ment, **1961:** 277
Citizens Committee on Natural Resources, **1963:**
    196n.
Citizens Committee for Tax Reduction and Re-
    vision in 1963, **1963:** 177
Ciudad Juarez, Mexico, **1963:** 307
Civil Aeronautics Board, **1961:** 121; **1962:** 13 (pp.
    34, 38), 93 (p. 237), 129; **1963:** 186
Civil Aeronautics Board, Chairman (Alan S.
    Boyd), **1963:** 29, 186
    Reorganization Plan 3 of 1961, **1961:** 163
Civil Air Patrol Cadets, **1962:** 173
Civil aviation, **1962:** 93 (p. 237), 129; **1963:** 30
    (p. 67), 179, 186, 242
Civil defense, **1961:** 5, 205, 302, 503; **1962:** 320;
    1963: 12 (p. 18), 82
    Annual exercises, remarks, **1961:** 154
    Fallout shelters, **1961:** 205, 302, 410, 415 [4], 455
        [13], 488 [13, 21], 503; **1962:** 7 (p. 10), 13
        (p. 28), 279 [11], 320; **1963:** 21 (p. 33)
    Federal aid, **1961:** 205

Civil defense — *continued*
    News conference remarks, **1961:** 415 [4], 455 [13],
        488 [13, 21]; **1962:** 40 [8], 279 [11]
    Responsibilities, **1961:** 295, 386
    State directors, message, **1963:** 166
Civil Defense Committee, Governors Conference,
    1961: 410, 503
Civil and Defense Mobilization, Office of, **1961:**
    205
    Change of name.
        See Emergency Planning Office of.
    Director (Frank B. Ellis), **1961:** 5, 295, 302
Civil rights, **1961:** 11, 205; **1962:** 7 (p. 8), 174, 288,
    359, 362, 399, 483; **1963:** 30 (p. 71), 59, 73,
    90, 153, 192, 220, 226, 230, 232, 236, 237,
    271, 290, 294, 302, 309, 311, 339, 340,
    349, 351, 360, 365, 366, 372, 397, 427, 444,
    462, 456 [3], 473
    See also Integration.
    Albany, Ga., **1962:** 316 [8]
    Birmingham, Ala.
        See main heading.
    Demonstrations, **1963:** 169 [1, 4, 14], 202 [20]
        230, 248, 305 [20], 320 [12], 328 [3, 9], 356
        [22]
        March on Washington, **1963:** 305 [20], 328 [3,
            9], 336
    District of Columbia, **1963:** 22, 35 [15], 230
    Employment, **1961:** 62 [10], 92 [12], 68, 116, 477
    Equal employment opportunity.
        See main heading.
    Federal aid, proposed termination in states
        violating, **1963:** 134 [5], 135, 144 [13]
    Freedom Riders, **1961:** 291 [10]
    Government employees recreational associa-
        tions, **1961:** 137
    Housing, **1961:** 62 [10], 92 [12]; **1962:** 8 [18],
        279 [16], 515 [2, 10], 545; **1963:** 10, 82,
        230, 248, 305 [7], 356 [9]
        In Washington D.C., **1962:** 142
    Legal counsel, **1963:** 12 (p. 14), 91
    Messages to Congress, **1963:** 82, 248
    Negro leadership, **1963:** 320 [9]
    News conference, remarks, **1961:** 8 [9], 15 [22],
        25 [8], 62 [10], 71 [14], 92 [8, 12], 171 [6],
        291 [10], 455 [7]; **1962:** 8 [18], 27 [18],
        198 [8], 279 [16], 302 [12], 316 [8], 378 [6],
        515 [2, 10]; **1963:** 89 [8, 15], 107 [18], 144
        [13], 169 [1, 4, 14, 19], 202 [1, 20], 305
        [4, 7, 20], 320 [6, 7, 9, 12], 328 [3, 9], 356
        [9, 22], 448 [4, 16], 459 [4, 11]
    Public accommodations.
        See Public accommodations, equal access.
    Radio address, question of, **1963:** 169 [19]
    Voting rights, **1961:** 8 [9], 92 [12], 286, 455 [7]
        See also main heading, Voting Rights.

Civil Rights Act of 1963, **1963:** 248
Civil rights bill, **1963:** 248, 305 [4, 7], 328 [7]
Civil rights, Commission on, **1961:** 62 [10]; **1962:**
        142, 246, 555; **1963:** 59, 82, 107 [18], 134
        [5], 135, 144 [13, 18], 202 [20], 248
    Chairman (John A. Hannah), **1963:** 135
    Conference, **1961:** 55
Civil Rights, Committee on (1947), **1963:** 248
Civil service, **1962:** 12, 323, 533; **1963:** 4n., 221, 366
    See also Government employees.
    Entrance examination, **1963:** 228
Civil Service Act, **1962:** 12
Civil Service Commission, **1962:** 43, 55, 143, 304,
        448; **1963:** 44, 148, 357, 405 [13], 448 [27],
        452
    Hearing examiner positions, review of standards,
        1961: 121
    Status of women study, **1961:** 504
Civil Service Commission, Chairman (John W.
        Macy, Jr.), **1961:** 465, 504; **1962:** 163, 304,
        323; **1963:** 4, 76, 129, 130, 148, 174, 238,
        357, 452
Civil Service League, National, **1962:** 167
Civil Service Retirement Act, **1962:** 447
Civil War, **1961:** 418, 461, 462, 473; **1962:** 3, 109,
        159, 552; **1963:** 92, 136, 192, 226, 227, 228,
        265, 276, 278, 279, 303, 381, 451
Civil War Centennial Commission, **1961:** 92 [8];
        1962: 159n.
Civilian Conservation Corps., **1963:** 378
Civilian nuclear power, **1962:** 100, 289, 335, 382,
        408
Clark, Judge Charles E., **1962:** 21
Clark, Sen. Joseph S., **1961:** 499; **1962:** 89 [5], 278,
        394, 395, 451-455; **1963:** 376, 445
Clark, Gen. Mark W., **1962:** 175
Clark, Justice Tom C., **1961:** 234
Clark, William, **1962:** 15
Classification Act, **1962:** 55, 447
Clay, Henry, **1962:** 349; **1963:** 2, 73, 99, 334, 381
Clay, Gen. Lucius D., **1961:** 325, 334 [3]; **1962:** 4,
        139 [5, 8], 145, 546 [12], 549; **1963:** 118,
        267, 268, 269, 270, 272, 333, 338
    Letter to, **1963:** 111
    News conference remarks on, **1963:** 89 [20], 169
        [17], 328 [1]
Clay Committee, **1963:** 89 [20], 111, 118, 120 [6]
Clayton, William L., **1962:** 20 [5], 74, 199
Clayton Act, **1962:** 93 (p. 241)
Clement, Gov. Frank G., **1963:** 192
Cleveland, Grover, **1962:** 439, 482; **1963:** 23, 228
Cleveland, Harlan, **1961:** 358n.; **1963:** 359
Cleveland, Ohio, **1961:** 454n.; **1962:** 311, 340 [10],
        401, 480
    Newspaper strike, **1963:** 35 [11], 75 [13], 107 [16]
Cliburn, Van, **1962:** 527n.
Cliff, Edward P., **1963:** 376
Clifford, Clark M., **1961:** 168n.; **1963:** 405 [12]

Clifton, Maj. Gen. Chester V., **1963:** 335
Clinton, Gordon S., **1961:** 472n.
Clooney, Rosemary, **1962:** 15, 233
Clothing Workers, Amalgamated, **1962:** 198 [15]
Clyde, Gov. George D., **1963:** 385
Coal, **1963:** 193, 381
    Mine disasters, **1963:** 155
    News conferences remarks, **1963:** 459 [25]
    Pipelines construction, **1962:** 102
    Slurry development, **1962:** 69
    Unemployment in industry, **1962:** 50 [3], 410 [1];
        1963: 110, 175 [2], 228
Coal industry, **1961:** 133
Coal mines, soil conservation, **1961:** 278
Coal and Steel Community, European, **1961:** 222,
        481; **1963:** 341
Coast and Geodetic Survey, **1961:** 100; **1963:** 396
Coast Guard, **1961:** 100; **1962:** 128, 243 [5], 255,
        330; **1963:** 388, 396
    171st anniversary, **1961:** 311
Coast Guard Academy, **1962:** 243 [5], 330; **1963:** 82
Coast Guard, Commandant (Adm. Alfred C.
        Richmond, **1961:** 311
Coat of arms, Presidential, **1961:** 11, 155
Cobalt, ocean deposits, **1961:** 49, 100
Cochran, Jacqueline, **1962:** 475
Cocoa prices, **1962:** 86
Codacci-Pisanelli, Guiseppe, **1962:** 500
Coerr, Wymberley, DeR., **1961:** 71 [6]
Coffee, **1963:** 99, 266, 326
Coffee Agreement, International, **1962:** 86, 126,
        410 [3], 418, 546 [20]
Coffin, Frank, **1961:** 119 [2]; **1962:** 326
Cohen, Malcolm, **1962:** 274n.
Cold war, **1962:** 50 [25], 109; **1963:** 12 (pp. 13, 17),
        21 (p. 31), 43, 82, 232, 260 [18], 320 [10],
        407, 426
    Nation's response to, **1961:** 185
Cole, David, **1961:** 40n., 256, 258 [11]; **1962:** 21
Colee, Harold, **1963:** 465
Coleman, William L., **1962:** 3
Collective bargaining, **1961:** 87, 121; **1962:** 75
        [1, 17], 121, 129, 152 [2, 17, 18], 162, 164,
        210 [13], 256, 369, 378 [20], 516; **1963:** 18,
        92, 184, 187, 244, 248, 298, 306, 310, 337,
        466
    See also Labor disputes.
    News conference remarks, **1963:** 35 [11], 54 [6],
        75 [2]
Collective security, **1961:** 34, 66; **1962:** 199
Colleges, **1963:** 21 (p. 38), 134, 146, 221, 271, 465
    Athletics dispute, **1963:** 7, 107 [8]
    Community colleges, **1963:** 43
    Federal aid, **1961:** 11, 27, 46, 62 [27], 70, 71 [13,
        17], 94, 144, 334 [6]; **1962:** 37, 40 [2], 65,
        174, 186, 302 [4], 328, 394, 395, 431, 432,
        436, 437, 451, 456, 458, 459, 480, 481, 483,
        551 [10]; **1963:** 43, 426, 439, 478

Colleges — *continued*
    Church-connected schools, **1962:** 259 [4]
    Fellowships, **1963:** 43
    Foreign aid participation, **1963:** 118
    Housing, **1961:** 17, 46, 70, 94; **1962:** 7 (p. 8), 23,
        37, 414, 452; **1963:** 43
    Integration, **1963:** 82
    Land-grant, **1962:** 37, 109, 166, 197, 202, 540;
        1963: 43, 82, 92, 118, 226, 279, 469
    Physical fitness programs, **1963:** 325
    Research grants to, **1962:** 209; **1963:** 70
    Role in public affairs, **1963:** 136, 192, 226
    Student loans, elimination of anti-Communist
        affidavit, **1962:** 469
    Student loan program, **1963:** 43
    Summer intern program for students, **1962:** 250,
        349
    Training grants, **1963:** 43
    Work-study programs, **1963:** 43
College Housing Act, **1963:** 43
College of William and Mary, **1961:** 418
Colley, Nathaniel, **1962:** 257n.
Collier Trophy, **1961:** 243
Collier (Robert J.) Trophy for 1961, presentation,
    1962: 294
Collier (Robert J.) Trophy for 1962, presentation,
    1963: 406
Collins, Gen. James F., **1962:** 422
Collins, John F., **1961:** 212
Collins, LeRoy, **1961:** 178; **1962:** 49, 243n., 515 [7]
Collins, Rt. Rev. Thomas, **1963:** 390
Colmer, Repr. William M., **1963:** 107 [24]
Cologne, visit to, **1963:** 253, 254
Colombia, **1962:** 86, 170, 243, 258, 549 [6, 10];
    1963: 72, 107 [1], 163, 361, 478
    Assistance, **1963:** 118
    Cooperatives in, **1963:** 149
    Lleras Camargo, Alberto, **1961:** 512, 515, 516n.;
        1962: 64, 258
    News conference remarks, **1962:** 410 [3], 546 [20]
    Peace Crops project, **1961:** 187, 199, 213
    Rural electrification, **1962:** 499
    Tax reforms, **1963:** 118
    U.S. Ambassador Fulton Freemen, **1961:** 514n.
    Valencia, Guillermo Leon, **1962:** 258
    Visit to, **1961:** 512-516
Colombo Plan, 10th anniversary, **1961:** 266
Colonialism, **1962:** 212, 461, 522n.; **1961:** 1, 222 [9],
    387; **1963:** 12 (pp. 15, 16), 14, 115, 300n.,
    302, 394n.
Colorado, **1962:** 336, 337, 338; **1963:** 223, 226,
    248ftn. (p. 486)
    Gov. Steve L. R. McNichols, **1962:** 216, 336
Colorado River, **1963:** 301
Colorado River, salinity reduction, **1962:** 273
Colorado River Basin, **1962:** 313
Columbia Basin project, deferment of drainage
    payments, **1961:** 336

Columbia Broadcasting System, **1962:** 551n.
Columbia Law Review, **1962:** 498
Columbia River, **1963:** 179, 301
Columbia River Basin development, **1961:** 474
    Treaty with Canada, **1961:** 49, 83 [2]
Columbia River Basin, reclamation, **1963:** 41
Columbia University, **1962:** 498
Columbus, Christopher, **1961:** 84, 143; **1962:** 450;
    1963: 5, 97, 194, 410
Columbus Bend, Tex., **1963:** 474
Columbus Day, **1962:** 450; **1963:** 405 [10], 410
Columbus, Ind., telegram from high school stu-
    dents, **1961:** 455 [20]
Columbus,Ohio, **1962:** 3, 201, 396
Combs, Gov. Bert T., **1962:** 431, 457, 458; **1963:**
    108, 458
COMIBOL.
    See Bolivia.
Command and General Staff School, foreign
    officers at, **1963:** 183
Commemorative occasions.
    See Addresses, remarks, etc., on com-
        memorative or dedicatory occasions.
Commerce, Department of, **1961:** 62 [7], 71 [18], 83
    [7]; **1962:** 16 (p. 49), 93 (p. 237), 113, 275,
    487; **1963:** 125, 127, 248, 306, 361, 407
    Commercial facilities abroad, **1961:** 23
    Depressed areas redevelopment program, **1961:**
        7, 35 [15]
    Export expansion program, **1962:** 114; **1963:** 30
        (p. 65)
    Export markets, development, **1961:** 23
    Foreign travel in U.S. promotion, **1961:** 23
    Highway cost allocation study, **1961:** 58
    Housing, planning on, **1961:** 76
    Maritime functions, **1961:** 238
    News conference remarks, **1962:** 229 [8], 279 [12];
        1963: 328 [23], 405 [1]
    Nomination of Franklin D. Roosevelt, Jr. as
        Under Secretary, **1963:** 65 [5]
    Public works functions, **1962:** 380
    Textiles, research on, **1961:** 161
    Trade mission program, **1961:** 23
    Transportation planning, **1962:** 129
    Transportation problem **1961:** 310
Commerce, Secretary of (Luther H. Hodges), **1961:**
    23, 40, 58, 79, 87, 158, 161, 259, 288, 310,
    327, 415n., 428, 497; **1962:** 6n., 10, 113n.,
    162, 165, 248, 410n., 495; **1963:** 21 (p. 37),
    29, 30 (p. 68), 62, 85, 87, 94n., 130, 299,
    306, 361
    Highway program, study, **1961:** 17
    Letters, **1962:** 153, 487
    Memorandum, **1962:** 221
    News conference remarks on, **1961:** 35 [15], 71
        [18], 171 [6], 258 [11]; **1962:** 40 [17], 75
        [21]

Commerce Committee for the Alliance for Progress, **1962:** 177
Commercial Fisheries, Bureau of, **1961:** 100
Commission on Automation, Presidential, **1963:** 310
Commission on Campaign Costs, President's, **1961:** 403; **1962:** 152 [4], 219; **1963:** 151
Commission on Civil Rights, **1961:** 55, 62 [10]; **1962:** 142, 246, 555; **1963:** 59, 82, 107 [18] 134 [5], 135, 144 [13, 18], 202 [20], 248
Commission on Educational Exchange, U.S. Advisory, **1961:** 57
Commission on Equal Rights for Women, **1963:** 315
Commission of the European Economic Community, **1961:** 21; **1962:** 144
Commission on Federal Expenditures, Presidential, proposed, **1963:** 120 [6]
Commission of Fine Arts, **1962:** 27 [21]
Commission on Mental Illness and Health, Joint, **1962:** 65
Commission on Money and Credit, **1961:** 245; **1962:** 16 (p. 51), 151, 229 [1, 15]; **1963:** 30 (p. 67)
Commission on Organization of the Executive Branch of the Government, **1961:** 237
Commission on Registration and Voting Rights, President's, **1963:** 117, 167
Commission on the Status of Women, President's, **1962:** 43, 304, 347, 505n.; **1963:** 233, 409
Committee on Civil Defense, Governors' Conference, **1961:** 410, 503
Committee on Civil Rights (1947), **1963:** 248
Committee for Economic Development, **1961:** 245; **1962:** 194, 203, 210 [13, 16]; **1963:** 75 [14], 175
Committee on Economic Growth, Cabinet, **1963:** 30 (p. 68)
Committee for an Effective Congress, National **1962:** 340 [18]
Committee on Employment of the Handicapped, President's, **1962:** 49; **1963:** 174, 452
Committee on Equal Employment Opportunity, President's, **1961:** 68, 116; **1962:** 7, (p. 8), 38n., 255n., 344, 509n.; **1963:** 82, 220, 248
Committee on Equal Opportunity in the Armed Forces, **1962:** 257
  Report, **1963:** 251
Committee on Equal Opportunity in Housing, President's, **1962:** 515 [2]; **1963:** 49, 82
Committee on Federal Credit Programs, report, **1963:** 62
Committee on Federal Office Space, Ad Hoc, **1962:** 221
Committee on Government Contracts, President's, **1961:** 68

Committee on Government Employment Policy, President's, **1961:** 68
Committee on Government Organization, President's Advisory, **1961:** 29
Committee on the Implementation of the Federal Employee-Management Relations Program, President's Temporary, **1962:** 215n.
Committee on International Exchange of Persons, **1963:** 140n.
Committee on Juvenile Delinquency and Youth Crime, **1961:** 382; **1962:** 220; **1963:** 64
Committee on Labor-Management Policy, President's Advisory, **1961:** 17, 23, 33, 40, 87, 205; **1962:** 6, 164, 203n., 515 [17]; **1963:** 30 (p. 67), 206, 299, 310
Committee on Management, President's Advisory, **1961:** 29
Committee on Manpower Development and Training, National Advisory, **1962:** 412
Committee of the National Cultural Center, **1961:** 467
Committee on Natural Resources, **1963:** 252
Committee on Radiation, National Advisory, **1962:** 229 [19], 259 [19]
Committee to Strengthen the Security of the Free World, **1962:** 549 [10]; **1963:** 89 [20], 111, 118, 120 [6]
Committee on Trade and Economic Affairs, U.S. - Canada, **1961:** 45
Committee on Trade and Economic Affairs, U.S.- Japan, **1961:** 252, 444n., 455 [3]; **1962:** 531n.
Committee for Traffic Safety, President's, **1962:** 11
  Report, **1963:** 125
Committee for the Voluntary Payroll Savings Plan, Interdepartmental, **1961:** 75
Committee on Youth Employment, President's, **1961:** 470; **1962:** 360; **1963:** 64, 92, 141, 142, 248, 393
Commodity Credit Corporation, **1961:** 94; **1962:** 7 (p. 7), 25, 27 [3]; **1963:** 21 (pp. 36, 40), 45, 202 [18], 405 [1], 407
Common carriers, rate regulation, **1963:** 87
Common market.
  See European Economic Community.
Common market, Central American, **1963:** 99, 107 [1], 120 [12]
Commonwealth, British, **1963:** 202 [3]
Communications
  Defense facilities, **1961:** 99
  Scientific and technical, **1963:** 67
  Technological progress, **1963:** 215n.
  Transcontinental Telegraph Centennial, **1941:** 433
  U.S.-Canada mutual defense system, **1961:** 298
  U.S.-Latin America, **1962:** 551 [14]

[References are to items except as otherwise indicated]

Communications — *continued*
  U.S.-Soviet, **1962:** 546 [17], 551 [14]; **1963:** 232,
    320 [8]
    Direct line, **1963:** 232, 250, 319a.
  U.S.-Vatican, **1963:** 305 [3]
Communications Act, **1961:** 15 [26]
Communications Satellite Act of 1962
  Approval, **1962:** 355
  Proposed, **1962:** 39
Communications Satellite Corporation, **1962:** 355
  Letter to incorporators, **1962:** 476
Communications Satellite Corporation, United
    States, **1963:** 470
Communications satellites, **1961:** 11, 99, 205, 254,
    387; **1962:** 7 (p. 11), 39, 96, 109; **1963:**
    21 (p. 34), 331, 366, 477, 478
  Approval of bill, **1962:** 355
  Geneva conference, **1963:** 470
  Global system, proposed, **1963:** 430
  Industry's share in program, question of, **1961:**
    139 [21], 299
  News conference remarks, **1962:** 59 [1], 107 [12],
    302 [1, 2, 6, 20], 316 [16]
  Policy, statement, **1961:** 299
  Relay, **1963:** 55, 126n.
  Syncom II, **1963:** 331
  Telstar, **1962:** 285, 302 [1, 2, 6, 20], 398; **1963:**
    55, 416n.
Communications Workers of America, **1962:** 47
Communism, **1961:** 11, 18, 26, 153, 155, 162, 178,
    244, 283, 302, 376, 387, 435, 468, 477, 497,
    499; **1962:** 7 (p. 10), 22, 68, 83, 109, 174,
    243 [1], 250, 293, 310 [1], 400, 414n., 449,
    528n., 537, 549 [10], 551 [15, 17, 18, 23],
    557; **1963:** 12 (p. 19), 57, 72, 80, 162, 226
  See also Marxism-Leninism.
  Campaign remarks, **1962:** 439, 440, 460, 461, 483
  Costa Rica, **1963:** 104
  In Cuba, **1961:** 11, 35 [12], 119 [6], 138, 178
    See also Cuba.
  Labor organizations, **1963:** 162, 268
  News conference remarks, **1961:** 35 [12], 119 [6,
    13], 171 [6, 14, 15], 318 [9, 10, 11], 334 [11,
    26], 455 [14], 488 [3, 4]; **1962:** 8 [9, 10], 50
    [6], 59 [15], 89 [9], 115 [11], 139 [16], 259
    [15], 279 [10], 340 [20], 352 [11], 378 [1],
    410 [12], 515 [1, 12], 546 [22]; **1963:** 260 [7,
    8], 305 [6, 25], 405 [7]
  Threat to newly emerging nations, **1961:** 90
  Versus democracy, **1961:** 119 [13]; **1962:** 170, 440,
    459, 483; **1963:** 12 (pp. 15, 16, 18), 14, 71,
    99, 104, 105, 118, 134 [1], 221, 232, 258,
    260 [7, 8], 268, 269, 271, 290, 291, 294,
    378, 383, 437, 441, 455, 464, 468
Communist aggression and expansion, **1961:** 132,
    155, 205, 214, 277, 335, 483; **1962:** 13
    (p. 28), 226, 276, 389, 419; **1963:** 12 (p. 16),
    21 (p. 33), 118, 232, 349

Communist aggression — *continued*
  Africa, **1963:** 14, 112, 118, 478
  Asia, **1961:** 11, 38, 138, 302; **1962:** 210 [11],
    531; **1963:** 14, 89 [20], 112, 118, 144 [2, 3,
    5, 16], 316, 340, 349, 477
  Cambodia, **1963:** 114 [16]
  Campaign remarks, **1962:** 395, 439, 453
  Europe, **1963:** 35 [1], 112
  Greece, **1961:** 128n.
  India, **1963:** 21 (p. 34), 107 [14], 219
  Joint statements with foreign leaders, **1961:** 193,
    242, 376, 468
  Korea, **1963:** 118
  Laos, **1961:** 92 [1, 3, 6]; **1962:** 50 [22], 192, 198 [4,
    20]; **1963:** 118, 144 [2, 3, 5, 16], 477
  Latin America, **1961:** 1, 8 [13], 11, 81, 138, 193,
    205, 373; **1962:** 7 (p. 12), 8 [10], 20 [22], 27
    [2, 6]; **1963:** 65 [10, 14], 89 [10, 22], 104,
    107 [1, 7], 112, 118, 120 [21], 459 [25], 476
  Middle East and Near East, **1963:** 118, 169 [2],
    477
  News conference remarks, **1961:** 8 [13], 15 [14],
    92 [1, 3, 6], 119 [13], 139 [14, 15, 23], 171
    [14, 15]; **1962:** 8 [10], 20 [22], 27 [2, 6], 40
    [4, 14], 50 [6, 9, 22], 89 [4, 9], 139 [16], 198
    [4, 20], 210 [11]; **1963:** 89 [10, 18, 20], 260
    [11], 328 [1]
  Southeast Asia, **1961:** 171 [15]
  Viet-Nam, **1961:** 435, 505; **1962:** 7 (pp. 12, 13), 34,
    40 [4], 50 [9], 139 [16]; **1963:** 21 (p. 34),
    118, 144 [16], 340, 349, 356 [5], 399, 438
  Western Hemisphere, **1961:** 19, 171 [14]; **1962:** 50
    [6], 77, 89 [9], 529; **1963:** 14, 65 [14], 71, 89
    [10, 18], 107 [1, 7], 144 [8, 17], 328 [1],
    333, 477
Communist bloc, **1961:** 483, 505n.; **1962:** 3, 7 (p. 7),
    10, 24, 32, 461, 551 [17]; **1963:** 12 (p. 15),
    118, 134 [1], 232, 379, 382, 383, 407
  See also Satellite countries, Soviet; Sino-Soviet
    bloc; *specific countries.*
  Cuban activities.
    See Cuba.
  Cuban adherence to, **1963:** 107 [7]
  Foreign aid program, **1961:** 244; **1962:** 22, 170
  Nationalistic trends in, **1963:** 319a
  News conference remarks, **1961:** 25 [7], 71 [18],
    119 [6, 13], 291 [11], 415 [5], 488 [6]; **1962:**
    20 [13, 25], 229 [3], 245 [9], 340 [4, 21, 26],
    352 [11], 378, [11], 546 [22]; **1963:** 35 [5],
    54 [3], 75 [18], 89 [16, 17], 305 [3], 328
    [11], 459 [1, 10]
  Oil shipments to Cuba, **1963:** 89 [16]
  Sino-Soviet rift, **1963:** 12 (p. 17), 305 [13, 17],
    319a
  Trade with, **1961:** 71 [18]; **1962:** 22, 546 [22];
    1963: 35 [5], 107 [15], 405 [1], 407
Communist system, **1961:** 192

Community Chest campaign, **1961:** 259
Community development, **1961:** 17, 76, 436; **1962:** 13 (p. 31), 23, 25, 380; **1963:** 21 (p. 37), 230
Community Facilities Administration, **1961:** 15 [5], 17; **1962:** 23, 545
Community Health, Bureau of, proposed, **1961:** 27
Community health services and facilities, **1962:** 65, 288; **1963:** 50, 53, 66, 74, 75 [1]
Community Health Services and Facilities Act, **1962:** 65; **1963:** 53, 74
Community Health Services and Facilities Act, approval, **1961:** 406
Community Health Services and Facilities Act of 1961, **1963:** 53, 74
Community Planning and Services Act, Senior Citizens, **1963:** 185
Community recreation centers, **1961:** 496
Community relations services, proposed, **1963:** 248
Competition, business, **1962:** 93 (p. 241)
Comptroller General of the United States (Joseph Campbell), **1963:** 151
Conant, James B., **1961:** 477, 499; **1963:** 141, 270, and p. 902
Conciliation and Mediation Service, Federal, **1963:** 92, 202 [20]
Conelrad, **1961:** 154
Conference of African States on Development of Education, **1961:** 188
Conference of Appalachian Governors, **1963:** 127
Conference of the Business Committee for Tax Reduction in 1963, **1963:** 351
Conference of Christians and Jews, National, **1961:** 479
Conference on Export Expansion, White House, **1963:** 306, 361
Conference of Heads of State of African States, **1963:** 200, 228, 260 [20], 304, 394, 397
Conference of Independent African States (1958), **1961:** 125n.
Conference on Mental Retardation, White House, **1963:** 364
Conference on Milk and Nutrition, National, **1962:** 19
Conference on Peaceful Uses of Space, **1961:** 206
Conference on Science and World Affairs, message, **1961:** 347
Conference of State Civil Defense Directors, **1963:** 166
Conference of State Legislative Leaders, National, **1963:** 368
Conference on Trade Policy, **1962:** 199
Conflict of interests
  Business, **1961:** 25 [21]
  Federal Government, **1961:** 152, 171 [11]; **1962:** 198 [1,21]
Conflicts of interest and ethical standards
  Memorandum, **1963:** 31

Conflicts of interest — *continued*
  News conference remarks, **1963:** 120 [20], 328 [20], 448 [17]
Congo, Republic of (Brazzaville), **1961:** 236
  Youlou, Fulbert, **1961:** 235, 236
Congo, Republic of the (Leopoldville), **1961:** 26, 92, 368, 487; **1962:** 104, 346, 395, 396, 551 [1]; **1963:** 12 (p. 11), 14, 136, 232, 366, 381, 382, 383, 385, 394
  Adoula, Cyrille, **1961:** 499, 519; **1962:** 8 [19], 35, 302 [11], 316 [7], 340 [14]; **1963:** 28
  Communism in, **1963:** 478
  Economy, **1963:** 471
  Gizenga, Antoine, **1961:** 62 [8]
  Joint statements on, **1962:** 87, 419, 554
  Joint statements with foreign leaders re, **1961:** 51, 74, 173, 304, 519
  Kasavubu, Joseph, **1961:** 35 [1]; **1963:** 28
  Katanga.
    See main heading, Katanga.
  News conference remarks, **1961:** 8 [2], 15 [14, 15], 25 [13], 35 [1, 4, 13, 16], 62 [8]; **1962:** 8 [19], 40 [14, 23], 107 [5], 302 [11], 316 [3, 7], 340 [14], 352 [20]
  Tshombe, Moise, **1961:** 519
  U.N. actions in, **1961:** 11, 35 [1, 13, 16], 62 [8], 132, 173, 456
  United Nations operations, **1962:** 7 (p. 11), 24, 40 [14, 23], 107 [5], 302 [11], 316 [3], 319, 340 [14], 352 [20], 424, 557; **1963:** 12 (pp. 10, 18), 28, 278, 366, 416, 418, 471
  U.S. Ambassador Edmund A. Gullion, **1963:** 120 [16]
  U.S. Ambassador Clare H. Timberlake, **1961:** 15 [15]
  U.S. food for, **1961:** 8 [2]
Congress
  Adjournment, question of, **1962:** 259 [12], 302 [4]
  Ethical standards, **1963:** 120 [20]
  Exchange visits to Soviet parliament, proposed, **1962:** 50 [17]
  First Congress, documents, publication of, **1963:** 26
  Government employees, release of information to Congress, **1963:** 405 [13], 448 [27]
  House of Representatives
    Election of new Speaker, **1961:** 415 [11]
    Increase in membership, question of, **1961:** 25 [27], 318 [5]
    Rules Committee membership, **1962:** 50 [15], 259 [8], 551 [8]
    Rules Committee membership increase, **1961:** 8 [14], 15 [19]
  Intelligence sources of Members, **1963:** 144 [12]
  Investigations
    Bay of Pigs invasion, **1963:** 35 [2]
    Defense contracts, **1963:** 35 [2]
  Liaison with executive branch, **1961:** 25 [12]

Congress — *continued*
  Members, limitation of terms, **1963:** 35 [10]
  New England and Western Members, meeting
    with, **1963:** 75 [17]
  News conference remarks, **1963:** 305 [4, 20], 328
    [7, 9], 448 [21, 25], 459 [4, 6, 11, 13]
  President's service in, **1963:** 162
  Record of, **1962:** 75 [18]; **1963:** 120 [8]
  Relationship with executive branch, **1962:** 20 [7]
  Resolution on Cuba, **1962:** 378 [18], 485, 486
  Responsibilities toward regulatory agencies,
    1961: 121
  Senate filibuster in literacy test bill, **1962:** 179
    [17]
  Visit of Members to Yugoslavia, **1963:** 419
  Warheads, nuclear, approval of joint control,
    1963: 75 [19]
  White House reception for Members, **1961:** 71
    [2], 78
  Wives of Members, remarks to, **1963:** 157
Congress, letters to Members of.
  See also Congress, messages to.
  Aspinall, Repr. Wayne N., public lands, **1963:** 37
  Buckley, Repr. Charles A., capital improve-
    ments in depressed areas, **1962:** 111
  Byrd, Sen. Harry Flood, tariff decisions, **1962:** 98
  Cannon, Repr. Clarence, civil defense, **1962:** 320
  Chavez, Sen. Dennis, capital improvements in
    depressed areas, **1962:** 111
  Cooley, Repr. Harold D., wheat and feed grains,
    1961: 300
  Dirksen, Sen. Everett M., Berlin wall, **1962:** 357
  Dirksen, Sen. Everett, test ban treaty, **1963:** 354
  Eastland, Sen. James O., drugs, **1962:** 137, 321
  Ellender, Sen. Allen J., wheat and feed grains,
    1961: 300
  Halleck, Repr. Charles, Berlin wall, **1962:** 357
  Harris, Repr. Oren, Federal Trade Commission,
    1961: 337
  Hayden, Sen. Carl, civil defense, **1962:** 320
  Holifield, Repr. Chet, use of by-product steam
    from nuclear reactors, **1962:** 289
  Magnuson, Sen. Warren, civil defense, **1962:** 320
  Mansfield, Sen. Mike, test ban treaty, **1963:** 354
  McNamara, Sen. Pat, health insurance for older
    persons, **1961:** 341
  Mills, Repr. Wilbur D.
    Tariff decisions, **1962:** 98
    Tax bill, **1962:** 108
  Pell, Sen. Claiborne, interurban transportation,
    eastern seaboard, **1962:** 462
  President of Senate and Speaker of House of
    Representatives
    Army Department reorganization, **1962:** 9
    Balance of payments, report, **1962:** 114
    Capital improvements program, **1962:** 53
    Children of unemployed workers, Federal aid,
      1961: 22

Congress, letters to Members — *continued*
  President of Senate — *continued*
    Children's Bureau research functions, **1961:**
      289
    Coal pipelines construction, **1962:** 102
    Colleges and universities, Federal aid, **1961:** 70
    Communications satellites, **1962:** 39
    Criminal justice, administration of, **1963:** 91
    Depressed areas redevelopment, **1961:** 7, 44
    District of Columbia charter, **1963:** 122
    District of Columbia, Federal aid to, **1963:** 56
    District of Columbia, self-government, **1961:**
      286
    District of Columbia voting in Presidential
      elections, **1961:** 186
    Economic assistance for Eastern Europe, **1961:**
      69
    Election campaign costs, **1962:** 219; **1963:** 151
    Farm bill, **1961:** 127
    Federal Airport Act, **1961:** 141
    Federal employee organization dues, with-
      holding, **1962:** 154
    Federal employee training, **1962:** 143
    Federal research on natural resources, **1963:**
      252
    Federal Reserve System, **1962:** 151
    Feed grains, emergency program, **1961:** 39
    Foreign affairs academy, **1963:** 57
    Foreign assistance, **1961:** 207
    Foreign central banks, **1961:** 54
    Foreign governments, interest rates, **1961:** 82
    Government research and development con-
      tracts, **1962:** 163
    Health, Education, and Welfare, Assistant
      Secretary of, additional, **1961:** 129
    Health and hospital care, **1961:** 52
    Health insurance for older persons, **1961:** 32
    Highway system, interstate, **1961:** 79
    Housing and urban improvement, **1961:** 101
    Immigration laws, revision, **1963:** 311
    Income tax reduction, **1962:** 176
    International air transport, regulation, **1963:**
      186
    International human rights convention, **1963:**
      309
    International Monetary Fund, U.S. loans to,
      1962: 31
    Judgeships, creation of additional, **1961:** 28
    Juvenile delinquency, **1961:** 182
    Labor, Assistant Secretary of, additional,
      1961: 166
    Land conservation fund, **1962:** 128
    Minimum wage bill, **1961:** 24
    National Aeronautics and Space Council, **1961:**
      114
    National Cultural Center, **1961:** 77
    National Defense Education Act, **1961:** 144
    National forests development program, **1961:**
      377

Congress, letters to Members — *continued*
　President of the Senate — *continued*
　　National Service Corps, proposed, **1963:** 130
　　Nile Valley, preservation of antiquities, **1961:** 108
　　Occupational training, **1961:** 211
　　Oceanography, **1961:** 100
　　Peace Corps, **1961:** 213; **1962:** 64
　　Peace Corps appropriation bill, **1963:** 294
　　Public Health Service Institutes, additional, **1961:** 290
　　Ready Reserve, mobilization, **1962:** 366
　　Recreation facilities, **1963:** 63
　　Refugee aid, **1961:** 297
　　Research grants to colleges and universities, **1962:** 209
　　Saline water conversion, **1961:** 257
　　Secret Service protection, **1961:** 142
　　Senior Citizens Act, proposed, **1962:** 193
　　Small Business Act, amendment, **1962:** 72
　　Social security program, **1961:** 43
　　Supersonic civil air transport, **1963:** 242
　　Surplus Federal lands, transfer to States, **1962:** 195
　　Transportation policy, **1963:** 87
　　Transportation, National Capital region, **1963:** 208
　　Travelers, American, duty-free allowance, **1961:** 53
　　Unemployment compensation, **1961:** 22, 241 **1962:** 80, 136
　　Unemployment insurance system, strengthening of, **1963:** 185
　　U.S. Arms Control and Disarmament Agency, proposed, **1961:** 262
　　United States Study Commission — Texas, report, **1962:** 313
　　Urban affairs and housing department, proposed, **1961:** 130
　　Urban mass transportation, **1963:** 69
　　Urban transportation, **1961:** 246
　　Veterans, disability compensation, **1961:** 159
　　Virgin Islands, self-government, **1962:** 130
　　Water resources planning bill, **1961:** 284
　　Water resources, report, **1963:** 70
　　Welfare and Pension Plans Disclosure Act, **1961:** 194
　　Wheat sale to the Soviet Union, **1963:** 407
　　Youth employment, **1961:** 233
　　Russell, Sen. Richard B., civil defense, **1962:** 320
　　Thomas, Repr. Albert, civil defense, **1962:** 320
　　Vinson, Repr. Carl, civil defense, **1962:** 320
Congress, messages to.
　See also letters to Members of.
　Aeronautics and space activities, report, **1962:** 26
　Agriculture, **1961:** 85; **1962:** 25
　Atomic energy agreement, U.S.-France, **1961:** 355
　Balance of payments, **1963:** 306

Congress, messages to — *continued*
　Balance of payments deficit, **1961:** 23
　Budget, **1962:** 13; **1963:** 21
　Budget and fiscal policy, **1961:** 94
　Chilean reconstruction, **1961:** 81
　Civil rights and job opportunities, **1963:** 82, 248
　Conflict of interests, **1961:** 152
　Conservation of natural resources, **1962:** 69
　Consumer interest, protection of, **1962:** 93
　Defense budget, **1961:** 99
　District of Columbia, budget, **1963:** 22
　Economic recovery and growth, **1961:** 17
　Economic report, **1962:** 16; **1963:** 30
　Education, **1961:** 46; **1962:** 37; **1963:** 43
　Farm, **1963:** 45
　Federal pay reform, **1962:** 55
　Foreign assitance, **1961:** 90; **1962:** 83
　Free world defense and assistance, **1963:** 118
　Health and hospital care, **1961:** 27
　Health programs, **1962:** 65; **1963:** 53
　Highways, **1961:** 58
　Housing and community developments, **1961:** 76
　Inter-American Fund for Social Progress, **1961:** 81
　Manpower Report of the President, **1963:** 92
　Maritime strike of 1961, settlement, **1962:** 21
　Mental illness and retardation, **1963:** 50
　Mutual security program, report, **1962:** 237
　Natural resources, **1961:** 49
　Nuclear test ban treaty, **1963:** 324
　Peace Corps, **1961:** 63
　Policemen and firemen, retirement benefits, veto, **1961:** 383
　Public welfare programs, **1962:** 28
　Railroad rules dispute, **1963:** 310
　Regulatory agencies, **1961:** 121
　Reorganization Plans, **1962:** 23, 118.
　　See also Reorganization Plans, messages.
　Reorganization Plan No. 1, **1963:** 207
　Senior citizens, **1963:** 74
　State of the Union, **1961:** 11; **1962:** 7; **1963:** 12
　Tax reduction and reform, **1963:** 34
　Taxation, **1961:** 136
　Trade, **1962:** 22
　Trade agreements, **1962:** 76; **1963:** 9
　Transportation, **1962:** 129
　United Nations
　　U.S. participation, reports, **1962:** 92, 319
　U.S. purchase of bonds, **1962:** 24
　United States Arms Control and Disarmament Agency, report, **1962:** 29
　Urgent national needs, **1961:** 205
　Youth, **1963:** 64
Congress, reports to.
　See also Congress, letters to Members of; Congress, messages to.
　List, Appendix C., **1961:** p. 844; **1962:** p. 943; **1963:** p. 926

[*References are to items except as otherwise indicated*]

Congress, reports to, messages transmitting.
   See also Congress, letters to Members of;
      Congress, messages to.
   Aeronautics and space activities, **1962:** 26
   Balance of payments, **1962:** 114
   Economic report, **1962:** 16; **1963:** 30
   Federal salary comparability, **1963:** 148
   Government research and development con-
      tracts, **1962:** 163
   Manpower resources, **1963:** 92
   Mutual security program, **1962:** 237
   National forests development program, **1961:** 377
   United Nations, U.S. participation, **1962:** 92, 319
   United States Arms Control and Disarmament
      Agency, **1962:** 29
   United States Study Commission — Texas, **1962:**
      313
   U.S. participation in the United Nations, **1963:** 471
   Water resources, **1963:** 70
Congress on Medical Librarianship, Second Inter-
   national, **1963:** 247
Congressional award, presentation to Robert
   Frost, **1962:** 110
Congressional Club, **1963:** 157
Congressional Gold Medal, **1963:** 353
Congressional Medal of Honor, **1962:** 420; **1963:**
   109, 159
Conley, Reginald G., **1962:** 533n
Connally, John B., Jr. (Secretary of the Navy),
   1961: 16, 232; **1962:** 179 [4]; **1963:** 108,
   223, 472, 474, 475, 476, 478
Connally, Tom, death of, **1963:** 442
Connecticut, **1962:** 326, 472-474
   Civil rights, **1963:** 248ftn. (p. 486)
   Gov. John N. Dempsey, **1961:** 212; **1962:** 472-
      474; **1963:** 108, 427
Connor, John T., **1962:** 476n.
Conservation Association, American, **1963:** 196
Conservation Foundation, **1963:** 196
Conservation of natural resources, **1961:** 17, 49, 85,
      94; **1962:** 7 (p. 7), 13 (p. 30), 25, 128, 216,
      240, 332, 333, 336, 413, 425, 495; **1963:** 12
      (p. 14), 21 (p. 36), 34, 37, 41, 45, 47, 63, 70,
      127, 179, 193, 196, 252, 305 [14], 366, 376,
      377, 379, 380, 381, 383-385, 387, 388, 400,
      405 [5], 430, 474, 478
   Message to Congress, **1962:** 69
   News conference remarks, **1962:** 75 [23], 410 [7]
Conservation tour
   California, **1963:** 389
   Minnesota, **1963:** 378
   Montana, **1963:** 382, 383
   Nevada, **1963:** 390
   North Dakota, **1963:** 379
   Oregon, **1963:** 388
   Pennsylvania, **1963:** 376

Conservation tours — *continued*
   Utah, **1963:** 385, 386
   Washington, **1963:** 384, 387
   Wisconsin, **1963:** 377
   Wyoming, **1963:** 380, 381
Conservation, White House Conference on, **1962:**
   69, 216
Conservative Party, British, **1963:** 120 [19]
Constitution, U.S., **1961:** 11, 46, 55, 99, 205; **1962:**
      23, 92, 141, 174, 202, 278, 328, 349, 420,
      437, 446, 451, 454, 480, 523, 549, 551 [3,
      10, 11]; **1963:** 6, 23, 59, 82, 88, 114, 115,
      134 [5], 135, 230, 236, 237, 245, 248, 266,
      271, 312, 338, 340, 344, 354, 401, 433, 436,
      462, 468, 478
   Amendment, form of, **1963:** 169 [8]
   Amendments, proposed
      Anti-poll tax, **1962:** 340 [2]
      Prayers in public schools, **1962:** 259 [3, 20]
   Anti-poll tax amendment, proposed, **1963:** 82,
      108
   Defense of the Constitution, John Adams, **1963:**
      2
   Documentary publications on, **1963:** 26
   First amendment, **1961:** 26, 153
   14th Amendment, **1963:** 82, 248, 320 [6]
   15th Amendment, **1963:** 82
   News conference remarks, **1961:** 8 [10, 14], 25 [8],
      62 [27], 71 [13, 14], 83 [8, 9, 21], 291 [10];
      1962: 40 [3], 152 [13], 259 [3, 20], 279 [8],
      340 [2], 378 [6], 515 [13], 546 [23]; **1963:**
      144 [13], 169 [4], 356 [6], 459 [6]
   Provision on Presidential inability, **1961:** 319
   13th, 14th, and 15th amendments, **1962:** 555
   22nd amendment, **1962:** 551 [9]
   23rd amendment, ratification, **1961:** 103, 186
Constitution Hall, **1962:** 250
Constitutional Convention, **1962:** 452
Construction industry, **1961:** 76; **1962:** 16 (p. 44),
      108, 359
   Labor dispute, **1962:** 179 [7], 302 [15]
   Unemployment, **1962:** 115 [16]
Construction, Federal, acceleration to reduce un-
   employment, **1961:** 17
Construction programs, Federal, equal employ-
   ment opportunity, **1963:** 220
Construction workers trade union, German, **1963:**
   268
Construction workers, unemployment, **1961:** 76
Consultants, Government, **1963:** 31
Consumers, **1962:** 93 (pp. 236, 240), 170; **1963:** 92,
      177, 202 [2], 271, 291
   Credit, **1963:** 77
   Income, **1962:** 16 (p. 44), 115 [16], 229 [1]; **1963:**
      12 (pp. 12, 13), 21 (pp. 26, 28), 30 (p. 62),
      45
   Message to Congress, **1962:** 93

Consumers — *continued*
Protection of, **1962:** 93, 296; **1963:** 237
Cosmetics, **1963:** 53
Drugs, **1962:** 137, 316 [1, 4, 24], 321, 395, 396, 414, 442, 446, 459; **1963:** 53, 74, 121
Spending, **1962:** 7 (p. 6), 16 (pp. 44, 47), 89 [5], 93 (p. 235), 302 [7, 17], 549; **1963:** 21 (p. 27), 30 (pp. 57, 59, 60, 61, 62), 34, 35, 45, 77, 92, 110, 134, 169 [15], 175, 351, 465
Consumer Price Index, **1962:** 93 (p. 238)
Consumer's Advisory Council, **1962:** 93 (p. 238), 296
Continental Can Co., **1962:** 139 [8]
Continental Congress, **1963:** 43, 92
Continental defense, **1961:** 99, 302
Continental National Bank of Fort Worth, **1963:** 448 [23]
Contracts, Government, **1962:** 13 (p. 38), 55, 163, 373; **1963:** 6, 19, 30 (p. 59), 34, 134, 175 [2], 448 [24], 478
Conservation, **1963:** 45
Defense, **1961:** 35 [3], 83 [1]; **1962:** 50 [14], 89 [13, 19], 245 [17], 453
See also Defense contracts.
Depressed areas, **1961:** 17; **1962:** 59 [19], 414
Electrification of underdeveloped countries, **1962:** 499
Equal employment opportunity, **1961:** 92 [12], 116, 204, 281; **1963:** 230
Laborers and mechanics employed under, work-week, **1962:** 327
News conference remarks, **1961:** 35 [3], 71 [3], 83 [1], 92 [12]; **1962:** 50 [14], 59 [19], 89 [13, 19], 179 [15], 245 [17]
Patent policy on inventions made under, **1962:** 175 [15]
Reclamation, **1963:** 41
Scientific and technical work, review of, **1961:** 314
Contracts, labor.
See Labor contracts.
Contributions, charitable, tax deduction, **1963:** 34
Convention on the Abolition of Forced Labor, **1963:** 309
Convention on the Abolition of Slavery, the Slave Trade, **1963:** 309
Convention for the Avoidance of Double Taxation of Income, U.S.-Luxembourg, **1963:** 156
Convention on High Seas Fisheries of the North Pacific Ocean, **1963:** 352n.
Convention on the Political Rights of Women, **1963:** 309
Conway, Jack T., **1962:** 174; **1963:** 49
Conway, Rev. Michael J., **1962:** 483n.
Conway, Gen. Theodore J., **1961:** 419n.
Cook, Mercer, **1963:** 359n.

Cook County, Ill., **1961:** 155
Cooke, Edward, **1962:** 452
Cooley, Repr. Harold D., **1961:** 300; **1962:** 413; **1963:** 448 [14]
Coolidge, Calvin, **1961:** 258 [4], 497; **1962:** 198 [7], 550; **1963:** 193, 377
Coombs, Philip H., **1961:** 57, 188, 443n.
Cooper, Camila, **1963:** 199
Cooper, Dexter, **1963:** 301n.
Cooper, Janita, **1963:** 199
Cooper, Sen. John Sherman, **1962:** 179 [17], 457
Cooper, Sen. and Mrs. John S., **1963:** 137
Cooper, Maj. L. Gordon, Jr., **1963:** 190, 199, 202 [4], 406
Cooper, Mrs. L. Gordon, Jr., **1963:** 190, 199
Cooper, Mrs. L. Gordon, Sr., **1963:** 199
Cooper, R. Conrad, **1962:** 121
Cooperation, American Institute of, **1963:** 149n.
Cooperative for American Remittances to Europe (CARE), **1961:** 8 [25], 85, 187
Cooperative League of the U.S.A., **1963:** 149n.
Cooperative Research Act, **1963:** 43
Cooperative Research Act, amendment proposed, **1962:** 37
Cooperatives, **1963:** 118
Cooperatives, National Conference on, **1963:** 149
Cooperatives, tax provisions, **1961:** 136; **1962:** 16 (p. 57)
Coordinating Council of Organizations on International Trade, **1962:** 199n.
Coosa River project, **1963:** 193
COPE registration conference, **1963:** 362
Copper, exports from Cyprus, **1962:** 225
Copper, ocean deposits, **1961:** 49
Coquet, Benito, **1962:** 269
Corbett, Jack C., **1961:** 71 [6]
Cordell Hull Dam, **1963:** 192
Cordova, Argentina, **1963:** 84
Cork, Ireland, **1963:** 277
Corn, **1962:** 25, 259 [8]
Price supports, **1962:** 39; **1963:** 45
Storage payments, **1961:** 85
Cornell University, **1961:** 493; **1962:** 25
Corporal punishment in schools, **1963:** 202 [6]
Corporate profits, **1962:** 16 (p. 44)
Corporate taxes, **1961:** 33, 92 [18]; **1962:** 7 (p. 7), 13 (p. 33), 16 (p. 57), 229 [1], 328, 549
Investments abroad, **1961:** 23, 136
Tax credits to provide investment incentives, **1961:** 17, 136
Corps of Engineers, **1961:** 71 [15], 320; **1962:** 13 (p. 30), 330, 414, 445; **1963:** 21 (pp. 36, 42), 127, 192, 301
Corpus Christi, Tex., **1962:** 417
Corregidor, battle of, **1962:** 131
Correspondents Association, White House, **1962:** 158

Corridor cities concept, National Capital Region, **1962:** 525

Corson, John, **1963:** 44n.

Cortez, Hernando, **1961:** 432

Cosmetics, consumer protection, **1963:** 53

Cosmetics, safety testing, **1962:** 93 (p. 239)

Cosmopolitan magazine, **1963:** 319a note

Cosmos Club, membership in, **1962:** 8 [23]

Cost of living, **1961:** 15 [23], 415 [20], 455 [17]; **1962:** 13 (p. 32), 328, 367

See also Inflation.

Cost reduction program, Federal, **1963:** 21 (p. 41)

Costa Rica, **1963:** 72, 106, 431, 478

Economic and social development, **1963:** 104

El Bosque housing project, **1963:** 99, 103

Mora, Juan Rafael, **1963:** 99

News conference remarks, **1963:** 89 [10], 107 [1, 7, 17, 22], 120 [12]

Orlich, Francisco J., **1963:** 97, 99, 100, 102, 103, 106

Peace Corps projects in, **1963:** 294

San José, Central American President's Conference.

See San José, Costa Rica.

Tax reforms, **1963:** 118

Trade union movement, **1963:** 104

U.S. Ambassador Raymond Telles, **1963:** 98, 102, 103; 105, 223

Visit to, **1963:** 97-100, 102-106

Costa Rican Christian Democratic Youth, **1963:** 104

Costa, Zenobio da, **1962:** 175

Cotton, **1961:** 15 [27], 161; **1963:** 21 (p. 36), 306, 478

Acreage allotments, **1962:** 25

Exports and imports, **1961:** 258 [10], 478, 488 [19]; **1962:** 8 [4], 22, 25, 170, 365; **1963:** 45, 75 [17]

Marketing programs, **1963:** 169 [13]

News conference remarks, **1962:** 8 [4], 198 [11], 245 [9], 410 [3, 9]

Prices, **1962:** 25, 410 [3, 9]; **1963:** 45

Price supports, **1961:** 94

Textiles, **1961:** 258 [10], 428, 488 [19]

Cotton Advisory Committee, National, **1962:** 198 [17]

Couey, James H., **1963:** 464

Council on Aging, President's, **1962:** 193n., 245 [11]; **1963:** 74, 92

Council on the Arts, President's Advisory, **1963:** 240, 246

Council of Churches, World, **1962:** 68

Council of Economic Advisers, **1961:** 49; **1962:** 65, 69, 93 (p. 238), 129, 152 [18], 210, [13, 16], 245 [2], 378 [20]; **1963:** 30 (pp. 64, 66), 94, 310

Estimates of steel industry profits, **1961:** 354

Tax bill, review, **1961:** 139 [18]

Council of Economic Advisers, Chairman (Walter W. Heller), **1961:** 83 [18], 123, 139 [6]; **1962:** 47, 75 [5], 279 [19], 296n.; **1963:** 29, 30 (p. 68), 62, 65 [2], 77, 94n.

Public works appraisal, **1961:** 17

Council on Foreign Economic Policy, **1961:** 207

Council on International Monetary and Financial Problems, National Advisory, **1961:** 23; **1962:** 31

Council of National Defense, **1963:** 133

Council of Negro Women, National, **1962:** 27 [11]

Council on Physical Fitness, President's, **1963:** 64

Council for Science and Technology, Federal, **1961:** 49; **1962:** 8 [1], 69, 118, 547; **1963:** 53, 70, 252

Council of Senior Citizens, Golden Ring, **1962:** 202n.

Council of Senior Citizens, National, **1962:** 202n., 217

Council on Youth Fitness, President's, **1961:** 27, 48n., 293, 348, 496; **1962:** 65, 283, 291; **1963:** 325

Counselling of parents of mentally retarded children, **1961:** 413

Counts, J. Curtis, **1963:** 206

County Cork, Ireland, **1963:** 478

Courts, Federal, **1962:** 459; **1963:** 135, 248

See also Supreme Court of the United States.

Civil rights enforcement, **1963:** 202 [1], 230

Courts of Appeals, **1961:** 28; **1962:** 21, 420

Customs and Patent Appeals, **1962:** 340 [28]

District Courts, **1961:** 28, 270; **1962:** 21, 33, 247, 434; **1963:** 39

Judgeships, additional, **1961:** 28, 195

Judicial appointments in South, **1963:** 89 [8]

News conference remarks, **1963:** 35 [23], 144 [13], 169 [1, 4], 320 [6]

Rights to counsel, **1963:** 12 (p. 14)

School integration decisions, **1961:** 25 [8]

Cousteau, Capt. Jacques-Yves, **1961:** 134

Couve de Murville, Maurice, **1963:** 144 [2]

Cox, Archibald (Solicitor General), **1962:** 115 [12], 231, 245 [2]; **1963:** 320 [6]

Crabmeat imports, **1961:** 483

Craig, May, **1961:** 15 [36], 291 [14], 455 [19]; **1962:** 20 [11]

Craig, Mrs. May, **1963:** 75 [9]

Cramer, Robert S., **1963:** 319a note

Creative America, **1962:** 552n.

Credit, **1961:** 17, 76; **1962:** 16 (p. 44), 93 (p. 236), 152 [2], 549 [7]; **1963:** 21 (p. 32), 30 (pp. 63, 67), 94, 242, 306, 407, 462

Federal programs, memorandum, **1963:** 62

News conference remarks, **1963:** 305 [2], 405 [15]

Report of Commission on Money and Credit, **1961:** 245

Credit facilities for U.S. exporters, **1961:** 437, 497

Credit Insurance Association, Foreign, **1963:** 30 (p. 65), 306
Credit systems, **1961:** 245
Credit Union Day, **1963:** 417
Credit Union National Association, World Extension Department, **1961:** 423
Credit unions, tax exemption, **1961:** 136
Creek Indians, **1961:** 16
Crenesse, Pierre, **1961:** 214 n.
Crime, **1962:** 7 (p. 7), 20 [24], 395, 443, 446, 459, 497; **1963:** 30 (p. 65), 64, 82, 134, 230, 248, 363, 423, 478
Crime, organized, **1961:** 11, 94, 136
    Measures to combat crime, **1961:** 362
Crimea, **1963:** 457
Criminal Justice Act of 1963, **1963:** 91
Criminal prosecutions, right of counsel in, **1963:** 91
Critical materials.
    See Strategic and critical materials.
Crittenberger, Willis, **1962:** 175
Crommelin, Rear Adm. John, G., **1961:** 62 [28]
Cromwell, Oliver, **1962:** 63, 180
Cronkite, Walter, **1963:** 340
Crop insurance, **1962:** 440; **1963:** 193
Cropland Conversion Program, **1963:** 382
Cropland, decline in need for, **1962:** 25
Crop yields, **1963:** 217
Crosby, Francis, **1961:** 312
Cross of Casimir Pulaski, **1962:** 461
Crossfield, A. Scott, **1961:** 486n.; **1962:** 294n.
Crotty, Peter J., **1962:** 461
Cuba, **1961:** 78, 132, 138, 483; **1962:** 86, 226, 250, 395, 396, 459, 528, 535, 549 [4, 10], 556, 557; **1963:** 14, 168, 311, 316, 344, 354, 366, 382, 385, 390, 391, 439, 464, 468, 476
    Air attacks on U.S. vessels, **1963:** 75 [3, 5, 8, 20]
    Arms shipments from Communist countries, **1961:** 15 [14]
    Attempted invasion, **1961:** 119 [4], 132, 138, 334 [26]
        Prisoners, tractors in exchange for, question of, **1961:** 201, 258 [6]
        Taylor (Gen. Maxwell D.) investigation, **1961:** 258 [8]
    Bay of Pigs invasion, **1962:** 107 [6], 551 [3, 4]; **1963:** 35 [2], 89 [3], 134, 448 [10]
        Prisoners captured in, **1962:** 107 [9], 139 [12], 259 [11], 546 [12], 556
    Broadcasts throughout Latin America, **1961:** 25 [24]
    Castro, Fidel, **1961:** 15 [14], 25 [24], 119 [4, 6, 20], 132, 138, 139 [7], 171 [17], 201, 258 [6], 334 [18, 26], 483, 488 [1]
        See also main heading, Castro.
    Communism in, **1961:** 11, 35 [12], 119 [6], 138, 178; **1962:** 50 [6], 89 [9], 115 [11], 378 [1], 515 [1]; **1963:** 12 (p. 18), 14, 54 [7], 65 [10, 11, 14, 16], 73, 99, 105, 107 [13], 118, 120 [21], 134 [1], 356 [16]

Cuba — *continued*
    Communism in — *continued*
        Subversive activities, **1963:** 65 [14], 107 [1, 7], 144 [17]
    Communist technicians and supplies for, **1962:** 340 [21, 26], 352 [14, 17], 378 [1, 11]; **1963:** [4], 54 [2], 65 [11], 333, 459 [6], 462, 477
    Congressional resolution on, **1962:** 378 [18], 485, 486
    Diplomatic relations with, **1961:** 8 [13]
    Economy, **1963:** 75 [18], 118, 465 [1]
    Exile organizations
        Assistance, **1963:** 202 [11]
        Raids by, **1963:** 107 [13], 120 [5]
    Expulsion from Inter-American organizations, **1962:** 27 [2], 50 [18], 89 [9]
    Food from Communist China, **1961:** 8 [25]
    Government in exile, question of, **1963:** 144 [11]
    Guantanamo naval base, **1962:** 107 [14, 21], 378 [1], 485, 515 [7]; **1963:** 202
    Guerillas, movement to and from, control of, **1963:** 144 [8]
    Imprisonment of U.S. citizens, **1961:** 15 [32], 258 [6]
    Invasion brigade veterans, enlistment in U.S. Army, **1963:** 120 [5]
    Invasion, question of, **1962:** 352 [14], 378 [1]; **1963:** 134 [1], 356 [16]
        Assurances against, **1962:** 515 [1, 4, 11], 546 [3]
    Isolation of, **1963:** 107 [7], 144 [8]
    Joint statements on, **1962:** 419, 508, 529, 544, 554
    News conference remarks, **1961:** 8 [13, 15, 25], 15 [14, 32], 25 [23, 24], 35 [8, 12], 71 [8], 119 [4, 6, 20], 139 [1, 7], 171 [9, 12, 17], 258 [6, 8], 334 [26], 455 [9]; **1962:** 27 [2, 10], 50 [6, 18], 89 [9,], 107 [6, 9, 14, 21], 115 [11], 139 [12], 259 [11], 279 [10], 340 [21, 26], 352 [11, 14, 17, 19, 21], 378 [9, 11, 13, 16, 18], 515 [4, 6, 7, 11, 13, 15, 18, 19], 546 [3, 4, 10, 12, 15, 17]; **1963:** 35 [2, 4, 19, 24], 54 [2, 5, 7, 12], 65 [10, 11, 14, 16], 75 [3, 5, 8, 16, 18, 20], 89 [3, 6, 7, 9, 10, 16, 18], 107 [1, 2, 7, 13, 17], 120 [3, 5, 18, 21], 144 [8, 11, 12, 17], 202 [8, 11, 14], 305 [16, 23], 320 [10, 13], 328 [16, 22], 356 [14, 16, 19, 23], 448 [10, 13], 459 [6]
    Nuclear weapons test ban treaty, ratification, question of, **1963:** 356 [23]
    Nuclear weapons tests, question of, **1963:** 320 [13]
    OAS security measures against, **1963:** 144 [17]
    Oil shipments to, proposed embargo, **1963:** 89 [16]
    Poliomyelitis outbreak, **1961:** 71 [8]
    Position on San José conference, **1963:** 107 [7]
    Property of U.S. citizens, **1961:** 119 [4]
    Refugees from, **1962:** 378 [1], 556; **1963:** 107 [13], 120 [5], 134 [1], 144 [8, 11], 202 [11]

Cuba — *continued*
  Soviet bombers, missiles, and weapons in, **1962:**
    352 [17], 378 [1, 11], 488-493, 500, 520,
    521, 529, 551 [2, 14-16, 18, 20]; **1963:** 30
    (p. 65), 75 [5, 20], 84, 120 [3, 5], 144 [12],
    221, 319a, 426, 471, 477, 478
    Broadcast, **1962:** 485
    Proclamation, **1962:** 486
    Removal, **1962:** 494, 501, 515 [1, 4, 6, 11], 546
      [3, 15], 549 [8]; **1963:** 11, 12 (pp. 11, 15, 16,
      18, 19), 54 [2, 5], 75 [16, 18], 89 [9], 118,
      120 [3], 202 [14]
  Soviet propaganda in, **1963:** 65 [16]
  Soviet relations with, **1963:** 356 [23]
  Soviet troops in, **1962:** 549 [8], 515 [1]; **1963:** 35
    [4], 54 [2, 5, 7, 12], 120 [3, 5], 305 [23], 328
    [16, 22], 448 [13]
    Withdrawal, **1963:** 75 [3, 16, 18], 89 [6], 107
      [2], 120 [3], 144 [12], 202 [14]
  Special Adviser (John J. McCloy), **1963:** 11
  Statements, **1962:** 378 [1], 515 [1]
  Trade with, **1961:** 35 [8]; **1962:** 27 [10]
    Embargo, **1961:** 171 [12], 455 [9]; **1962:** 32, 89
      [9], 378 [1]
  Trade with free world, **1963:** 134 [1], 144 [8], 407
  Travel to, **1963:** 107 [17], 320 [10]
  U.S. aerial reconnaissance, **1962:** 501, 520, 521;
    1963: 35 [4], 54 [5], 75 [20], 89 [9]
  U.S. naval blockade, **1962:** 486, 488n., 492, 493,
    501, 515 [1], 551 [2]; **1963:** 35 [19], 134 [1],
    147, 225, 227, 351
  U.S. prisoners in, release, **1963:** 144 [8]
  U.S. relations with, **1963:** 120 [18], 305 [16, 23],
    320 [10]
    Diplomatic relations, question of resumption,
      1963: 89 [18]
    Voice of America broadcasts, **1962:** 532; **1963:**
      477
Cuban Invasion Brigade, presentation of flag to
    President, **1962:** 556
Cuban refugees, **1961:** 8 [15], 9, 19, 86, 132, 138, 139
    [7], 297
  Message to mothers, **1961:** 183
  Military training in U.S., question of, **1961:** 171
    [9]
  Voorhes (Tracy), report, **1961:** 8 [15]
Cuban Revolutionary Council, **1962:** 556n.
Cudlip, Merlin A., **1961:** 254n.
Cullerton, P.J., **1961:** 155; **1962:** 483
Cultural Center, National, **1961:** 77, 467; **1962:** 152
    [5], 301, 527, 552
Cultural Center Week, National, **1962:** 527n.
Cultural exchange, **1962:** 183
  U.S.-Poland, **1962:** 461
Cultural and educational exchange, **1961:** 78, 424
  Approval of bill, **1961:** 379
Cultural life in U.S., **1962:** 184, 243 [1]; **1963:** 5, 30
    (p. 66), 50, 92, 137, 204, 240, 246, 266, 327,
    385, 439

Cultural and Technical Interchange Between East
    and West Center for, **1963:** 231
Curran, Joseph, **1961:** 258 [11]
Currencies, **1963:** 77
Currencies, coinage, use of free silver for, **1961:** 484;
    1962: 16 (p. 55); **1963:** 30 (p. 67), 94
Currencies, foreign, **1962:** 16 (p. 50), 31, 302 [6],
    392; **1963:** 30 (pp. 59, 65), 89 [11], 118
Curtis, Charles, **1962:** 550
Curtis, George W., **1961:** 162, 418
Cushing, Richard Cardinal, **1961:** 1n., 212; **1963:**
    136
Cushman, Robert E., **1963:** 245
Cuss I, U.S.S., **1961:** 110
Custer, Gen. George A., **1963:** 257, 385, 425
Customs Bureau, **1962:** 448
Customs duties, reduction in duty-free allowance
    for American travelers, **1961:** 23, 53, 497
Cutler, Robert, **1961:** 95
Cutrer, Lewis, **1962:** 372n.
Cyclotron, **1961:** 342
CYO.
  See Catholic Youth Organization.
Cyprus, **1962:** 226, 325
  Ambassador Zenon Rossides, **1962:** 227, 339n.
  Archbishop Makarios, **1962:** 224, 225, 227, 249
  Kyprianou, Spyros, **1962:** 227
  U.S. Ambassador, Fraser Wilkins, **1962:** 227
  Visit of Vice President Johnson, **1962:** 339
Czechoslovakia, **1961:** 212, 483
Czestochowa, Poland, Cathedral, **1962:** 461

Daane, J. Dewey, **1961:** 123n.
Dachau concentration camp, **1962:** 168
Dacko, David, letter, **1961:** 167
Da Costa, Zenobio, **1962:** 175
DAG.
  See Development Assistance Group.
Dairy products, **1962:** 19, 25, 89 [18], 115 [20], 440;
    1963: 21 (p. 36), 45, 169 [13], 238
Dale, William, **1961:** 119 [2]
D'Alesandro, Thomas, **1962:** 446
Daley, Richard J., **1961:** 155, 454n.; **1962:** 482, 483;
    1963: 109, 110
Dallas, Tex., **1961:** 352; **1963:** 82, 477
Dallas Citizens Council, **1963:** 477
Dalton, Gov. John M., **1962:** 375n.; **1963:** 108
Dan River Mills, **1962:** 113n.
Dana, Charles, **1961:** 153
Danbury, Conn. **1963:** 270
Daniel, Gov. Price, **1962:** 68, 373n.
Daniels, Wilhelm, **1963:** 255
Dantas, San Tiago, **1962:** 146 n.
Dante, Allighieri, **1962:** 527; **1963:** 258
Dar-es-Salaam, Tanganyika, **1961:** 500
Darlington, Charles F., **1962:** 415
Darin, Bobby, **1962:** 201
Daugherty, Louise G., **1962:** 412n.
Davenport, Iowa, **1963:** 308

David, Donald K., **1962:** 194; **1963:** 175
Davidson, Rear Adm. John F., **1961:** 232
Da Vinci, Leonardo, **1962:** 546 [1]; **1963:** 5
Davis, Repr. Clifford, **1961:** 278
Davis, Gerald Lee, **1962:** 321
Davis, Brig. Gen. Howard A., **1963:** 441
Davis, Gov. Jimmie H., **1962:** 170, 171; **1963:** 108
Davis, Repr. John W., **1963:** 330
Davis, Pauline L., **1963:** 389
Davis, Sammy, **1962:** 233
Davis Cup, **1962:** 383
Dawes, Charles, **1962:** 275
Dawson, Repr. William L., **1961:** 155; **1962:** 483
Day, J. Edward (Postmaster General), **1961:** 244,
    339, 455 [11]; **1962:** 352 [8]; **1963:** 4, 107
    [6], 148, 153, 315, 317
Dean, Arthur H., **1961:** 80, 205, 358n.; **1962:** 107
    [2], 152 [15], 198 [13], 290, 302 [8], 316 [2,
    5, 17, 18]; **1963:** 3, 27
  Geneva test ban conference, **1961:** 326, 335
  News conference remarks, **1961:** 83 [6, 21], 139
    [23], 171 [1], 318 [2, 8], 334 [15]
  Statement re Soviet resumption of nuclear tests,
    1961: 340n.
Dean, Mrs. Ben J., Jr., **1962:** 150n.
Debates, television, **1962:** 352 [25]; **1963:** 448 [24]
Debt, consumer, **1962:** 93 (p. 240)
Debt, corporate, **1963:** 30 (p. 64)
Debt, national, **1961:** 33; **1962:** 13 (pp. 34, 35), 234,
    328, 549; **1963:** 21 (p. 41), 30 (p. 63), 34,
    62, 94, 175, 329, 351, 363, 450, 465, 477
  Interest on, **1963:** 30 (p. 63), 77 [1], 134, 175, 465
  Limit on, **1961:** 94; **1962:** 13 (p. 35), 245 [9]; **1963:**
    21 (p. 40), 30 (p. 63), 77, 94, 134
  Management, **1961:** 17, 75, 94; **1962:** 13 (p. 35),
    16 (p. 44), 230, 280; **1963:** 21 (p. 41), 30 (p.
    64), 94, 306
  News conference remarks, **1962:** 210 [13], 245 [9],
    316 [10]
  Reduction, **1961:** 17; **1963:** 21 (p. 40), 77, 144 [14]
Debt, private, **1961:** 234; **1962:** 30 (p. 64), 34
Debt, State-local, **1963:** 30 (p. 64)
Decade of development, **1961:** 90, 207, 346, 387,
    491; **1962:** 237; **1963:** 38, 101, 118, 366,
    430, 471
  Human skills, conference on, **1962:** 358
Decatur House, **1963:** 425
Decision-Making in the White House, Theodore C.
    Sorensen, **1963:** 370
Decker, Gen. George H., **1961:** 419n.; **1962:** 75 [20],
    226, 416, 423
Decker, Martin M., **1962:** 294n.; **1963:** 406n.
Declaration of Independence, **1961:** 450n.; **1962:**
    202, 278, 279 [8], 555; **1963:** 52, 294, 312,
    339
Dedicatory ocasions.
  See Addresses or remarks on commemorative or
    dedicatory occasions.

Defender space weapon, **1961:** 99
Defense Areas Agreement, U.S.-Brtish West Indies,
    message to Prime Minister Adams, **1961:**
    36
Defense budget, message to Congress, **1961:** 99
Defense Center, North American, **1963:** 222
Defense of the Constitution, John Adams, **1963:** 2
Defense contracts, **1961:** 35 [3]; **1962:** 50 [14], 89
    [13, 19], 245 [17], 453; **1963:** 77, 107 [4, 19,
    23], 120 [7], 134, 169 [5, 20], 175 [2], 478
  For depressed areas, **1961:** 17, 83 [1], 176
  For small business, **1961:** 83 [1]
  TFX aircraft, **1963:** 107 [4, 19, 23], 120 [7], 169
    [5], 328 [20], 448 [23], 475, 476
Defense, Department of, **1961:** 90, 176n., 497; **1962:**
    13 (pp. 28, 32), 71, 93 (p. 238), 129, 163,
    209, 237, 250, 257, 275, 276, 307, 328, 342,
    442, 487, 549; **1963:** 8, 11, 21 (pp. 40, 42),
    29, 30 (p. 69), 36, 77, 125, 166, 238n., 251,
    306, 329, 349, 353, 388
  Advanced Research Projects Agency, **1961:** 417n.
  Censorship in, **1962:** 50 [23]
  Central supply agency, **1961:** 436
  Civil defense functions, **1961:** 205, 295, 302, 455
    [13], 503; **1962:** 13 (p. 28), 320
  Construction program, **1961:** 99
  Cost reduction program, **1962:** 282
  Defense, national.
    See National securitv.
  Defense contracts in depressed areas, **1961:** 17,
    83 [1], 176
  Defense strategy, reappraisal, **1961:** 11
  Information, release to press, **1962:** 410 [8], 515
    [7, 14, 19]
  News conference remarks, **1961:** 15 [2, 8, 35], 25
    [4], 62 [18], 71 [9, 18], 83 [1], 171 [16], 318
    [9, 14], 334 [22], 455 [4, 13, 20], 488 [10];
    1962: 20 [2, 15], 40 [5], 50 [14, 23], 59 [17], 75
    [20], 89 [13, 19], 139 [1, 5], 179 [15], 245 [17],
    259 [21], 302 [8], 340 [8], 410 [8], 515 [3, 5, 7,
    14, 19]; **1963:** 54 [4, 5], 75 [3], 89 [9], 107
    [23], 144 [9], 202 [22], 328 [4], 459 [10]
  Space program, 1962: 340 [8]; **1963:** 30 (p. 58)
Defense Establishment, **1961:** 99
Defense Mobilization, Office of, **1961:** 161
Defense procurement, **1961:** 302; **1962:** 13 (p. 36);
    1963: 77 [1], 134, 169 [5, 20]
  Buy American policy, **1961:** 497
Defense program **1961:** 11, 62 [6, 29, 30], 99, 302
Defense spending, **1961:** 23, 90, 94, 99, 302, 343,
    436, 440, 448, 497, 499; **1962:** 7 (p. 10), 13
    (pp. 28, 35), 14, 24, 140, 162, 250, 280, 282,
    314, 328, 392, 400, 456, 549, 551 [13]; **1963:**
    12 (p. 18), 21 (pp. 27, 39), (pp. 58, 59, 63,
    64), 34, 77 [1], 85, 118, 134, 166, 175, 306,
    351, 361, 430, 465, 476-478

[References are to items except as otherwise indicated]

Defense spending — *continued*
News conference remarks, **1961:** 119 [8], 291 [9]
415 [7]; **1962:** 8 [21], 75 [10], 89 [4], 139
[1], 179 [5], 245 [9], 259 [15], 302 [6, 9],
316 [20], 352 [11], 410 [12]; **1963:** 107 [4,
19, 21, 23], 120 [7, 11, 21], 169 [5, 20], 305
[2], 320 [10], 328 [23], 459 [6]
Defense support.
See Military assistance and defense support.
Defense, Secretary of (Robert S. McNamara),
1961: 5, 23, 99, 135, 205, 242, 244, 259,
262, 302, 353, 466, 497; **1962:** 9, 109,
140n., 163, 328, 486, 549, 551 [3, 21], 554;
1963: 3, 8n., 49, 62, 94n., 166, 175 [4], 181,
236n., 238n., 251, 306, 354, 393, 396, 399,
414n., 477
Action on Maj. Gen Edwin A. Walker, **1961:** 139
[11]
Memorandum to, **1963:** 29, 62
News conference remarks on, **1961:** 8 [7, 19], 15
[2, 24], 25 [4, 5], 62 [6, 29, 30], 71 [18], 92
[15], 139 [11], 291 [15], 318 [9], 334 [22],
415 [1, 7]; **1962:** 20 [2], 40 [5, 17], 50 [9],
59 [12], 75 [20], 89 [8], 139 [1, 2, 5, 11],
152 [11], 179 [16], 279 [17], 316 [6, 19],
378 [19], 515 [1], 546 [5]; **1963:** 35 [22], 54
[5, 7, 12], 75 [20], 107 [4, 19, 23], 120 [1]
169 [5, 20], 260 [15], 305 [2], 320 [2], 328
[1, 17, 20], 356 [17], 405 [16], 448 [3, 15],
459 [5]
On steel price increase, **1961:** 354
Order on military dependents abroad, **1962:** 59
[12]
Report, **1962:** 282
Deficits, **1963:** 465
Deficit spending, **1961:** 205, 302; **1962:** 203, 234, 243
[2], 328, 392, 549; **1963:** 12 (p. 12), 21 (pp.
(p. 27, 28, 29), 30 (pp. 60, 61), 34, 65 [2, 4],
77 [4], 89 [7], 94, 120 [11, 21], 175, 306
News conference remarks, **1961:** 62 [25], 291 [7];
1962: 27 [27], 210 [16], 245 [6], 279 [19],
316 [10], 340 [19]
Deflation, **1962:** 546 [6]; **1963:** 77, 134 [3, 4]
De Gasperi, Alcide, **1961:** 239n.; **1963:** 35 [17]
De Gaulle, Charles, **1961:** 11, 205, 212, 215, 216,
217, 231, 355, 373, 481; **1962:** 184, 234,
513; **1963:** 5, 340
Joint statement with, **1961:** 223
Meeting with, question of, **1963:** 144 [10]
Message, **1961:** 140
News conference remarks on, **1961:** 15 [22], 119
[19], 139 [19], 222, 258 [18], 488 [11];
1962: 8 [13], 20 [20], 59 [5], 107 [13], 198
[3, 6], 210 [7], 229 [2, 9], 302 [16], 546 [1];
1963: 35 [24], 54 [3, 8], 65 [3, 8, 17], 65 [9,
15], 144 [10], 260 [15, 17], 320 [2, 4, 15,
16], 328 [21]

De Gaulle, Mme., **1961:** 216, 222
De Keyser, Henry L., **1962:** 236
Delaware, **1963:** 461
Gov. Elbert N. Carvel, **1963:** 108, 461
Delaware Basin Commission, **1961:** 445n.
Delaware-Maryland Turnpike, dedication, **1963:**
461
Delaware River, **1963:** 379
Delaware River Basin compact, **1962:** 69, 391
Delaware River Basin compact, signing, remarks,
1961: 445
Delaware River and Bay Authority, approval,
1962: 391
Delinquency, juvenile.
See Juvenile delinquency.
Della Porta, Glauco, **1963:** 288
Delta Sigma Theta Sorority, **1963:** 10
Del Vecchio, Charles, **1962:** 158
DeMart, George, **1962:** 328
De Martino, Gen. Umberto, **1963:** 303
De Miranda, Francisco, **1963:** 73
Democratic Convention (1956), **1961:** 239
Democratic National Committee, **1962:** 233; **1963:**
23, 35 [9]
President's birthday dinner, **1961:** 209
Remarks, **1961:** 3
Democratic National Committee, Chairman (John
M. Bailey), **1961:** 3, 8 [20], 209, 498; **1962:**
15, 229 [6], 233n., 346n.; **1963:** 24, 151,
204, 459 [15]
Democratic Party, **1961:** 3, 498; **1962:** 3, 15, 186,
201, 233, 459; **1963:** 94, 118, 146, 204, 223,
228, 340, 349, 378, 427, 445, 463, 466, 467,
472, 474, 478
Campaign remarks, **1962:** 396, 414, 431, 436-440,
446, 451-456, 458, 472, 473, 480-483
Convention (1956), **1962:** 77; (1964), **1963:** 35 [9]
Dinner, **1963:** 202 [21]
Midwestern conference, **1962:** 346
New York City primary, **1961:** 334 [24]
News conference remarks, **1961:** 8 [20], 334 [24],
455 [19]; **1962:** 20 [26], 40 [13], 179 [12],
245 [7, 9], 259 [8], 279 [15], 302 [14, 19],
340 [12, 18], 378 [21], 410 [2], 515 [8];
1963: 35 [9], 120 [13], 202 [21], 356 [22],
448 [4], 459 [12]
Responsibility of President as head, **1961:** 448
Texas, **1963:** 478
Young Democrats, **1963:** 146, 356 [19]
Democratic Party of California, **address, 1961: 477**
Democratic Party of Cook Co., Ill, address, **1961:**
155
Democratic Party of New York, **1961:** 8 [20]
Democratic State Committeewomen of California,
1963: 228
Democratic Women, Campaign Conference for,
1962: 205
Democracy, **1962:** 180, 201, 250, 300, 363, 410 [1],
544

Demonstrations, civil rights, **1963:** 169 [1, 4, 14], 202 [20], 230, 248, 305 [20], 320 [12], 328 [3, 9], 356 [22]

De Morias, Mascarenhas, **1962:** 175

Dempsey, Gov. John N., **1961:** 212; **1962:** 472-474; **1963:** 108, 427

Denges, Msgr. Joseph F., **1962:** 162

Dennis, C. L., **1963:** 95n.

Dennison, Adm. Robert L., **1962:** 135, 148n., 149, 521; **1963:** 147

Dennison, hydrofoil ship, **1962:** 129

Dental and medical education, **1962:** 7 (p. 8), 37, 65, 288.

See also Medical and dental education.

Dentists, shortage of, **1963:** 53, 134

Dentists, training of, **1961:** 27, 52

Denton, Repr. Winfield K., **1962:** 456, 458

Denver, Colo., **1963:** 202 [13]

Denver, Colo., White House Regional Conference, **1961:** 454n.

De Oliveira Campos, Roberto, **1963:** 335

Depletion allowances, **1963:** 34

De Poix, Capt. Vincent P., **1962:** 148n.

Depreciation allowances, **1962:** 7 (p. 6), 13 (p. 33), 16 (p. 47), 162, 328, 468; **1963:** 12 (p. 12), 30 (p. 62), 34, 92, 131

Mining property, **1961:** 391

News conference remarks, **1962:** 8 [15], 139 [13], 152, [2, 14], 229 [1, 4], 245 [18], 279 [19]

Statement, **1962:** 286

Textile machinery, **1961:** 161, 497

Depressed areas, **1961:** 7, 11, 17, 33, 44, 46, 49, 85, 94; **1962:** 7 (p. 6), 16 (p. 43), 165, 380, 395, 396, 414, 431, 438, 439, 446, 451, 452, 453, 549; **1963:** 21 (pp. 32, 36, 40), 30 (p. 58), 110, 130, 162, 175 [2], 228, 241, 248, 363, 378, 445, 455, 463, 465 [5]

Defense contracts, **1961:** 17, 83 [1], 176

Education, **1963:** 43, 50

Federal aid, **1963:** 127, 193

Food distribution, **1961:** 15 [3], 17, 85

Foreign investment in, **1962:** 279 [12]

Government contracts, **1962:** 59 [19], 89 [13, 19], 453

Health services, **1963:** 50

Manpower development and training program, **1961:** 205

News conference remarks, **1961:** 15 [3, 13], 25 [25], 35 [3, 15], 83 [1], 334 [10]; **1962:** 20 [26], 59 [19], 89 [13, 19], 115 [16], 229 [1], 279 [12], 410 [1]

Public works in, **1962:** 111, 229 [1]; **1963:** 21 (p. 37), 123

Redevelopment.

See Area redevelopment.

TVA area, **1961:** 98

Depressions, **1963:** 30 (p. 60), 105, 127, 379, 400, 401

Depressions — *continued*

1919 depression, **1963:** 162, 462, 466

1929 depression, **1962:** 22, 25; **1963:** 85, 92, 110, 162, 216

Dericoyard, J. P., **1961:** 487n.

Desai, M. J. **1961:** 452n.

De San Martin, Jose, **1961:** 78, 515

Desegregation.

See Integration

De Seversky, Maj. Alexander, **1962:** 475

De Tocqueville, Alexis, **1963:** 552; **1963:** 94, 430

Detroit, Mich., **1962:** 89 [13], 174, 179 [2], 378 [10], 433, 436, 437; **1963:** 400

Food distribution to needy families, **1961:** 17

White House Regional Conference, meeting, **1961:** 454n.

DetroitLions, **1961:** 496

De Valera, Eamon, **1962:** 353n.; **1963:** 274, 278, 282, 283, 415

De Valera, Mrs. Eamon, **1963:** 282, 283

DeValle, José Cecilio, **1963:** 99

Development Act, International, **1961:** 207, 346

Development Agency for Northeast Brazil, **1961:** 285

Development Assistance Committee, **1961:** 91, 481

Development Assistance Group (OECD), **1961:** 91, 192, 193, 222 [2]

Joint statement with Chancellor Adenauer, **1961:** 120

Development Association, International, **1963:** 21 (p. 35), 391

Development Loan Fund, **1961:** 90, 184

Director (Frank Coffin), **1961** 119 [2]

Reassignment of functions.

See International Development, Agency for.

Development Service, German, **1963:** 258

Dever, Paul A., **1963:** 427

Devers, Gen. Jacob L., **1962:** 422; **1963:** 203

DeVoto, Bernard, **1961:** 212

Dewey, Thomas E., **1962:** 219, 482; **1963:** 151, 455, 459 [6]

Dhahran, U.S. base, **1962:** 50 [12]

Diabetes, **1963:** 51

Dick, Mrs. Jane Warner, **1963:** 359n.

Dickens, Charles, *A Christmas Carol,* **1963:** 465

Dickieson, Alton C., **1962:** 398

Diefenbaker, John G., **1961:** 25 [1], 190, 192, 273; **1962:** 477; **1963:** 54 [8]

Joint statement with, **1961:** 45, 193

Telephone conversation, **1961:** 298

Diefenbaker, Mrs. John G. **1961:** 190

Diem, Ngo Dinh, **1963:** 340, 438, 459 [5]

Diem, Ngo Dinh, letters, **1961:** 435, 505

Diesel fuel tax, **1961:** 58

Diggs, Repr. Charles C., Jr., **1962:** 362, 436

Dillon, C. Douglas.

See Treasury, Secretary of the.

Dilworth, Richardson, **1961:** 264; **1962:** 394, 395, 451-455; **1963:** 455

Dingell, Repr. John D., **1962:** 433, 436

Diphtheria, eradication, **1962:** 65

Diplomacy, private, **1961:** 8 [24]

Diplomatic Papers, U.S., publication, letter, **1961:** 353

Diplomats, Foreign, discrimination against, **1963:** 82

Dirk, Black Watch officer's, presentation to President, **1963:** 457

Dirksen, Sen. Everett McK., **1961:** 139 [10]; **1962:** 238, 357; **1963:** 320 [2, 13], 354, 356 [1, 23], 382, 422

Disability insurance, **1961:** 17

Disabled persons, Federal aid, **1962:** 28, 328; **1963:** 21 (p. 38), 74

   Veterans, **1962:** 367

DiSalle, Gov. Michael V., **1962:** 3, 396, 431,.432, 480

Disarmament, **1961:** 11, 80, 99, 193, 205, 302, 347, 365, 387, 442; **1962:** 7 (p. 11), 13 (p. 38), 29, 186, 310 [3], 319, 493, 503, 551 [18]; **1963:** 12 (pp. 16, 18), 14, 20, 75 [18], 116, 136, 232, 319a., 426, 449, 471

  See also Arms inspection and control.

  Broadcast, **1962:** 71

  Geneva conference.

    See main heading, Geneva conference.

    Interviews for radio and TV, **1961:** 214, 483

  Joint statements with foreign leaders, **1961:** 45, 51, 66, 120, 135, 146, 230, 242, 411, 519; **1962:** 160, 544; **1963:** 292

  Letter to Secretary Rusk, **1962:** 90

  Messages to Premier Khrushchev, **1962:** 48, 62, 73

  News conference remarks, **1961:** 8 [5, 7], 62 [19, 21], 83 [6], 222, 318 [2, 8]; **1962:** 8 [8, 20], 40 [1, 9, 11], 50 [2-4, 13], 107 [16], 152 [1, 8, 15], 179 [8], 316 [18]

  Soviet proposals, **1961:** 62 [19], 483

  Ten-nation conference, **1961:** 192, 408

  U.S.-Soviet talks, **1961:** 365

  Women demonstrators, **1962:** 8 [20]

Disarmament Advisory Committee, **1963:** 439

Disarmament Agency, U.S.

  See United States Arms Control and Disarmament Agency.

  Ten-nation conference at Geneva, **1961:** 192, 408

Disarmament Conference, **1963:** 250

Disasters, natural

  Earthquakes

    Chile, **1961:** 81, 94; **1962:** (1960), 542n.

    Iran, **1962:** 364

    Famine in Kenya, **1962:** 18

  Floods, **1961:** 83 [2]

    In Viet-Nam, **1961:** 505

Discoverer earth satellite, **1961:** 99

Discrimination.

  See Civil rights; Integration.

Disease immunization program, **1962:** 7 (p. 8), 65, 288

Disease prevention, **1963:** 21 (p. 37), 50, 53, 64, 134, 326, 366, 374, 434

  Livestock, **1963:** 217

  Mental illness, **1963:** 313

Disraeli, Benjamin, **1963:** 64, 455

Distinguished Civilian Service Awards Board, **1963:** 76 and p. 900

Distinguished Federal Civilian Service Awards, presentation, **1962:** 323; **1963:** 238

Distinguished Service Medal, **1963:** 199, 345

  Anderson, Adm. George W., Jr., **1963:** 318

  Burke, Adm. Arleigh A., **1961:** 303

  Decker, Gen. George H., **1962:** 416

  Dennison, Adm. Robert L., **1963:** 147

  Lemnitzer, Gen. Lyman L., **1962:** 422

  Norstad, Gen. Lauris, **1963:** 8

  O'Donnell, Gen Emmett, **1963:** 345

  White, Gen. Thomas D., **1961:** 260

Distinguished Service Medal, American Legion, acceptance, **1962:** 70

Distinguished Service Medal, NASA, **1962:** 61

District of Columbia, **1961:** 152, 467; **1962:** 59 [3], 203; **1963:** 64, 222, 226, 230, 248, 255, 291, 316, 327, 334, 340, 381, 412, 461

  Aquarium, construction of, **1962:** 546 [24]

  Area redevelopment, **1962:** 525

  Budget message, **1963:** 22

  Buildings, **1963:** 412

  Civil rights, **1963:** 22, 35 [15], 230, 305 [20], 328 [3, 9], 336, 356 [22]

  Civil War Centennial Commission, **1962:** 159n.

  Commissioner Walter N. Tobriner, **1963:** 66, 122n., 456

  Crime, **1963:** 230

  Cultural activities, **1962:** 552

  D.C. Transit Co., **1962:** 27 [11]

  Destruction (1814), **1962:** 70

  District Court, **1962:** 434

  Education, **1963:** 10, 22, 35 [15], 43

  Federal aid, **1963:** 56

  Federal funds for, **1962:** 546 [24]

  General Hospital, **1963:** 22

  Highway program, **1963:** 22, 208, 456

  Home rule, **1962:** 130; **1963:** 122

  Housing, **1963:** 35 [15], 230

  Housing, racial discrimination in, **1962:** 142

  Indecent publications law, amendment, disapproval, **1962:** 479

  Junior college, proposed, **1963:** 22

  Junior Village, **1962:** 546 [24]

  Juvenile delinquency, **1962:** 243 [4]

  Lafayette Park, **1962:** 27 [21], 512

  Lincoln Park, **1962:** 27 [11]

  Mental health responsibilities, **1963:** 66

  Metropolitan Club, **1961:** 415 [14]

  Moscow communications link, **1963:** 232, 250, 319a.

District of Columbia — *continued*
  National Capital Park System, **1962:** 362
  News conference remarks, **1963:** 35 [15], 169 [14],
    202 [6], 305 [14, 19, 20], 328 [3, 9], 356 [4,
    22], 448 [16], 459 [16]
  Pennsylvania Avenue redevelopment, **1962:** 221
  Race relations in, **1963:** 169 [14]
  Saint Elizabeths Hospital, **1963:** 22, 66
  Schools, **1963:** 35 [15], 202 [6], 230
  Scientific and industrial exposition, permanent,
    proposed, **1962:** 181
  Self-government, letter, **1961:** 286
  Senior citizens, **1963:** 74
  Sewage disposal problems, **1963:** 305 [14]
  Teachers College, **1963:** 22
  Transportation, **1963:** 208
  USO building, destruction of, **1962:** 27 [21]
  Voting rights, **1963:** 122
    In presidential elections, **1961:** 186
      Ratification of constitutional amendment,
        statement, **1961:** 103
      Welfare measures, **1963:** 22
      Wilson memorial, **1961:** 399
      Youth, **1963:** 35 [15], 305 [19]
      Youth resources, **1962:** 546 [24]
District Courts, **1962:** 21, 33
Dividends
  Stock market, **1962:** 210 [10]
  Taxes on, **1961:** 136
  Veterans insurance, **1961:** 15 [4], 17, 35 [3]; **1962:**
    517
  Withholding tax, proposed, **1962:** 7 (p. 7), 13 (p.
    33), 16 (p. 57), 108, 115 [2], 179 [1], 229
    [4], 340 [16], 410 [2], 468, 549 [6]
Dixon, Paul Rand, **1961:** 119 [11]
Dobrynin, Anatoly F., **1962:** 160, 179 [6], 279 [20],
    302 [13]; **1963:** 75 [18]
Dockworkers strike.
  See Maritime labor disputes.
Doctors, shortage of, **1963:** 43, 53, 134
Documents, historical, publication, **1963:** 26, 245
DOD.
  See Defense, Department of.
Dodd, Sen. Thomas J., **1962:** 472, 474
Doherty, Gerard F., **1963:** 427
Dojcinovic, Vera, **1962:** 351
Dolan, Joseph, F., **1963:** 181
Dollar, **1962:** 31; **1963:** 305 [12]
  Canadian, **1963:** 89 [11]
  Gold relationship, **1963:** 391
  Holdings by foreign countries, **1961:** 23, 82
  News conference remarks, **1961:** 8 [19], 15 [2, 23],
    35 [10], 62 [3]; **1962:** 229 [15], 259 [14],
    302 [6], 316 [19], 410 [1, 2]

Dollar — *continued*
  Stability, **1961:** 8 [19], 11, 15 [2, 23], 23, 35 [10],
    62 [3], 205, 302, 497; **1962:** 7 (p. 13), 14,
    16 (pp. 43, 50), 22, 151, 229 [15], 234, 259
    [14], 280, 302 [6], 328, 392; **1963:** 21 (p.
    29), 30 (p. 63), 67 [17], 94, 110, 118, 134,
    175, 306, 363, 391, 407
Dolloff, Maynard C., **1962:** 326
Domestic peace corps, proposed, **1962:** 243 [4];
    1963: 12 (p. 13), 176, 305 [19], 465
Dominican Republic, **1971:** 78, 483, 488 [1]; **1962:**
    7 (p. 12), 8 [10], 17, 86; **1963:** 88, 311, 459
    [18]
  Balaguer, Joaquin, **1961:** 517
  Military coup, **1963:** 405 [7], 448 [11]
  Statement on situation, **1961:** 517
  Tax reforms, **1963:** 118
  U.S. relations with, **1963:** 448 [11]
Dominick, Repr. Peter H., **1962:** 336; **1963:** 345
Donelson, Maj. Andrew Jackson, **1963:** 264
Donnelley, Dixon, **1961:** 123n.
Donohue, F. Joseph, **1961:** 234
Donovan, James, **1962:** 556
Dooley, Dr. Thomas A., III, presentation of medal
    to family, **1962:** 228
Dooley, Mrs. Thomas A., II, **1962:** 228
Doolittle, Lt. Gen. James H., **1961:** 168n.; **1963:**
    221, 405 [12]
Dorfman, Ben D., **1961:** 478
Dorfman, Robert, **1961:** 458n.
Dostoievsky, Feodor, **1962:** 527
Doty, Paul, **1961:** 347n.
Douglas, Kirk, **1963:** 24
Douglas, Sen. Paul H., **1961:** 35 [10], 152, 155, 158;
    1962: 58n., 93 (p. 240), 481, 483; **1963:**
    109, 110
  Area redevelopment report, **1961:** 7
Douglas, Stephen A., **1962:** 349
Douglas, Justice William O., **1961:** 487
Douglas Aircraft Company, **1961:** 281n.; **1962:** 551
    [13]
Douglass, Frederick, **1962:** 362
Douglass (Frederick) Home, incorporation into
    National Capital Park System, **1962:** 362
Dow Chemical Company, **1961:** 248
Dow-Jones Average, **1963:** 356 [12]
Dowling, Walter C., **1961:** 334 [3, 21]; **1962:** 198
    [14]
Downey, John T., **1962:** 243 [6]
Draft rejectees, training and rehabilitation, **1963:**
    393
Draper, William F., portrait of President by, **1963:**
    160n.
Driver License Register, Federal, **1962:** 11
Drouin, Mark Robert, **1961:** 192

Drugs, **1963:** 53, 407
  Addiction, **1962:** 411
  Consumer protection, **1962:** 93 (p. 235), 137, 202,
      316 [1, 4, 24], 340 [2], 321, 395, 396, 414,
      442, 446, 459; **1963:** 53, 74, 121
Drug Abuse, President's Advisory Commission on
      Narcotic and, report, **1963:** 121
Drug prices, **1961:** 119 [11]
  Distribution of, **1962:** 316 [24]
  Illegal traffic in, **1962:** 273
  Letters to Senator Eastland, **1962:** 137, 321
  Regulation, **1962:** 7 (p. 8), 93 (p. 239), 411
    Approval of bill, **1962:** 442
  Use in treating mental illness, **1963:** 50
  White House Conference on Narcotic and Drug
      Abuse, **1962:** 218, 411
Drummond, Roscoe, **1963:** 356 [7]
Dryden, Hugh L., **1961:** 177, 178; **1962:** 107 [1],
      378 [17], 533n.
Dryfoos, Orvil, death of, **1963:** 205
Dubinsky, David, **1961:** 40n.; **1962:** 200, 202; **1963:**
      139
Dublin, Ireland
  Easter Rising (1916), **1963:** 281
  Mayor Robert Briscoe, **1962:** 233
  Mayor Sean Moore, **1963:** 279
  Visit to, **1963:** 274, 278, 279
Dublin, N.H., **1963:** 277
Dubord, Richard J., **1962:** 326
DuBridge, Dr. Lee A., **1963:** 76n.
Duck stamp program, **1962:** 69
Duke, Angier Biddle, **1963:** 275
Dulles, Allen W., **1961:** 485, 497; **1962:** 107 [6],
      512; **1963:** 405 [16]
Dulles, John Foster, **1961:** 480; **1962:** 259 [1], 507n.,
      512; **1963:** 76
Dulles, Mrs. John Foster, **1962:** 512
Dulles International Airport, dedication, **1962:** 512
Dulski, Repr. Thaddeus J., **1962:** 461
Duluth, Minn., **1963:** 378, 390
Duncan, John P., Jr., **1962:** 127n.
Dunganstown, Ireland, family reunion at, **1963:**
      276n.
Dunsany, Lord, **1962:** 158
Durante, Jimmy, **1962:** 201
Dutton, Frederick G., **1963:** 31n.
Duty-free allowance for American travelers, re-
      duction, **1961:** 23, 497
  Letter to Speaker Rayburn, **1961:** 53
Duvalier, Francois, **1963:** 169 [12]
Dyhenfurth, Norman G., **1963:** 158n., 296
Dynasoar space weapon, **1961:** 99

"E" awards for exports promotion, **1962:** 113
"E" flag award, **1961:** 495
Eagle missile, **1961:** 99
Eagle, national emblem, **1963:** 259, 426
Eagle, training barque, **1962:** 330
Earhart, Amelia, **1963:** 315

Earthquakes
  Chile (1960), **1962:** 542n.
    Reconstruction, U.S. assistance, **1961:** 81, 94
  Distinction from underground nuclear explosions,
      1963: 89 [4], 319a
  Iran, **1962:** 364
  Yugoslavia disaster, **1963:** 421
East Coast Memorial to Missing at Sea, **1963:** 203
East-West negotiations, **1963:** 328 [21]
East-West tensions, **1963:** 260 [4]
Easter Rising, Dublin (1916), **1963:** 281
Eastern Air Lines, **1961:** 50; **1962:** 245 [1], 256
Eastland, Sen. James O., **1962:** 137, 321
Eau Claire, Wis., **1962:** 328
Eckhart, Felix von, **1962:** 152 [19]
ECLA.
  See Economic Commission for Latin America,
      U.N.
Economic Advisers, Council of.
  See Council of Economic Advisers.
Economic assistance and development, **1961:** 23,
      69, 102, 123, 146, 149, 193, 202, 207, 210,
      236, 267, 285, 304, 343, 346, 389, 409, 430,
      436, 497; **1962:** 7 (p. 12), 25 40 [4], 50 [9],
      83, 126, 146, 147, 163, 249, 254, 273, 280,
      314, 340 [4], 358, 392, 526, 549 [10]; **1963:**
      6, 30 (p. 64), 57, 61, 72, 80, 81, 89 [20],
      107 [1, 22], 111, 116, 120 [12, 21], 124, 169
      [17], 217, 262, 306, 477
  See also Foreign assistance; Mutual security pro-
      gram; Technical assistance to less-
      developed and new countries; Military
      assistance and defense support.
  Development lending, **1963:** 118
  French TV and radio interview, **1961:** 214
  Joint statements with foreign leaders, **1961:** 112,
      230, 288, 309, 376, 411, 510
  Message to Congress, **1961:** 90
  News conference remarks, **1961:** 92 [6, 10], 119
      [2], 171 [15], 291 [14], 334 [16], 415 [15],
      448 [3]
Economic Assistance Mission, United States, **1961:**
      517
Economic boycotts, **1961:** 71 [20]
Economic Club of New York, **1962:** 546 [6], 549
Economic Commission for Latin America, U.N.,
      1961: 122; **1962:** 86
Economic Community, European.
  See main heading, European Economic
      Community.
Economic community, Latin American, **1963:** 107
      [1], 120 [12]
Economic Cooperation Administration, **1963:** 124n.
Economic cooperation conferences of African
      nations, **1961:** 107, 175, 304, 430
Economic Cooperation and Development, Organ-
      ization for.
  See Organization for Economic Cooperation and
      Development.

[References are to items except as otherwise indicated]

Economic Cooperation, African and Malagasy
Organization for, **1961:** 107n.
Economic cooperation, international, **1963:** 260 [8]
Economic Development, Committee for, **1961:** 245;
1962: 194, 203, 210 [13, 16]; **1963:** 75,
[14], 175
Economic Growth, Cabinet Committee on, **1963:**
30 (p. 68)
Economic growth, U.S., **1961:** 11, 33, 119 [18], 136,
149, 207, 222, 245, 258 [4, 15, 16], 477;
1962: 6n., 13 (p. 35), 16 (p. 45), 22, 108,
151, 195, 199, 234, 273, 280, 328, 392, 545,
549; **1963:** 12 (p. 12), 21 (pp. 27-30, 37-39,
43), 30 (pp. 57, 59-62, 65, 68-70), 34, 43,
74, 77, 92, 94, 128, 131, 134, 145, 175, 177,
188, 193, 208, 248, 306, 329, 349, 351, 380,
385, 391, 445, 461, 465, 466, 471, 474, 475,
478
Campaign remarks, **1962:** 432, 439, 458
News conference remarks, **1962:** 50 [3], 152 [2],
210 [16], 229 [1], 302 [18], 316 [13], 410
[1]; **1963:** 35 [14], 65 [4], 75 [14], 120 [11],
144 [14, 15], 305 [2, 18], 356 [12], 405 [18]
Economic isolation, **1961:** 497
Economic report to Congress, **1962:** 16; **1963:** 30
Economic and Social Council, Inter-American,
1961: 122
"Economic Surveys by the OECD-United States,"
1963: 175ftn. (p. 387)
Economics and Commerce, Association for International Exchange of Students in, **1963:** 128
Economy, national, **1961:** 11, 22, 23, 33, 37, 43, 44,
49, 53, 58, 76, 85, 87, 90, 93, 94, 121, 136,
185, 205, 245, 274, 302, 332, 354, 454, 458,
499; **1962:** 3, 7 (pp. 5-7), 13 (p. 27), 22, 23,
25, 47, 53, 55, 77, 80, 91, 93 (p. 235), 108,
111, 151, 162, 164, 165, 174, 176, 194, 230,
234, 243 [2], 250, 335, 346, 359, 385, 392,
421, 438, 449, 459, 468, 483, 517, 549;
1963: 12 (pp. 12, 15), 21 (pp. 26, 27, 29, 30,
37, 41, 43), 30 (p. 57), 45, 50, 53, 62, 64,
74, 77 [4], 82, 87, 92, 94, 110, 118, 119,
123, 128, 134, 149, 175, 177, 185, 187, 188,
197, 220, 228, 306, 310, 319a, 329, 337,
340, 349, 351, 363, 369, 407, 427, 436, 445,
465, 466, 470, 477
Broadcast, **1962:** 328
Effect of strikes, **1963:** 54 [6]
Message to Congress, **1961:** 17; **1962:** 16; **1963:**
30
News conference remarks, **1961:** 8 [21], 15 [4, 9,
23, 27], 25 [16, 25], 35 [3, 6, 14], 62 [4, 7],
83 [12, 18], 92 [2, 18], 119 [14, 18], 139 [6,
16], 171 [21], 119 [14, 18], 139 [6, 16], 171
[21], 258 [4, 15, 16], 291 [7], 334 [10, 12,
14], 415 [20, 21], 455 [16], 488 [17]; **1962:**
8 [7], 27 [27], 40 [9], 50 [3], 59 [16], 75 [5,
7], 89 [5], 116 [16], 198 [10, 12], 210 [10,

Economy — *continued*
News conference remarks — *continued*
13, 16], 229 [12, 16], 245 [1, 2, 6, 7, 9, 17],
259 [8, 18], 279 [3, 19], 302 [5, 6, 17, 18],
316 [10], 340 [19], 410 [1, 2], 546 [6]; **1963:**
54 [6], 65 [2, 4], 75 [14], 107 [9, 21], 120
[11, 21], 144 [14, 15, 21], 169 [15], 305 [5],
328 [7, 15], 405 [18], 459 [4]
Role of Indians in, **1963:** 86, 113
Stabilization, **1963:** 131
Statement, **1962:** 229 [1]
White House Conference on National Economic
Issues, **1962:** 164, 203, 210 [13]
Ecuador, **1961:** 483; **1962:** 302 [9], 325; **1963:** 432
Arosemena Monroy, Carlos, **1962:** 299, 300, 302
[9], 303
Assistance and development, **1962:** 303
Ecumenical Council, Catholic Church, **1962:** 430
Editorial Cartoonists, American Association, **1963:**
172
Editors and Publishers, Business, White House
Conference of, **1962:** 410
Edmondson, Repr. Ed, **1961:** 441
Edmondson, Gov. J. Howard, **1961:** 441n.
Education, **1961:** 33, 46, 57, 70, 178, 302, 436, 454,
477, 499; **1962:** 3, 6n., 7 (p. 9), 13 (pp. 28,
31, 32), 16 (p. 46), 109, 171, 174, 195, 200,
255, 359, 360, 540, 549; **1963:** 10, 19, 21
(pp. 32, 38, 39), 22, 30 (pp. 61, 68-70), 43,
92, 130, 134, 136, 160, 175, 176, 177, 192,
226, 228, 240, 246, 271, 279, 310, 319, 323,
332, 340, 342, 363, 366, 378, 379, 385, 387,
390, 393, 401, 423, 445, 460, 462, 464-469,
473, 478
See also Schools; Students.
Adult, **1963:** 74, 92
Appalachian region, **1963:** 127
Bond issues, **1963:** 465
Business investment, **1963:** 465
Campaign remarks, **1962:** 394-396, 414, 431, 432,
436-439, 451, 452, 456, 458, 480, 481, 483
Central America, **1963:** 103
Civil rights.
See Integration.
Community colleges, **1963:** 43
Congo, Republic of the, **1961:** 487
Cuban refugees, **1961:** 19
District of Columbia, **1963:** 10, 22, 35 [15], 43
Equal opportunity, **1963:** 10, 82, 228, 320 [7]
Ethiopia, **1963:** 397n.
Exchange programs, **1963:** 128, 140, 231, 308,
332
Facilities expansion, **1963:** 21 (pp. 38, 39)
Federal aid, **1961:** 11, 46, 71 [13, 17], 83 [8, 9, 16],
94, 144, 255, 291 [8, 16], 318 [17], 334 [6],
398, 462, 473; **1962:** 7 (p. 9), 13 (p. 32),
16 (p. 46), 37, 40 [2, 3], 75 [18], 107 [19],
186, 209, 259 [4, 12], 302 [4], 328, 394-396,

Education — *continued*
  Federal aid — *continued*
     459, 480, 481, 483, 551 [10]; **1963:** 21
     (p. 38), 30 (pp. 65, 69), 43, 50, 74, 77, 82,
     89 [7], 92, 141, 162, 226, 228, 240, 248,
     279, 358n., 426, 469, 478
  Foreign educators, visit of, **1962:** 51
  Foreign students in U.S., **1961:** 205, 443
  Handicapped children, **1963:** 447
  Indian and Eskimo children, **1961:** 71 [5], 94
  Indian Institute of Technology, U.S. consortium,
    1961: 460
  Indians, **1962:** 331; **1963:** 86, 113
  Land-grant colleges, **1961:** 71 [17], 462, 473
  Latin America, **1963:** 12 (p. 17), 105, 326
  Medical and dental, **1961:** 27, 52, 94; **1962:** 7 (p.
    8), 8 [24], 13 (p. 31), 37, 65
    See also Medical and dental education.
  Mentally retarded, **1961:** 413; **1963:** 50
  Message to Congress, **1962:** 37; **1963:** 43
  Negroes, **1963:** 10, 226, 237, 248, 328 [12], 339,
    355, 444
  News conference remarks, **1961:** 71 [5, 12, 13,
    17], 83 [8, 9, 16], 171 [6], 291 [8, 16], 318
    [17], 334 [6]; **1962:** 8 [1, 24], 20 [17, 23],
    40 [2, 3], 75 [18], 107 [19], 259 [4, 12], 302
    [4], 378 [21]; **1963:** 35 [15], 75 [1], 89 [1, 7],
    120 [21], 144 [20], 320 [1, 7], 328 [12], 448
    [7], 459 [11]
  Older persons, **1963:** 74, 75 [1]
  Pacific Islands Trust Territory, **1962:** 297
  Private and parochial schools.
    See main heading, Private and parochial schools.
  Puerto Rican immigrants, **1963:** 10
  Research, **1963:** 43
  Rural areas, **1962:** 25; **1963:** 43, 45
  Scholarships, **1963:** 10, 43, 221, 294, 400
  Scholarships for National Guardsmen and
    reservists, proposed, **1962:** 20 [17]
  Science, **1961:** 94, 318 [17]
  Science and engineering, **1962:** 8 [1], 13 (p. 32),
    37, 547; **1963:** 21 (p. 38), 30 (p. 69), 43,
    64, 92, 136, 226, 366
  Students.
    See main heading, Students.
  Teacher of the Year Award, **1962:** 188
  Teachers.
    See main heading, Teachers; training.
  Television, educational, **1962:** 20 [23], 37, 93
    (p. 327), 156, 166; **1963:** 137, 445
  Textbooks, **1963:** 22
  UNESCO meeting of Asian ministers of educa-
    tion, **1962:** 122
  U.S. system, **1963:** 448 [7]
  Veterans, **1963:** 21 (p. 39)
  Vocational, **1961:** 46, 144, 413
    See also Occupational training.
  Women, **1962:** 156

Education — *continued*
  Youth, **1963:** 12 (p. 13), 43, 64, 110
Education, American Council on, **1961:** 144
Education, Commissioner of, **1961:** 144
Education, Commissioner of (Francis Keppel),
  oath of office ceremony, **1962:** 540
Education, Conference of African States on, **1961:**
  188
Education, Office of, **1962:** 37, 188; **1963:** 21 (p. 38),
  43, 50, 82, 358, 447
Education Act, National Defense, **1961:** 144, 398;
  1962: 469
  News conference remarks, **1961:** 71 [13], 291,
    [18], 318 [17]
Education Association, National, **1963:** 469
Education Associations, State, **1963:** 469
Education Improvement Act of 1963, National,
  1963: 43, 185
Educational and cultural exchange, **1961:** 57, 78,
  379, 424
Educational and Cultural Exchange Act,
  Mutual, **1961:** 379
Educational Exchange, United States Advisory
   Commission on, **1961:** 57
Educational-information-propaganda program
  in Latin America, **1961:** 276
Educational Television Act, approval, **1962:** 166
EEC.
  See European Economic Community.
EFTA.
  See European Free Trade Association.
Egan, Gov. William A., **1961:** 298
Egger, Rowland A., **1961:** 184
Eglin Air Force Base, Fla., **1962:** 172, 173
Egypt, **1961:** 108
  See also United Arab Republic.
  Missile production in, **1963:** 120 [10]
E. I. du Pont de Nemours and Co., **1962:** 33
Eichelberger, Clark M., **1963:** 101
Eielson Air Force Base, Alaska, **1962:** 493
Einstein, Albert, **1963:** 435
Eisendrath, Rabbi Maurice N., **1961:** 463n.
Eisenhower, Dwight D., President, **1961:** 1, 77, 78
  90, 112, 205, 249, 392, 480, 497; **1962:** 66,
  74, 86, 157, 184, 199, 219, 232, 234, 252,
  314, 422, 453, 459, 506 n., 507 n., 512, 527
  549 [9, 10], 551 [3, 9, 10, 13], 553; **1963:**
  6, 8, 76, 77 [1], 94, 132, 134, 151, 175 ftn.
  (p. 391), 204, 208, 268, 297, 316, 324, 327,
  333, 338, 340, 349, 354, 420, 455, 460 n.
  Agreement on procedures during Presidential
    inability, **1961:** 319
  Library, Abilene, Kans., **1962:** 546 [7]; **1963:** 207
  Meeting with Emperor Haile Selassie, **1963:**
    395 n.
  Meeting with King Mohamed V of Morocco
    (1959), **1963:** 114, 115 n., 116

Eisenhower — *continued*
  News conference remarks on, **1961:** 8 [12, 27, 30,
    32], 15 [8, 20, 24, 25], 35 [8], 71 [13], 83
    [24], 92 [1, 18], 139 [14], 258 [19], 318 [6],
    455 [1, 4, 5], 488 [8]; **1962:** 8 [21], 20 [14],
    27 [27], 40 [8, 13], 59 [1], 115 [10], 152 [5],
    198 [7, 11], 210 [4, 20], 229 [3], 245 [9, 17],
    259 [1, 5, 7, 8, 15], 279 [22], 302 [14, 18],
    340 [27], 352 [11], 378 [9, 20], 410 [6], 546
    [7]; **1963:** 35 [10], 65 [2, 12], 120 [11, 21],
    202 [16], 356 [23], 405 [8], 459 [6]
  Nuclear test ban treaty proposal (1959), **1963:**
    319a
  People-to-people program, **1961:** 455 [1]
  Policy on China, **1962:** 259 [1, 5, 7]; **1963:**
    202 [16]
  Restoration of military rank, **1961:** 62 [2], 88
  TV debate, question of, **1962:** 210 [20]
  Visit to Japan, question of, **1961:** 171 [19]
Eisenhower, Mrs. Dwight D., **1961:** 249; **1962:** 152,
  [5], 527 n.
Eisenhower, Milton, **1961:** 201
El Alto airport, Bolivia, loan, **1961:** 184
El Bosque (Costa Rica) housing project, **1963:** 99,
  103
El Chocon-Los Colorados project, Argentina,
  1961: 389
Eleanor Roosevelt Cancer Foundation, **1961:** 215,
  414
Eleanor Roosevelt Memorial Foundation, **1963:**
  139, 408
Election campaign, Congressional, addresses or re-
  marks
  September 20, Harrisburg, Pa., **1962:** 394, 395
  September 21, Columbus, Ohio, **1962:** 396
  September 27, Wheeling, W. Va., **1962:** 414
  October 5, Cincinnati, Ohio, **1962:** 432
  October 5, Erlanger Ky., **1962:** 431
  October 5, Detroit, Mich., **1962:** 433
  October 6, Detroit, Mich., **1962:** 436
  October 6, Flint, Mich., **1962:** 437
  October 6, Muskegon, Mich., **1962:** 438
  October 6, St. Paul, Minn., **1962:** 439
  October 7, St. Cloud, Minn., **1962:** 440
  October 10, Baltimore, Md., **1962:** 446
  October 12, Newark, N.J., **1962:** 450
  October 12, Aliquippa, Pa., **1962:** 451
  October 12, Pittsburgh, Pa., **1962:** 452
  October 13, McKeesport, Pa., **1962:** 453
  October 13, Monessen, Pa., **1962:** 454
  October 13, Washington, Pa., **1962:** 455
  October 13, Indianapolis, Ind., **1962:** 456
  October 13, Louisville, Ky., **1962:** 457-458
  October 14, Niagara Falls, N.Y., **1962:** 460
  October 14, Buffalo, N.Y., **1962:** 461
  October 17, Stratford, Conn., **1962:** 472
  October 17, New Haven, Conn., **1962:** 473
  October 17, Waterbury, Conn., **1962:** 474

Election campaign — *continued*
  October 19, Cleveland, Ohio, **1962:** 480
  October 19, Springfield, Ill., **1962:** 481
  October 19, Chicago, Ill., **1962:** 482, 483
Election campaign costs, **1961:** 8 [31], 171 [11],
  488 [14]; **1962:** 219; **1963:** 151
  President's commission, **1961:** 403
Election of 1936, **1961:** 474
Election campaign of 1960, **1961:** 3, 447, 448, 483;
  1962: 89 [13], 107 [6], 115 [6], 201, 259
  [1, 7, 10], 346, 414; **1963:** 113 n., 223,
  229, 305 [18, 22]
  News conference remarks, **1961:** 8 [20], 25 [4, 8,
    20], 455 [4, 7]
  "Speeches of Senator John F. Kennedy, Presi-
    dential Campaign of 1960," **1961:** 371 n.
Election campaigns
  1962, **1962:** 15, 210 [20], 279 [13, 23, 26], 316
    [13], 340 [23, 24], 346, 350, 352 [5, 10],
    378 [9, 11, 21], 459
  1964, **1962:** 115 [6]; **1963:** 65 [13], 202 [2, 9, 19],
    328 [13]
Election campaign of 1964, question of TV debates,
  1961: 15 [26]
Election Finance, Registry of, **1963:** 151
Elections
  Free, right of, **1962:** 115 [25]
  1960, **1962:** 162, 472; **1963:** 405 [8]
  1962, **1962:** 27 [9], 302 [14], 378 [3], 515 [8],
    551 [7]
    Statement, **1962:** 502
  1964, **1962:** 245 [7]; **1963:** 305 [24], 328 [7], 340,
    356 [22], 405 [8, 11, 18, 19], 448 [22],
    465 [4]
Elections 1964
  Kentucky primary, **1963:** 120 [13]
  New Hampshire primary, **1963:** 459 [7]
  1968, **1963:** 35 [22]
  Presidential, Puerto Rico, voting in, **1963:** 35 [6]
  Voting rights.
    See main heading, Voting rights.
Electoral college, **1961:** 8 [31]
Electoral reform, **1961:** 8 [31]
Electric power industry, **1963:** 21 (p. 36), 175 [1]
Electric power transmission, **1962:** 69, 335
Electric Workers, International Brotherhood of,
  1962: 247
Electrical companies, Government charges of
  fraud, **1961:** 25 [21]
Electricians, labor contract, **1962:** 20 [19]
Electrification of less developed countries, **1962:**
  499
Electrification, rural, **1963:** 21 (p. 39), 45, 105, 149,
  193
Electronic data processing, **1963:** 21 (p. 42)
Electronic data processing and computers, **1961:**
  417
Electronics trainees, Alaskan, **1962:** 317

Eliot, Dr. Martha M., **1962:** 132
Eliot, T.S., **1963:** 455
Elizabeth, Queen Mother, **1963:** 457
Elizabeth II, **1961:** 227, 231; **1963:** 297
Elizabethville, Katanga, **1963:** 88
Elk Hills oil reserves, **1963:** 6
Ellender, Sen. Allen J., **1961:** 287, 300; **1962:** 170, 171, 413
Elliot, Repr. Carl, **1963:** 193, 194
Elliott, Byron K., **1963:** 368
Elliott, Lloyd H., **1963:** 426
Ellis, Clyde T., **1962:** 499
Ellis, Frank B., **1961:** 5, 295, 302; **1962:** 27 [24]
El Paso, Tex., **1963:** 202 [13], 223, 248ftn. (p. 486), 307, 478
El Paso, Tex., capture of airliner hijackers, **1961:** 312
El Paso, Tex., Chamizal Zone, **1962:** 279 [21]
   Mayor Judson Williams, **1963:** 223
El Paso International Airport, **1963:** 223
El Salvador
   Rivera, Julio A., **1963:** 99, 100, 102, 106
   Tax reforms, **1963:** 118
El Salvador, U.S. recognition of government, **1961:** 35 [2]
Emancipation Proclamation, **1963:** 10, 12 (p. 14), 82, 153, 248, 249, 339
   Centennial, **1962:** 7 (p. 8), 246, 399, 401, 555; **1963:** 59, 153
Emergency Broadcasting System, National, **1961:** 154
Emergency Planning Office of, **1961:** 205, 386; **1962:** 8 [15], 39, 410 [11], 445; **1963:** 166
   See also Civil and Defense Mobilization, Office of.
   Director (Edward A. McDermott), **1962:** 40 [17], 445
   Director (Frank B. Ellis), **1962:** 27 [24]
Emergency, national, question of, **1962:** 379 [19]
Emergency Conference on Pacific Northwest Timber Damage, **1962:** 495
Emerging nations.
   See Less-developed countries and new nations.
Emerson, Ralph Waldo, **1963:** 53, 204, 387
Emmet, Robert, **1963:** 278
Employee-management relations in government, **1961:** 250, 494
Employee organizations, **1961:** 494
Employment, **1961:** 17, 20, 133, 136, 274, 454, 470, 497, 498, 499; **1962:** 6n., 7 (pp. 6, 14), 13 (p. 27), 16 (pp. 42, 45), 22, 28, 91, 108, 162, 165, 174, 176, 205, 230, 234, 280, 328, 380, 405, 549; **1963:** 12 (pp. 11-13), 21 (pp. 26, 27, 29, 38), 30 (pp. 57-62, 68, 70, 71), 34, 64, 134, 177, 187, 188, 193, 242, 248, 290, 301, 310, 329, 336, 351, 366, 379, 391, 393, 400, 401, 407, 445, 458, 464, 466, 468, 478

Employment — *continued*
   Aerospace industry, **1962:** 373
   Agriculture, **1961:** 85
   American Indians, **1963:** 86, 113
   Apprenticeship programs, **1963:** 220
   Automation, effect of, **1962:** 50 [3]
   Cuban refugees, **1961:** 19
   Effect of automation, **1961:** 23, 25 [25], 136, 139 [8], 171 [6], 211
   Equal opportunity.
      See Equal employment opportunity.
   Farm, **1962:** 25; **1963:** 74, 110
   Federal.
      See Government employees.
   Government, **1961:** 68, 152, 436, 504
   Handicapped workers, **1963:** 92, 174, 357
   Industrial, **1963:** 110, 113
   Labor force, growth, **1963:** 92
   Lumber industry, **1962:** 307
   Mexican agricultural workers, **1961:** 400; **1962:** 345
   Migratory labor, **1963:** 74, 130
   Minority groups, **1963:** 210
   Negroes, **1963:** 10, 110, 220, 328 [12], 444, 462
   News conference remarks, **1961:** 15 [23], 25 [25], 62 [10], 71 [12], 83 [12], 92 [12], 119 [8, 18], 139 [8], 455 [7, 19]; **1962:** 8 [4], 50 [3], 89 [5], 210 [13], 229 [1], 302 [4, 18], 410 [1], 546 [6]; **1963:** 65 [1], 75 [1, 14], 120 [8, 11], 144 [21], 305 [18], 328 [7, 12], 356 [8], 448 [7]
   Older persons, **1963:** 74, 92
   Public works, **1963:** 123
   Racial quotas, **1963:** 328 [12], 356 [8]
   Rural, **1963:** 21 (p. 36)
   Services, **1963:** 21 (p. 38)
   Statistics, committee for review of, **1961:** 458
   Steel industry, **1963:** 110, 131
   Tariff reduction, effect of, **1962:** 22, 170
   Tax incentives, **1963:** 175 [2]
   Women, **1961:** 455 [19], 504; **1963:** 92, 409
   Young people, **1961:** 233, 234, 470, 477; **1962:** 7 (p. 6), 13 (p. 31), 16 (p. 56), 28, 89 [5], 174, 186, 220, 229 [1], 288, 302 [4], 328, 336, 337, 360
      See also Youth; employment and training.
Employment Act of 1946, **1962:** 16 (p. 42), 53, 91, 176; **1963:** 30 (pp. 57, 58, 59), 92, 175, 188, 436, 466
Employment of the Handicapped, President's Committee on, **1962:** 49; **1963:** 174, 452
Employment Opportunity, Committee on Equal, **1963:** 82, 220, 248
Employment Opportunities Act, Youth, **1963:** 30 (p. 71), 43, 75 [14], 89 [1], 110, 120 [8], 127, 142
Employment Service, Federal-State, **1963:** 74

Employment Service, United States, **1961:** 17, 136;
  1962: 13 (p. 31), 16 (p. 56), 28, 91; **1963:**
  21 (p. 38), 92, 305 [15]
Employment, Youth, President's Committee on,
  1961: 470; **1963:** 64, 92, 141, 142, 248,
  393
Encyclicals, Pope John XXIII, **1963:** 136, 213
Enders, John F., **1963:** p. 901
Energy Study, National, **1963:** 301
Engels, Friedrich, **1961:** 153
Engineering, Brazilian Military Institute of, **1962:**
  335
Engineering Extension Service, Federal-State,
  1963: 30 (p. 69)
Engineering research, **1963:** 68
Engineers
  Education, **1963:** 92
  Shortage of, **1962:** 8 [1], 37, 546 [8], 547, 549;
    1963: 43
Engineers, Corps of, **1961:** 71 [15], 320; **1962:** 13
  (p. 30), 330, 414, 445; **1963:** 21 (pp. 36,
  42), 127, 192, 301
England.
  See United Kingdom.
Engle, Sen. Clair, **1962:** 337, 338, 340 [15]; **1963:**
  228, 389
Engle, Fred J., **1963:** 389
English Channel, **1962:** 226
Eniwetok Island, **1962:** 342
Enrico Fermi award, **1962:** 530
Enterprise system, **1961:** 81, 93, 121, 497; **1962:** 10,
  16 (p. 42), 38, 39, 75 [2], 139 [9, 11], 152
  [2, 17], 162, 165, 174, 181n., 203, 212, 242,
  273, 278, 296, 310 [1], 355, 410 [1, 3],
  542n., 549, 551 [12]; **1963:** 12 (pp. 13, 16),
  12 (p. 37), 30 (p. 65), 77, 87, 128, 131, 169
  [17], 175 [3], 188, 193, 202 [2], 221, 242,
  301, 361, 468
Enterprise, U.S.S., **1962:** 148
Enthoven, Alain C., **1963:** 238
Equal employment opportunity, **1961:** 62 [10], 68,
  116, 332, 477, 499; **1962:** 7 (p. 8), 16 (p.
  45), 200, 242, 257, 344, 399; **1963:** 10, 92,
  142, 230, 237, 320 [7], 339, 362, 452, 478
  Agreements, signing of, **1962:** 38, 255; **1963:** 19
  Business, **1963:** 230
  In Government service, **1962:** 13 (p. 38), 304;
    1963: 230
  Joint statement with labor leaders, **1962:** 509
  Message to Congress, **1963:** 248
  Minority groups, **1963:** 210
  Negroes, **1962:** 302 [18]; **1963:** 82, 92, 110, 220,
    230, 248, 336, 444, 462
  Under Government contracts, **1961:** 92 [12]
  Women, **1961:** 455 [19], 504; **1962:** 43, 156, 304,
    347; **1963:** 233, 409

Equal Employment Opportunity, President's
  Council on, **1961:** 68, 116; **1962:** 7 (p. 8),
  38n., 225n., 344, 509n.; **1963:** 82, 220, 248
  See also Equal employment opportunity.
  Government contractors' plans for progress,
    1961: 204, 281
Equal opportunity, **1963:** 305 [24], 368
Equal Opportunity in the Armed Forces, Commit-
  tee on, **1962:** 257
Equal Opportunity in the Armed Forces, Presi-
  dent's Committee on, report, **1963:** 251
Equal Opportunity in Housing, President's Com-
  mittee on, **1962:** 515 [2]; **1963:** 49, 82
Equal Pay Act of 1963, **1963:** 233
Equal rights.
  See also Civil rights.
  Women, **1961:** 455 [19], 488 [5]
Equal Rights for Women, Commission on, **1963:**
  315
Erdmann, Mrs. Marian, **1963:** 383
Erhard, Ludwig, **1961:** 62 [23]; **1963:** 262, 263n.,
  265, 266, 454
Erlander, Tage, **1961:** 71 [4]
Erlanger, Ky., **1962:** 431
Escapees.
  See Refugees and escapees.
Escola Superior de Guerra of Brazil, **1962:** 496
Eskimo children, schools for, **1961:** 71 [5]
Eskimo electronic trainees, **1962:** 317
Esselstyn, Dr. Caldwell B., **1962:** 112n.
Estate tax on property located abroad, **1961:** 136
Estes, Billie Sol, **1962:** 198 [1, 7, 11, 17], 210 [6, 12
  18]
Ethical standards,
  Business, **1961:** 25 [21]; **1962:** 10
  Congress, **1963:** 120 [20]
  Executive branch, **1963:** 31, 120 [21]
  Federal Government, **1961:** 152, 171 [11]
  Government employees, **1962:** 13 (p. 38), 198 [1,
    21]; **1963:** 31, 248, 448 [17, 27]
Ethiopia, **1962:** 325; **1963:** 455
  Assistance, **1963:** 397n, 398
  Economic and social development, **1963:** 398
  Emperor Haile Selassie I, **1963:** 200n, 394, 395, 397,
    398, 416
  Five Year Plan, **1963:** 398
  Invasion of (1936), **1963:** 395n.
  Peace Corps projects in, **1963:** 294, 397n.
  U.S. relations with, **1963:** 395
  U.S. tourists in, **1963:** 397
  Visit to, proposed, **1963:** 398
Ethiopian Herald, **1963:** 294
Euratom.
  See European Atomic Energy Community.
Europe, **1961:** 222, 480; **1962:** 207, 254, 506, 507, 521,
  549; **1963:** 8, 12 (p. 15), 16, 88, 162, 171, 179,
  228, 266, 383
  Agricultural exports to, **1962:** 185

[References are to items except as otherwise indicated]

Europe — *continued*
  Assistance, **1963:** 72, 89 [20], 98
  Drug control, **1962:** 411
  Exchange students, **1963:** 140
  Labor movement, **1963:** 162
  Refugee camps, **1961:** 297
  Unification, **1963:** 156
  U.S.-Soviet issues in, **1963:** 75 [18]
Europe, Action Committee for United State of,
    1963: 32
Europe, Central and Eastern, **1961:** 11, 302, 483, 509,
    515
  Economic assistance to Eastern Europe, letter
    1961: 69
  News conference remarks, **1961:** 71 [1], 291 [17],
    318 [10], 415 [18]
  Radio Free Europe broadcasts to, **1961:** 71 [1]
European, Eastern, **1962:** 7 (p. 12), 389; **1963:** 12
    (p. 15), 105, 262, 271, 290, 291, 366, 373,
    382, 383, 385, 405 [1], 424, 437, 455, 459
    [22], 464
  See also specific countries.
  Economic growth, **1963:** 188
  Liberation, **1963:** 54 [7]
  Radio Free Europe broadcasts to, **1963:** 437
  Trade, **1963:** 407, 426
  U.S. wheat sale to, **1963:** 407
Europe, Illinois Trade Mission to, **1963:** 422
Europe, Western, **1961:** 11, 23, 34, 90, 115, 120, 122,
    123, 219, 220, 302, 476, 515, 516; **1962:** 25,
    68, 77, 86, 103, 168, 199, 284, 363, 395, 400,
    456, 531, 541, 543, 551 [21, 22]; **1963:** 12 (pp.
    15, 18), 134 [1], 221, 232, 257, 258, 266, 268,
    271, 287-291, 351, 361, 366, 373, 378, 383,
    385, 390, 413, 418, 424, 455, 465-467, 476-
    478
  Assistance, **1963:** 54 [3], 65 [13], 72, 89 [20], 124,
    134 [30, 260 [3, 13]
  Chickens, imports from U.S., **1963:** 75 [17], 259
  Communist threat to, **1963:** 35 [1], 112
  Defense of, **1962:** 13 (p. 29), 70, 74, 115 [18], 302
    [6], 316 [6, 20]; **1963:** 12 (p. 15), 35 [12, 17,
    24], 54 [3, 8], 65 [3, 6, 8, 9, 15, 17, 19], 89
    [7, 14], 107 [11], 253, 257, 260 [1, 13, 15],
    263, 266, 272, 290, 291, 295, 303, 320 [15],
    340
  Economic and political integration, **1961:** 242,
    318 [1], 481, 483; **1962:** 7 (p. 13), 20 [20],
    22, 169, 170, 198 [3, 16], 248, 251, 278,
    279 [4, 8]
  Economic, political and social development,
    1963: 12 (p. 15), 14, 20, 32, 35 [17], 54 [3],
    65 [8], 80, 118, 132, 150, 188, 253, 258,
    262, 266, 291, 292, 295, 378, 468
  Economy, **1962:** 74, 174, 186, 194, 203, 205, 210
    [13, 16], 230, 234, 245 [6], 310 [1], 328,
    458, 459, 546 [6]

Europe — *continued*
  Fiscal policy, **1963:** 253
  Foreign aid programs, **1962:** 75 [10], 549 [10];
    1963: 12 (p. 15), 21 (pp. 35, 39), 80, 253,
    306
  Manpower resources, **1963:** 72
  Natural resources, **1963:** 72
  News conference remarks, **1961:** 62 [26], 71 [18],
    222, 318 [1], 415 [5], 455 [16], 488 [17];
    1962: 20 [20], 40 [14], 59 [12], 75 [2, 10],
    115 [18], 198 [3, 6, 16], 210 [13, 16], 229
    [5], 245 [6], 259 [6, 9, 14], 279 [4, 6, 8, 25],
    302 [6, 9], 316 [6, 19, 20], 340 [7, 25], 378
    [4], 410 [1, 12], 546 [6]; **1963:** 35 [1, 12, 17,
    24], 54 [3, 8, 10], 65 [3, 6, 8, 9, 13, 15, 17,
    19], 75 [17], 89 [7, 14], 107 [11, 15], 120
    [12, 14, 19], 175 [3], 260 [1, 2, 5, 13, 15, 16,
    18], 305 [9, 11], 320, 356 [18], 448 [1]
  Nuclear weapons, **1962:** 279 [25], 551 [22], 557;
    1963: 65 [6, 9, 15], 89 [14]
  Postwar recovery, **1961:** 222
  Soviet proposal on withdrawal of U.S. troops,
    1961: 483
  Steel industry, **1963:** 175 [3]
  Teachers from, **1962:** 341
  Trade, **1963:** 35 [17], 75 [17], 102, 107 [15], 292
  Trade with Communist bloc, **1961:** 71 [18]
  Trade with Latin America, **1962:** 86, 126, 144, 279
    [6], 302 [9], 378 [4]
  Trade with U.S., **1961:** 455 [16]; **1962:** 7 (p. 14), 8
    [22], 16 (p. 46), 22, 75 [2], 76, 259 [2], 279 [6],
    410 [1]
  U.S. Armed Forces, **1962:** 7 (p. 10), 198 [6], 259 [6,
    14], 295, 309, 422, 537, 549 [9], 557; **1963:** 35
    [17], 65 [3, 15, 17, 19], 260 [13], 448 [1], 478
    Military dependents, **1962:** 59 [12]
    U.S. assistance, **1962:** 13 (p. 29), 250
  U.S. exports, **1963:** 118
  U.S. investments, **1961:** 136, 488 [17], 499; **1962:** 22
  U.S. relations with, **1962:** 74, 278, 279 [4]; **1963:** 20,
    54 [3, 10], 120 [19], 260 [2, 5], 295, 320 [16]
  Visit of Vice President Johnson, **1962:** 339
  Voting participation, **1963:** 167
European Atomic Energy Community, **1961:** 222,
    481; **1963:** 54 [3]
European Coal and Steel Community, **1961:** 222,
    481; **1962:** 341
European Community, **1963:** 262
European Economic Community, **1961:** 21, 239,
    424, 483, 497, 499; **1962:** 7 (p. 14), 13 (p.
    36), 16 (p. 49), 31, 86, 108, 114n., 126, 162,
    170, 174, 194, 199, 250, 273, 310 [1], 328,
    400, 449, 531, 541; **1963:** 9, 12 (p. 16), 14,
    15, 30 (p. 65), 150, 152, 175 [3], 260 [13],
    266, 278, 291, 326, 391
  Joint statements, **1962:** 144, 183, 554
  Joint statements with Chancellor Adenauer on,
    1961: 120, 193, 481

[References are to items except as otherwise indicated]

European Economic Community — *continued*
  News conference remarks, **1961:** 222, 318 [1], 455 [15, 16], 488 [17];**1962:** 8 [4, 22], 20 [20], 40 [14], 75 [2], 115 [23], 198 [16], 210 [16, 19], 229 [1, 9], 245 [6], 259 [2], 279 [4], 302 [9], 340 [2], 378 [4]
  President (Walter Hallstein), **1962:** 144
    Joint statement, **1961:** 189
    Message, **1961:** 21
  Trade negotiations with, **1963:** 169 [21]
  Trade with U.S., **1962:** 8 [22], 16 (p. 49), 22, 75 [2], 76, 259 [2]
  U.K. membership, **1961:** 222 [8], 318 [1], 519
  U.K membership, proposed, **1962:** 7 (p. 14), 20 [20], 22, 88, 160, 198 [16], 210 [19], 229 [9], 248, 251, 279 [4], 549 [2], 554
  U.K. membership, question of, **1963:** 20, 35 [17], 54 [3, 11], 65 [8], 75 [17], 260 [8]
  U.S. policy on, **1962:** 210 [19]; **1963:** 35 [17]
  U.S. relations with, **1963:** 45
  U.S. trade with, **1963:** 175 [3], 202 [5]
European Economic Community, Commission of the, **1961:** 21; **1962:** 144
European Economic Cooperation, Organization for.
  See Organization for European Economic Co-operation.
European Free Trade Association, **1962:** 160, 378 [1]
European Migration, Intergovernmental Committee for, **1961:** 297
European Monetary Agreements, **1961:** 222
European Payments Union, **1961:** 222
Ev (Dirksen) and Charlie (Halleck) show, **1961:** 139 [10]
Evans, Upshur, **1962:** 412n.
Everett, Edward, **1963:** 140
Everett, Repr. Robert A., **1963:** 192
Evers, Martin, **1962:** 432
Everson case, Supreme Court decision, **1961:** 62 [27], 71 [13]
Everton, John S., **1961:** 367n.
Evian-les-Bains, France, **1961:** 222 [1]
Evins, Repr. Joe L. **1963:** 192
Exchange controls, foreign, **1961:** 497, 499
Exchange of persons, **1961:** 57
  American Field Service, **1963:** 308
  Association for International Exchange of Students in Economics and Commerce, **1963:** 128
  Cultural and Technical Interchange between East and West, Center for, **1963:** 231
  Experiment in International Living, **1962:** 363
  Farm leaders, Latin American, **1963:** 404n.
  Fulbright program, **1963:** 140, 332
  Teachers, **1961:** 48; **1962:** 341
  U.S.-Ethiopia, **1963:** 397n.
  U.S.-Japan, **1963:** 424n.
  U.S.-Poland, **1962:** 461

Excise taxes, **1961:** 58, 136; **1962:** 7 (p. 7), 13 (p. 34), 16 (p. 56), 128, 129, 328, 395, 549 [5]; **1963:** 21 (p. 30)
Executive branch, **1962:** 13 (p. 38), 20 [7], 107 [15, 19, 20], 139 [11], 275, 296, 448; **1963:** 35 [23], 50, 57, 70, 82, 91, 94, 135, 146, 166, 209, 232, 237, 240, 246, 248, 252, 310, 328 [9], 336, 409, 427, 430, 445, 448 [17, 25], 458
  Civil rights policy, **1963:** 89 [8]
  Ethical standards, **1963:** 31, 120 [20]
  Land management functions, **1963:** 37
  Liaison with Congress, **1961:** 25 [12]
  Reorganization, **1961:** 11, 111; **1963:** 207
Executive Employees Standards Act, proposed, **1961:** 152
Executive Office of the President, **1962:** 250; **1963:** 166
Executive orders, list, Appendix B., **1961:** p. 840; **1962:** p. 938; **1963:** p. 922
Executive privilege.
  See Privileged information.
Exiles.
  See Refugees and escapees.
Expense accounts, **1961:** 136, 185; **1962:** 16 (p. 57), 158
Experiment in International Living, **1962:** 363
Exports, **1961:** 11, 23, 136, 497; **1962:** 7 (p. 15), 13 (p. 36), 14, 16 (pp. 44, 49), 22, 76, 162, 170, 199, 280, 328, 449, 549 [2, 10]; **1963:** 21 (p. 40), 75 [11], 77 [4], 118, 131, 175, 306, 310, 391, 422, 455
  See also specific commodities.
  Agricultural, **1962:** 7 (p. 14), 8 [22], 22, 25, 144, 185; **1963:** 21 (p. 35), 30 (p. 65), 45, 75 [17], 118, 202 [18], 259, 407
  Agricultural commodities, **1961:** 23, 85, 127
  Chickens, **1963:** 75 [17], 259
  Cotton, **1961:** 258 [10], 488 [19]; **1962:** 8 [4], 25
  Expansion program, **1962:** 7 (p. 14), 16 (p. 49), 114, 280; **1963:** 21 (p. 37), 228
  "E" awards, **1962:** 113
  Increase, **1963:** 118
  Industrial, **1963:** 30 (p. 65)
  Industrial goods, **1962:** 22
  Iron and steel, **1961:** 354
  Latin American, **1963:** 54 [10]
  Livestock, **1962:** 185
  News conference remarks, **1961:** 35 [8], 71 [18], 258 [10], 488 [17, 18, 19]; **1962:** 8 [4, 22], 27 [10], 139 [5], 259 [2], 316 [19], 340 [16], 378 [2], 410 [1]
  Swedish, **1963:** 361
  To Communist countries, **1961:** 71 [18]
  To Cuba, **1961:** 35 [8]; **1962:** 27 [10]
  U-2 aircraft, **1962:** 378 [2]
  Wheat, **1963:** 45, 89 [11], 202 [18]
Export Control Act, **1963:** 407
Export Coordinator, Office of, **1962:** 114n.

Export credit facilities, statement, **1961:** 437
Export credit insurance, **1961:** 437, 497
Export expansion program, **1961:** 497
   "E" flag awards, **1961:** 495
Export Expansion, White House Conference on,
   1963: 306, 361
Export-Import Bank of Washington, **1961:** 23, 90,
      94; **1962:** 7 (p. 12), 13 (pp. 29, 38), 16 (p.
      49), 275, 549 [10]; **1963:** 21 (pp. 35, 40), 30
      (p. 65), 54 [1], 118, 306, 361, 459 [9]
   Credit facilities, **1961:** 437, 497
   Meriwether (Charles M). nomination, **1961:**
      62 [14, 28], 71 [22]
   News conference remarks, **1961:** 62 [14, 28], 71
      [22], 83 [3]
   President (Harold F. Linder), **1961:** 23, 437;
      1963: 62
Extension Service, Federal-State Engineering,
   1963: 30 (p. 69)

Fahs, Charles B., **1962:** 122n.
Fair Deal, **1962:** 439
Fair employment practices.
   See Equal Employment Opportunity.
Fair Labor Standards Act, **1961:** 17, 24; **1962:** 458;
   1963: 30 (p. 67), 92
Fairchild, Edward T., **1961:** 339
Faivovich, Angel, **1962:** 543n.
Fall River, Mass., **1961:** 155; **1962:** 384
Fallon, Repr. George H., **1962:** 466; **1963:** 461
Fallout, radioactive, **1961:** 49, 205, 410, 442, 440;
   1962: 65, 71, 320
   See also Radioactive fallout.
   Effect on food, **1962:** 19
   Milk, **1962:** 20 [11, 18], 316 [22]
   News conference remarks, **1961:** 258 [12], 455
      [18], 488 [21]; **1962:** 20[11, 18], 229 [19], 259
      [19], 316 [22], 352 [7, 18]
Fallout shelters, **1961:** 205, 302, 410, 503; **1962:** 7 (p.
      10), 13 (p. 28), 279 [11], 320; **1963:** 21 (p. 33),
      166
   News conference remarks, **1961:** 415 [4], 455 [13],
      488 [13, 21]
Family Circle magazine, **1963:** 319a note
Family of Man Award, acceptance, **1963:** 455
Family Services, Bureau of, **1962:** 28
Family welfare programs, **1963:** 64
Faneuil Hall, **1963:** 266
Fanfani, Amintore, **1961:** 318 [7]; **1962:** 352 [3]
   Joint statement with, **1963:** 20
   Visit of, **1961:** 239, 242; **1963:** 15, 16, 20
Fannin, Gov. Paul, **1961:** 475n., 476n,; **1963:** 108
FAO.
   See Food and Agriculture Organization.
Far East.
   See Asia, South Asia, and Southeast Asia.
Farah, Empress, **1962:** 138
Farben, I. G., Co., **1963:** 89 [12]
Farbstein, Repr. Leonard, **1963:** 89 [15]

Farm bill, **1961:** 83 [19], 127; **1962:** 201, 205, 459
   Campaign remarks, **1962:** 394-396, 437
   News conference remarks, **1962:** 89 [18], 259 [8],
      302 [4], 340 [2], 378 [21]
Farm cooperatives, **1961:** 85; **1962:** 440
Farm credit, **1961:** 37 [3], 85; **1962:** 440
Farm Credit Administration, Governor (R. B.
   Tootell), **1963:** 62
Farm economy, **1961:** 11, 17, 39, 83 [19], 85, 94,
      113, 316, 436; **1962:** 3, 7 (p. 7), 13 (p. 30),
      16 (p. 44) 19, 25, 127, 197, 413; **1963:** 12
      (p. 14), 21 (p. 35), 30 (pp. 58, 61), 34, 45,
      61, 105, 110, 149, 189, 193, 197, 201, 217,
      379, 400, 404, 465, 478
   Campaign remarks, **1962:** 395, 396, 439, 440, 473,
      481, 484
   News conference remarks, **1962:** 8 [11], 259 [8],
      352 [4]; **1963:** 202 [2, 12, 15, 18], 305 [18],
      405 [1]
Farm groups, meeting, **1961:** 15 [27]
Farm housing, **1961:** 76, 94
Farm machinery, **1963:** 407
Farm prices and income.
   See Farm economy.
Farm program, **1961:** 15 [27], 23, 85, 113, 127; **1962:**
      7 (p. 7), 25, 127, 459; **1963:** 12 (p. 14), 21
      (p. 35), 197, 202 [2, 12, 15, 18]
   Campaign remarks, **1962:** 440, 456, 481
   Message to Congress, **1963:** 45
   News conference remarks, **1962:** 198 [11], 245 [9],
      410 [3]
   Wheat referendum, **1963:** 45, 169 [13], 189, 197,
      201, 202 [2, 12, 15, 18]
Farmers affected by imports, assistance to, **1962:** 22

Farmer Cooperatives, National Council of, **1963:**
   149n.
Farmers Home Administration, **1961:** 85, 94; **1962:**
      25; **1963:** 21 (pp. 36, 42), 45, 110, 478
Farmers Organization, National, **1962:** 352 [4]
Farmers Union, National, **1963:** 404n.
Farms, low income, **1961:** 85
Fascell, Repr. Dante B., **1962:** 77n., 89 [2], 179 [4];
      1963: 465-467
Fascism, **1961:** 373; **1963:** 395n.
Faubus, Gov. Orval E., **1961:** 440; **1963:** 108, 400,
      401
Faulhaber, James H., **1962:** 122n.
Faulkner, William, **1963:** 455
   Death of, **1962:** 281
Faust, Johann, **1963:** 266
Fay, Paul B., Jr., **1963:** 174
Fayette County, Tenn., eviction of tenant farmers,
      1961: 8 [9]
Fayetteville, Ark., **1962:** 361
Faysal, Crown Prince, **1962:** 429
FBI.
   See Federal Bureau of Investigation.

FCC.
See Federal Communications Commission.
"Featherbedding," **1963:** 30 (p. 68)
Fecteau, Richard G., **1962:** 243 [6]
Federal Advisory Council on the Arts, proposed,
1962: 37
Federal aid to States, **1962:** 549; **1963:** 21 (pp. 31,
36), 35 [21], 209
Air pollution control, **1962:** 65
Airports, **1961:** 94, 141
Area redevelopment, **1962:** 165; **1963:** 92, 228
Civil defense, **1961:** 205; **1963:** 166
Conservation, **1962:** 128
Crime control, **1963:** 30 (p. 65), 64
Depressed areas, **1963:** 127, 193
Disease immunization, **1962:** 65
Education, **1961:** 11, 46, 71 [13, 17], 83 [8, 9, 16],
94, 144, 255, 291 [8, 16], 318 [17], 334 [6],
398, 462, 473; **1962:** 7 (p. 9), 13 (p. 32), 16
(p. 46), 37, 40 [3], 328, 438, 439, 451, 452,
456, 458, 459, 480, 483, 551 [10]; **1963:** 21
(p. 38), 30 (pp. 65, 69), 43, 50, 74, 77, 82,
89 [7], 92, 141, 162, 226, 228, 240, 248,
279, 358n., 426, 469, 478
Flood insurance, **1962:** 89 [11]
Forest development, **1961:** 85
Health programs, **1963:** 30 (p. 65), 51
Health services and facilities, **1961:** 14, 27, 37, 94,
406
Highways, **1961:** 17, 35 [3], 37, 58, 83 [7], 261;
1962: 21 (pp. 27, 32, 36); **1963:** 13 (p. 31),
16 (p. 44), 129
Hospitals, **1962:** 115 [27]; **1963:** 53
Libraries, **1963:** 43
Mental health program, **1963:** 50, 66
Mississippi, termination, question of, **1963:** 134
[5], 135, 144 [13]
Old age assistance grants, **1963:** 74 .
Outdoor recreational programs, **1962:** 69
Public works, **1962:** 16 (p. 52), 53, 229 [1]
Recreational and cultural programs, **1963:** 30 (p.
66), 63
Surplus lands, transfer, **1962:** 195
Transportation, **1963:** 30 (p. 65), 69
Urban renewal, **1962:** 23
Water pollution control, **1961:** 49
Water resources development, **1962:** 69
Welfare services, **1962:** 28; **1963:** 22
Withdrawal in event of civil rights violation,
question of, **1963:** 135, 144 [13]
Federal Airport Act, **1961:** 141, 374
Federal Appalachian Regional Commission, **1961:**
176n.
Federal Apprenticeship Act, **1963:** 248
Federal Aviation Act, **1962:** 129
Federal Aviation Act of 1958, **1963:** 242

Federal Aviation Agency, **1961:** 121, 374; **1962:** 93
(p. 236); **1963:** 21 (p. 42), 29, 238, 242
Federal Aviation Agency, Administrator (Najeeb
E. Halaby), **1962:** 512; **1963:** 29, 238n.
Federal Bureau of Investigation, **1962:** 7 (p. 7), 443;
1963: 144 [13], 360, 365
Director (J. Edgar Hoover), **1961:** 15 [36], 312,
362; **1962:** 231, 497
Meriwether (Charles M.) files, **1961:** 71 [22]
National Academy, graduation exercises, **1962:**
497
News conference remarks, **1962:** 152 [12], 198 [1,
7, 17], 210 [6, 18], 378 [6]
Federal Communications Commission, **1961:** 121;
1962: 13 (p. 38), 27 [16], 93 (p. 237), 316
[16], 352 [23]
Chairman (Newton N. Minow), **1962:** 27 [16],
302 [20], 515 [16], 532
Reorganization Plan, **1961:** 151
Federal Council for Science and Technology, **1961:**
49, 417; **1962:** 8 [1], 69, 118, 187, 547;
1963: 53
Report, **1963:** 70, 252
Federal Credit Programs, Committee on, report,
1963: 62
Federal Credit Union Act, amendment, **1963:** 417
Federal Deposit Insurance Corporation, **1963:** 306
Federal Driver License Register, **1962:** 11
Federal employees.
See Government employees.
Federal Executive Pay Act of 1956, **1962:** 151
Federal Executives, Boards of, regional, **1961:** 465
Federal Expenditures, Presidential Commission
on, proposed, **1963:** 120 [6]
Federal Extension Service, **1962:** 25
Federal Flood Insurance Act (1956), **1962:** 89 [11]
Federal Hazardous Substances Labeling Act of
1960, **1963:** 53
Federal Highway Administrator (Rex M.
Whitton), **1963:** 164
Federal Home Loan Bank Board, **1961:** 17
Chairman (Joseph P. McMurray), **1961:** 62 [4];
1962: 279 [9]; **1963:** 49, 62
Reorganization Plan, **1961:** 237
Federal Housing Administration, **1961:** 15 [5], 17,
76, 258 [22]; **1962:** 16 (p. 44), 23, 480, 545
Federal Industrial Relations Commission, **1963:**
133
Federal Maritime Board, **1961:** 121, 370
Termination, **1961:** 238
Federal Maritime Commission, **1961:** 370, 401;
1962: 129; **1963:** 306
Establishment, **1961:** 238
Federal marshals, use in civil rights enforcement,
1963: 202 [1]

Federal Mediation and Conciliation Service, **1961:**
256, 270n; **1962:** 179 [7], 247n., 298, 302
[15], 379, 376, 390, 421, 428; **1963:** 18, 92,
202 [20], 206
  Director (William E. Simkin), **1962:** 390; **1963:**
  206
Federal National Mortgage Association, **1961:** 15
[5], 17; **1962:** 16 (p. 44), 23, 323, 545
New loan program, proposed, **1961:** 76
Federal Office Space, Ad Hoc Committee on, **1962:**
221
Federal Power Act, **1962:** 69
Federal Power Commission, **1961:** 49, 121, 152;
1962: 69, 93 (p. 237)
  Civilian nuclear power, study, **1962:** 100
Federal Property and Administrative Services Act
of 1949, **1962:** 195; **1963:** 207
Federal Radiation Council, **1961:** 258 [12]; **1962:**
19, 71
Federal Register, Presidential documents published
in, Appendix B, **1963:** p. 921
Federal Reserve Act, **1961:** 23; **1962:** 151
Federal Reserve Banks, notes to replace silver cer-
tificates, **1961:** 484
Federal Reserve System, **1961:** 17, 23, 76; **1962:** 16
(pp. 44, 50), 151, 203, 229 [15], 234, 549 [3,
7]; **1963:** 30 (pp. 63, 65, 67), 54 [1], 306
  Board of Governors, **1962:** 16 (p. 54), 151; **1963:**
  305 [22], 306, 328 [15], 349
    Chairman (William McC. Martin, Jr.), **1961:**
    83 [18], 123, 258 [16]; **1962:** 151, 549 [3];
    1963: 54 [1], 62, 94n.
  News conference remarks, **1961:** 25 [16], 62 [4],
  258 [16], 291 [2]
Federal Salary Reform Act of 1962, **1963:** 4, 21 (p.
43), 53, 148
  Advisory Panel on, **1963:** 44, 148
  Report, **1962:** 55
Federal Savings and Loan Insurance Corporation,
1962: 93 (p. 237)
Federal-State Employment Service, **1963:** 74
Federal-State Engineering Service, **1963:** 30 (p. 69)
Federal-State-local governmental responsibilities,
1961: 17, 33, 465; **1962:** 27 [7]; **1963:** 30
(p. 65)
  Civil defense, **1961:** 205, 455 [13], 503; **1962:** 13
  (p. 28), 320; **1963:** 166
  Civil rights, **1963:** 82, 230, 232, 237, 248
  Community development, **1961:** 436
  Community relations services, **1963:** 248
  Conservation, **1962:** 128, 495; **1963:** 376, 377
  Depressed areas, **1961:** 7
  Drug control, **1962:** 218, 411
  Education, **1961:** 46, 477; **1962:** 37; **1963:** 43, 92,
  141, 469
  Employment, **1963:** 21 (p. 38), 174, 464
  Equal employment opportunity, **1963:** 220
  Family welfare programs, **1963:** 64

Federal-State-Local — *continued*
  Health services, **1962:** 65; **1963:** 50, 51, 53
  Highway program, **1961:** 35 [3], 58
  Manpower development, **1963:** 423
  Mental health, **1961:** 492
  Narcotics control, **1962:** 218
  Older persons, **1962:** 193; **1963:** 74
  Public welfare, **1962:** 306
  Public works, **1962:** 229 [1]; **1963:** 123
  Recreational facilities, **1962:** 13 (p. 30); **1963:** 63
  Traffic safety, **1963:** 125
  Transportation, **1963:** 12 (p. 14), 69
  Transportation planning, **1962:** 129
  Urban renewal, **1962:** 23
  Voting rights, **1963:** 117
Federal Surplus Property Disposal Act, amend-
ment proposed, **1962:** 69
Federal Trade Commission, **1961:** 119 [11], 121,
337; **1962:** 13 (p. 38), 93 (p. 237), 139 [1,
4], 162, 296
  Reorganization Plan, **1961:** 180
Federal Trade Commission, Chairman (Paul Rand
Dixon), **1961:** 119 [11]
Federal Water Pollution Control Act, **1963:** 377
Federation of Catholic Universities, **1963:** 342
Fedorenko, N.T., **1963:** 27n.
Feed Grain Act of 1963, **1963:** 189n.
  Approval of, **1963:** 197
Feed grains, **1961:** 15 [27], 316, 436; **1962:** 13 (p.
30), 25, 127, 340 [2], 413, 549; **1963:** 21, (p.
35), 45, 169 [13], 189, 197, 202 [2, 12, 15],
407, 465
  Campaign remarks, **1962:** 439, 440, 456
  Emergency program
    Approval of bill, **1961:** 89
    Letters, **1961:** 39, 300
    Statement, **1961:** 113
  News conference remarks, **1962:** 259 [8], 410 [3]
  Price supports, **1961:** 39
  Surpluses, **1961:** 39, 102
Feighan, Repr. Michael A., **1962:** 480
Feinsinger, Nathan P., **1961:** 245; **1962:** 253; **1963:**
184
Fekini, Mohieddine, **1962:** 467n.
Feldman, George, **1962:** 476n.
Feldman, Myer, **161:** 444; **1962:** 296n., 462
Felix, Dr. Robert H., **1961:** 490
Fellowships, **1963:** 43
Fellowships, oceanographic research, **1961:** 100
Fenoaltea, Sergio, **1961:** 242; **1962:** 339n., 361n.,
524; **1963:** 191, 293
Fermi, Enrico, **1962:** 524, 530
Fermi (Enrico) award, **1962:** 530
Fertilizers, **1963:** 110
Festival of the Cities of the New World, **1963:** 412
Fettinger, John G., **1963:** 435
FHA.
  See Federal Housing Administration.

Field and regional governmental activites, **1961:** 465

Fifielski, Edwin P., **1962:** 343n.

Fighters.

    See Aircraft, military.

Figueres, Jose, **1961:** 78

Finan, Thomas B., **1962:** 446

Financiers, **1963:** 422

Fine Arts, Commission of, **1962:** 27 [21]

Finger injury, the President's, **1963:** 169 [16]

Finland

    Karjalainen, Ahti, **1961:** 421n.

    Kekkonen, Urho K., **1961:** 421, 422, 424, 451, 488 [4]; **1962:** 52

    Purchase of United Nations bonds, **1962:** 82

Finletter, Thomas K., **1961:** 25 [2, 17], 221, 393; **1963:** 36

Finley, David, **1962:** 262; **1963:** 425

Finnegan, Repr. Edward R., **1962:** 483

Fire prevention, **1963:** 325

Fire prevention, forests, **1961:** 85

Firemen, benefits, veto, **1961:** 383

First Armored Division, **1962:** 519, 521

First Family, record album, **1962:** 546 [19]

Fiscal policy, **1962:** 13 (pp. 35-37), 16 (p. 44), 151, 176, 234, 250, 280, 340 [19], 410 [1], 549; **1963:** 30 (pp. 58, 61, 63, 66), 30 (p. 63), 34, 94, 107 [9], 134 [4], 144 [14], 175, 187, 188, 260 [5, 8, 13], 266, 291, 305 [12, 22], 306, 328 [23], 381, 387, 391, 436, 465

Fiscal policy, message to Congress, **1961:** 94

Fish and wildlife resources, **1961:** 49, 65, 100; **1962:** 69, 128; **1963:** 217, 377

Fishbein, Dr. Morris, **1962:** 222

Fisher, Adrian S., **1962:** 8 [20]; **1963:** 89 [4]

Fisher, Patrick J., **1962:** 376

Fisheries of the North Pacific Ocean, Convention on High Seas, **1963:** 352n.

Fisheries, Commercial Bureau of, **1961:** 100

Fisheries, U.S.-Canadian discussion, **1963:** 179

Fishery products, shipping of, **1962:** 129

Fisk, James B., **1961:** 8 [1], 62 [21]

Fissionable materials, **1961:** 387; **1962:** 71

Fitzgerald, Lord Edward, **1963:** 278

Fitzgerald, Ella, **1962:** 201

Fitzgerald, John Frances, **1961:** 220; **1962:** 450; **1963:** 264, 277, 281

Fitzgerald Field House, University of Pittsburgh, **1962:** 452

Fitzpatrick, Howard, **1963:** 427

Fitness clinics, regional, **1963:** 325

Fiumicino airport, Rome, **1963:** 287

Flag of Cuban Invasion Brigade, acceptance, **1962:** 556

Flag of West Virginia, presentation to President, **1963:** 195

Flaming Gorge Dam project, **1963:** 386

Flat, U.S., **1962:** 505n.

Fleigers, Serge, **1961:** 222 [4]

Fleming, Robben W., **1962:** 421

Fleming, Thomas F., **1963:** 465

Flemming, Arthur S., **1963:** 460n.

Fliegerhorst Barracks, Germany, **1963:** 263

Flight Engineers International Association, **1961:** 50; **1962:** 245 [1], 253, 256, 516

Flight safety plaque, presentation to Strategic Air Command, **1962:** 535

Flint, Mich., **1962:** 437

Flood control, **1961:** 17, 49, 83 [2], 94, 445; **1962:** 69, 332, 333, 414; **1963:** 21 (p. 36), 45, 193, 376

Flood Control Act, **1962:** 313

Flood insurance, **1962:** 89 [11], 152 [10]

Floods

    Idaho, **1961:** 83 [2]

    Viet-Nam, **1961:** 505

Florence, Italy, **1963:** 5

Florida, **1961:** 112, 518; **1962:** 77, 171, 183; **1963:** 35 [9], 356 [22], 464, 466, 467, 469

    Gov. Farris Bryant, **1961:** 499; **1962:** 77; **1963:** 108, 465-468

    News conference remarks, **1962:** 179 [4]. 378 [22], 515 [9]

Florida Barge Canal, proposed, **1963:** 465

Florida East Coast Railway, **1963:** 414

Flour, **1963:** 407

    Exports, **1963:** 45

    For overseas relief, **1963:** 45

Flying Tiger Lines, **1961:** 50

Fogarty, Repr. John E., **1961:** 488 [8]; **1963:** 435

Foley, Edward H., **1961:** 234

Foley, John, **1962:** 446

Folk dancing, **1963:** 137

Følling, Dr. Ivar Asbjørn, **1962:** 534

Folsom, Marion B., **1963:** 44n.

Fonda, Henry, **1962:** 201

Fong, Sen, Hiram L., **1963:** 229

Food, **1962:** 7 (p. 8), 25, 93 (p. 235); **1963:** 130, 217, 383, 407, 458

    Conservation, **1963:** 45

    Consumer protection, **1963:** 74

    For Chinese refugees in Hong Kong, **1962:** 245 [10]

    For Communist China, question of, **1961:** 8 [25]; **1962:** 89 [14], 210 [2], 243 [6]

    For Communist countries, question of, **1962:** 75 [4], 229 [3]; **1963:** 405 [1], 407

    For Cuban refugees, **1961:** 19

    For Egypt, **1962:** 229 [10]

    For fallout shelters, **1962:** 279 [11]

    For Kenya, **1962:** 18

    For needy and unemployed people, **1961:** 8 [10], 11, 17, 35 [3], 71 [7], 85; **1962:** 452, 453; **1963:** 74, 455

Food — *continued*
  Stamp plan, **1961:** 15 [3], 85, 436; **1962:** 13 (p.
    30), 16 (p. 44), 25, 318, 328, 414, 440;
    1963: 21 (p. 36), 45, 74, 127, 445
  For overseas relief, **1962:** 25, 107 [10], 133; **1963:**
    33, 217, 459 [13]
  For prisoners in Cuba, **1962:** 107 [9]
  For Togo, **1962:** 103n., 105
  For underprivileged of the world, **1961:** 35 [11],
    62 [11], 139 [2]
  From ocean, **1962:** 216
  Pollution control, **1963:** 53
  Prices, **1963:** 197, 202 [2, 12, 15, 18]
  Production and distribution, **1963:** 41, 187
  Radioactive fallout, effect of, **1962:** 19, 20 [11,
    18], 316 [22]
  School programs, **1963:** 89 [5], 135, 193, 423, 458
  Shortages, **1963:** 310, 405 [1]
  Storage, **1963:** 175
  Surplus, **1963:** 351
  World Food Congress, **1963:** 33, 217, 218
  World food program, **1962:** 319; **1963:** 471
Food and Agriculture Act of 1962, **1963:** 21 (p. 36),
    45
  Approval, **1962:** 413
Food and Agriculture Organization, U.N., **1963:** 33
    217, 455
Food Bank, World, **1962:** 293
Food Congress, World, **1962:** 478; **1963:** 33, 217,
    218
Food and Drug Administration, **1962:** 13 (p. 31), 93
    (pp. 236, 238), 137, 296, 316 [1, 4, 24], 323;
    1963: 21 (p. 37), 53
Food, Drug and Cosmetic Act, **1963:** 53, 74
Food Machinery and Chemical Corporation of
    New York City, **1961:** 119 [3]
Food for Peace, Director (George McGovern),
    1961: 15ftn. (p. 39), 85, 207, 482; **1962:** 8
    [6], 293
  News conference remarks, **1961:** 35 [11], 62 [11],
    139 [2]
Food for Peace Committee, report, **1961:** 6n.
Food for peace program, **1961:** 6, 11, 90, 207, 285,
    482; **1962:** 7 (p. 12), 8 [6], 13 (p. 29), 25,
    105, 107 [10], 133, 293, 413, 446, 478;
    1963: 21 (p. 35), 45, 118, 217, 326, 366,
    439, 445
  Bolivia, **1961:** 184
  Latin America, **1961:** 78, 102
    Mission, **1961:** 11, 15 [34]
  News conference remarks, **1961:** 15 [34], 139 [2]
Food production.
  See Agricultural productivity.
Food Program, World, **1963:** 471
Food surpluses.
  See Agricultural surpluses; Food for peace pro-
    gram.

Football Hall of Fame award, acceptance, **1961:**
    496
Forand, Aime J., **1962:** 81, 202, 217; **1963:** 138
Forced Labor, Convention on the Abolition of,
    1963: 309
Ford, Benson, **1961:** 375
Ford, Henry, II, **1961:** 40n; **1962:** 234; **1963:** 145n.,
    169 [15], 351
Ford Foundation, **1961:** 245; **1962:** 340 [13]; **1963:**
    22, 355, 423, 430
Ford Motor Co., **1963:** 77 [1]
Fordham, Jefferson B., **1961:** 152
Foreign affairs, **1961:** 129, 456, 521; **1962:** 7 (p. 9),
    13 (p. 36)
  News conference remarks, **1961:** 15 [8], 171 [10],
    291 [15], 415 [8, 12]
Foreign Affairs Academy, proposed, **1963:** 57
Foreign Affairs magazine, 40th anniversary, 1962:
    387
Foreign affairs organization, guidelines, **1961:** 207
Foreign Aid and Related Agencies Appropriation
    Act, 1963, **1963:** 6
Foreign assistance, **1961:** 6, 11, 185, 244, 277, 333;
    1962: 13 (pp. 36, 38), 16 (p. 50), 20 [26],
    22, 25, 74, 77, 107 [10], 133, 163, 170, 199,
    232, 237, 243 [1], 280, 302 [6], 316 [19],
    340 [4], 392, 410 [12], 455, 549 [10]; **1963:**
    6, 12 (p. 16), 21 (pp. 32, 35), 30 (p. 64), 57,
    77, 89 [10, 20], 111, 217, 221, 255, 258,
    262, 291, 306, 316, 333, 340, 342, 361, 366,
    378, 385, 455, 459 [6, 11, 13], 465, 477
  See also Economic assistance and development;
    Military assistance and defense support;
    Mutual security program; Technical
    assistance to less-developed and new
    countries; Alliance for Progress; *specific
    countries.*
Afghanistan, **1963:** 344n.
Africa, **1961:** 139 [4]; **1962:** 549 [10], 254, 314;
    1963: 12 (p. 17), 124, 338, 342
Algeria, **1962:** 75 [15]
Appropriations, **1961:** 343; **1963:** 118
Argentina, **1961:** 202, 389; **1963:** 35 [19]
Asia, **1962:** 314; **1963:** 12 (pp. 15, 17, 19), 89 [20],
    124, 328 [1], 338, 342
Austria, **1962:** 168n.
Berlin, **1962:** 40 [14]
Bolivia, **1961:** 184, 409; **1962:** 216; **1963:** 118,
    431n.
Brazil, **1961:** 285; **1962:** 126, 146, 177
Cambodia, **1962:** 107 [15]; **1963:** 89 [20], 459 [1]
Cameroon, **1962:** 87
Caribbean area, cooperation with Canada, **1963:**
    179
Central African Republic, **1961:** 167
Central America, **1961:** 99
Chile, **1961:** 81, 94; **1963:** 61, 118

Foreign assistance — *continued*
China, Republic of, **1961:** 309; **1962:** 549 [10];
1963: 72n., 118
Clay Committee, on, **1963:** 89 [20], 111, 118, 120
[6]
Colombia, **1962:** 410 [3]; **1963:** 118
Congo, Republic of the, **1961:** 8 [2]; **1962:** 236
Cuban exile organizations, **1963:** 202 [11]
Cyprus, **1962:** 227, 249
Denial to nations practicing discrimination,
1963: 89 [15]
Dominican Republic, **1962:** 17
Drain on U.S. balance of payments, **1963:** 134 [3]
Eastern Europe, **1961:** 69
Ecuador, **1962:** 303
Egypt, **1962:** 229 [10]
Ethiopia, **1963:** 397n., 398
Expenditures, **1963:** 328 [23]
France, **1963:** 72
Funds for, **1962:** 389
Germany, **1963:** 72, 134 [3]
Greece, **1961:** 128, 135, 222; **1963:** 118, 328 [1],
338
Honduras, **1963:** 118
India, **1961:** 460; **1962:** 50 [10], 83, 89 [4], 340 [4],
515 [3, 5], 549 [10]; **1963:** 118, 169 [17], 202
[3], 219, 285, 328 [1], 356 [25]
Indonesia, **1961:** 146; **1963:** 459 [13]
Iran, **1962:** 147, 364; **1963:** 118, 328 [1], 338
Israel, **1963:** 120 [10], 169 [2]
Italy, **1963:** 72, 134 [3]
Ivory Coast, **1962:** 212
Jordan, **1963:** 169 [2]
Kenya, **1962:** 18
Korea, **1961:** 468; **1962:** 549 [10]; **1963:** 72, 328
[1], 338
Laos, **1961:** 92 [6. 15], 318 [15]; **1962:** 40 [14];
1963: 78, 81, 202 [10]
Latin America, **1961:** 1, 11, 15 [34], 78, 81, 90,
102, 313, 324, 491; **1962:** 3, 7 (p. 12), 40
[14], 77, 89 [4], 177, 245 [12], 279 [1], 314,
378 [4]; **1963:** 12 (p. 17), 21 (p. 35), 72,
100, 107 [1, 22], 118, 120 [12], 124, 146,
320 [14], 338, 342, 431, 462, 477, 478
Legislation, **1962:** 89 [4], 279 [1], 302 [19], 352
[11]; **1963:** 328 [1]
Less developed countries and new nations, **1961:**
23, 34, 41, 62 [23, 26], 63, 90, 112, 139 [2],
167, 193, 205, 207, 214, 244, 299, 302, 343,
346, 481, 497; **1962:** 7 (pp. 12, 13), 13 (pp.
29, 36, 38), 25, 65, 75 [10], 83, 109, 183,
245 [5], 276 [1, 6], 358, 392, 499, 549;
1963: 12 (p. 15), 20, 21 (pp. 34, 39), 38, 57,
101, 118, 124, 176, 217, 239, 253, 278, 292,
294, 328 [1]
Letters and messages to Congress, **1961:** 90, 207,
322, 343
Liberia, **1961:** 430

Foreign assistance — *continued*
Mansfield Committee, **1963:** 89 [20]
Marshall plan, 15th anniversary message, **1963:**
124
Message to Congress, **1962:** 83; **1963:** 118
Mexico, **1962:** 268; **1963:** 118
Middle East, **1963:** 12 (p. 17), 169 [2], 338, 459
[13]
Morocco, **1963:** 116
Nigeria, **1961:** 304; **1962:** 83
Pakistan, **1961:** 267, 283; **1962:** 50 [10], 83, 216;
1963: 118, 285, 328 [1], 338
Peace Corps.
See main heading.
Peru, **1961:** 318 [15], 376
Phillipines, **1963:** 239
Poland, **1961:** 11; **1962:** 229 [3], 245 [9], 302 [10],
1963: 35 [5]
Reduction, **1963:** 120 [21], 338n.
Reorganization of program, **1962:** 229 [5]
Ryukyu Islands, **1962:** 99
Somali Republic, **1962:** 526
Statement, **1962:** 389
Sudan, **1961:** 411
Tanganyika, **1961:** 288; **1962:** 83, 539
Television remarks, **1962:** 400
Togo, **1962:** 103n., 105
Turkey, **1961:** 222; **1963:** 118, 328 [1], 338, 443
United Kingdom, **1963:** 118
Venezuela, **1961:** 510; **1963:** 118
Viet-Nam, **1961:** 488 [3], 505; **1962:** 40 [4, 14], 50
[9], 59 [11], 546 [14], 549 [10]; **1963:** 89
[20], 118, 305 [10], 338, 349, 356 [18], 399
Western Europe, **1962:** 13 (p. 29), 250; **1963:** 54
[3], 65 [13], 72, 89 [20], 124, 134 [3], 260
[3, 13]
Yugoslavia, **1962:** 3, 77, 229 [3], 245 [9], 302 [10];
1963: 35 [5], 420n.
Foreign Assistance Act of 1948, **1963:** 124n.
Foreign Assistance Act of 1961, **1961:** 436; **1963:**
118
Approval, **1961:** 346
Foreign Assistance Act of 1962, **1962:** 83
Approval, **1962:** 314
Foreign Assistance Act of 1963, **1963:** 89 [15], 118n.
Foreign central banks, **1961:** 497
Interest on deposits held in U.S., **1961:** 82
Interest on U.S. Government securities, **1961:** 23,
54
Foreign Credit Insurance Association, **1961:** 437;
1963: 30 (p. 65), 306
Foreign currencies, **1961:** 497; **1962:** 16 (p. 50), 31
302 [6], 392; **1963:** 30 (pp. 59, 65), 89 [11],
118
Foreign economic activities of Government agen-
cies, study, **1961:** 207
Foreign Economic Policy, Council on, **1961:** 207
Foreign educators, visit of, **1962:** 51

Foreign exchange controls, **1961:** 497, 499
Foreign government deposits held in U.S., **1961:** 23, 82
Foreign Intelligence Advisory Board, President's (Killian committee), **1961:** 168, 258 [9], 291 [15]; **1963:** 405 [12]
Foreign intelligence program, **1962:** 13 (p. 38)
Foreign investment companies, termination of tax benefits, **1961:** 136; **1962:** 13 (p. 34)
Foreign military officers, remarks, **1963:** 183, 335
Foreign ministers meetings
　Council of foreign Ministers in 1949, **1961:** 329n.
　Geneva, **1962:** 73
　Geneva conferences.
　　See main heading, Geneva conference.
　New York City, **1962:** 352 [6]
　North Atlantic Treaty Organization, **1961:** 25 [6], 171 [14], 291 [5, 15], 318 [7], 334 [19], 488 [11, 12]; **1962:** 160, 179 [16], 198 [14]; **1963:** 65 [6], 107 [11], 179
　On Berlin, proposed, **1962:** 59 [5]
　Organization of American States, **1962:** 485, 486, 529; **1963:** 65 [10]
　Ottawa, **1963:** 179
　Punta del Este conference.
　　See main heading, Punta del Este conference.
　Southeast Asia Treaty Organization, **1961:** 38, 92 [1], 97
　Western powers, **1961:** 334 [2], 364, 519
Foreign policy, **1962:** 7 (p. 15), 22, 92, 170, 226, 243 [1], 275, 282, 446, 454, 459, 466, 551 [1]; **1963:** 32, 38, 57, 81, 88, 116, 134 [1, 2], 198, 221, 256, 262, 307, 338, 344, 359, 361, 383, 385, 407, 420, 433, 445, 465 [1], 477
　Assistance, **1963:** 118
　Bipartisanship, **1963:** 118
　Diplomatic recognition of government, criteria for, **1963:** 120 [12]
　Middle East, **1963:** 169 [2]
　News conference remarks, **1962:** 107 [15], 229 [21], 259 [21], 316 [16], 546 [9]; **1963:** 35 [1], 54 [3, 4], 65 [3], 120 [12], 169 [2], 202 [8], 320 [5, 10], 328 [1], 448 [1], 459 [5, 6]
"Foreign Relations of the United States," publication, **1961:** 353
Foreign Service, **1962:** 55, 64, 107 [15], 243 [5], 254, 272, 275, 325, 546 [9], 550, 553; **1963:** 4n., 19, 88, 192, 221, 256
　Former Peace corpsmen, recruitment for, **1963:** 129
　Officers, remarks to, **1963:** 88
Foreign Scholarships, Board of, remarks, **1961:** 57
Foreign Service Academy, proposed, **1963:** 120 [16]
Foreign Service Act, **1962:** 55; **1963:** 129
Foreign Service Association, American, **1962:** 275
Foreign Service Institute, **1962:** 276; **1963:** 120 [16]
Foreign Service Reserve, **1963:** 129

Foreign students in the United States, **1961:** 181, 205, 282
　Meeting on, **1961:** 443
Foreign visitors.
　See Visitors, foreign leaders.
Forest fire prevention, **1961:** 85
Forest resources, **1963:** 127
Forest Service, **1961:** 17, 85; **1962:** 307n.; **1963:** 63, 430
　Report on forest development program, **1961:** 377
Forestry Association, American, **1963:** 196
Forestry research, **1961:** 85
Forests, national, **1961:** 17, 85, 94, 441; **1962:** 7 (p. 7), 13 (p. 30), 25, 69, 128, 307, 414; **1963:** 63, 193, 209, 325
　Development, **1961:** 49, 377
　Highways, **1961:** 49, 58
Formosa (Taiwan), **1961:** 119 [7]; **1962:** 115 [17, 21], 259 [1, 5, 7]
　See also China, Republic of.
Formosa Resolution (1954), **1962:** 259 [1, 7]; **1963:** 202 [16]
Fort Bragg, N.C., remarks, **1961:** 419
Fort Chaffee, Ark. **1961:** 440
Fort Drive Parkway, National Capital area, proposed, **1963:** 208
Fort Hood, Tex., **1962:** 519n.
Fort Knox, Ky., **1962:** 162, 410 [12]
Fort Lauderdale (Fla.) News, **1963:** 35 [2]
Fort Lewis, Wash., **1962:** 152 [3]
Fort Polk, La. **1962:** 152 [3]
Fort Smith, Ark., remarks, **1961:** 440
　Mayor Robert R. Brooksher, Jr., **1961:** 440n.
Fort Stewart, Ga., **1962:** 519
Fort Worth, Tex., **1963:** 448 [23], 475, 476, 478
Fortas, Abe, **1962:** 257n.
Fortune magazine, **1963:** 465
Foss, Joe J., **1962:** 398
Fosse, Bob, **1962:** 158
Foster, Dr. John S., Jr., **1963:** 328 [2], 334
Foster, John Watson, **1962:** 512
Foster, William C., **1961:** 388; **1962:** 107 [2], 316 [18], 352 [18]
　See also United States Arms Control and Disarmament Agency, Director.
Foundations, tax-exempt, **1962:** 340 [13]; **1963:** 26, 92, 245
Founding Fathers, **1963:** 23, 26
Fountain, Repr. L. H., **1962:** 198 [1, 7]
Four Freedoms, **1963:** 46
4-H Club, National, message, **1961:** 67
4-H Clubs, **1963:** 404
Four-power alliance, World War II, **1961:** 292
Fourth of July, John Adams toast, **1961:** 397
Fowler, Henry H., **1962:** 14; **1963:** 351
Foy, Fred C., **1963:** 361

France, **1961:** 302, 483, 499; **1962:** 206, 341, 549 [2, 5], 551 [5]; **1963:** 144 [10], 267, 296, 301, 316, 462, 465, 467
   Algerian crisis.
     See main heading, Algerian crisis.
   Alliance in War of Independence, **1963:** 112
   Ambassador Hervé Alphand, **1963:** 112
   Arms sales to Israel, **1963:** 120 [10]
   Assistance, **1963:** 72
   Atomic energy for mutual defense, agreement with U.S., **1961:** 355
   Berlin crisis.
     See main heading, Berlin crisis.
   Cease-fire agreement with Algeria, **1962:** 97
   Couve de Murville, Maurice, **1963:** 144 [2]
   De Gaulle, Charles.
     See main heading, De Gaulle, Charles.
   Economic growth, **1962:** 74, 194, 203, 210 [13]
   German-French treaty, **1963:** 65 [17], 260 [6]
   Institute of High Studies for National Defense, **1963:** 112
   Mona Lisa, loan to U.S., **1962:** 546 [1]; **1963:** 5, 16, 112
   National War College **1963:** 112
   Naval forces, withdrawal from NATO, question of, **1963:** 260 [15]
   News conference remarks, **1961:** 25 [19], 62 [12], 119 [18, 19], 139 [19], 222 [1, 3, 7], 258 [2, 18], 318 [7], 334 [2], 455 [8, 15]; **1962:** 8 [16], 50 [9], 59 [5], 75 [10], 107 [13], 152 [8, 19], 198 [3], 210 [13], 229 [9], 259 [9, 14, 21], 340 [3], 546 [1]
   Non-aggression pledge, **1963:** 320 [4]
   Nuclear test ban treaty, question of signing, **1963:** 35 [3]
   Nuclear weapons, **1962:** 152 [8], 198 [3], 229 [9], 259 [9, 21], 551 [22], 557; **1963:** 12 (p. 16), 35 [24], 54 [3, 8], 65 [6, 17], 260 [9], 320 [2, 15]
   Nuclear weapons tests, **1961:** 222 [3], 455 [8]; **1963:** 75 [19]
   Policy on Germany and Berlin, **1961:** 292
   Relations with Germany, **1963:** 35 [17], 65 [17], 266
   Troops in Germany, **1963:** 272
   U.S. Ambassador James M. Gavin, **1961:** 218, 393; **1962:** 229 [9], 316 [12]
   U.S. forces in, **1963:** 448 [1]
   U.S. investments in, **1963:** 77 [1]
   Visit to, **1961:** 216-223
   Wage levels, **1962:** 162, 174
Franco, Francisco, **1962:** 229 [11]
Franco Montoro, André, **1962:** 54
Frankfurt, Germany, **1963:** 361
   Mayor Werner Bockelmann, **1963:** 264-266
   Paulskirche address, **1963:** 266
   Visit to, **1963:** 264-266
Frankfurter, Justice Felix, **1962:** 352 [1, 13], 353, 393n.; **1963:** p. 902

Frankfurter, Mrs. Felix, **1962:** 353
Franklin, Benjamin, **1961:** 125, 145, 209, 212, 215, 216, 217, 222, 397, 520; **1962:** 161, 168n., 170, 274, 452; **1963:** 2, 226, 245, 268, 271, 278, 387
Franklin, John, **1961:** 40n.
Franz, Alwin F., **1961:** 254n.
Fraser, Donald, **1962:** 439
Fraser, Rt. Hon. Hugh, **1963:** 221
Frazier, Repr. James B., Jr., **1962:** 340 [24]
Frederick Douglass Home, incorporation into National Capital Park System, **1962:** 362
Fredericksburg, Va., **1961:** 461
Fredericksburg (Va.), Battle of, **1963:** 276, 278
Free Trade Union Development, Institute for, **1962:** 324
Free University of Berlin, address, **1963:** 271
Free World, Committee to Strengthen the Security of the, **1963:** 89 [20], 111, 118, 120 [6]
Freedom House, **1963:** 32
Freedom From Hunger Campaign, **1961:** 139 [2], 482; **1962:** 478; **1963:** 217
Freedom From Hunger Foundation, United States, **1961:** 482; **1963:** 33
Freedom From Hunger Week, National, **1963:** 33
Freedom of information, **1963:** 232
Freedom Riders, **1961:** 198, 291 [10]
Freedom of speech and religion, **1963:** 105
Freedom Train, **1962:** 350
Freeman, Fulton, **1961:** 514n.
Freeman, Gordon M., **1963:** 174
Freeman, Orville L.
   See Agriculture, Secretary of.
Freeman, Mrs. Orville L., **1962:** 15
Freeman, Gen. Paul L., **1963:** 263
Freeport, Tex., **1963:** 474
   Dedication of saline water conservation plant, **1961:** 248
Freidin, Jesse, **1963:** 206
French Lick, Ind., **1962:** 346
French, Marjorie L., **1962:** 188
French Revolution, **1963:** 5
Fresno, Calif., **1962:** 338
Freund, Paul A., **1963:** 245
Frey, Roger, **1961:** 219n.
Friedel, Repr. Samuel N., **1962:** 446
Friedman, Rabbi Herbert A., **1962:** 133n.
Friedman, Richard, **1962:** 483
Friskie, Mr. and Mrs. Edward A., **1962:** 329
Friskie, Michael, **1962:** 329n.
Frondizi, Arturo
   Joint statement with, **1961:** 389
   Letter, **1961:** 149

Frost, Robert, **1961:** 56, 65, 212, 501; **1962:** 110, 378 [15], 527n., 549 [10]; **1963:** 42, 390, 439, 440, 468
Fry, Franklin C., **1961:** 35 [11]

Fryingpan-Arkansas project, **1962:** 69, 336, 337;
  1963: 376
  Approval, **1962:** 332
Fuel oil, **1961:** 62 [13]
Fuel taxes, **1963:** 34, 63
Fulbright, Sen. J. William, **1961:** 57n., 307, 379,
       440; **1962:** 180n., 261, 361; **1963:** 88, 105,
       188, 260 [13], 375, 400, 401
  Educational exchange program, **1963:** 140, 332
  Foreign policy statements, **1961:** 171 [10], 318 [9,
       10]
  Memorandum on role of military in educating pub-
       lic on communism, **1961:** 318 [9]
  News conference remarks on, **1961:** 171 [10], 318
       [9, 10]
  Teacher exchange program, **1962:** 341
Fulbright Act, **1961:** 379
  Anniversary, remarks, **1961:** 307
Fulbright-Hays Act, **1961:** 379
Fulmer, Gene, **1963:** 331
Fulton, Repr. Richard R., **1963:** 192
Fundraising campaigns
  Eleanor Roosevelt Foundation, **1963:** 139, 408
  Navy Relief Fund, **1962:** 326
  Radio Free Europe, **1961:** 71 [1]
  Red Cross, **1961:** 59, 60; **1962:** 67
  Savings bonds, **1962:** 14
  United Community, **1963:** 369
  United Community campaigns, **1961:** 375
  United Givers Fund, **1961:** 259
  United Negro Colleges Development, **1963:** 355
Furtado, Celso, **1961:** 285
Future Farmers of America, **1963:** 404

Gabon, Republic of, **1962:** 368
  U.S. Ambassador Charles F. Darlington, **1962:**
       415
Gabrielson, Ira, **1963:** 196n.
Gagarin, Maj. Yuri, **1961:** 117n., 171 [13], 178, 318
       [17]; **1962:** 59 [2]
Gainsbrugh, Martin S., **1961:** 458n.
Gaither (H. Rowan, Jr.) report of 1958, **1961:** 15
       [37]
Gaitskell, Hugh, **1963:** 25
Gaitskell, Mrs. Hugh, **1963:** 25
Galatti, Stephen, **1962:** 284
Galbraith, J. Kenneth, **1962:** 245 [3], 316 [14]; **1963:**
       120 [16], 215
Gallagher, Repr. Cornelius E., **1961:** 448; **1962:** 450
Gallati, Stephen, **1963:** 308
Gallup, George H., **1962:** 302 [14]
Gallup Poll, **1961:** 83 [14]; **1962:** 27 [26], 302 [14],
       316 [10]; **1963:** 356 [22]
Galway, Ireland, **1963:** 280
Galway, N.Y., **1963:** 277
Gambiez, Gen. Fernand, **1963:** 112
Gambling, **1962:** 443, 446
Gandhi, Indira, **1961:** 452

Gandhi, Mohandas K. (Mahatma), **1961:** 452; **1963:**
       215
Gann, George, **1961:** 119 [2]
Garcia, Arturo, **1961:** 373n.
Garcia, Hector, **1961:** 25 [14], 36n.
Gardner, Mrs. Arthur, **1962:** 527
Gardner, Ralph W., **1961:** 209
Garibaldi, Giuseppe, **1961:** 84
Garland, Judy, **1962:** 534
Garmatz, Repr. Edward A., **1962:** 446
Garrison, O. L., **1963:** 466
Garrison, William Lloyd, **1961:** 212
Garrison Dam, **1963:** 379
Garrison Diversion project, **1962:** 69
  Upper Missouri River Basin, statement, **1961:**
       247
Garroway, Dave, **1961:** 14
Garst, Jonathan, **1961:** 102
Gary, Ind., **1963:** 363
Garza, Joe A., **1963:** 473
Gas, natural, **1962:** 93 (p. 237)
Gas rate increase, backlog of cases before FPC,
       1961: 121
Gas resources, **1963:** 179
Gascoigne, Maj. Gen. Sir Julian, **1961:** 518n.
Gasoline tax, **1961:** 58; **1962:** 128; **1963:** 63
Gaston, A. G., Motel, **1963:** 181
Gates, Thomas S. (former Secretary of Defense),
       1961: 8 [19]
Gathings, Repr. E. C., **1963:** 400, 401
GATT.
  See General Agreement on Tariffs and Trade;
       Geneva Conferences.
Gaulle, Charles de.
  See De Gaulle, Charles.
Gavan, Maj. Gen. Paul A., **1961:** 461
Gavin, Gen. James M., **1961:** 218, 393; **1962:** 229 [9],
       316 [12]
Gatwick, England, **1963:** 284, 286
Gaza Strip, **1963:** 278
  U.N. troops in, **1961:** 35 [16]
Gemini space project, **1962:** 378 [14]; **1963:** 175 [4],
       202 [4]
General Agreement on Tariffs and Trade, **1961:** 23,
       189; **1962:** 303, 477, 484; **1963:** 9, 169 [21],
       202 [5, 18], 292.
  See also Trade Agreement Act.
  Provisional Cotton Textile Company, **1961:** 428
General Aniline and Film Corp., **1963:** 89 [12]
General Dynamics Corp., **1962:** 390; **1963:** 107 [23],
       120 [7], 448 [23]
General Electric Company, **1961:** 281n.
General Medical Sciences, Division of, **1962:** 65,
       470
General Medical Sciences, Institute of, proposed,
       1961: 290
General Motors Corp., **1961:** 350; **1962:** 33, 302
       [7]

General Services Administration, **1961:** 17, 83 [25], 119 [3], 171 [4]; **1962:** 93 (p. 238), 129, 221, 307; **1963:** 125, 388

General Services Administrator (Bernard L. Boutin), **1962:** 221, 260; **1963:** 26, 62, 207

General Services Administrator (John L. Moore), **1961:** 83 [25], 353n.

Geneva, Treaty of, **1963:** 78

Geneva Agreement of 1962, **1963:** 285

Geneva agreement on Viet-Nam (1945), **1961:** 505

Geneva conferences

Disarmament, **1962:** 29, 41, 42, 48, 62, 71, 73, 82, 90, 109, 116, 126, 134, 273, 290, 310 [3], 319, 346, 348, 518; **1963:** 20, 58, 232, 250

Disarmament proceedings in 1920's and '30's, **1961:** 222

Foreign ministers, **1962:** 73

Foreign ministers, 1959, proposals on Germany and Berlin, **1961:** 292

GATT, **1961:** 189

Heads of government in 1955, **1961:** 483

Indochina (1954), **1961:** 92 [1]; **1962:** 27 [8], 40 [4], 50 [9]

Laos, **1961:** 222 [6], 258 [20], 230, 231, 309, 415 [6]; **1962:** 179 [6, 16], 239, 251, 259 [22], 279 [5], 301, 308, 312, 316 [7], 352 [16]; **1963:** 78, 79, 81, 134 [2], 144 [3, 5, 16], 169 [9], 285

News conference remarks, **1962:** 8 [20], 27 [22], 40 [11, 14], 50 [2], 75 [3, 7, 9, 13, 19], 89 [1, 10, 12], 107 [2, 4, 16], 115 [3], 152 [, 8, 15], 179 [8], 245 [4], 279 [5], 302 [8], 316 [2, 18], 352 [2], 378 [17]

Nuclear test ban or suspension, **1961:** 11, 80, 112, 205, 214, 230, 231, 326, 387, 408, 442, 483

Break up of negotiations by U.S.S.R., **1961:** 446

News conference remarks, **1961:** 8 [1], 83 [6, 21], 92 [13], 139 [23], 171 [1], 222, 258 [3], 318 [2, 8], 334 [15]

U.S.-U.K. bank proposal, **1961:** 345, 357

Nuclear test suspension, **1962:** 8 [17], 27 [22], 71, 316 [2, 18]; **1963:** 20, 75 [12], 107 [20], 305 [1], 316

Radio Conference on Space Communications, **1963:** 470

Tariffs, **1962:** 76

Tariffs and trade, **1963:** 9, 169 [21], 179, 202 [5, 18], 292, 361

Tariff negotiations, **1961:** 318 [1]

Ten-nation disarmament commission, **1961:** 192, 408

U.S.-Communist China, U.S. prisoners, **1961:** 15 [32], 415 [6]

U.S. Representative Arthur H. Dean, resignation, **1963:** 3

Geneen, Harold S., **1963:** 450

Geographic Society, National, **1962:** 262; **1963:** 296n.

Geological research, Project Mohole, **1961:** 100, 110

Geological Survey, **1963:** 430

Geological Survey, Director (Thomas B. Nolan), **1961:** 490

George Washington University, **1962:** 325

George Washington University, remarks, **1961:** 162

George I, King, **1963:** 426

Georgetown University, **1962:** 325

Georgia, **1963:** 162, 356 [22], 465

Gov. Carl E. Sanders, **1963:** 108

Gov. S. Ernest Vandiver, **1961:** 334 [1]

Geraldini family, **1962:** 450

Gerhardsen, Einar, visit of, **1962:** 178, 182, 183

Gerhardsen, Madame, **1962:** 178, 183

German Development Service, **1963:** 258

German Revolution of 1848, **1963:** 266

Germany, **1961:** 33, 231, 302, 473, 483; **1962:** 4, 74, 109, 250, 254, 310 [3], 507, 551 [5, 22]; **1963:** 12 (p. 18), 192, 259, 271, 285, 291, 295, 361, 366, 385, 413, 426, 462, 465, 467

Adenauer, Konrad.

See main heading, Adenauer, Konrad.

Aid to less-developed countries, **1961:** 25 [19], 41, 62 [23]

Ambassador Wilhelm Grewe, **1962:** 198 [14]

Assistance, **1963:** 72, 134 [3]

Autobahn to Berlin, **1961:** 483, 488 [7]

Berlin.

See main heading, Berlin crisis.

Communique of 1944 re, **1961:** 329n.

Economic growth, **1962:** 74, 194, 203; **1963:** 266

Erhard, Ludwig.

See main heading, Erhard, Ludwig.

European development, role in, **1963:** 260 [1, 18]

French troops in, **1963:** 272

German-French treaty, **1963:** 65 [17], 260

I. G. Farben Co., **1963:** 89 [12]

Loan to Bolivia, **1961:** 184

Lübke, Heinrich, **1963:** 258, 259, 262

Mathilde mine disaster, **1963:** 454

Mission of Belgrade conference representatives re, **1961:** 364, 365

Missile technicians in Egypt, **1963:** 120 [10]

News conference remarks, **1961:** 25 [19], 62 [23, 26], 119 [18], 258 [2], 291 [1, 11, 17, 19], 318 [4], 334 [2, 3, 5, 11, 21], 415 [13, 18, 22], 455 [6, 15], 488 [4, 6, 7, 10, 18]; **1962:** 8 [16], 27 [23], 75 [19], 152 [16, 19], 179 [5, 16, 198 [14], 210 [9], 245 [13], 259 [6, 14], 316 [4, 24], 340 [7], 410 [5]; **1963:** 35 [17, 24], 54 [7, 8], 65 [13, 17], 89 [12], 107 [3], 120 [10], 144 [9], 260 [1, 4, 7, 12, 13, 18], 320 [2], 328 [11], 356 [19], 448 [1, 28], 459 [19]

Germany — *continued*
Nuclear forces, question of, **1963:** 54 [8], 260 [7]
Nuclear weapons, **1961:** 455 [15], 483
Peace corps, establishment of, **1963:** 258, 294
Relations with France, **1963:** 35 [17], 65 [17], 266
Reunification, question of, **1961:** 41, 120, 480,
    481, 483; **1963:** 260 [4], 271, 320 [2]
Schroeder, Gerhard, **1962:** 507n., 508
Soviet aide memoire re, **1961:** 225n., 291 [1, 11,
    17, 19], 318 [4]
    U.S. reply, **1961:** 292
Strauss-Gilpatric agreement on military procure-
    ment, **1963:** 77 [1], 448 [1]
Thalidomide, use in, **1962:** 316 [4, 24]
Trade union movement in, **1963:** 268
U.K. troops in, **1963:** 272
U.S. Ambassador Walter C. Dowling, **1961:** 334
    [3, 21]; **1962:** 198 [14]
U.S. Ambassador George C. McGhee, **1963:** 256,
    272
U.S. armed forces, **1961:** 497, 499
U.S. expenditures in agreement on, **1963:** 77 [1]
U.S. forces in, **1962:** 259 [6, 14], 439; **1963:** 65
    [13], 144 [9], 266a, 272, 448 [1, 28]
U.S. relations with, **1963:** 260 [1, 12]
Visit of Vice President Johnson, **1961:** 325
Visit to, **1963:** 253-259, 261-273
Von Brentano, Heinrich, **1961:** 25 [19], 41, 62 [23,
    26], 120
Wage levels, **1962:** 162, 174, 410 [5]
Zinn, Georg August, **1963:** 265-266a
Germany, East, **1961:** 138, 292, 302, 483; **1962:** 8
    [16], 50 [1], 74, 152 [16], 179 [16], 302 [2,
    13], 551 [19]; **1963:** 54 [7], 291, 356 [19]
News conference remarks, **1961:** 258 [2], 291 [1],
    318 [4, 10], 334 [21, 23], 415 [18], 455 [15],
    488 [18]
Refugees from, **1961:** 291 [1], 302, 318 [10]
Soviet peace treaty with, question of, **1961:** 258
    [2], 291 [1], 292, 318 [4], 387, 483
Ulbricht, Walter, **1961:** 291 [1], 483
U.S. convoy blocked, **1963:** 459 [19]
U.S. recognition, question of, **1963:** 320 [2]
Gerontology, **1963:** 74
Gerrymandering, **1961:** 25 [27]
Gerstenmaier, Eugen, **1963:** 266
Gesell, Gerhard A., **1962:** 257; **1963:** 251
Gettysburg Address, copy inscribed to President of
    Brazil, **1961:** 105
Gettysburg, Battle of, **1963:** 249, 276
Gewin, Judge Walter P., **1962:** 420
Ghana
Accra, **1961:** 125n.
Nkrumah, Kwame, **1961:** 72, 73, 74, 181, 273, 331
Peace Corps project, **1961:** 331
Volta River project, **1961:** 273, 415 [15]
Ghent, Treaty of, **1961:** 397
GI bill of rights, **1961:** 62 [27]

Giaimo, Repr. Robert N., **1962:** 473; **1963:** 410n.,
    423
Gibbon, Edward, **1961:** 496
Gibbons, Repr. Sam M., **1963:** 465-467
Gilbraltar, **1962:** 226
Gift taxes, **1963:** 34
Gilbert, Carl J., **1962:** 449
Gill, Lewis M., **1962:** 376
Gill, Repr. Thomas P., **1963:** 229
Gilliland, Edwin R., **1962:** 547n.
Gilman, Leonard Walter, **1961:** 312
Gilpatric, Roswell L., **1961:** 355, 455 [18]; **1962:**
    172, 378 [14], 422, 423; **1963:** 76n., 77 [1],
    203, 328 [20]
Gilruth, Robert R., **1961:** 177; **1962:** 61, 323, 374n.
Ginzberg, Eli, **1962:** 412n.
Girl Scouts, **1963:** 305 [19]
Girls Nation, **1963:** 322
Gizenga, Antoine, **1961:** 62 [8]; **1962:** 396
Gladieux, Bernard L., **1962:** 167n.
Gladstone, William E., **1962:** 349
Glass, import duties, **1963:** 9
Glass, tariffs on, **1962:** 98, 115 [23], 245 [16]
Glasser, Melvin A., **1962:** 132
Gleason, John S., Jr. (Ambassador, Veterans Af-
    fairs), **1961:** 461, 492; **1963:** 4, 49n., 62,
    130, 148, 174
Glen Lake, Mich., high school seniors, remarks,
    1962: 252
Glenn, David, **1962:** 61
Glenn, Lt. Col. John H., **1961:** 177; **1962:** 56, 60,
    63, 68, 77, 171, 323, 373; **1963:** 199, 406
    NASA Distinguished Service Medal, **1962:** 61
    News conference remarks on, **1962:** 50 [19], 59 [1,
    3]
    Telephone conversation with, **1962:** 57
Glenn, Mrs. John H., Jr., **1962:** 56, 61
Glenn, Mr. and Mrs. John H., Sr., **1962:** 61
Glenn, Lynn, **1962:** 61
Global Marine Exploration Company, **1961:** 110
Glueck, Rabbi Nelson, **1961:** 1n.
GNP (gross national product).
    See National product.
Goa, Indian attack on, **1962:** 8 [14]
Goethe, Johann Wolfgang von, **1961:** 418; **1962:**
    527; **1963:** 192, 266, 271
Goheen, Robert F., **1962:** 533n.
Gold
Holdings abroad by U.S. citizens, **1961:** 23
Outflow from U.S., **1961:** 8 [18, 19], 11, 17, 23,
    25 [16, 19], 62 [3], 82, 119 [14], 205, 239,
    455 [17], 488 [17], 497; **1962:** 7 (p. 13), 16
    (p. 43), 22, 59 [12, 17], 115 [2, 23], 139 [1,
    5], 152 [11], 162, 174, 194, 203, 210 [13],
    229 [4], 230, 234, 250, 259 [2], 280, 302 [6],
    316 [19], 328, 392, 395, 410 [12]; **1963:**
    77, 120 [11], 134, 306, 363, 448 [1]

Gold — *continued*
  Reserves, **1963:** 77 [1], 306, 310, 391, 405 [1], 407
  Speculation in **1961:** 497
  Standard, **1963:** 305 [12]
  U.S. reserves, **1962:** 162, 174, 199, 280, 340 [25], 410 [12]

Gold Medal, Congressional, **1963:** 353
Goldberg, Arthur J., **1963:** 76n., 85, 298, 310.
  See also Labor, Secretary of.
  Appointment to U.S. Supreme Court, **1962:** 352 [1, 13], 393
Golden Ring council of Senior Citizens, **1962:** 202n.
Goldhaber, Maurice, **1961:** 361
Goldner, Herman, **1963:** 464
Goldstein, Louis, **1962:** 446
Goldstein, Mortimer D., **1961:** 123n.
Goldwater, Sen. Barry, **1961:** 448, 488 [17]; **1962:** 40 [8], 158, 316 [13], 439, 458; **1963:** 202 [9], 305 [24], 328 [13], 345, 356 [14], 405 [8], 427n. 448 [2, 24], 462
Golf, President's playing, **1963:** 305 [11]
Gómez Valderrama, Pedro, **1963:** 323n.
Gomulka, Wladyslaw, **1961:** 119 [17]
Gonzalez, Henry B., **1961:** 434, 455 [5]
Good, Dr. Frederick L., **1961:** 212
Good Housekeeping magazine **1963:** 319a note
Good Neighbor Policy, **1962:** 86, 264
Goodman, Benny, **1962:** 158
Goodwin, Richard N., 258 [17], 334 [7]
Gopallawa, William, **1962:** 106
Gorbach, Alfons, visit of, **1962:** 168, 169
Gordon, Kermit (Director, Bureau of the Budget), **1963:** 4, 29, 30 (p. 68), 62, 143, 144 [14], 148, 306, 371
Gordon, Robert Aaron, **1961:** 458n.
Gore, Sen. Albert , **1962:** 139 [9], 207; **1963:** 192
Gore, Jack, **1963:** 35 [2]
Gorman, Patrick E., **1963:** 187
Gossett, William T., **1962:** 541, 549 [2]
Goulart, João (President of Brazil), **1962:** 177
  Messages, **1962:** 146, 490
  News conference remarks, **1962:** 75 [22], 115 [14], 139 [14]
  Visit of, **1962:** 124, 125, 126
Government contracts.
See also Contracts, Government.
Government contracts, President's Committee on, **1961:** 68
Government employees, **1961:** 11, 60; **1963:** 98, 230, 317, 325
  Appearance and testimony before congressional committees, **1963:** 405 [13], 448 [27]
  Conflict of interests and ethical standards, **1961:** 152, 171 [11]
  Distinguished Federal Civilian Service Awards, **1962:** 323; **1963:** 238
  Employee-management relations, **1961:** 250, 494; **1962:** 154, 215

Government employees — *continued*
  Employee organizations, **1962:** 215n.
    Withholding of dues, proposed, **1962:** 154
  Ethical standards, **1962:** 13 (p. 38), 198 [1, 21]; **1963:** 31, 248, 448 [17, 27]
  Equal employment opportunities, **1961:** 68, 504; **1962:** 13 (p. 38), 304; **1963:** 230
  Handicapped, **1963:** 357
  Lie detector tests, question of, **1963:** 120 [1]
  Limitation on employment, **1961:** 436
  National Capital Region, **1962:** 525
  Officials, suits against, **1962:** 434; **1963:** 448 [27]
  Older persons, **1963:** 74, 96
  Pay, **1961:** 251, 396; **1962:** 7 (p. 7), 13 (p. 37), 163, 167, 187, 210 [21], 229 [1], 448; **1963:** 4, 21 (pp. 32, 40, 41, 43), 22, 44, 53, 134, 148, 175 [4]
    Approval of bill, **1962:** 447
    Message to Congress, **1962:** 55
  Peace Corpsmen, former, recruitment for Federal civilian service, **1963:** 129
  Personnel management, **1962:** 12; **1963:** 351
  Political pressure on, **1963:** 35 [16]
  Postal employees, **1961:** 291 [7], 396; **1962:** 13, (p. 37), 50 [21], 447
  Productivity, **1962:** 448; **1963:** 21 (p. 41), 371
  Recreational associations, memorandum, **1961:** 137
  Reduction, **1962:** 549; **1963:** 21 (p. 41), 24, 77, 144 [14], 175, 363, 371
  Retirement, **1962:** 447
  Savings bonds, purchase of, **1961:** 75
  Scientific and technical, **1962:** 187, 448
  Students, summer employees, **1962:** 250, 349; **1963:** 334
  Training, **1962:** 143
  Training for overseas service, **1963:** 57
  Unemployment insurance, **1961:** 94
  Women, **1962:** 156, 304
  Young people, **1963:** 171
Government Employment Policy, President's Committee on, **1961:** 68
Government officials
  Coordination of policy statements, **1961:** 35 [7]
  News briefings, **1961:** 25 [5]
Government Organization, President's Advisory Committee on **1961:** 29
Government organization and operations, consultants on, **1961:** 29
Government regional and field activities, coordination , **1961:** 465
Governors' Appalachian conference, **1961:** 176
Governors' Committees , on Employment of the Handicapped, **1963:** 452
Governors' Conference, Appalachian,, **1963:** 127
Governors' Conference, Civil Defense Committee of, **1961:** 410, 503

Governors' Conference, National, **1963:** 35 [21]
Governors, telegram on public works, **1961:** 37
Grabowski, Bernard F., **1962:** 473, 474
Grace, J. Peter, **1962:** 177
Grady, Henry, **1963:** 401
Grady, J. Harold, **1962:** 446
Gragson, Oran, **1963:** 390
Graham, Beardsley, **1962:** 476n.
Graham, Frank P., **1961:** 418n.
Graham, Philip L., **1962:** 476
Graham, William F. (Billy), **1961:** 26; **1962:** 68;
    1963: 52
Grain, **1963:** 45.
    See also Specific grains.
    Feed grains, **1961:** 15 [27], 39, 89, 102, 113, 300,
        316, 436; **1962:** 13 (p. 30), 25, 127, 259
        [8], 340 [2], 410 [3], 413, 439, 440, 456,
        549; **1963:** 21 (p. 35), 45, 169 [13], 189,
        197, 202 [2, 12, 15], 407, 465
    For Communist China, question of, **1962:** 210 [2]
    Prices, **1961:** 83 [19]
    Purchases by Soviet Union, **1963:** 405 [1, 15, 17]
    Storage, **1961:** 85; **1962:** 25, 198 [11], 210 [12];
        1963: 175, 189
    Withholding from market, **1962:** 352 [4]
Grain Cooperatives, National Federation of, **1963:**
    149n.
Grand Coulee Dam **1961:** 474; **1962:** 335; **1963:**
    384, 389
Grand Forks, N. Dak., **1963:** 379
Grand Prairie, Tex., **1963:** 478
Grand Turk Island, **1962:** 61n.
Grant, Maj. Gen. U.S., 3rd, **1961:** 92 [8]
Grant, Ulysses S., **1963:** 257
Grattan, Henry, **1963:** 278
Graven, David, **1962:** 439
Gray, David, **1962:** 233
Gray, Gordon, **1961:** 168n., 418n.; **1963:** 425
Gray, Horace, **1962:** 393n.
Gray, Repr. Kenneth J., **1962:** 58n., 481
Grayson, Adm. Cary T., **1962:** 36
Great Basin National Park, **1962:** 69; **1963:** 390
Great Britain.
    See United Kingdom.
Great Cities program, **1963:** 22
Great Falls, Montana, Mayor Marian Erdmann,
    1963: 383
Great Lakes, **1963:** 179, 411
Great Lakes fisheries, **1961:** 49
Great Lakes Steel Corp. **1962:** 139 [9]
Greece, **1961:** 84, 178, 397, 473; **1962:** 70, 226, 349
    Ancient, **1962:** 291; **1963:** 325, 334, 381, 448
    Assistance, **1961:** 135, 222; **1963:** 118, 328 [1],
        338
    Caramanlis, Constantine, **1961:** 128, 135, 457
    Communist aggression in, **1961:** 128n.
    Defense, **1963:** 333, 477
    Election in, **1963:** 448 [2]
    Immigration quota, **1963:** 311

Greece — *continued*
    Message to people, **1962:** 78
    News conference remarks, **1962:** 229 [3], 352 [11]
    Visit of Vice President Johnson, **1962:** 339
Greek Olympic Games, **1961:** 496
Greeley, Horace, **1961:** 153
Green, Dr. Constance M., **1963:** 245
Green, Repr. Edith, **1961:** 474; **1963:** 10n., 409
Green, Howard, **1961:** 45
Green, Theodore F., **1962:** 259 [5]
Green, Repr. William J., Jr., **1962:** 278; **1963:** 445
Green River, **1963:** 386n.
Greenleaf, Simon, **1961:** 429n.
Greensboro, N.C., Mayor David Schenck, **1963:**
    230
Greenville, N.C., USIA transmitter, **1963:** 55
Greenwood, Miss., **1963:** 120 [22]
Greers Ferry Dam project, **1963:** 400
Gregg, Dr. Donald E., **1962:** 323
Gregory, Dick, **1963:** 120 [22]
Gretel (yacht), **1962:** 383; **1963:** 216n.
Grewe, Wilhelm (West German Ambassador),
    1961: 480n.; **1962:** 198 [14]
Griffin, Repr. Robert P., **1962:** 252
Grissom, Capt. Virgil I., **1961:** 296; **1962:** 61; **1963:**
    406
Griswold, A. Whitney, **1962:** 234
Gromyko, Andrei A. (Soviet Foreign Minister),
    1961: 92 [16], 364, 365, 415 [3, 9, 13, 18];
    1962: 73, 96, 116, 134, 419, 485, 551 [16];
    1963: 35 [3], 144 [2], 314, 356 [4], 366, 405
    [3]
    News conference remarks on, **1962:** 8 [2], 27 [4],
        40 [19], 59 [5], 107 [18], 115 [9], 179 [6],
        302 [2]
Gronouski, John A., **1963:** 328 [5], 356 [13], 392,
    408
Grosvenor, Melville, **1962:** 262; **1963:** 296
Grover, Wayne C. (Archivist of the United States),
    1962: 260
Gruening, Sen. Ernest, **1962:** 317; **1963:** 405 [12]
Gruenther, Gen. Alfred M., **1962:** 36, 295n., 351n.;
    1963: 8, 133
GSA.
    See General Services Administration.
Guadalcanal, **1963:** 109
Guadalupe River Basin, **1962:** 313
Guadelupe Island, **1961:** 110
Guam, access to, **1962:** 342
Guantanamo City, Cuba, poliomyelitis outbreak,
    1961: 71 [8]
Guantanamo naval base, Cuba, **1962:** 107 [14, 21],
    378 [1], 485, 515 [7]; **1963:** 202 [8]
Guatemala
    News conference remarks on, **1963:** 120 [12, 16]
    Ydigoras, Miguel, **1963:** 99, 100, 102, 106
Gubbrud, Gov. Archie, **1962:** 335
Grudeman, Edward, **1961:** 274

[References are to items except as otherwise indicated]

Guerrilla warfare, **1961:** 99, 139 [14], 214; **1962:** 40 [4], 226, 276, 343, 439; **1963:** 12 (p. 18), 21 (p. 32), 144 [8], 168, 183, 221, 445, 476, 477
Guide book, White House, **1962:** 262
Guinea, Republic of Sékou Touré, **1962:** 444
Gulf of Mexico, **1962:** 198 [9], 417
Gullion, Edmund A., **1963:** 120 [16]
Guri Hydro-electric Dam, Venezuela, **1961:** 510
Gursel, Cemal, **1961:** 439; **1963:** 443
Guthman, Edwin O., **1962:** 231
Gutierrez, José Mario, **1962:** 269n.
Guy, Gov. William L., **1963:** 379
Guzman Neyra, Alfonso, **1962:** 271n.

Habermeyer, Howard W., **1961:** 385
Hadrian, Emperor, **1963:** 381
Hagans, Rev. Reed, **1962:** 3n.
Hagerstown, Md., **1962:** 328
Hagerty, James C., **1962:** 515 [16]
Haggerty, Cornelius J., **1963:** 206
Haile Selassie I, **1963:** 200n., 416
    Visit of, **1963:** 394, 395, 397, 398
Hailsham, Lord, **1963:** 260 [14], 285, 286, 314, 320, [8], 328 [6]
Haines, Maj. Gen. Ralph E., Jr., **1962:** 519
Haines, Wesley, **1962:** 182n.
Haiti, **1963:** 75 [15], 169 [12], 311
    Duvalier, Francois, **1963:** 169 [12]
Halaby, Najeeb E. (Federal Aviation Agency Administrator), **1962:** 512; **1963:** 29, 238n.
Halaby, Mrs. Najeeb E., **1962:** 512
Hall, David, **1963:** 174
Hall, Paul, **1961:** 258 [11]
Halleck, Repr. Charles A., **1961:** 128, 139 [10]; **1962:** 357; **1963:** 120 [11], 353, 444
Hallstein, Walter, **1961:** 21, 189; **1962:** 144
Halstead, Anna Roosevelt, **1963:** 408n.
Hamilton, Alexander, **1961:** 165, 520; **1962:** 278, 330; **1963:** 2, 245
Hamilton, Bermuda, visit, **1961:** 518, 519
Hamilton, Fowler (Administrator, Agency for International Development), **1962:** 212, 232, 243, 499; **1963:** 6
Hammar, Conrad, **1962:** 439
Hammarskjold, Dag, **1961:** 449; **1962:** 7 (p. 11), 319; **1963:** 28, 366
    See also United Nations Secretary General.
    Death of, **1961:** 393
    Posthumous award, Parvin Foundation, **1961:** 487
Hammond, A. J. Dowuona, **1961:** 188n.
Hams, Polish, **1962:** 546 [22]
Hanau, Germany, visit to, **1963:** 263
Handicapped children, concert for, **1961:** 327
Handicapped, President's Committee on Employment of the, **1963:** 174, 452
Handicapped persons, Government employment, **1963:** 357

Hanford Atomic Reactor, **1963:** 376, 384
Hanford, Wash., **1961:** 474
    Nuclear reactor, **1962:** 289, 382, 408
Hanlon, Paul, **1962:** 386
Hanna Nickel Smelting Co., **1962:** 340 [27]
Hannah, John A, 1961, **1961:** 55; **1962:** 246; **1963:** 135
Hannan, Bishop Philip M., **1961:** 178
Hanoi, North Viet-Nam, **1961:** 171 [8], 435, 505
Hansen, Gov. Cliff, **1963:** 381
Hansen, Repr. Julia B., **1961:** 474
Hansen, Morris H., **1962:** 533n.
Harbor and river improvement, **1962:** 69, 128
Harden, Clifford, **1962:** 549ftn. (p. 887); **1963:** 118
Harding, Warren G., **1962:** 36, 439, 482: **1963:** 407
Hardy, Repr. Porter, Jr., **1962:** 107 [15]
Harkins, Gen. Paul D., **1962:** 226; **1963:** 448 [3], 459 [5]
Harlan, John M., **1963:** 82, 171, 237
Harmon, Tom, **1961:** 496
Harmon Trophy, presentation, **1961:** 486; **1962:** 475
Harriman, W. Averell, **1961:** 488 [9]; **1962:** 27 [17], 248, 515 [3, 5]; **1963:** 124n., 144 [2, 5], 160, 169 [9], 260 [14], 285, 286, 305 [8], 314, 316, 320 [4], 328 [6], 421, 459 [14]
Harriman, Mrs. Florence, **1963:** 133
Harris, Eric Lloyd, **1962:** 324
Harris, Rev. Frederick Brown, **1963:** 351
Harris, Repr. Oren, **1961:** 25 [9], 337, 385; **1962:** 316 [1], 442; **1963:** 374, 400, 401, 447
Harris, Sam, **1962:** 476n.
Harris, Thomas E., **1963:** 206
Harrisburg, Pa., **1962:** 394, 395
Harrison, Gov. Albertis S., Jr., **1963:** 108
Harrison, George M., **1961:** 40n.; **1963:** 95n., 299
Hart, Parker T., **1963:** 120 [16]
Hart, Sen. Philip A., **1962:** 93 (p. 242), 231, 252, 362, 433, 437; **1963:** 93
Hartke, Sen. Vance, **1962:** 346n., 456
Hartsfield, William B., **1961:** 334 [1]
Harvard-Radcliffe Orchestra, **1962:** 271
Harvard University, **1961:** 14, 162, 496; **1962:** 109, 156, 234, 238, 540; **1963:** 2, 144 [6], 254, 271, 379, 440, 477
Harvey, Repr. James, **1962:** 231
Harvey, Mary, **1963:** 319a note
Harvey, William, **1961:** 413
Harvey Aluminum Company, **1961:** 171 [4]
Hasan al-Rida al-Sanusi, Crown Prince, visit of, **1962:** 467, 471
Hassan II, King, **1963:** 114-116
Hatcher, Andrew T., **1961:** 334 [7]; **1962:** 115 [3], 139 [2]
Hathaway, William D., **1962:** 326
Hatheway, Louise A. **1961:** 65
Hauge, Gabriel, **1963:** 175
Havana, **1962:** 556n.; **1963:** 72, 468

Hawaii, **1962:** 139 [3]; **1963:** 381, 464
  Gov. John A. Burns, **1963:** 229, 230
  Visit to, **1963:** 229, 230
Hawaii, airports, Federal aid, **1961:** 141
Hawley- Smoot Tarriff, **1962:** 199
Haworth, Leland, **1961:** 361
Hayden, Sen. Carl, **1961:** 415 [12]; **1962:** 320
  50th anniversary as Member of Congress, **1961:**
    475, 476
Hayes, A. J., **1962:** 298n., 376n.; **1963:** 162
Hayes, Samuel P., **1961:** 119 [2]
Hays, Brooks, **1962:** 190
Hays, Repr. Wayne L., **1961:** 379; **1962:** 414
  Teacher exchange program, **1963:** 140, 332
Hayworth, Don, **1962:** 437
Heads of state and government, joint statements
    with.
  See also Joint statements with leaders of
    foreign governments.
Heads of state and government, meetings
  Addis Ababa conference of African leaders,
    1963: 200, 228, 260 [2], 304, 394, 397
  Joint statement on, **1962:** 160
  Monrovia conference of African leaders, **1961:**
    175, 304, 430
  NATO Council, question of, **1961:** 25 [6]
  News conference remarks, **1961:** 8 [24], 25 [6],
    258 [13], 318 [23], 455 [6]; **1962:** 50 [2, 5],
    75 [8], 89 [6], 115 [9], 245 [13]; **1963:** 65
    [19], 107 [1, 7, 17, 22], 144 [1, 3, 7, 10], 169
    [6], 305 [8], 320 [8], 328 [8]
  San José meeting of Presidents of Central
    America, Panama, and U.S., **1963:** 89
    [10], 97-100, 102-106, 107 [1, 7, 17, 22],
    118, 120 [12], 134 [1]
  Summit conferences, question of, **1963:** 305 [8],
    320 [8], 328 [8]
  Yaounde conference on economic cooperation,
    1961: 107
Heads of state and government, message to.
  See also Messages to heads of state and
    government.
Health, **1963:** 130, 176, 455
  Benefits of milk, **1962:** 19
  Central America, **1963:** 103
  Cigarette smoking, effect on, **1962:** 210 [17], 229
    [18]; **1963:** 202 [17]
  Effect of pesticides, **1962:** 352 [24]
  Medical information, international exchange,
    1963: 247
  Mental health.
    See main heading.
  Narcotic and drug abuse, report, **1963:** 121
  Older persons, **1963:** 74
  Radioactive fallout, effect on, **1963:** 316

Health, Education, and Welfare, Department of,
    1961: 100, 297, 398; **1962:** 11, 28, 37, 65, 93
    (p. 237), 137, 198 [2], 209, 259 [4], 311,
    323, 487; **1963:** 21 (p. 40), 22, 43, 53, 64, 66
    82, 125, 233, 248, 358n., 377, 423, 448 [21]
  Additional Assistant Secretary, proposed, **1961:**
    129
  Cuban refugees, responsibility for, **1961:** 297
  News conference remarks, **1961:** 83 [4], 291 [18],
    488 [8]
Health, Education, and Welfare, Secretary of,
    1961: 144
Health, Education, and Welfare, Secretary of
    (Anthony J. Celebrezzez), **1962:** 323n.,
    329, 401, 411n., 450, 540; **1963:** 43, 50,
    53, 62, 66n., 74, 76n., 130, 141, 248, 392,
    393, 410, 435
  Oath-of-office ceremony, **1962:** 311
Health, Education, and Welfare, Secretary of
    (Abraham A. Ribicoff), **1961:** 3, 22, 32,
    43, 48, 52, 70, 212, 244, 289, 290, 294, 427;
    1962: 77, 221n., 132, 193, 202, 220
  Chairman, President's Council on Youth Fitness,
    1961: 27
  Cuban leaders, assistance, **1961:** 86
  Cuban refugees, study, **1961:** 9, 19
  Government action on mental health, **1961:** 492
  Juvenile delinquency control, **1961:** 182, 382
  News conference remarks on, **1961:** 25 [3], 83 [9],
    488 [8]; **1962:** 115 [13], 279 [18]
  Resignation, **1962:** 288
  Vocational education program, **1961:** 46
Health Care for the Aged, National Committee on,
    1963: 459 [12], 460
Health and Human Development, National
    Institute of, **1963:** 53, 74, 447
Health, National Institutes of, **1963:** 21 (p. 37), 50,
    144 [6], 435
Health of the President, **1961:** 258 [7]; **1962:** 316
    [11]; **1963:** 305 [11]
Health insurance, **1963:** 50, 74
Health insurance under social security.
  See Social Security.
Health Organization, World, **1963:** 53, 366
Health professions, **1963:** 50, 53
Health Professions Educational Assistance Act of
    1963, **1963:** 374
Health Professions Educational Assistance Act,
    proposed, **1962:** 37
Health programs, **1961:** 14, 27, 52, 94, 406; **1962:**
    7 (p. 8), 13 (pp. 28, 31), 195, 288, 414;
    1963: 12 (p. 14), 21 (p. 32, 37, 39), 22, 30
    (p. 65), 51, 53, 54 [6], 64, 83, 87, 92, 134,
    175, 240, 313, 325, 364, 374, 434, 462, 474,
    478

Health programs — *continued*
See also Medical care.
  Children, **1961:** 25 [3], 27
  Children and youth, **1962:** 19, 65, 132, 291, 395,
    470; **1963:** 50, 64, 369
  Cuban refugees, 1961: 19
  International, **1963:** 53
  Maternity, **1963:** 50
  Mental health and retardation.
    See also Mental health and mental health
      programs.
  Message to Congress, **1962:** 65; **1963:** 50, 53
  Older persons, **1963:** 75 [1, 6]
  People-to-people program, **1961:** 146
Health Research Center, National Environmental,
  1963: 448 [21]
Health Research Facilities Construction Program,
  1962: 470
Health Services and Facilities Act,Community,
  1961: 406
Healy, James J., **1961:** 256; **1962:** 21; **1963:** 18
Heard, Alexander, **1961:** 403; **1963:** 192
Hearing examiners, regulatory agencies, **1961:** 121
Hearst, William R., Jr., **1962:** 11n.
Hearst, William Randolph, Foundation, **1963:** 48n.
Heart disease, **1962:** 65; **1963:** 74, 434
Heart Disease and Cancer, President's Conference
  on, **1961:** 83 [4]
  And cigarette smoking, **1962:** 210 [17]
Heber Springs, Ark., **1963:** 400
Hebert, Repr. F. Edward, **1961:** 35 [10]; **1962:**
  170, 171
Hebrew Congregations, Union of American,
  Trustees, remarks, **1961:** 463
Hechler, Repr. Ken, **1962:** 252, 414; **1963:** 249
Heckscher, August, **1963:** 246
Heeney, Arnold, **1961:** 45
Heilbron, Louis H., **1963:** 226
Heineman, Ben W., **1962:** 386n.
Heisbourg, Georges, **1963:** 152
Held, Adolph, **1962:** 81, 202
Helicopters, U.S., in Vietnamese conflict, **1963:**
  169 [9]
Helicopter services, subsidies, **1962:** 129
Heller, Walter W. (Chairman, Council of
    Economic Advisors), **1963:** 29, 30 (p. 68),
    62, 65 [2], 77, 94n.
  See also Council of Economic Advisers, Chair-
    man.
Hell's Canyon power project,**1963:** 175 [1]
Hemingway, Ernest, **1962:** 161n., 527
  Death of, **1961:** 268
Hempstone, Smith, **1962:** 340 [14]
Henry, Joseph, **1963:** 430
Henry, Patrick, **1961:** 473
Hepatitis, **1962:** 65
Heraldry, Army Institute of, **1963:** 76
Herbert, William J., **1962:** 298n.

Hercules, Pollaiuolo paintings, **1963:** 16
Herman, George, **1962:** 551
Hermitage, Andrew Jackson home, **1963:** 194
Hernandez, José, **1962:** 86
Heroin, **1962:** 411
Herrera, Felipe, **1961:** 95, 517
Herrling, William, **1962:** 186
Hershey, Lt. Gen. Lewis B., **1961:** 348, 496; **1962:**
  208n.; **1963:** 393
Herter, Christian A. **1961:** 480; **1962:** 74, 199, 541,
    549 [2]; **1963:** 75 [17], 76, 179, 306
  Appointment as Special Representative for
    Trade Negotiations, **1962:** 510
  News conference remarks on, **1962:** 20 [5], 40 [15]
Hesse, Germany, Minister-President Georg August
  Zinn, **1963:** 265, 266, 266a
Hickenlooper, Sen, Bourke, **1962:** 30n., 107 [5], 549
  [4]; **1963:** 105
Hicks, Marion, **1963:** 476
Hope, hospital ship, **1961:** 146
Hopkins, Marvin B., **1963:** 221
Horbein, Thomas F., **1963:** 158n.
Horne, John E., **1962:** 58n.; **1963:** 62, 118n.
Horsky, Charles A. (President's Advisor for
    National Capital Affairs), **1963:** 35 [15]
Hospitals and medical care facilities, **1961:** 14, 37,
    94, 406; **1962:** 7 (p. 7), 65, 174, 202, 288,
    395, 480; **1963:** 12 (p. 14), 21 (pp. 38, 39),
    22, 53, 74, 123, 134, 193, 290, 364, 401,
    445, 447, 461, 472, 478
  See also Medical care.
  Central America, **1963:** 103
  Construction, **1963:** 107 [24], 120 [8]
  Fallout shelters in, **1962:** 320
  Federal aid, **1963:** 53
  Mental hospitals, **1963:** 50, 51, 66, 447, 465 [5]
  Message and letter to Congress, **1961:** 27, 52
  Modernization, **1963:** 53
  Narcotic addicts, **1962:** 115 [27]
  News conference remarks, **1962:** 115 [27], 210 [1],
    279 [24]
  Older persons, **1963:** 12 (p. 14), 22, 74, 75 [1, 6],
    138, 459 [11, 12], 460, 461
High, Robert King, **1961:** 498; **1963:** 467
High Mountain Sheep power project, Idaho, **1963:**
  175 [1]
High School Symphony Orchestra, National, **1962:**
  322
Hightower, John M., **1961:** 119 [8]
Highways, **1961:** 94, 205; **1962:** 7 (p. 7), 395; **1963:**
    109, 127, 208, 456, 461
  Accident prevention, **1962:** 11, 93 (p. 236)
  Bolivian, **1961:** 184
  Dislocation of families, **1962:** 129
  Eastern seaboard, **1962:** 391
  Federal aid, **1961:** 17, 35 [3], 37, 58, 83 [7], 261;
    1962: 13 (p. 31), 16 (p. 44), 129
  Forest highways and access roads, **1961:** 49, 58;
    1962: 69

Highways — *continued*
    Interstate system, **1961:** 58, 436, 476; **1962:** 414;
        1963: 21 (pp. 27, 32, 36, 39), 30 (p. 67),
        127
    Latin America, **1963:** 118, 164
    Letter to Governors, **1961:** 37
    Message and letter to Congress, **1961:** 58, 79
    National Capital Region, **1963:** 22, 208, 456
    News conference remarks, **1961:** 35 [3], 83 [7]
    Ouachita National Forest road, **1961:** 441
    Safety, **1963:** 125
    Trust fund, **1961:** 312, 318 [16, 22]; **1962:** 13 (p.
        31); **1963:** 21 (pp. 27, 32, 36)
Highway Act of 1956, **1961:** 58
Highway Act of 1961, **1961:** 261
Highway Congress, Pan American, **1963:** 164
Highway Projects, Policy Advisory Committee,
    1963: 456
Highway Safety, Office of, **1962:** 11, 93 (p. 236);
    1963: 125
Hijacking of airplanes, comment on, **1961:** 312, 318
    [16, 22]
Hill, Sen. Lister, **1961:** 278; **1963:** 193, 194, 247,
    374, 435, 447
Hill-Burton Act, **1962:** 174, 279 [24]; **1963:** 21
    (p. 38), 50, 53, 74, 193
Hills, Lee, **1963:** 134
Hirohito, Emperor, **1962:** 531
Hiroshima, **1963:** 107 [20], 328 [17]
Hiss, Alger, **1962:** 515 [16]
Historic Preservation, National Trust for, **1963:** 425
Historical Publications Commission, National,
    1963: 26, 245
Historical Society, Massachusetts, **1963:** 2, 245
Hitch, Charles J., **1961:** 25 [4]
Hitler, Adolf, **1962:** 310 [3], 551 [15]
Hoang Thuy Nam, **1961:** 435
Hoban, James, **1963:** 278
Hobby, Oveta Culp, **1962:** 40 [8]
Hodges, Luther H.
    See Commerce, Secretary of.
Hodges, Mrs. Luther H., **1961:** 227
Hoff, Gov. Philip H., **1963:** 427
Hoffman, Paul G., **1963:** 124n.
Hofstadter, Robert, **1962:** 161n.
Hokkaido, Japan, **1963:** 27
Holding companies, personal, tax treatment, **1963:**
    34
Holifield, Repr. Chet, **1962:** 408; **1963:** 384
Holland.
    See Netherlands.
Holland, Repr. Elmer J., **1961:** 139 [8]; **1962:** 395,
    452, 453, 455
Holland, Mrs. Elmer J., **1962:** 453
Holland, Sen. Spessard L., **1962:** 77
Holleman, Jerry R., **1961:** 116
Hollywood, Calif., **1963:** 228
Holmes, Oliver Wendell, **1962:** 109, 393n.

Holt, Harold E., **1962:** 383n.
Holton, Karl, **1963:** p. 901
Holum, Kenneth, **1961:** 247
Holy Roman Empire, **1963:** 152
Holyoake, Keith, **1961:** 66
Homaira, Queen, **1963:** 343, 344, 347
Home, Lord, **1961:** 112, 258 [18], 318 [7]; **1962:**
    73, 89 [12], 419, 554; **1963:** 52, 144 [2],
    285, 305 [17], 328 [6]
Home Builders, National Association of, **1962:** 545
Homer, Arthur B., **1961:** 354n.
Homestead Act, **1961:** 462; **1962:** 69, 202
Homestead Air Force Base, Fla., **1962:** 520
Honduras, **1962:** 546 [20], 549 [6]
    Assistance, **1963:** 118
    News conference remarks, **1963:** 405 [7], 459 [18]
    Villeda Morales, Ramón, **1962:** 528, 529, 546
        [20]; **1963:** 99, 100, 102, 106
Honduras, British, **1963:** 294
Hong Kong, Chinese refugees in, **1962:** 210 [2, 5],
    245 [10]
Honolulu, Hawaii, **1962:** 196n.
    Center for Cultural Interchange Between East
        and West, **1963:** 231
    Mayor Neil S. Blaisdell, **1963:** 229, 230
    Mayors Conference, **1963:** 229, 230
Honorary degrees acceptance, **1961:** 162, 418; **1962:**
    234; **1963:** 221, 226, 232, 271, 379, 426,
    439
Hoover, Herbert, President, **1961:** 497; **1962:** 199,
    234, 439, 512, 550, 551 [9]; **1963:** 94, 193,
    216, 245, 344, 382, 407
    Library, Stanford University, **1962:** 546 [7]
    Library, West Branch, Iowa, **1963:** 207
    News conference remarks on, **1962:** 340 [20],
        546 [7]
Hoover, J. Edgar, **1962:** 231, 497
    See also Federal Bureau of Investigation,
        Director.
Hoover Commission, **1961:** 35 [10], 244, 314
Hoover Dam-Lake Mead outdoor recreational
    complex, **1963:** 390
Hope, Bob, **1961:** 215; **1963:** 353
    Racial discrimination, **1963:** 82
    U.S., abroad, **1963:** 118
Hot Springs, Va., **1962:** 478
Hotel and restaurant workers, wages, **1961:** 171 [20]
Hound Dog Missile, **1961:** 99; **1962:** 554, 557
Houphouet-Boigny, Felix, **1962:** 216, 238
    Visit of, **1962:** 206, 207, 212
Houphouet-Boigny, Madame, **1962:** 206
Houser, Theodore, **1963:** 44n., 175
Housing, **1961:** 11, 17, 31, 58, 94, 264, 436, 448, 454,
    477; **1962:** 7 (p. 7), 13, (pp. 28, 31), 16 (p.
    44), 23, 93 (p. 238), 174, 202, 545; **1963:** 21
    (pp. 32, 37), 30 (pp. 58, 59), 110, 130, 134,
    144 [20], 175, 177, 230, 237, 240, 248, 271,
    290, 366, 458, 462, 466, 468

Housing — *continued*
Campaign remarks, **1962:** 395, 396, 414, 437, 438, 452, 454-456, 458, 473, 481
College, **1961:** 17, 46, 70, 94; **1962:** 7 (p. 8), 23, 37, 414, 452; **1963:** 43
Department of Urban Affairs and Housing, proposed, **1962:** 7 (p. 7), 13 (p. 38), 20 [1, 7, 8], 23, 27 [7, 25], 40 [8], 59 [7], 190, 437, 458, 459
District of Columbia, **1963:** 35 [15], 230
Equal opportunity, **1963:** 49
Farm, **1961:** 76, 94
For dislocated families, **1962:** 129
Group facilities, **1963:** 74
Indians, **1961:** 371
Kenosha, Wis., eviction of needy families, **1961:** 96
Latin America, **1963:** 54 [10], 99, 103, 118, 462
Low income, **1963:** 21 (p. 37)
Message and letter to Congress, **1961:** 76, 101
Mexico City project, **1962:** 269
Military personnel, **1963:** 169 [20]
Negroes, **1963:** 134
News conference remarks, **1961:** 15 [5, 36], 62 [4, 10], 92 [12]; **1962:** 8 [18], 198 [10], 229 [1, 16], 279 [16], 302 [7], 515 [2, 10]
Older persons, **1961:** 76, 448, 477; **1962:** 7 (p. 8), 13 (p. 31), 328, 395, 437, 452, 454, 456, 458, 545; **1963:** 21 (p. 37), 74, 75 [1], 77 [2], 445, 478
On Indian reservations, **1963:** 113
Public, **1961:** 17, 76; **1962:** 414; **1963:** 423, 445
Racial discrimination, **1962:** 8 [18], 279 [16], 515 [2, 10], 545; **1963:** 10, 82, 230, 248, 305 [7], 356 [9]
In Washington, D.C., **1962:** 142
Racial discrimination ban, **1961:** 62 [10], 92 [12]
Rental, **1963:** 74
Rural, **1962:** 25, 93 (p. 238); **1963:** 21 (p. 36), 45, 74
Single persons, **1963:** 74
Urban, **1962:** 23, 190; **1963:** 21 (p. 37), 423, 445
Veterans, **1961:** 76, 94
Housing, President's Committee on Equal Opportunity in, **1962:** 515 [2]; **1963:** 49, 82
Housing Act of 1961, **1961:** 264; **1962:** 13 (p. 31), 16 (p. 44), 37, 69, 93 (p. 238), 129, 340 [10], 414, 452, 454, 456, 458, 473, 481, 545; **1963:** 21 (p. 37), 74, 376
Housing and Home Finance Administrator (Robert C. Weaver), **1961:** 31, 58, 70, 264, 371
Housing and Home Finance Agency, **1961:** 15 [5], 17, 20, 49, 76, 96; **1962:** 23, 53, 69, 93, (p. 238), 129, 323, 487; **1963:** 74, 127, 423

Housing and Home Finance Agency, Administrator (Robert C. Weaver), **1961:** 31, 58, 70, 264, 371; **1962:** 20 [8], 27 [25], 40 [8], 59 [7], 153, 198 [2], 279 [18], 323n.; **1963:** 49, 62, 69, 74, 130
Housing and Urban Affairs Department, **1961:** 11, 76, 130
Houston, Sam, **1961:** 16
Houston, Tex., **1962:** 369n., 372-374, 378 [22]; **1963:** 35 [9], 190, 473, 474
Mayor Lewis Cutrer, **1962:** 372n.
Ministers Conference (1960), **1962:** 549
Howard University, **1962:** 325; **1963:** 10n.
Howe, Alan T., **1963:** 146
Howe, Louis, **1962:** 260
Howes, Sally Ann, **1962:** 158
Hoyt, Palmer, **1961:** 153n.
Hruska, Sen. Roman L., **1961:** 476n.
Hubbard Medal, **1963:** 296
Huff, Sam, **1961:** 496
Hughes, Gov. Harold E., **1963:** 108
Hughes, Richard J., **1961:** 448, 455 [5]; **1962:** 174, 450
Hull, Cordell, **1962:** 22, 170, 199; **1963:** 192
Human Development, Institute of Child Health and, **1963:** 53
Human relations committees, municipal, proposed, **1963:** 230
Human rights, **1963:** 136, 192, 366
Human Rights Week, **1961:** 504
Human Skills in the Decade of Development, Conference on, **1962:** 358
Hume, Paul, **1963:** 173
Humphrey, Don, **1961:** 119 [2]; **1962:** 340 [29]
Humphrey, George M., **1962:** 340 [15, 27]; **1963:** 351
Humphrey, Sen. Hubert H., **1961:** 8 [25], 63, 244, 388; **1962:** 107 [19], 186, 199, 205, 254, 296n., 414, 439, 440; **1963:** 75 [12], 170, 328 [4], 349, 378, 416
Hungary, **1961:** 138; **1962:** 229 [3]; **1963:** 54 [7], 134 [1], 144 [8], 278
Hunt, Reed O., **1963:** 119
Hunting stamps, **1961:** 49; **1962:** 69
Huntley, Chet, **1963:** 349
Huntville, Ala., **1962:** 371, 340 [17]; **1963:** 169 [4], 236, 350, 448 [18]
Hurd, Owen, **1963:** 384
Hurley, Neil C., Jr., **1963:** 361
Hurst, John Fletcher, **1963:** 232
Husayn, Ibrahim, **1962:** 339n.
Hutcheson, Judge Joseph C., Jr., **1962:** 420
Hutchinson, William T., **1963:** 245
Hutton, Hugh, **1963:** 172
Hyannis, Mass., **1962:** 290n., 321n., 517n., 518.; **1963:** 179n., 180n.

Hyannis, Mass., releases from, **1961:** 266, 267, 269, 270, 271, 286, 311, 313, 314, 343-348, 367, 384, 386

Hyannis Port, Mass., **1961:** 268n., 298n., 397, 483n.; **1963:** 144 [1], 169 [6], 338, 340, 348

Hyde Park, N.Y., **1962:** 260, 546 [7]; **1963:** 193, 207

Hydroelectric power projects, **1961:** 17, 49, 121, 445, 474; **1962:** 69, 332; **1963:** 21 (p. 36), 175 [1], 179, 192, 193, 301, 376, 379, 384, 386, 389, 400, 401, 474, 478
    See also Power projects.

Hydrogen bomb, **1962:** 179 [13]
    See also Atomic bomb; Nuclear weapons; Nuclear weapons test.
    Soviet explosion, **1961:** 426, 442, 446

IA-ECOSOC.
    See Inter-American Economic and Social Council.

Iakovos, Archbishop, **1961:** 1n.

IAM.
    See International Association of Machinists.

Iba, Zambales (Philippines), **1963:** 239n.

Ibadan, Nigeria, **1963:** 331n.

Ibn-Saud, King Abdul Aziz, **1962:** 46

ICA.
    See International Cooperation Administration.

ICBM (Intercontinental Ballistic missile), **1961:** 99, 222

ICC.
    See Interstate Commerce Commission.

Ice Patrol, International, **1961:** 100

Idaho, **1963:** 175 [1], 248ftn. (p. 486)

Idaho, floods, **1961:** 83 [2]

I.G. Farben Co., **1963:** 89 [12]

Ikeda, Hayato (Prime Minister of Japan), **1961:** 444; **1962:** 99, 531; **1963:** 424
    Visit of, **1961:** 249, 252

Illegitimacy in U.S., **1963:** 423

Illinois, **1962:** 410 [1]; **1963:** 228, 248ftn. (p. 486), 363, 378, 422, 463
    Area redevelopment, **1962:** 58
    Candidates for public office, **1962:** 481-483
    District Court for Northern District, **1962:** 33
    Food distribution, **1961:** 15 [3], 17
    Gov. Otto Kerner, **1961:** 155, 244, 454; **1962:** 58, 481, 483; **1963:** 109, 422
    Unemployment, **1961:** 83 [18]

Illinois Trade Mission to Europe, **1963:** 422

Illiteracy, **1963:** 14, 22, 226, 248
    Adults, **1963:** 455
    Latin America, reduction, **1963:** 118

Illiteracy in U.S., **1962:** 7 (p. 9), 16 (p. 47), 288; **1963:** 43, 393, 423

Immigration to U.S., **1963:** 191, 311, 420n.
    French, **1963:** 191
    German, **1963:** 255, 265
    Irish, **1963:** 274, 276, 277, 278, 280, 281, 282
    Italian, **1963:** 235, 287, 288

Immigrants, Norwegian, **1962:** 178

Immigration laws, **1961:** 318 [21]; **1962:** 261; **1963:** 35 [13], 235, 311

Immigration and Naturalization Service, **1962:** 512
    Commissioner (Gen. J.M. Swing), **1961:** 312

Immigration to U.S. of refugees from Communist China, **1962:** 210 [2]

Imports, **1961:** 8 [18], 11, 23, 488 [17, 18, 19], 497, 499; **1962:** 7 (p. 15), 14, 16 (p. 44), 22, 139 [1, 5], 170, 214, 280, 340 [16], 410 [1], 449; **1963:** 30 (p. 65), 34, 131, 175 [3], 306, 418, 459 [25]
    Agricultural, **1962:** 8 [22]
    Bicycles, **1962:** 484
    Carpets, **1963:** 9
    Carpets, tile, and glass, **1962:** 98, 115 [23], 245, [16]
    Coffee, **1962:** 418
    Controls, **1963:** 202 [13]
    Cotton, **1961:** 258 [10], 478, 488 [19]; **1962:** 8 [4], 365; **1963:** 45, 75 [17]
    Crabmeat, **1961:** 483
    Economic boycotts, **1961:** 71 [20]
    From Communist bloc, **1962:** 546 [22]
    From Cuba, **1961:** 35 [8]; **1962:** 27 [10]
    Glass, **1963:** 9
    Lamps, discharge, **1963:** 9
    Lead from South Africa, **1963:** 202 [13]
    Lumber from Canada, **1962:** 307
    Oil, **1962:** 8 [15], 27 [24], 410 [11]; **1963:** 73, 459 [14, 25]
    Polish and Yugoslav, U.S. tariffs on, **1963:** 118
    Raw materials, **1962:** 199
    Residential fuel oil, **1961:** 62 [13]
    Restrictions, **1963:** 77
    Sugar, **1962:** 279 [7]
    Textiles, **1962:** 8 [15], 20 [21], 410 [9]; **1963:** 45, 75 [17]
    Tropical products from less developed countries, **1962:** 22
    Wool, **1962:** 8 [4]; **1963:** 75 [17], 459 [25]

In the Clearing, Robert Frost, **1962:** 110n.

Inaugural address, **1961:** 1
    Comments on, **1961:** 8 [28], 463

Inaugural, first anniversary, **1962:** 15

Inaugural, second anniversary, **1963:** 24, 35 [16]

Income
    Corporate.
        See Profits, corporate.
    National, **1963:** 118, 175, 306, 329, 351
    Older persons, **1963:** 74

Income, personal, **1962:** 13 (p. 27), 16 (p. 46), 328;
    1963: 21 (p. 30), 30 (pp. 58, 60-62, 68), 34,
    35 [14], 45, 74, 185, 193, 401, 407, 423,
    468, 478
Income taxes, **1961:** 15 [10], 17, 136; **1962:** 16 (p.
    43), 33, 129, 162, 328; **1963:** 30 (pp. 59, 63)
  Campaign contributions, proposed credit for,
    1963: 151
  Convention, U.S-Luxembourg, **1963:** 156
  Foreign central banks, **1961:** 23, 54
  News conference remarks, **1962:** 27 [7], 59 [16],
    115 [2], 179 [1], 229 [1, 4], 245 [18], 340
    [16], 410 [2], 515 [17]
  Reduction, **1962:** 176, 245 [18], 515 [17], 549
    Presidential standby authority, proposed,
    1962: 7 (p. 6), 13 (p. 35), 16 (p. 51), 27
    [27], 176, 245 [18], 259 [18]
  Reduction and revision, **1963:** 12 (p. 12), 21 (p.
    29), 30 (pp. 60-63), 34, 74, 77, 92, 134, 175
    [2], 177, 233, 363, 465
  Withholding tax on dividends and interest, pro-
    posed, **1962:** 7 (p. 7), 13 (p. 33), 16 (p. 57),
    108, 115 [2], 179 [1], 229 [4], 340 [16], 410
    [2], 468, 549 [6]
Incontro Club, Valdagno, Italy, **1963:** 191
Independence, Mo., **1961:** 448; **1962:** 546 [7];
    1963: 207
Independence Hall, address, **1962:** 278
Independence movement, Communist bloc, **1963:**
    319a
Independence of nations, **1962:** 278; **1963:** 260
    [11], 304
India, **1961:** 11, 26, 244, 387; **1962:** 70, 341, 363,
    554; **1963:** 85, 118, 232, 260 [13], 285, 455,
    457, 477
  Air support in case of attack by Communist
    China, requests for, **1963:** 75 [10]
  Ambassador B. K. Nehru, **1963:** 296
  Assistance, **1962:** 50 [10], 83, 89 [4], 340 [4],
    515 [3, 5], 549 [10]; **1963:** 118, 169 [17],
    202 [3], 219, 285, 328 [1], 356 [25]
  Bokaro steel mill, **1963:** 169 [17]
  Chinese invasion of, **1962:** 500, 515 [3, 5, 20],
    551 [20], 554
  Communist China, invasion of, **1963:** 12 (p. 16),
    21 (p. 34), 107 [14], 118, 214, 219, 285,
    320 [3], 459 [3]
  Communist China, relations with, **1963:** 459 [3]
  Defense of, **1963:** 89 [20], 107 [14]
  Dispute with Pakistan, **1962:** 8 [14], 20 [3], 50
    [10], 551 [1], 554, 557; **1963:** 278, 349,
    356 [25]
  Harriman (W. Averell) mission, **1962:** 515 [3, 5]
  Institute of Technology, U.S. participation in
    development, **1961:** 460
  Military survey team, U.S.-U.K., **1963:** 107 [14]
  Nehru, Jawaharlal, **1961:** 11, 35 [1], 452, 455
    [14], 456, 460; **1962:** 50 [10], 316 [14],
    363, 554

India — *continued*
  News conference remarks, **1961:** 35 [1], 171 [14],
    455 [14]; **1962:** 8 [14], 20 [3], 50 [10], 89
    [4], 245 [3, 9], 316 [14], 340 [4], 352 [11],
    515 [3, 5, 18, 20]
  Peace Corps projects, **1963:** 294
  Radhakrishnan, Sarvepalli, **1963:** 214, 215, 217,
    218, 219
  Social and economic development, **1963:** 219
  Soviet aircraft, purchase of, **1962:** 245 [3, 9],
    316 [14]
  U.S. Ambassador Ellsworth Bunker, **1961:** 244
  U.S. Ambassador J. Kenneth Galbraith, **1962:**
    245 [3], 316 [14]; **1963:** 120 [16], 215
  Visit by Mrs. John F. Kennedy, **1963:** 214
Indians, American, **1963:** 23, 465 [5], 468
  Acoma, **1962:** 340 [22]
  Cherokee and Creek, **1961:** 16
  Education, **1963:** 86, 113
  Electronics trainees, **1962:** 317
  First public housing loan, **1961:** 371
  Navajos, **1962:** 240
  Remarks to representatives, **1962:** 331
  Reservations, **1963:** 130, 305 [19]
  Schools for children, **1961:** 71 [5], 94
  Seneca Nations, opposition to Kinzua Dam
    project, **1961:** 71 [15], 320
  Sioux, **1963:** 257
  Treaties with U.S., **1961:** 71 [15]
  Welfare programs, **1963:** 86, 113
Indian Affairs, American Association on, **1963:** 113
Indian Affairs, Bureau of, **1961:** 71 [5]; **1963:**
    21 (p. 36), 113
Indian Affairs, Commissioner of (Philleo Nash),
    1963: 113
Indian Ocean, **1962:** 216
Indian Ocean expedition, **1961:** 100
Indiana, **1962:** 410 [1], 456; **1963:** 248 ftn. (p. 486),
    378, 379
  Gov. Matthew E. Welsh, **1962:** 279 [14], 346 n.,
    456
Indiana Dunes, proposed national park, **1962:**
    75 [23]
Indianapolis, Ind., **1962:** 456
Indians, American, National Congress of, **1963:** 86
Indochina, **1962:** 50 [9], 226; **1963:** 89 [20]
  See also Cambodia; Laos; Viet-Nam.
Indochina, Geneva conference (1954), **1961:** 92 [1]
Indonesia, **1963:** 455
  Assistance, **1963:** 459 [13]
  Assistance and development, **1961:** 146
  Dispute with Maylasia, **1963:** 459 [13]
  Dispute with Netherlands, **1961:** 119 [21]; **1962:**
    8 [3, 19], 139 [10], 210 [22], 251, 316 [3, 7],
    323, 334, 340 [14], 346; **1963:** 12 (p. 18),
    232

Indonesia — *continued*
  Independence, anniversary, **1962:** 334
  Mission of Don Humphrey to, **1962:** 340 [29]
  Oil negotiations with American companies, **1963:** 212, 224
  Soviet assistance, **1962:** 352 [11]
  Sukarno, Achmed, **1961:** 119 [21], 143, 146, 359, 364, 365; **1962:** 334, 340 [29]; **1963:** 212, 224, 459 [13]
  U.S. Ambassador Howard P. Jones, **1961:** 146
  Visit of Robert F. Kennedy, **1962:** 243 [1]
Industrial capacity, U.S., **1961:** 11, 15 [23], 17, 33, 90
Industrial Conference Board, National, remarks, **1961:** 33
Industrial National Bank of Rhode Island, **1962:** 113 n.
Industrial Payroll Savings Committee, United States, campaign, **1963:** 450
Industrial plant and equipment, modernization, **1961:** 33, 136
Industrial Relations Commission, Federal, **1963:** 133
Industrial revolution, **1963:** 217, 239
Industries affected by imports, assistance to, **1961:** 499
Industry, labor and agriculture, meeting of leaders, **1961:** 8 [18]
Industry, U.S., **1962:** 22, 449; **1963:** 21 (pp. 32, 37), 134, 136, 192, 193, 196, 206, 271, 301, 361, 378, 400, 451, 452, 460, 462, 474, 478
  Accident prevention, **1963:** 119, 155
  Capacity, **1962:** 13 (p. 27), 174, 229 [1], 410 [1], 549; **1963:** 12 (p. 12), 30 (pp. 58, 61, 62, 68), 34, 94, 175, 179, 248
  Consumer protection, **1963:** 53, 74, 121, 237
  Depreciation allowances.
    See main heading, Depreciation allowances.
  Development, **1963:** 63
  Employment, **1963:** 110, 113
  Exports.
    See main heading, Exports.
  Federal aid, **1963:** 242
  Imports, effect of, **1962:** 22; **1963:** 459 [25]
  Investments abroad, **1963:** 12 (p. 17), 77 [1], 118, 266, 306, 319, 418, 436
  Manpower needs, **1963:** 92
  Modernization of plant and equipment, **1962:** 7 (pp. 6, 14), 13 (p. 33), 152 [2], 162, 174, 199, 229 [1], 280, 286, 328, 395, 549; **1963:** 30 (pp. 61-63), 34, 131, 175, 306, 363, 465
  News conference remarks, **1962:** 139 [13], 152 [2], 229 [1], 410 [1], 546 [6]
  Occupational training, **1963:** 141
  Permanent exposition in Washington, D.C., proposed, **1962:** 181
  Physical fitness films, **1963:** 325

Industry — *continued*
  Pollution of air and water from, prevention, **1963:** 366
  Productivity, **1963:** 21 (pp. 29, 39), 30 (pp. 58, 59), 34, 77 [4], 110, 177
  Research, **1963:** 21 (p. 37), 30 (p. 69), 34
  Salaries, comparability with Government, **1963:** 148
  Technology, **1963:** 30 (pp. 68, 69)
Infant care, **1963:** 50, 434, 447
Infant mortality, **1962:** 65, 132; **1963:** 64, 455
Infantile paralysis, **1963:** 51
Inflation, **1961:** 17, 33, 354, 366, 497; **1962:** 7 (p. 6), 13 (p. 27), 14, 16 (p. 45), 22, 162, 174, 203, 230, 234, 243 [2], 273, 280, 328, 549, 551 [12]; **1963:** 21 (pp. 29, 41), 30 (pp. 61, 64), 75 [11], 77, 110, 134 [3], 175, 290, 306, 351, 363, 465
  In Brazil, **1962:** 546 [18]
  News conference remarks, **1961:** 15 [23], 334 [14]; **1962:** 139 [1], 152 [2], 210 [21], 229 [1], 245 [6], 279 [19], 340 [19], 410 [1, 5], 546 [6, 18]
Information
  Availability, **1962:** 410 [1, 8], 515 [7, 14, 19], 546 [21]; **1963:** 54 [12], 75 [9], 89 [9], 120 [3], 232
  Latin America, expansion of program, **1961:** 276
  Manpower resources development, **1963:** 92
  Medical, international exchange, **1963:** 247
  Nuclear technology, dissemination of, **1963:** 54 [8]
  Polls abroad, USIA, **1963:** 75 [4]
  Press, self-restraint in publishing intelligence data, **1961:** 153, 185
  Privileged, **1961:** 8 [23], 334 [7]; **1962:** 40 [5], 107 [15]
    Scientific and technical, communication of, **1963:** 67
    Soviet missiles in Cuba, **1963:** 89 [9]
    Stockpiles of critical materials, **1962:** 40 [17]
    U.S. activities in Berlin, **1962:** 357
    U.S. activities in Viet-Nam, **1962:** 50 [9]
    USIA broadcasts in Germany, **1963:** 144 [9]
Information Agency, United States, **1961:** 8 [23], 92 [14], 205
Injunctions in labor disputes
  Aerospace industry, **1963:** 39
  Longshoremen's strike, **1962:** 428
  Military aircraft industry, **1962:** 247
Inland waterways, **1962:** 13 (p. 34), 129; **1963:** 21 (p. 31)
Inner tubes, tax, **1961:** 58
Inouye, Sen. Daniel K., **1963:** 229
Insect pest control, **1961:** 49, 85
Insecticides, **1963:** 110
Inspection, nuclear tests.
  See Nuclear weapons tests, inspection and control.

Institute of Child Health and Human Development, **1963:** 53
Institute for Free Trade Union Development, **1962:** 324
Institute of General Medical Sciences, **1963:** 53
Institute of Health, National, **1963:** 21 (p. 37), 50, 144 [6], 435
Institute of Research on Exceptional Children, **1963:** 447
Institute of Wildlife Management, **1963:** 196
Insurance, **1963:** 134
  Accident, **1963:** 119
  Crop, **1962:** 440
  Disability, **1961:** 17; **1963:** 74
  Exports, **1962:** 16 (p. 49)
  Export credit, **1961:** 437, 497
  Flood, **1962:** 89 [11], 152 [10]
  Health, **1963:** 50, 74.
    See also Social Security.
  Mortgage, **1962:** 23, 545; **1963:** 21 (p. 37), 74, 445, 466
  News conference remarks, **1961:** 15 [4, 17], 25 [25], 35 [3, 14], 62 [7], 139 [3]
  Old-age and survivors, **1961:** 17; **1963:** 74
  Premiums, tax treatment of, **1963:** 34
  Retirement, **1963:** 74
  Unemployoment, **1961:** 11, 15 [17], 17, 22, 25 [25], 35 [3, 14], 62 [7], 93, 94, 241, 323, 339, 384, 385, 436, 499; **1963:** 21 (p. 38), 30 (p. 67), 92, 185, 402
    See also Unemployment insurance.
  Veterans, **1961:** 15 [4], 35 [3], 139 [3]; **1962:** 16 (p. 44), 517
Insurance Association, Foreign Credit, **1963:** 30 (p. 65), 306
Insurance companies, tax provisions, **1961:** 136; **1962:** 16 (p. 57)
Integration, **1963:** 305 [25]
  See also Civil rights.
  Armed forces, **1963:** 251
  Atlanta, **1961:** 334 [1]
  Birmingham, Ala.
    See main heading, Birmingham.
  News conference remarks, **1961:** 25 [8], 62 [10], 334 [1]
  New Orleans, **1961:** 25 [8], 55
  Parochial schools in New Orleans, **1962:** 152 [13]
  Public accommodations, **1963:** 21 (p. 37), 82, 144 [13], 230, 248, 462, 465 [3]
  Public colleges and universities, **1961:** 62 [10]
  Public schools, **1961:** 55, 352, 405; **1962:** 198 [8]; **1963:** 82, 169 [4], 248, 350, 356 [2, 8, 22], 455, 462
  Sit-ins protesting segregation, **1963:** 202 [2]
  State universities, **1963:** 82
  Supreme Court decisions, **1963:** 230, 237, 248
    University of Alabama, **1963:** 169 [4], 202 [1], 234, 236, 237, 243

Integration — *continued*
  University of Mississippi, **1962:** 420, 459, 551 [10]; **1963:** 35 [23], 82
Intellectual life in U.S., **1963:** 192
Intelligence activities, U.S., **1961:** 168, 258 [8, 9]
Intelligence advisory board, President's, **1961:** 168; **1963:** 405 [12]
Intelligence data, publication by newspapers, **1961:** 153, 185
Intelligence program, foreign, **1962:** 13 (p. 38); **1963:** 54 [4, 5, 12], 144 [12], 202 [14]
Interagency Committee on Oceanography, **1963:** 430
Interagency steering committee on international air transportation policy, **1963:** 186
Interagency Textile Administrative Committee, **1961:** 428
Inter-American Center, proposed, **1962:** 229 [8]
Inter-American Community, **1961:** 192
Inter-American conference (1889), **1962:** 556
Inter-American Conference for the Maintenance of Peace (1936), **1961:** 122
Inter-American Conference of Ministers of Labor, **1963:** 163
Inter-American Congress (1825), **1963:** 99
Inter-American cooperation, **1963:** 97-99, 103-106, 118, 149, 429, 468, 473
  Appropriation, **1961:** 208
  Armed forces, **1963:** 168
  U.S.-Canada, **1963:** 179
Inter-American cooperation, appropriation, **1961:** 208
Inter-American Defense Board, **1962:** 27 [2], 117, 378 [1]
Inter-American Development Bank, **1961:** 78, 81, 95, 184, 389, 491, 510, 513, 517; **1962:** 13 (p. 29), 83, 86; **1963:** 21 (p. 35), 118, 431n.
  Board of Governors meeting, **1961:** 119 [20], 122
  News conference remarks, **1961:** 119 [20], 318 [15, 24]
  President (Felipe Herrera), **1961:** 95, 517
Inter-American Economic and Social Conference, **1963:** 107 [22]
  See also Punta del Este conferences.
Inter-American Economic and Social Council, **1961:** 81, 122, 184, 491; **1962:** 86
  Ministerial meeting, **1961:** 78, 210
  Selection of panel of experts, **1961:** 491
Inter-American Fund for Social Progress, **1961:** 81, 90
Inter-American Highway, **1963:** 164
Inter-American Institute of Agricultural Sciences, **1963:** 430
Inter-American Press Association, **1963:** 468
Inter-American Symposium, **1962:** 513

Inter-American system, **1963:** 14, 99, 102, 464

Inter-American Treaty of Reciprocal Assistance
(Rio Pact), **1962:** 273, 485, 486; **1963:** 89
[19]

Intercity transportation, **1962:** 129

Interdepartmental committee for payroll savings,
1961: 75

Interdepartmental Highway Safety Board, **1963:**
125

Interdepartmental task force on Latin America,
proposed, **1961:** 11

Interest, withholding of taxes, **1961:** 136

Interest, withholding tax proposed, **1962:** 7 (p. 7),
13 (p. 33), 16 (p. 57), 108, 179 [1], 229 [4],
340 [16], 410 [2], 468, 549 [6]

Interest equalization tax, foreign investors, proposed, **1963:** 306

Interest on national debt, **1963:** 30 (p. 63), 77 [1],
134, 175, 465

Interest rates, **1961:** 94; **1962:** 16 (p. 44), 280,
340 [19]; **1963:** 21 (p. 41), 30 (p. 58), 34,
94, 175, 188, 306

  Consumer purchases, **1962:** 93 (p. 240)

  Deposits of foreign central banks and governments, **1961:** 23, 82

  Foreign aid, **1962:** 549 [10]

  Loans for public facility projects, **1961:** 15 [5]

  Long and short-term securities, **1961:** 17, 25 [16]

  Mortgages, **1961:** 15 [5], 17, 62 [4], 76; **1962:** 16
(p. 44), 93 (p. 238); **1963:** 74, 305 [22],
306

  News conference remarks, **1963:** 305 [22], 328
[23], 405 [15]

  Railroad retirement fund, **1963:** 402

  United Nations bonds, **1962:** 24

Inter-Faith Chapel, Kings Point, dedication, **1961:**
156

Intergovernment Committee for European Migration, **1961:** 297

Intergovernmental Oceanography Commission,
UNESCO, **1961:** 100; **1963:** 430

Intergovernmental Relations, Advisory Commission on, **1963:** 368

Interhandel Co., **1963:** 89 [12]

Interior, Department of the, **1961:** 247; **1962:** 69,
100, 240, 307, 425, 487; **1963:** 47, 63, 113,
155n., 209, 301, 390

  Saline water conversion, **1961:** 257

  Urban land reserves study, **1961:** 76

Interior, Secretary of the (Stewart L. Udall), **1961:**
48, 65, 247, 445; **1962:** 13 (p. 31), 50 [20],
128, 216, 317, 333, 335, 337, 404, 425, 495,
531, 550; **1963:** 37, 47, 62, 63, 113, 130,
155, 207, 301, 376-387, 389, 390

  Natural resources programs, **1961:** 49

Interior — *continued*
  News conference remarks on, **1961:** 62 [13], 71
[5], 171 [11]

  Passamaquoddy Tidal Basin project, **1961:** 197

  Solicitation of campaign funds by friend, **1961:**
171 [11]

Interlochen, Mich., **1962:** 322n.

Internal Revenue Code, **1962:** 129; **1963:** 74, 118

Internal Revenue Service, **1961:** 94, 136, 488 [14];
1962: 7 (p. 7), 13 (p. 33), 198 [1], 229 [1],
340 [13], 448, 468, 549; **1963:** 21 (p. 42),
306

  Joint Conference of field officers, remarks, **1961:**
157

Internal Revenue Service, Commissioner
(Mortimer M. Caplin), **1961:** 157; **1962:**
340 [13]

International Act for Peace and Security, military
assistance, **1961:** 207

International agreements (1961)
  Antarctic Treaty, **1961:** 253

  Charter of Punta del Este, **1961:** 324n., 376n.,
389, 491, 510

  International Coffee Agreement, **1962:** 86, 126,
410 [3], 418, 546 [20]

  Nuclear test ban treaty.
    See main heading, Nuclear test ban treaty.

  Organization for Economic Cooperation and
Development Convention, **1961:** 91

  Textile agreement, **1961:** 428

  U.S.-British West Indies, mutual defense agreement, **1961:** 36

  U.S.-Canada, Columbia River Basin development, **1961:** 49, 83 [2]

  U.S.-France, atomic energy for mutual defense,
1961: 355

  U.S.-Luxembourg, commerce and taxation,
1963: 156

  U.S.-Mexico, agricultural credit agreement,
1962: 268

  U.S.-Mexico, Chamizal Zone Agreement, **1963:**
307

  U.S.-Pan American Union, funds for Alliance
for Progress, **1961:** 491

  U.S.-U.K., Nassau agreement, **1962:** 554, 557

  U.S.-U.K. Polaris missile agreement, **1963:** 35
[18], 54 [8]

  U.S.-U.S.S.R. air transport agreement, **1963:**
448 [20]

  U.S.-U.S.S.R. direct communications link, **1963:**
250

International Air Transport Association, **1963:** 186

International Association of Machinists, **1962:** 247,
298, 376, 390, 410 [6]; **1963:** 39, 162

Development, **1962:** 20 [3], 83, 168, 234, 544

[References are to items except as otherwise indicated]

International Atomic Energy Agency, **1963:** 430
International Bank for Reconstruction and Board of Governors, remarks, **1962:** 392
International Bank for Reconstruction and Development, **1961:** 90, 283; **1963:** 54, 391
President (Eugene R. Black), **1961:** 119 [2], 244, 273; **1962:** 27 [12], 50 [10], 392
Volta River project, **1961:** 273
International Boundary and Water Commission, U.S.-Mexico, **1962:** 94
International Brotherhood of Electrical Workers, **1962:** 247
International Christian Leadership, Inc., **1962:** 68n., **1963:** 52n.
Remarks, **1961:** 26
International Coffee Agreement, **1962:** 86, 126, 410 [3], 418, 546 [20]
International Conference on Middle Level Manpower, **1963:** 294
International Congress on Medical Librarianship, **1963:** 247
International Control commission, Laos, **1963:** 144 [2], 169 [9]
See also Laos.
International cooperation, **1963:** 68, 217, 219, 260 [8]
International Cooperation Administration, **1961:** 81, 90, 167, 285
See also International Development, Agency for.
Abolishment proposed, **1961:** 207
Director (Henry R. Labouisse), **1961:** 119 [2], 288
International Council of Scientific Unions, **1961:** 100
International Court of Justice, **1962:** 8 [19], 107 [5], 340 [14], 498; **1963:** 366, 471
International Credit Union Day, message, **1961:** 423
International Development Act, **1961:** 207, 346
International Development, Agency for, **1961:** 346, 460, 510; **1962:** 7 (p. 12), 13 (p. 29), 83, 177, 237, 243 [1], 272, 276, 326, 358, 550; **1963:** 6, 21 (p. 35), 61n., 118, 306, 356 [15], 361, 404n., 455
International Development, Agency for, Administrator (David E. Bell), **1963:** 118, 169 [10], 306, 338
International Development, Agency for, Administrator (Fowler Hamilton), **1961:** 395, 466; **1962:** 212, 232, 243, 499; **1963:** 6
Electrification projects, **1962:** 499
News conference remarks, **1962:** 139 [11], 229 [5], 340 [11], 410 [12]
Overseas Directors, remarks, **1962:** 232
Proposed, **1961:** 90, 205, 207, 244
International Development Association, **1962:** 392; **1963:** 21 (p. 35), 391

International Development, Citizens Committee for, remarks, **1961:** 277
International Economic and Social Development, National Conference on, **1961:** 244
International Exchange of Persons, Committee on, **1963:** 140n.
International Federation of Catholic Universities, **1963:** 342
International Finance Corporation, **1963:** 391
International Freedom from Hunger Campaign, **1963:** 33
International Geophysical Year (1957-58), **1962:** 59 [1]
International groups.
See Addresses or remarks to international groups.
International health programs, **1963:** 53
International human rights convention, **1963:** 309
International Ice Patrol, **1961:** 100
International Indian Ocean Expedition, **1961:** 100
International Joint Commission, U.S. and Canada, **1962:** 123
Report, **1961:** 197
International Labor Organization, **1963:** 305 [21], 309
International Ladies Garment Workers Union, **1962:** 200
International law, **1961:** 387; **1962:** 498, 515 [13]
International Law Commission, **1963:** 366
International Living, Experiment in, **1962:** 363
International Longshoremen's Association, **1962:** 421; **1963:** 18
International Monetary Financial Problems, National Advisory Council on, **1961:** 23; **1962:** 31
International Monetary Fund, **1961:** 11, 23, 497; **1962:** 13 (p. 32), 16 (p. 50), 31, 114n., 280; **1963:** 30 (p. 65), 306, 391
Board of Governors, remarks, **1962:** 392
Managing Director (Per Jacobsson), **1962:** 546 [6]; **1963:** 77, 161, 391
News conference remarks, **1963:** 35 [19], 305 [12], 328 [23]
International Organization of Masters, Mates and Pilots, **1961:** 270; **1962:** 21
International Passamaquoddy Engineering Board, **1961:** 197
International Peace Corps Secretariat, **1963:** 176, 294
International Peace and Security Act, **1961:** 207
Internatinal Polyphonic Contest, **1962:** 352 [3], 361
International security, **1963:** 58, 72, 112, 114, 115, 217, 314, 316, 391
International Telecommunication Union, **1963:** 470
International Textile Agreement, **1961:** 428
International Tin Agreement, **1961:** 409
International Trading Co., **1962:** 89 [14]
International transportation, **1962:** 129

International Typographical Union, **1963:** 75 [2, 13], 107 [16]
International Union of the American Republics, **1961:** 122
International Union of Operating Engineers, **1962:** 247
International Wage Policy Committee, **1962:** 121
Inter-Parliamentary Council, **1962:** 500
Interstate commerce, **1963:** 248, 305 [7]
Interstate Commerce Act, **1962:** 129; **1963:** 310
Interstate Commerce Commission, **1961:** 121; **1962:** 8 [18], 13 (p. 38), 93 (p. 237), 129; **1963:** 82, 125, 310
Interstate Commerce Commission, Chairman (Laurence K. Walrath), **1963:** 62
Interstate commerce, movement of household goods, **1962:** 93 (p. 237)
Interviews of the President, transcripts
  British Broadcasting Company, **1961:** 229
  Cronkite, Walter (CBS television), **1963:** 340
  Editor of Izvestia, **1961:** 483
  Huntley, Chet, and David Brinkley, **1963:** 349
  Lawrence, William, **1962:** 459
  Press interviews, **1962:** 551, 557
  Radiodiffusion-Television Francaise, **1961:** 214
  Roosevelt, Mrs. Franklin D., **1962:** 156
  Stein, Robert, **1963:** 319a
Intrepid, U.S.S., **1962:** 213
Inventories, business, **1962:** 16 (p. 44)
Inventories, tax provisions, **1961:** 136
Investments, **1962:** 13 (pp. 27, 36, 37), 302 [7], 328, 410 [2, 3, 12]; **1963:** 12 (p. 13), 35 [14], 65 [2], 77, 94, 175, 177, 230, 478
  Capital goods, **1961:** 33; **1962:** 7 (p. 6), 16 (p. 47), 89 [5], 152 [2], 170, 177, 199, 229 [1, 16], 286, 358; **1963:** 21 (p. 39), 30 (pp. 59, 61, 68), 34, 175 [1, 2], 306, 351, 363, 391, 436, 462, 468
  Communications satellite corporation, **1962:** 107 [12]
  Depressed areas, **1962:** 165
  Dividends, tax treatment, **1963:** 34
  Foreign, in U.S., **1961:** 23; **1962:** 7 (p. 14), 279 [12], 280; **1963:** 306, 391
  Housing, **1962:** 545
  News conference remarks, **1961:** 139 [18], 488 [17]
  Private, in less developed nations, **1963:** 118
  Stock options, tax treatment of, **1963:** 34
  Tax credit incentive plan, **1961:** 17, 136, 139 [18]. 161
  Tax credit plan, **1962:** 7 (p. 6), 13 (p. 33), 16 (p. 48), 108, 114n., 115 [2, 15], 152 [2, 9, 14], 162, 174, 229 [1], 259 [16, 18], 279 [19], 280, 286, 328, 395, 410 [2], 468, 549 [6]; **1963:** 12 (p. 12), 30 (p. 62), 34, 92, 110, 118, 131, 465
  Textile industry, **1961:** 161

Investments — *continued*
  U.S. abroad, **1961:** 13, 136, 488 [17], 497, 499; **1962:** 16 (pp. 49, 57), 22, 75 [10], 108, 126, 152 [11], 177, 199, 203, 212, 259 [2], 279 [12], 280, 302 [6], 316 [19], 358, 410 [12], 549 [2]; **1963:** 12 (p. 17), 77 [1], 118, 266, 306, 319, 418, 436
  In Peru, **1961:** 376
  "Tax havens," **1961:** 136, 497
Iowa, **1963:** 248ftn. (p. 486)
  Gov. Harold E. Hughes, **1963:** 108
Iowa State University, **1962:** 25
Iran, **1961:** 483; **1962:** 70, 226, 352 [11], 363; **1963:** 333, 361, 477
  Assistance, **1963:** 118, 328 [1], 338
  Bilateral Agreement of Cooperation (1959), **1962:** 147
  Earthquake, U.S. relief, **1962:** 364
  Shah Mohammad Reza Pahlavi, **1962:** 138, 141, 147, 364; **1963:** 60
  Visit of Vice President Johnson, **1962:** 339
IRBM (Intermediate range ballistic missiles), **1962:** 485, 489
Ireland, **1962:** 75 [9], 233; **1963:** 275, 283. 295, 297, 418
  Ambassador Thomas J. Kiernan, **1962:** 233n.
  De Valera, Eamon, **1962:** 353n.; **1963:** 274, 278, 282, 283, 415
  Easter Rising (1916), **1963:** 281
  Economic and social development, **1963:** 278, 418
  Lemass, Sean F., **1963:** 278, 281, 283, 415, 416, 418
  U.S. Ambassador Matthew H. McCloskey, **1962:** 233; **1963:** 24, 275
  Visit to, **1963:** 274-282
Ireland, Northern, test ban treaty, **1963:** 314, 324
Irish Brigade in Civil War, **1963:** 276, 278
Irish Guards, **1963:** 150
Iron, **1961:** 354; **1963:** 378, 455
Iron Curtain countries.
  See Communist bloc.
Irrigation, **1961:** 17, 49; **1963:** 21 (p. 36), 383, 386, 389, 478
Irrigation projects, **1962:** 69, 335, 337
Isbrandtsen Co., Inc., **1962:** 113n.
Isaiah, **1961:** 1
Isolationism, **1962:** 198 [6], 199, 284, 458
Israel
  Arms purchases, **1963:** 120 [1]
  Assistance, **1963:** 120 [10], 169 [2]
  Exports to, **1963:** 361
  Farm machinery loan, **1961:** 83 [3]
Issenmann, Bishop Clarence G., **1962:** 3n.
Italian-Americans, **1962:** 450
Italian Migration, American Committee on, **1963:** 235
Italian Mount McKinley Expedition, **1961:** 305

Italy, **1961:** 499; **1962:** 230, 363, 551 [22]; **1963:** 5, 15, 16, 107 [3], 235, 260 [3, 10], 295, 311, 361, 378
  Ambassador Sergio Fenoaltea, **1962:** 339n., 361n.,, 524; **1963:** 191, 293
  Assistance, **1963:** 72, 134 [3]
  Balance of payments, **1963:** 16
  Brosio, Manlio, **1961:** 84n.
  Centennial of unification, remarks, **1961:** 84
  Economic growth, **1962:** 74, 194, 203; **1963:** 15, 16, 191
  Fanfani, Amintore, **1961:** 239, 242, 318 [7]; **1962:** 352 [3]; **1963:** 15, 16, 20
  Incontro Club, remarks, **1963:** 191
  Investment in capital goods, **1961:** 33
  Leone, Giovanni, **1963:** 290-293
  Martino, Gaetano, **1961:** 84
  Marzotto, Count Giannino, **1963:** 191
  Missile bases in, **1963:** 35 [18]
  Music contest, **1962:** 352 [3], 361
  News conference remarks, **1961:** 119 [18], 318 [7]
  Paintings, display in U.S., **1963:** 16
  Piccioni, Attilio, **1963:** 291-293, 373
  Renaissance, **1963:** 325
  Segni, Antonio, **1961:** 239, 242; **1962:** 352 [3]; **1963:** 16, 260 [10], 287, 290, 291, 292, 293
  Unemployment, **1963:** 16
  U.S. Ambassador G. Frederick Reinhardt, **1961:** 242
  U.S. expenditures in, **1963:** 77 [1]
  U.S. forces in, **1962:** 259 [14]
  U.S. relations with, **1963:** 260 [10], 287, 290, 292, 293
  Visit to, **1963:** 287-293
  Visit of Vice President Johnson, **1962:** 339
  Voting participation, **1963:** 167
Ivory Coast, Felix Houphouet-Boigny, **1962:** 206, 207, 212, 216, 238
Iwo Jima, **1963:** 109
Izaak Walton League of America, **1963:** 196
Izvestia, **1962:** 27 [1]
Izvestia, interview by editor of, **1961:** 483, 488 [4, 7]

Jackson, Andrew, **1962:** 35, 170, 252, 349, 439, 452, 482; **1963:** 23, 146, 187, 194, 228, 312, 322, 370
Jackson, Lady Barbara Ward, **1963:** 136
Jackson, Sen. Henry M., **1961:** 3, 152, 472n., 474; **1962:** 107 [3], 408; **1963:** 41, 54 [4], 384, 387
Jackson, Miss., **1963:** 135, 230, 248
Jackson Hole National Monument, Wyo., **1963:** 383, 387, 388, 390
Jacksonville, Fla., Mayor Haydon Burns, **1962:** 190n.
Jacobs, Andrew, Jr., **1962:** 456
Jacobsson, Per, **1962:** 546 [6]; **1963:** 77, 161, 391
Jakomas, Andrew, **1962:** 453n.
Jagan, Cheddi, **1961:** 483; **1963:** 328 [10]

Jamaica, **1963:** 328 [10], 311
James, Henry, **1962:** 281
Jamestown, Va., **1962:** 77
Jannus, Tony, 50th anniversary of flight, **1963:** 464
Japan, **1961:** 220, 483, 497, 499; **1962:** 22, 74, 395, 449; **1963:** 21 (p. 39), 77 [1], 199, 221, 228, 266, 328 [23], 361, 378, 385, 455
  Cotton exports to U.S., **1963:** 75 [17]
  Detection stations, nuclear tests, proposed, **1963:** 27
  Economy, **1962:** 328, 531; **1963:** 12 (p. 15)
  Emperor Hirohito, **1962:** 531
  Fisheries dispute with Canada, **1963:** 352
  Foreign aid programs, **1963:** 21 (p. 35)
  Ikeda, Hayato, **1961:** 249, 252, 444; **1962:** 99, 351; **1963:** 424
  Investment in capital goods, **1961:** 33
  Kosaka, Zentaro, **1961:** 455 [3]
  Legion of Merit award to Japenese officer, **1962:** 139 [15]
  News conference remarks, **1962:** 8 [4], 75 [16], 245 [4], 279 [6, 12]
  Ohira, Masayoshi, **1962:** 531n.
  Peace treaty with, **1963:** 78
  Ryukyu Islands, interest in, **1962:** 99
  Trade, **1962:** 8 [4], 22, 98, 170, 199
    Delegation to U.S., **1962:** 531
  Trade agreement with, **1963:** 9
  Trade with U.S., **1961:** 258 [10], 455 [3, 16], 488 [19]
  U.S. Ambassador Edwin O. Reischauer, **1962:** 275
  U.S. exports, **1963:** 118
  U.S. investments, **1961:** 136
  U.S.-Japan committee on trade and economic affairs, **1961:** 252, 444n., 455 [3]
  U.S.-Japan cultural conference, **1963:** 424
  Visit of President Eisenhower, question of, **1961:** 171 [19]
  Visit of Robert F. Kennedy, **1962:** 243 [1]
Jarman, Repr. John, **1961:** 441
Jarring, Gunnar, **1962:** 161n.
Jarret, Rev. Tally H., **1963:** 390
Jarring, Madame, **1962:** 161n.
Jarvis, Joseph B., **1962:** 122n.
Javits, Sen. Jacob, **1962:** 515 [15]; **1963:** 459 [12], 460
Jay, John, **1963:** 387
Jean,'Prince, **1963:** 150, 152, 154, 156, 157
Jefferson, Thomas, **1961:** 72, 78, 125, 145, 165, 397, 418, 473, 496, 498, 499, 520; **1962:** 15, 37, 50 [25], 86, 161, 170, 201, 234, 270, 274, 278, 287, 371, 439, 452, 461, 482, 527, 555 [10]; **1963:** 12 (p. 19), 23, 46, 73, 146, 192, 204, 226, 227, 228, 245, 255, 271, 279, 294, 297, 300, 385, 387, 469
Jefferson-Jackson dinner, address, **1962:** 186
Jenkins, Herbert T., **1961:** 334 [1]

[References are to items except as otherwise indicated]

Jennings, Donald, **1962:** 438

Jensen, Repr. Ben. F., **1962:** 127n.

Jensen, Vernon H., **1962:** 421

Jerstad, Luther C., **1963:** 158n., 296

Jessup, Judge Philip C., tribute to, **1962:** 498

Jewish High Holy Days, message, **1963:** 346

Jewish High Holy Days, statement, **1961:** 351;
   1962: 379

Jews and Christians, National Conference of, **1961:**
   479

JFK, the Man and the Myth, Victor Lasky, **1963:**
   356 [7]

Joan of Arc, **1962:** 70

Jodoin, Claude, **1963:** 179

John Birch Society, **1961:** 139 [14]; **1962:** 40 [13],
   546 [22]

John F. Kennedy Center for the Performing Arts,
   1963: 327n.

John, Sir Caspar, **1963:** 203

John XXIII, Pope, **1962:** 430; **1963:** 107 [10], 202
   [7], 217
   Death of, **1963:** 213
   Medal of Freedom, **1963:** p. 903

Johnson, Alston, **1963:** 3d, 48

Johnson, Christopher, **1961:** 222 [8]

Johnson, Edwin C., **1962:** 336

Johnson, Repr. Harold T., **1962:** 337, 338; **1963:**
   389

Johnson, James A., **1963:** 12 (p. 19)

Johnson, Repr. Lester R., **1962:** 186

Johnson, Lynda Bird, **1962:** 150n.

Johnson, Lyndon B., President, **1963:** 118n.
   See also Congress, letters to members — Presi-
     dent of the Senate; Vice President (Lyn-
     don B. Johnson).
   Medal of Freedom awards, presentation, **1963:**
     p. 899
   Proclamation — a period of mourning for John
     F. Kennedy, **1963:** p. 899

Johnson, Mrs. Lyndon B., **1961:** 78, 203; **1962:** 68;
   1963: 473

Johnson, Sherman E., **1963:** 238

Johnson, Repr. Thomas F., **1962:** 446

Johnson Act, **1963:** 405 [15], 407

Johnson Island, nuclear tests, **1963:** 328 [2]

Johnston, Logan T., **1961:** 354n.

Johnston, Sen. Olin D., **1961:** 26n.; **1962:** 241

Johnston, Mrs. Olin D., **1961:** 26n.

Johnston Island, nuclear tests, **1962:** 316 [9], 378
   [8], 503

Joint Chiefs of Staff, **1962:** 59 [4], 75 [16], 186, 226,
   378 [1, 19], 416, 422, 521; **1963:** 221, 312,
   318n., 354, 396
   Chairman (Gen. Lyman L. Lemnitzer), **1961:**
     260, 279n., 303, 415 [1]; **1962:** 20 [2, 14],
     75 [20], 139 [15], 226, 294, 295n.; 302 [16],
     316 [20]

Joint Chiefs of Staff — *continued*
   Chairman (Gen. Maxwell D. Taylor), **1962:** 423;
     1963: 35 [2], 399, 405 [16], 448 [3]
   News conference remarks on, **1961:** 15 [2], 258
     [3], 291 [15], 318 [9], 415 [4, 10]; **1963:** 320
     [2], 328 [2], 356 [17, 24]
   Term of office, limitation, question of, **1963:** 356
     [24]

Joint Commission on Mental Illness and Health,
   1962: 65

Joint Federal-State Committee on the Appalachian
   Region, **1963:** 127

Joint Intelligence Board, Chairman (John A.
   McCone), **1961:** 392

Joint statement on fair employment practices, **1962:**
   509

Joint statement on nuclear tests, U.S.-U.K., **1962:**
   41, 134

Joint statements with leaders of foreign govern-
   ments
   Afghanistan, King Mohammed Zaher, **1963:** 347
   Algeria, Prime Minister Ben Bella, **1962:** 466
   Argentina, President Frondizi, **1961:** 389
   Australia
     Deputy Prime Minister McEwen, **1962:** 88
     Prime Minister Menzies, **1961:** 51; **1962:** 251
   Austria, Chancellor Gorbach, **1962:** 169
   Bolivia, President Paz, **1963:** 432
   Brazil, President Goulart, **1962:** 126
   Cameroon, President Ahidjo, **1962:** 87
   Canada, Prime Minister Diefenbaker, **1961:** 45,
     193
   Canada, Prime Minister Pearson, **1963:** 179, 180
   Chile, President Alessandri Rodriguez, **1962:** 544
   China, Republic of, Vice President Chen, **1961:**
     309
   Congo, Republic of, President Youlou, **1961:** 236
   Cyprus, Archbishop Makarios, **1962:** 227
   Ecuador, President Arosemena Monroy, **1962:**
     303
   Ethiopia, Emperor Haile Selassie I, **1963:** 398
   Finland, President Kekkonen, **1961:** 424
   France, President de Gaulle, **1961:** 223
   Germany, Chancellor Adenauer, **1961:** 120, 481;
     1962: 508; **1963:** 262
     Foreign Minister von Brentano, **1961:** 41
   Ghana, President Nkrumah, **1961:** 74
   Greece, Prime Minister Caramanlis, **1961:** 135
   Honduras, President Villeda Morales, **1962:** 529
   India, Prime Minister Nehru, **1961:** 456
   India, President Radhakrishnan, **1963:** 219
   Indonesia, President Sukarno, **1961:** 146
   Iran, Shah Mohammad Reza Pahlavi, **1962:** 147
   Ireland, Prime Minister Lemass, **1963:** 418
   Italy
     Foreign Minister Piccioni, **1963:** 373
     Prime Minister Fanfani, **1961:** 242; **1963:** 20
     President Segni, **1963:** 292

Joint statements with leaders — *continued*
Ivory Coast, President Houphouet-Boigny, **1962:** 212
Japan, Prime Minister Ikeda, **1961:** 252
Korea, Chairman Park, **1961:** 468
Laos, Prince Souvanna Phouma, **1962:** 312
Laos, King Sri Savang Vatthana, **1963:** 81
Liberia, President Tubman, **1961:** 430
Libya, Crown Prince Hasan al-Rida al-Sanusi, **1962:** 471
Luxembourg, Grand Duchess Charlotte and Prince Jean, **1963:** 156
Mexico, President López Mateos, **1962:** 94, 273
Morocco, King Hassan II, **1963:** 116
New Zealand, Deputy Prime Minister Marshall, **1962:** 248
Prime Minister Holyoake, **1961:** 66
Nigeria, Prime Minister Balewa, 1961: 304
Norway, Prime Minister Gerhardsen, **1962:** 183
Pakistan, President Ayub Khan, **1961:** 283; **1962:** 403
Panamá, President Chiari, **1962:** 242
Peru, President Prado, **1961:** 376
Rwanda, President Kayibanda, **1962:** 388
Saudi Arabia
Crown Prince Faysal, **1962:** 429
King Saud, **1962:** 45
Somali Republic, Prime Minister Abdirascid Ali Scermarche, **1962:** 526
Soviet Union, Premier Khrushchev, **1961:** 225
Sudan, President Abboud, **1961:** 411
Tanganyika, Prime Minister Nyerere, **1961:** 288; **1963:** 304
Togo, President Olympio, **1962:** 105
Tunisia, President Bourguiba, **1961:** 173
United Kingdom
Foreign Secretary Home, **1962:** 419
Prime Minister Macmillan, **1961:** 97, 112, 230, 345, 357; **1962:** 42, 160, 348, 554; **1963:** 285
Venezuela, President Betancourt, **1961:** 510; **1963:** 73
Yugoslavia, Marshal Tito, **1963:** 421
Joint statement with President Hallstein, European Economic Community, **1961:** 189; **1962:** 144
Joint U.S.-Japan Committee on Trade and Economic Affairs, **1961:** 252, 444n., 455 [3]; **1962:** 531n.
Jones, Howard P., **1961:** 146
Jones, John Paul, **1961:** 232
Jones, Lewis Webster, **1961:** 479n.
Jones, Robert, **1963:** 319a note
Jones, Repr. Robert E., **1963:** 193, 194
Jones, Theodore A., **1963:** 49
Jones, Judge Warren L., **1962:** 420
Jones, William C., **1961:** 26n.
Jordan, assistance, **1963:** 169 [2]

Joseph P. Kennedy, Jr. Foundation, international awards, **1962:** 534
Joseph P. Kennedy, Jr., U.S.S., **1962:** 384
Journal American, **1963:** 405 [16]
Journeymen and Apprentices of the Plumbing and Pipe Fitting Industry, United Association of, **1962:** 247
Joyce, James, **1963:** 278
Juarez, Benito, **1961:** 78; **1962:** 264, 556
Judicial Conference of the United States, **1961:** 28, 121
Judiciary, Federal, **1962:** 8 [12]; **1963:** 44, 89 [8], 91, 166, 248.
See also Courts, Federal; Supreme Court.
Additional judgeships, **1961:** 28
Juliana, Queen, **1963:** 132
Junior Chamber of Commerce, **1962:** 47
Junior Red Cross, **1962:** 351
Junior Village, Washington, D.C., **1962:** 546 [24]; **1963:** 22
Jupiter missile, **1963:** 35 [18]
Justice, Department of, **1961:** 121; **1962:** 33, 93 (p. 237), 129, 139 [1, 4], 198 [1], 279 [16], 476; **1963:** 6, 31, 82, 89 [12], 107 [17], 120 [22], 135, 169 [1], 181, 248, 305 [20], 320 [6], 405 [15], 407, 448 [24]
See also Attorney General.
Antitrust Division, **1961:** 25 [21]
News conference remarks, **1961:** 92 [12], 119 [4, 11], 455 [7]
Justice, International Court of, **1963:** 366, 471
Juvenile delinquency, **1961:** 11, 15 [36], 182; **1962:** 7 (p. 7), 132, 220, 243 [4], 395; **1963:** 22, 30 (p. 65), 43, 64, 74, 230, 248, 351, 363, 423
Juvenile Delinquency Act of 1961, **1963:** 64, 423
Juvenile Delinquency and Youth Crime, Committee on, **1961:** 382
Juvenile Delinquency and Youth Crime, President's Committee on, **1962:** 220; **1963:** 64
Juvenile Delinquency and Youth Offenses Control Act, **1961:** 382; **1962:** 220n.

Kaidi, Ahmed, **1962:** 465n.
Kaiser, Edgar F., **1962:** 204, 476n.
Kambona, Oscar, **1963:** 300, 302
Kamchatka, **1963:** 27
Kamel, Mostafa, **1961:** 334 [9]
Kamen, Charles, **1961:** 334 [9]
Kan, Dr. Osamu, **1961:** 444
Kanga, Victor, **1962:** 85n.
Kanpur, India, **1961:** 460n.
Kansas, **1963:** 248ftn. (p. 486)
Gov. John Anderson, Jr., **1963:** 108
Kansas City, Mo., **1961:** 179n., 462n.; **1963:** 248ftn. (p. 486)

Karth, Repr. Joseph E., **1962:** 439

Kasavubu, Joseph, **1961:** 35 [1]; **1963:** 28

Kashmir, **1961:** 283; **1963:** 366
  Dispute, **1962:** 8 [14], 20 [3], 50 [10]
  India-Pakistan dispute, **1963:** 278, 349, 356 [25]
  United Nations operations, **1963:** 471

Kasongo, Maurice, **1961:** 487n.

Kastenmeier, Repr. Robert W., **1962:** 186

Katanga, **1961:** 368; **1962:** 302 [11], 340 [14], 352 [20]; **1963:** 28, 88

Katmandu, Nepal, **1963:** 158n.

Katzenbach, Nicholas de B. (Deputy Attorney General), **1962:** 180n.; **1963:** 171

Kaye, Danny, **1962:** 201, 527n.

Kayibanda, Grégoire, **1962:** 267, 388

Keane, Thomas, **1961:** 155

Kearsarge, U.S.S., **1962:** 427n.; **1963:** 190n.

Keating, Sen. Kenneth B., **1962:** 340 [6]; **1963:** 144 [12], 345

Kee, Repr. Elizabeth, **1962:** 414; **1963:** 249

Keenan, Joseph, **1961:** 40n.

Kefauver, Sen. Estes, **1961:** 119 [11]; **1962:** 93 (p. 239), 139 [9], 316 [1], 442; **1963:** 192, 194, 223

Kefauver-Harris drug control amendments, **1963:** 53

Keita, Mobido, visit of, **1961:** 359, 363, 364, 365

Kekkonen, Taneli K., **1961:** 422n.

Kekkonen, Urho K., **1961:** 488 [4]; **1962:** 52
  Visit of, **1961:** 421, 422, 424, 451

Kekkonen, Mme. Urho K., **1961:** 422

Keldsen, Irving, **1962:** 439

Keller, Charles Jr., **1963:** 49

Kelley, Claude B., **1961:** 65n.

Kelley, Nicholas, **1962;** 167

Kelly, Repr. Edna F., **1963:** 359n.

Kelly, Gene, **1963:** 24

Kelly, John V., **1963:** 275

Kelsey, Dr. Frances O., **1962:** 296, 316 [1, 4], 323

Kenin, Herman D., **1961:** 330n.

Kennan, George F., **1961:** 25 [13]; **1962:** 245 [9], 551 [15]; **1963:** 328 [21]

Kennedy, Caroline, **1961:** 73, 212; **1962:** 201, 205; **1963:** 172, 465 [6]

Kennedy, David, **1962:** 476n.

Kennedy, Edward M., **1962:** 20 [9], 89 [2], 115 [19], 198 [19], 259 [10], 340 [18], 352 [10], 395, 546 [19]; **1963:** 348, 427, 459 [25]

Kennedy, John F., **1962:** 483
  Assasination, **1963:** p. 890
  Cartoons on, **1963:** 172
  Center for Performing Arts, **1963:** 327n.
  Medal of Freedom, posthumous award, **1963:** p. 903
  Mourning for, proclamation, **1963:** p. 899

Kennedy, John F., personal reminiscences
  Candidacy in 1960 Presidential election, **1963:** 465 [4]
  Congressional service, **1963:** 162, 474
  82nd Airborne Division, **1961:** 419
  Election campaign (1956), **1963:** 223
  Friendship with Senator Smathers, **1962:** 77
  Football, **1961:** 496
  Naval experiences, **1961:** 232, 496
  Navy service, **1963:** 183
  Nurmi, Paavo, **1961:** 422
  Paris, wish for assignment to, **1961:** 218
  Political life, **1961:** 418
  Presidential campaign (1960), **1963:** 445
  Service in Congress, **1962:** 189; **1963:** 162, 474
  Service in Navy, **1963:** 183
  Study in London, **1962:** 180; **1963:** 171
  United Nations conference, San Francisco, **1961:** 501
  Visits abroad
    Cordova, Argentina, **1963:** 84
    Germany (1945), **1963:** 265, 270
    Ireland, **1963:** 415
    Paris, **1963:** 476
  Visit to Acapulco, Mexico, **1962:** 189
  Visit of Amintore Fanfani in 1956, **1961:** 239
  Visit to Klagenfurt, Austria, **1961:** 224
  Visits to London prior to World War II, **1961:** 227, 228

Kennedy, John F., President, Hugh Sidey, **1963:** 356 [7]

Kennedy, John F., speeches in presidential campaign, **1961:** 371n.

Kennedy, Mrs. John F., **1961:** 73, 78, 128n., 162, 165, 173, 181, 190, 192, 217, 218, 219, 224, 280, 327, 404n., 411, 421n., 431, 452n., 471, 507, 508, 509, 511, 512, 515, 516; **1962:** 36, 109, 150, 152 [5], 155n., 168, 178n., 180, 183, 184n., 189, 205, 206, 258, 262, 263, 270-272, 322n., 384, 402, 430, 490, 496, 505, 511, 515 [9], 527n., 528n., 546 [1], 556n.; **1963:** 25, 71, 72, 115, 116, 126n., 133, 137, 152, 156, 157, 171, 214, 457, 473, 475, 476, and p. 900
  News conference remarks on, **1961:** 15 [1], 71 [2], 222, 488 [5]

Kennedy, John F., Jr., **1961:** 15 [1]

Kennedy, Joseph P., **1962:** 179 [10], 384, 515 [9], 551 [23]; **1963:** 126, 348, 465

Kennedy, Mrs. Joseph P., **1962:** 384, 515 [9]; **1963:** 465

Kennedy, Joseph P., Jr., **1962:** 384; **1963:** 348, 476
  Foundation, international awards, **1962:** 534

Kennedy, Patrick, **1963:** 276n.

Kennedy, Patrick J., role in government of Boston, **1961:** 220

Kennedy, Robert F.
  See Attorney General.
Kennedy, Thomas, **1961:** 40n.
Kenosha, Wis., eviction of needy families, **1961:** 96
Kent, Carleton, **1961:** 35 [14]
Kentucky, **1963:** 135, 175 [2], 228, 241, 248ftn. (p.
      486), 378, 455, 463, 465
  Candiates for public office, **1962:** 431, 457, 458
  Democratic primary, **1963:** 120 [13]
  Food distribution to needy families, **1961:** 15 [3],
      17
  Gov. Bert T. Combs, **1962:** 431, 457, 458; **1963:**
      108, 458
  News conference remarks, **1962:** 115 [27], 410 [1]
  Unemployment, **1961:** 83 [18]
Kenya, **1962:** 18
Keppel, Francis, **1962:** 540; **1963:** 358
Kerner, Gov. Otto, **1961:** 155, 244, 454; **1962:** 58,
      481, 483; **1963:** 109, 422
Kerr, Clark, **1961:** 40n.; **1962:** 109n.; **1963:** 184
Kerr, Sen. Robert S., **1961:** 206, 441, 476n.; **1962:**
      449
Kerr-Mills Act, **1962:** 229 [13]; **1963:** 74
Key, V. O., **1961:** 403
Key West, Fla., **1961:** 97n.; **1962:** 160, 521, 553
  Discussions with Prime Minister Macmillan,
      1961: 112
Keys, Grant, **1962:** 480
Kharlamov, Mikhail, **1962:** 27 [4]
Khartoum, **1961:** 402n., 404
Kheel, Theodore, **1963:** 18
Khemisti, Mohammed, **1962:** 465n.
Khrushchev, Nikita S., **1961:** 155, 205, 209, 214, 215,
      226, 229, 231, 242, 302, 322, 340n., 365,
      387, 483; **1962:** 7 (p. 6), 41, 71, 74, 90, 160,
      174, 186, 395, 396, 414n., 440, 459, 483,
      485, 491n., 494, 500, 501, 507n., 549, 551
      [6, 13, 15, 17-19]; **1963:** 81, 110, 134, 168,
      232, 314, 316, 319a, 382, 426, 455
  Attendance at U.S. session, question of, **1961:** 8
      [5], 15 [6], 35 [5]
  Messages, **1961:** 2, 118, 132, 271, 522; **1962:** 42,
      48, 60, 62, 73, 96, 239, 435, 492, 493; **1963:**
      1, 27
  News conference remarks on, **1961:** 8 [5, 6, 8, 17,
      22, 24, 30], 15 [6], 25 [13], 35 [4, 5], 62
      [19], 71 [16], 83 [6, 10], 92 [4], 119 [5], 139
      [23], 222, 258 [4, 13, 16, 21], 291 [20], 318
      [4], 334 [11, 17], 488 [4]; **1962:** 27 [23], 50
      [2], 59 [1, 18], 75 [4, 14], 89 [1], 107 [1],
      115 [7], 179 [8], 245 [4, 8, 13], 259 [22],
      279 [17, 20], 302 [13], 340 [9], 352 [6], 378
      [15], 515 [1, 4, 6, 7, 12], 546 [3, 15, 17];
      1963: 35 [7, 24], 54 [5, 7, 10], 65 [19], 75
      [18], 120 [18], 144 [2, 3, 4, 7], 169 [9, 18],
      320 [8], 328 [8], 405 [3], 448 [18]

Khrushchev, Nikita S. — *continued*
  Vienna meeting, **1961:** 225
  Vienna meeting with (1961), 1962: 308, 551 [5,
      16, 18; **1963:** 65 [19], 79, 144 [3], 169 [9]
  Visit to U.S. in 1959, **1961:** 483
Khyber Pass, **1961:** 279
Kiernan, Thomas J., **1962:** 233n.
Kiesinger, Kurt-Georg, **1963:** 266
Kiev, **1962:** 233
Kilday, Paul J., **1961:** 434
Kilkenny, Minn., **1963:** 277
Killarney, W. Va., **1963:** 277
Killian, James R., **1963:** 405 [12]
Killian (James R.) Committee.
  See President's Foreign Intelligence Advisory
      Board.
Killingsworth, Charles C., **1962:** 298, 386
Killion, George L., **1962:** 476n.
Kilmer, Gordon B., **1962:** 231
Kimball, Adm. Dan, **1961:** 403; **1962:** 298n.
King, Rev. A. D., **1963:** 181
King, Repr. Cecil R., medical care bill.
  See King-Anderson medical care bill.
King, Gov. John W., **1963:** 108, 427
King, Martin Luther, **1962:** 279 [9], 302 [12], 378 [6]
King, Philip Gidley, **1962:** 383
King, Rufus, **1962:** 383
King-Anderson medical care bill, **1962:** 202, 210 [1,
      4, 8], 229 [13], 279 [2]; **1963:** 75 [6], 138
  See also Social security
King County, Wash., **1961:** 474
Kingry, Mary Ann, **1962:** 231
Kinkaid, Adm. Thomas C., **1963:** 203
Kings Point, N.Y., **1961:** 156
Kinsolving, Arthur L., **1963:** 455
Kinzua Dam project, opposition by Seneca Nation,
      1961: 71 [15], 320
Kiphuth, Robert J., **1963:** p. 901.
Kirk, Dr. Samuel A., **1962:** 534n.; **1963:** 447
Kirkpatrick, Rear Adm. Charles L., **1963:** 321
Kirtland Air Force Base, N. Mex., **1962:** 538
Kirwan, Repr. Michael J., **1961:** 474
Kitona, Congo, **1961:** 519
Kittredge, George Lyman, **1963:** 247, 440
Kitty Hawk, U.S.S., **1963:** 225, 228
Klagenfurt, Austria, **1961:** 224
Kluczynski, Repr. John C., **1962:** 483
Kluttz, Jerry, **1963:** 24
Klutznick, Philip, **1961:** 358n.; **1963:** 139
Knebel, Fletcher, **1961:** 83 [22]
Knights of Labor,, **1963:** 85
Knighton, William H. Y., Jr., **1962:** 158
Knous, Robert L., **1962:** 336
Knoxville, Tenn. interracial visits in, **1963:** 169 [14]
Koelbel, Herbert, **1963:** 271
Kohler, Foy D., (U.S. Ambassador to Soviet
      Union), **1962:** 279 [5], 302 [13]; **1963:** 144
      [4], 169 [9], 459 [2]

Koht, Paul, **1962:** 161n.; **1963:** 133
Koirala, Matrika Prasad, **1963:** 296
Kolwezi, **1963:** 28
Komar torpedo boats, Cuban, attack on U.S.,
        question of, **1963:** 54 [12]
Kong Le, Gen., **1963:** 134 [2], 144 [5]
Korea, **1961:** 26, 232, 309; **1962:** 70, 77, 226, 352
        [11], 531, 549 [9, 10], 551 [22]; **1963:** 12 (p.
        19), 72, 134 [1], 183, 194, 221, 366, 378,
        394, 477
    Anniversary of revolution, **1961:** 131
    Assistance, **1961:** 468; **1963:** 72, 328 [1], 338
    Communist aggression, **1963:** 118
    Defense of, **1963:** 194
    Military government in, **1963:** 107 [5], 120 [4]
    News conference remarks, **1963:** 107 [5, 7], 120
        [4], 320 [3, 11], 328 [1]
    Park, Chung Hee, **1961:** 468
    United Nations operations, **1963:** 471
    U.S. Ambassador Samuel D. Berger, **1963:** 120
        [16]
Korea, North, **1961:** 138; **1962:** 549 [10]
Korean-type war waged by Communists, **1961:** 231,
        244
Korean War, **1961:** 212, 222 [4], 387, 512; **1962:** 24,
        25, 75 [19], 139 [16], 258, 330, 398, 402,
        407, 420, 551 [15]; **1963:** 34, 92, 168, 175,
        183, 227, 228, 325, 455, 457, 465, 472
Korth, Fred (Secretary of the Navy), **1962:** 294,
        309, 323n.; **1963:** 318, 328 [20], 448 [6, 22],
        459 [16]
Kosaka, Zentaro, **1961:** 455 [3]
Kosciusko, Thaddeus, **1962:** 461
Kossuth, Louis, **1963:** 266
Koterba, Edward V., **1961:** 258 [1]
Kowal, Chester, **1962:** 461n.
Kramer, Ferdinand, **1963:** 49
Kraus, Dr. Hans, **1961:** 496
Kraus-Weber survey on youth fitness, **1962:** 291
Kreisky, Bruno, **1962:** 168n., 169
Krim, Arthur B., **1962:** 201; **1963:** 204
Krock, Arthur, **1963:** 134 [6], 356 [7]
Krol, Archbishop John, **1962:** 278
Kubitschek de Oliveira, Juscelino, **1961:** 13
Kublai Khan, **1961:** 435
Kuchel, Sen. Thomas H., **1962:** 337; **1963:** 387
Kuznetsov, V. V., **1963:** 27
Kwajalein Island, **1962:** 342
Kyprianou, Spyros, **1962:** 227

Labaree, Leonard W., **1963:** 245
Labor, **1961:** 400; **1962:** 13 (p. 31), 14, 16 (p. 44), 22,
        101, 170, 200, 234, 242, 280, 328, 358, 359;
        1963: 21 (p. 37), 30 (pp. 68, 70), 34, 94,
        103, 110, 141, 175, 177, 185, 226, 228, 230,
        305 [20], 306, 423, 452, 462, 465, 466
    Child, **1963:** 85
    Civil rights responsibilities, **1963:** 230
    Migratory, **1963:** 74, 130

Labor — *continued*
    Mobility, **1963:** 77
    News conference remarks, **1962:** 20 [19], 89 [5],
        245 [7], 279 [3], 410 [2], 546 [20]
    Responsibility for price stability, **1961:** 497
    Statistics, **1963:** 405 [11]
    Trade union movement, **1962:** 324, 509; **1963:** 85,
        104, 139, 162, 163, 268, 270, 339
        Latin America, **1963:** 163
Labor, agriculture, and industry,meeting of lead-
        ers, **1961:** 8 [18]
Labor, Department of, **1961:** 152; **1962:** 13 (p. 31),
        50 [3], 65, 101, 129, 352 [1], 358, 405;
        1963: 30 (p. 70), 50, 74, 92, 110, 119, 125,
        240, 248, 423
    Additional Assistant Secretary, proposed, **1961:**
        166
    Federal contracts in depressed areas, **1961:** 17
    Fiftieth anniversary, **1963:** 85
    Status of women study, **1961:** 504
    Vocational education program, study, **1961:** 46
Labor, Secretary of (Arthur J. Goldberg), **1961:** 22,
        24, 40, 50, 68, 87, 116, 182, 194, 274, 323,
        330, 400, 427, 428, 470, 497, 499; **1962:**
        6n., 38, 43n., 66, 136, 174, 220, 253, 255,
        324
    Employment statistics review, **1961:** 458n.
    Government action on mental health, **1961:** 492
    Letters, **1962:** 215, 345, 393
    Memorandum, **1962:** 221
    News conference remarks on, **1961:** 35 [3], 83
        [12], 171 [6], 258 [11]; **1962:** 8 [7], 27 [18],
        40 [17, 23], 59 [19], 75 [5, 21], 89 [19], 139
        [7], 179 [2, 7], 198 [5], 245 [1], 302 [15],
        340 [17]
    Reports, **1962:** 215, 345
    Resignation, **1962:** 393
Labor, Secretary of (W. Willard Wirtz), **1962:** 360,
        378 [7], 405, 509, 516; **1963:** 18, 30 (p. 68),
        69, 74, 76n., 85, 92, 119, 130, 141, 162,
        163n., 179, 220, 244, 248, 298, 299, 310,
        337, 361, 393, 414
    News conference remarks, **1963:** 75 [11], 305 [5]
        405 [11]
Labor, Secretary of, employee-management rela-
        tions functions, **1961:** 494
Labor contracts
    Automobile industry, **1962:** 174
    Electricians, **1962:** 20 [19]
    Steel industry, **1962:** 40 [22], 115 [4, 15], 139 [1, 4,
        9, 11]
    Trans World Airlines, **1962:** 516
Labor Day, **1963:** 339, 340
    Message to youth, **1962:** 360
    Statement, **1961:** 332; **1962:** 359
Labor disputes, **1961:** 455 [17]; **1962:** 174, 230, 302
        [15]; **1963:** 92, 363
    See also Collective Bargaining.

Labor disputes — *continued*
  Aerospace industry, **1962:** 244, 298, 369, 376, 378
    [20], 390, 410 [6]; **1963:** 39
  Air carriers, **1961:** 50
  Airlines, **1962:** 204, 245 [1], 253, 256, 516; **1963:**
    298
  Automobile industry, **1961:** 334 [12], 350
  Compulsory arbitration, question of, **1963:** 75
    [13]
  Construction industry, **1962:** 179 [7], 302 [15]
  Emergency measures in States, **1963:** 120 [9]
  Government employees, strikes prohibited, **1961:**
    494
  Legislative proposal re, **1961:** 269
  Maritime industry, **1962:** 21, 139 [3], 421, 428;
    1963: 18, 54 [9], 411
  Maritime strike, **1961:** 256, 258 [11], 269, 270
  Metropolitan Opera Association orchestra, **1961:**
    330
  Military aircraft industry, **1962:** 247; **1963:** 39
  Missile workers, Huntsville, Ala., **1962:** 340 [17]
  Newspaper strikes, **1962:** 179 [2]; **1963:** 35 [11],
    54 [6], 75 [2, 13], 107 [16], 120 [9]
  Railroads, **1962:** 66, 198 [5], 378 [7], 386; **1963:**
    95, 120 [17], 184, 244, 298, 299, 305 [5],
    310, 328 [14], 337, 414
  Steel industry, **1962:** 75 [1, 17], 121, 410 [6]; **1963:**
    134
Labor force, women in, **1963:** 233
Labor-management conference, **1961:** 83 [20]
Labor-management panel, **1961:** 171 [6]
Labor-Management Panel, National, **1963:** 206
Labor-Management Policy, President's Advisory
    Committee on, **1961:** 17, 23, 33, 87, 205,
    499; **1962:** 203n., 515 [17]; **1963:** 30 (p. 67),
    206, 299, 310
  Establishment, **1961:** 40
  Reports, **1962:** 6, 164
Labor-management relations, **1961:** 15 [16], 17, 33,
    40, 121, 205; **1962:** 40 [22], 75 [1, 17], 129
    203, 210 [13], 244, 245 [2], 405, 551 [12];
    1963: 75 [2, 13], 77 [4], 92, 131, 134 [3], 163,
    206, 233, 244, 310, 402, 446, 448 [7, 16]
  See also Management.
Labor-Management Relations Act.
  See Taft-Hartley Act.
Labor Ministers, Inter-American Conference of,
    message, **1963:** 163
Labor movement, **1961:** 499
Labor Organizations, **1962:** 54, 101; **1963:** 85, 120
    [9], 134 [3], 187, 206, 411
  AFL-CIO, **1961:** 169, 414, 499; **1962:** 47, 203,
    247, 279 [3], 324, 405; **1963:** 39, 75 [11,
    14], 77, 85, 162, 174, 268, 362, 462
  Airlines Pilots Association, **1961:** 50; **1962:** 204,
    245 [1], 516
  Amalgamated Clothing Workers, **1962:** 198 [15]
  American Federation of Musicians, **1961:** 330

Labor organizations — *continued*
  Automobile, Aerospace and Agriculture -
    Implement Workers of America, **1963:** 39
  Codes of ethical practice **1961:** 25 [21]
  Communism in, **1963:** 162, 268
  Communications Workers of America, **1962:** 47
  Costa Rica, **1963:** 104
  Economic boycotts, **1961:** 71 [20]
  Fair employment practices program, **1962:** 509
  Flight Engineers International Association, **1961:**
    50; **1962:** 245 [1], 253, 256, 516
  Government employees, **1962:** 154, 215n.
  International Association of Machinists, **1962:**
    247, 298, 376, 390, 410 [6]
  International Brotherhood of Electrical
    Workers, **1962:** 247
  International Ladies Garment Workers Union,
    1962: 200
  International Longshoremen's Association, **1962:**
    421
  International Organization of Masters, Mates
    and Pilots, **1962:** 21
  International Union of Operating Engineers,
    1962: 247
  Knights of Labor, **1963:** 85
  Locomotive Engineers, Brotherhood of, **1963:**
    310
  Locomotive Firemen and Enginemen, Brother-
    hood of, **1963:** 310
  Longshoremen's Association, International,
    1963: 18
  Machinists, International Association of, **1963:**
    39, 162
  Meat Cutters and Butcher Workmen of North
    America, Amalgamated, **1963:** 187
  Mine, Mill and Smelter Workers, **1963:** 202 [13]
  National Maritime Engineers Beneficial
    Association, **1962:** 21
  Newly emerging nations, **1962:** 174
  Order of Railroad Telegraphers, **1962:** 386
  Railroad Trainmen, Brotherhood of, **1963:** 310
  Railway Conductors and Brakemen, Order of,
    1963: 310
  Railway and Steamship Clerks, Brotherhood of,
    1963: 95n., 298
  Steelworkers Union, United, **1963:** 131, 466
  Switchmen's Union of North America, **1963:** 310
  Typographical Union, International, **1963:** 75
    [2, 13], 107 [16]
  United Aerospace Workers, **1962:** 390
  United Association of Journeymen and Appren-
    tices of the Plumbing and Pipe Fitting
    Industry, **1962:** 247
  United Automobile Workers, **1961:** 334 [12], 350;
    1962: 174, 179 [9], 298
  United Brotherhood of Carpenters and Joiners
    of America, **1962:** 247

Labor organizations — *continued*
United Steelworkers of America, **1961:** 274, 366;
1962: 20 [19], 75 [1], 115 [4], 121, 139 [1,
9, 11], 152 [12, 14], 162, 385
Welders, United International Union of, **1963:** 39
Labor Organizations, International, **1963:** 305 [21],
309
Labor Party, British, 1963: 120 [19]
Labor Relations Board, National, **1961:** 121; **1963:**
82
Reorganization Plan, **1961:** 200
Labor Statistics, Bureau of, **1962:** 55, 93 (p. 238),
139 [1]; **1963:** 21 (p. 43), 148
Labor surplus areas.
See Depressed areas.
Laboratories, nuclear research, **1963:** 328 [2]
Laborers and mechanics employed by Government,
workweek, **1962:** 327
Labouisse, Henry R., **1961:** 119 [2], 288
Lackey, Dent, **1962:** 460
La Esperanza Sugar Mill, Bolivia, loan, **1961:** 184
La Farge, Oliver, **1961:** 371n., **1963:** 113
Lafayette, Marquis de, **1962:** 184; **1963:** 126, 294
Lafayette College, **1962:** 416
Lafayette Park, Washington, D.C., **1962:** 27 [21],
512
La Flore, ship model, gift to President, **1963:** 112
Lagos, Nigeria, **1961:** 430
Lagos, Nigeria, meeting of African leaders, **1962:**
103, 105, 212
Lake Mead, **1963:** 390
Lake Michigan, **1962:** 279 [14]; **1963:** 109
Lake Superior, **1963:** 377, 378
Lake Tahoe, **1963:** 390
Laking, G. R., **1962:** 248
Lalla Nezha, Princess, **1963:** 115
Lamar, Lucius, **1962:** 420
La Morita resettlement project, Venezuela, **1961:**
509
Lancaster, Burt, **1962:** 534
Land, Edwin H., **1963:** p. 901
Land Conservation Commission, propose, **1962:**
128
Land-Grant College Act, **1962:** 540; **1963:** 228, 381,
445, 469
Land-grant colleges, **1961:** 71 [17], 462, 473; **1962:**
37, 109, 166, 197, 202, 540; **1963:** 43, 82,
92, 118, 226, 279, 469
Land-Grant Colleges and State University,
Association of, **1961:** 462
Land Management, Bureau of, **1961:** 17
Land reforms, **1963:** 326, 468
Land reserves, urban, **1961:** 76
Land-use program, **1963:** 21 (p. 36)
Land and Water Conservation Fund, **1963:** 63
Landis, James M., **1961:** 25 [9]
Landon, Alfred, **1962:** 199

Lands, public **1962:** 69; **1963:** 209, 279
Acquisition program, **1963:** 63
Conservation, **1963:** 45
Conservation fund proposed, **1962:** 69, 128, 336
Federal surplus lands, transfer to States, **1962:**
195
Laws, revision, **1963:** 37
Lands, public domain, **1961:** 94
Langer, William L., **1961:** 168n.
Languages, teaching of, **1963:** 43
Lankford, Repr. Richard E., **1962:** 446
Lansing, Robert, **1962:** 512
Laos, **1961:** 11, 138, 146, 205, 244, 387, 483; **1962:**
7 (p. 12), 226, 278, 323, 346, 349, 395, 396;
1963: 12 (p. 11), 88, 227, 238, 285, 316,
382, 383, 390, 459 [6], 476, 477
Agreement on, **1962:** 308, 312, 316 [7], 419; **1963:**
78, 79, 81, 134 [2], 144 [3, 5, 16], 169 [9],
285
Statement, **1962:** 301
Arms for, **1961:** 83 [11], 92 [1], 119 [10], 171 [8]
Assistance, **1961:** 92 [6, 15], 318 [15]; **1963:** 78,
81, 202 [10]
Cease-fire, **1962:** 50 [22], 59 [4], 179 [6], 198 [4,
20]
Cease-fire, question of, **1961:** 92 [1, 3], 97, 119 [10],
132, 139 [9], 258 [20]
Coalition government, **1962:** 8 [9], 115 [8], 198 [4],
229 [22], 239, 259 [22], 301; **1963:** 81, 144 [5]
Communist aggression, **1962:** 50 [22], 192, 198 [4,
20]; **1963:** 118, 144 [2, 3, 5, 16], 447
Communist threat to, **1961:** 92 [1, 3, 6]
Geneva conference on, **1961:** 222 [6], 258 [20],
415 [6]; **1962:** 179 [6, 16], 239, 251, 259
[22], 279 [5], 301, 308, 312, 316 [7], 352
[16]; **1963:** 78, 79, 81, 134 [2], 144 [3, 5,
16], 169 [9], 285
International control commission, **1961:** 8 [29],
25 [26], 71 [11], 171 [8], 193, 231, 258 [20],
1962: 316 [7]; **1963:** 144 [2], 169 [9]
Joint statements, **1962:** 160, 419
Joint statements with foreign leaders re, **1961:** 51,
66, 97, 112, 193, 225, 230, 309, 456
King Savang Vatthana, **1961:** 51, 66; **1962:** 50
[22], 308; **1963:** 78, 79, 81
Kong Le, Gen., **1963:** 134 [2], 144 [5]
News conference remarks, **1961:** 8 [29], 15 [14,
15, 25 [13, 26], 71 [11], 83 [11], 92 [1, 3, 6,
9, 13, 15], 119 [10], 139 [9], 171 [8], 222 [6],
258 [20], 318 [15], 415 [6]; **1962:** 8 [9], 27
[8, 17, 23], 40 [14], 50 [9, 22], 59 [4], 115
[8], 179 [6, 8, 16], 198 [4, 20], 210 [4, 11],
229 [22], 245 [8, 13], 259 [22], 279 [5], 316
[7, 17], 352 [16]; **1963:** 75 [18], 144 [3, 5,
16], 169 [9, 11], 202 [10], 320 [2]
Pathet Lao, **1961:** 92 [1]; **1963:** 134 [2], 144 [5],
169 [9]
Phoumi Nosavan, **1963:** 144 [5]

Laos — *continued*
  Plaine des Jarres, **1963:** 134 [2], 144 [5]
  Prince Souvanna Phouma, **1961:** 83 [11]; **1962:**
    50 [22], 115 [8], 239, 308, 312; **1963:** 78,
    81, 134 [2], 144 [5]
  Quinim Pholsena, **1962:** 308n.
  Soviet control, degree of, **1963:** 144 [5]
  United Nations operations, **1963:** 366
  U.S. Ambassador Winthrop G. Brown, **1961:** 15
    [15]
  U.S. Ambassador Leonard Unger, **1963:** 120 [16]
  U.S.-Soviet talks on, **1963:** 144 [2, 5]
Laramie, Wyo., **1963:** 381
Larkin, Felix E., **1962:** 412n.
LaRoche, Chester J., **1961:** 496n.
Larson, Leonard W., **1962:** 222
Lasky, Victor, *JFK, the Man and the Myth,* **1963:**
    356 [7]
Las Vegas, Nev., **1962:** 398, 443; **1963:** 390
  Mayor Oran Gragson, **1963:** 390
Latin America, **1961:** 13, 34, 57, 155, 189, 220, 275,
    476, 483; **1962:** 15, 22, 70, 74, 77, 186,
    216, 226, 250, 254, 276, 299, 300, 335, 389,
    395, 400, 449, 453, 461, 499, 513, 528, 531,
    541-543, 551 [17, 21]; **1963:** 12 (p. 15), 16,
    98, 137, 162, 171, 256, 266, 271, 277, 308,
    311, 330, 334, 338, 378, 381, 382, 383, 390,
    424, 428, 432, 445, 455, 468, 476
  See also American Republics, Inter-American;
    Organization of American States; West-
    ern Hemisphere; *specific countries.*
  Agricultural leaders in U.S., **1963:** 404
  Air Force Chiefs of Staff, remarks, **1963:** 168
  Alliance for Progress.
    See main heading.
  Assistance, **1962:** 3, 40 [14], 77, 89 [4], 177, 245,
    [12], 279 [1], 314, 378 [4]; **1963:** 12 (p. 17),
    21 (p. 35), 72, 100, 107 [1, 22], 118, 120
    [12], 124, 146, 320 [14], 338, 342, 431, 462,
    477, 478
  Assistance and development, **1961:** 1, 11, 15, [34],
    78, 81, 90, 102, 119 [20], 313, 324, 376, 491
  Communist activity, **1961:** 1, 8 [13], 11, 81, 138,
    193, 205, 373, 499
  Communist expansion, **1962:** 7 (p. 12), 8 [10], 20
    [22], 27 [2, 6]
  Communism in, **1963:** 65 [10, 14], 89 [10, 22], 104,
    107 [1, 7], 112, 118, 120 [21], 459 [25], 476
  Cuban relations with, **1961:** 132
  Cuban subversion in, 1963: 65 [14], 107 [1, 7]
    144 [17]
  Cultural exchange with U.S., **1961:** 78
  Defense, **1963:** 89 [10], 99, 102, 144 [17]
  Democracy in, **1963:** 120 [12]
  Development programs, **1963:** 107 [22], 118
  Dictatorships, **1963:** 405 [7]
  Diplomatic corps, reception for, **1961:** 71 [2], 78

Latin America — *continued*
  Economic and social development, **1961:** 78, 81,
    83 [13], 149, 222, 318 [24], 515; **1962:** 83,
    86, 170, 245 [12], 264, 265, 544, 549 [6];
    1963: 12 (p. 17), 54 [10], 72, 103, 105, 107
    [1, 7, 22], 118, 120 [12], 219, 291, 319, 320
    [14], 323, 326, 333, 429, 459 [22], 464
  Economic community, **1963:** 107 [1], 120 [12]
  Exchange students, **1963:** 65 [14], 140
  Exchange teachers from, **1962:** 341
  Exports, **1962:** 258, 273, 418
  Food for peace, **1961:** 78, 102
    Mission, **1961:** 11, 15 [34]
  Food for peace program, **1962:** 7 (p. 12), 13
    (p. 29)
  Foreign investment in, **1962:** 177, 410 [3]
  Free trade area, **1962:** 126; **1963:** 118
  Good Neighbor Policy, **1962:** 86, 264; **1963:** 72
  Highways, **1963:** 118, 164
  Joint statements, **1962:** 160, 544
  Labor ministers conference, **1963:** 163
  Labor Movement, **1962:** 546 [20], **1963:** 162, 268
  Land reforms, **1963:** 118
  Manpower resources, **1963:** 72
  Military assistance and defense support, **1963:**
    464
  Natural resources, **1963:** 72
  News conference remarks, **1961:** 8 [13], 15 [34],
    25 [14, 23, 24], 35 [2, 11], 71 [2], 83 [13],
    92 [7], 119 [20], 222, 258 [17], 291 [3], 318
    [24], 334 [16]; **1962:** 8 [8, 10], 20 [22], 27
    [2, 6, 15], 40 [14], 89 [4], 198 [9], 245 [12],
    259 [17], 279 [1, 6], 302 [9], 352 [11], 378
    [1, 4, 16], 410 [3], 515 [15], 546 [18, 20];
    1963: 35 [17], 54 [10], 75 [18], 89 [10], 107
    [1, 3, 7, 17, 21, 22], 120 [12, 15, 16, 19, 21],
    144 [17], 260 [18], 320 [14], 405 [7], 459 [6,
    22]
  Nuclear threat to, **1962:** 485, 486, 491
  Nuclear weapons ban, proposed, **1962:** 515 [15]
  Peace Corps projects, **1962:** 325; **1963:** 74, 120
    [15], 294
  Punta del Este conference.
    See main heading, Punta del Este conference.
  Students, **1962:** 310, 324, 496; **1963:** 104
  Tax reforms, **1963:** 118
  Technological training, **1963:** 163
  Trade, **1962:** 22; **1963:** 35 [17], 77, 118
    With Europe, **1962:** 7 (p. 15), 86, 126, 144, 279
      [6], 302 [9], 378 [4]
  U.N. Economic Commission, **1961:** 122, 491
  U.S. broadcasts to, **1962:** 7 (p. 12), 532
  U.S. communications with, **1962:** 551 [14]
  U.S. educational-information-propaganda
    program, **1961:** 205, 276
  U.S. Foreign Service officers in, **1963:** 120 [16]
  U.S. relations with, **1963:** 120 [19]
  Visit to, question of, **1963:** 107 [3]
  Voice of America broadcasts to, **1963:** 326n., 477

[*References are to items except as otherwise indicated*]

Latin America, Economic Commission for, **1962:** 86

Latin America, President's Task Force on, **1961:** 15 [34], 25 [23], 258 [17], 276

Latin American Citizens, League of United, **1963:** 473

Laughlin, Donald M., **1962:** 481

Launch Operations Center, Cape Canaveral, Fla., **1962:** 370

Laundry workers, exclusion from minimum wage bill, **1961:** 171 [20], 251

Lausche, Sen. Frank J., **1962:** 3, 396, 432, 480; **1963:** 202 [14]

Lavoisier, Antoine Laurent, **1961:** 413

Law, international, **1962:** 498, 515 [13]

Lawford, Peter, **1962:** 201, 233

Lawrence, David, **1962:** 36

Lawrence, Gov. David L., **1961:** 3, 179; **1962:** 89 [13], 278, 394, 395, 452-455; **1963:** 49, 445

Lawrence, William, **1962:** 459, 551

Lawrence, William H., **1961:** 291 [9]

Lead imports from South Africa, **1963:** 202 [13]

League of Nations, **1963:** 101, 319a, 394, 395

League for Peace, Women's, **1962:** 152 [15]

League of United Latin American Citizens, **1963:** 473

League of Women Voters, **1962:** 156

Leavenworth, Kans., **1963:** 183

Lebanon, **1962:** 339; **1963:** 455

Leber, Georg, **1963:** 268

Lee, Glenn, **1963:** 384

Lee, John M., **1963:** 36

Lee, Peggy, **1962:** 201

Lee, Richard C., **1962:** 473; **1963:** 230, 423

Lee, Gen. Robert E., **1961:** 162; **1963:** 278

Lee, William A., **1963:** 110

Leedom, Boyd, **1962:** 68n.

Lefevre, Theo, **1961:** 174

Legal counsel, right to, **1963:** 12 (p. 14)

Leger, Alexis, **1962:** 161n.

Legion of Merit, award to Japanese officer, **1962:** 139 [15]

Legislation, statements upon approval
  Aeronautics and Space Act, amendment, **1961:** 147
  Agriculture Act, **1961:** 316
  Area Redevelopment Act, **1961:** 158
  Atomic Energy Commission authorization bill, **1962:** 408
  Brick and tile industry, income, **1961:** 391
  Cape Cod National Seashore Park, **1961:** 315
  Chilean reconstruction, **1961:** 208
  Communications Satellite Act, **1962:** 355
  Community Health Services and Facilities, **1961:** 406
  Delaware River and Bay Authority, **1962:** 391
  Direct Courts, jurisdiction in suits against Government officials, **1962:** 434

Legislation — *continued*
  Drug reform bill, **1962:** 442
  Educational Television Act, **1962:** 166
  Eisenhower, Dwight D., restoration of military rank, **1961:** 88
  Eleanor Roosevelt Foundation, **1963:** 139
  Equal Pay Act of 1963, **1963:** 233
  Federal Airport Act, extension, **1961:** 374
  Federal Credit Union Act, **1963:** 417
  Federal Water Pollution Control Act Amendments, **1961:** 294
  Feed grains, emergency program, **1961:** 89
  Feed grains bill, **1963:** 197
  Food and Agriculture Act, **1962:** 413
  Foreign Assistance Act, **1962:** 314
  Foreign Assistance Act of 1961, **1961:** 346
  Frederick Douglass Home, incorporation into National Capital Park System, **1962:** 362
  Fryingpan-Arkansas Reclamation Project, **1962:** 332
  General Motors Corp., distribution of shares, **1962:** 33
  Health Professions Educational Assistance Act of 1963, **1963:** 374
  Highway Act of 1961, **1961:** 261
  Housing Act of 1961, **1961:** 264
  Inter-American cooperation, **1961:** 208
  Judgeships, additional, **1961:** 195
  Juvenile Delinquency and Youth Offenses Control Act, **1961:** 382
  Mann Creek Federal Redamation Project, **1962:** 333
  Manpower Development and Training Act, **1962:** 91
  Maternal and Child Health and Mental Retardation Planning Bill, **1963:** 434
  Mental retardation facilities and community health centers, construction, **1963:** 447
  Mexican farm workers, recruitment, **1961:** 400
  Migration and Refugee Assistance Act, **1962:** 261
  Minimum wage, **1961:** 169
  Mutual Educational and Cultural Exchange Act, **1961:** 379
  National Cultural Center Act, amendment, **1963:** 327
  National Defense Education Act, extension, **1961:** 398
  National Institute of Child Health and Human Development, establishment, **1962:** 470
  Navajo Irrigation Project, **1962:** 240
  Office of Emergency Planning, **1961:** 386
  Outdoor Recreation Bill, **1963:** 209
  Pacific Islands Trust Territory, administration, **1962:** 297
  Padre Island National Seashore, **1962:** 417
  Peace Corps Act, **1961:** 380
  Philippines war damage bill, **1962:** 315
  Point Reyes, National Seashore, **1962:** 377

[References are to items except as otherwise indicated]

Legislation — *continued*
Postal Service and Federal Employees Salary
Act, **1962:** 447
Princess Anne County School Board, Virginia,
relief of, **1961:** 369
Public Welfare Amendments Act, **1962:** 306
Public Works Acceleration Act, **1962:** 380
Railroads
Prevention of shutdown, **1963:** 337
Railroad Retirement Act, amendment, **1961:** 384
Retirement and unemployment insurance
systems, **1963:** 402
Rayburn (Sam) commemorative medal, **1962:**
409
Reclamation projects, **1963:** 41
Revenue Act, **1962:** 468
Saline water conversion program, **1961:** 381
San Juan-Chama Reclamation Project, **1962:** 240
Shipping Act, amendments, **1961:** 370, 401
Social Security Amendments of 1961, **1961:** 263
Soil Conservation and Domestic Allotment Act,
1962: 425
Space program, expansion, **1961:** 296
Student loans, elimination of anti-Communist
affidavit, **1962:** 469
Tariff revision, **1962:** 214
Trade Expansion Act, **1962:** 449
Unemployment Compensation Act, Temporary
Extended, **1961:** 93
Uniformed services pay raise bill, **1963:** 396
United Nations loan bill, **1962:** 424
U.S. Arms Control and Disarmament Agency,
1961: 388
Veterans disability compensation, **1962:** 367
Welfare and Pension Plans Disclosure Act,
amendments, **1962:** 101
Woodrow Wilson Memorial Commission, **1961:**
399
Work Hours Act, **1962:** 327
World Food Congress, meeting in U.S., **1962:**
478
Legislation, Vetoes and Memorandums of
Disapproval.
See Veto Messages and Memorandums of
Disapproval.
Legislative branch, **1963:** 44, 82, 94, 166, 232, 310,
319a, 419, 448 [17]
Legislative program, **1962:** 7 (p. 5), 205, 346, 385,
393, 551 [9,11]; **1963:** 12 (p. 12), 21 (p.
34), 23, 34, 43, 45, 50, 74, 110, 118, 187,
228, 230
Campaign remarks, **1962:** 394-396, 414, 431, 432,
436-439, 446, 451-456, 458, 472-474, 480,
481, 483
Measures approved, comment on, **1961:** 499

Legislative program — *continued*
News conference remarks, **1961:** 25 [12], 71 [12],
83 [14], 119 [14, 22], 139 [16], 415 [12],
455 [7], 488 [16]; **1962:** 75 [18], 107 [19],
152 [9], 229 [7], 245 [9], 259 [8, 12, 16],
302 [4], 316 [13], 340 [2], 378 [21]; **1963:**
35 [14], 75 [1, 6, 7, 14], 89 [1, 7], 107 [9,
21, 24], 120 [8, 21], 144 [15], 305 [4], 328
[7]
Public attitude towards, **1963:** 144 [15]
Lehman, Herbert H., **1963:** p. 901
Leidesdorf, Samuel D., **1963:** 455n.
Leighty, G.E., **1962:** 386n.; **1963:** 299n.
Leimena, Johannes, **1961:** 146
Lejeune, Dr. Jerome, **1962:** 534n.
Lemass, Sean, **1963:** 278, 281, 415, 416, 418
LeMay, Gen. Curtis E., **1961:** 260, 265, 455 [4], 486;
1962: 172, 294, 423; **1963:** 89 [9], 168, 221,
312
Lemnitzer, Gen. Lyman L., **1961:** 260, 279n., 303,
415[1]; **1962:** 226, 294, 295n., 423; **1963:**
356 [17]
Appointment as NATO, Supreme Commander,
1962: 302 [16]
Distinguished Service Medal, **1962:** 422
News conference remarks on, **1962:** 20 [2, 14], 75
[20], 139 [15], 302 [16], 316 [20]
Lend-lease, **1961:** 11
Lending institutions, tax provisions, **1961:** 136
L'Enfant, Pierre Charles, **1961:** 219; **1962:** 221n.
Lengede, Germany, **1963:** 454
Lenin, Nikolai, **1961:** 483
Lennon, Francis X., **1962:** 472
Lenroot, Katharine F., **1962:** 132
Leone, Giovanni, **1963:** 290-293
Leonidas, **1961:** 162, 418; **1962:** 349
Leopoldville, Congo, **1963:** 256
See also Congo, Republic of the (Leopoldville).
Parvin Foundation awards, **1961:** 487
Lerner, Alan Jay, **1963:** 204
Lesinski, Repr. John, **1962:** 433, 436
Less developed countries and new nations, **1961:** 1,
57, 129, 135, 146, 192, 207, 214, 220, 231,
254, 275, 277, 285, 299, 313, 343, 346, 389,
411, 497; **1962:** 7 (p. 10), 16 (p. 47),
35, 74, 303, 449; **1963:** 12 (pp. 16, 17)
See also specific countries.
Assistance, **1962:** 7 (pp. 12, 13), 13 (p. 29), 25, 65,
75 [10], 83, 109, 183, 245 [5], 279 [1, 6],
358, 392, 499, 549; **1963:** 12 (p. 15), 20, 21
(pp. 34, 39), 38, 57, 101, 118, 124, 176,
217, 239, 253, 278, 292, 294, 328 [1]
Assistance and development, **1961:** 23, 34, 41, 62
[23, 26], 63, 90, 12, 139 [2], 167, 193, 205,
207, 214, 244, 299, 302, 343, 346, 481, 497
Presidential contingency fund, **1961:** 205
United Nations, **1961:** 387

Less developed countries — *continued*
　Communication satellite system, participation,
　　1961: 299
　Cooperative movement in, **1963:** 149
　Economic development, **1961:** 91, 222; **1962:** 7
　　(p. 12), 22, 25, 83, 319; **1963:** 21 (p. 34),
　　65 [8], 101, 219, 260 [8], 271, 319a
　Electrification, **1962:** 499
　Exports, **1962:** 22, 144
　Health problems, **1962:** 65
　Joint statements with foreign leaders re, **1961:**
　　66, 242, 252
　Malnutrition in, **1963:** 217
　News conference remarks, **1961:** 62 [23, 26], 139
　　[2], 222, 258 [10]
　Overpopulation, **1962:** 245 [5]
　Private investment in, **1963:** 118
　Textile exports, **1961:** 258 [10]
　Trade, **1963:** 202 [5], 262
　Trade unions, **1962:** 174
Lester, Richard A., **1961:** 425, 504n.; **1962:** 505n.;
　　1963: 409
Le Tourneau-Westinghouse Co., **1962:** 113n.
Letson, John W., **1961:** 334 [1]
Lewis, Fulton, Jr., **1962:** 40 [8]
Lewis, Meriwether, **1962:** 15
Lewis, Sinclair, **1962:** 161n.
Libby Dam, **1961:** 83 [2]
Libby Dam Project, **1963:** 383
Liberal arts, **1963:** 136
Liberia
　Economic mission to, **1961:** 430
　Tubman, William V.S., **1961:** 175, 429, 430
Libonati, Repr. Roland V., **1962:** 483
Libraries, **1963:** 226
　Federal aid, **1963:** 43
　Presidential, reorganization, **1963:** 207
　Robert Frost Library, **1963:** 440
Library, Dwight D. Eisenhower, Abilene, Kans.,
　　1962: 546 [7]
Library, Franklin D. Roosevelt, Hyde Park, N.Y.,
　　1962: 260, 546 [7]
Library, Harry S. Truman, **1961:** 448; **1962:** 546 [7]
Library, Herbert Hoover, Stanford University,
　　1962: 546 [7]
Library Association, American, **1961:** 144; **1963:** 43
Library of Congress, **1962:** 546 [7]
Library services, **1963:** 74
Library Services Act, **1963:** 43
Library Week, National, **1961:** 126
Libreville, Gabon, **1962:** 368
Libya
　Ambassador Mohieddine Fekini, **1962:** 467n.
　Crown Prince Hasan al-Rida al-Sanusi, **1962:**
　　467, 471
　Quaddafi, Wanis, **1962:** 467n.
Lie detector tests, **1963:** 120 [1]
Life expectancy, **1963:** 14, 74, 75 [1], 85

Life Insurance, National Service, **1962:** 16 (p. 44),
　　517
Life magazine, **1962:** 260n., 546 [23]; **1963:** 245
Life magazine, 25th anniversary, remarks, **1961:** 64
Lifesaving awards, **1962:** 182
Limerick, Ireland, **1963:** 281
Limerick, Maine, **1963:** 277
Lincoln, Abraham, **1961:** 84, 105, 165n., 433, 452,
　　462; **1962:** 3, 35, 68, 109, 202, 243 [2], 252,
　　264, 278, 362, 399, 551 [3], 552, 555; **1963:**
　　16, 23, 59, 82, 86, 153, 159, 226, 228, 237,
　　248, 265, 278, 279, 294, 302n., 325, 336,
　　340, 356 [22], 370, 381, 451, 453, 462
Lincoln, Murray D., **1961:** 6n.
Lincoln Center, New York City, **1961:** 467
Lincoln College, **1961:** 331
Lincoln Memorial, **1962:** 399
Lincoln Park, Washington, D.C., **1962:** 27 [11]
Lindbergh, Col. Charles A., **1961:** 486; **1962:** 7 (p.
　　11), 61, 243 [3], 475; **1963:** 199, 472
Linder, Harold F. (President, Export-Import
　　Bank) **1963:** 62
　See also Export-import Bank of Washington,
　　President.
Lindsey, Jake W., **1962:** 420
Linear electron accelerator, **1961:** 94
Link, Arthur S., **1962:** 36; **1963:** 245
Lippmann, Walter, **1961:** 139 [23]
Lisagor, Peter, **1962:** 59 [9]; **1963:** 35 [7]
Liston, Charles (Sonny), **1962:** 27 [19]
Literacy tests for voting, **1962:** 27 [18], 179 [17];
　　1963: 82
Litschgi, A. Byrne, **1962:** 476n.
Little Big Horn, **1963:** 385
Little Red River, **1963:** 401
Little Rock, Ark., **1963:** 401
Livermore, Calif., **1963:** 328 [4]
Livestock, **1963:** 197, 217
Livestock exports, **1962:** 185
Living standards, **1961:** 483
Lleras Camargo, Alberto, **1961:** 512, 515, 516n.;
　　1962: 64, 258
Lloyd George, David, **1961:** 133
Loan guarantee program, Federal, **1962:** 16 (p. 55);
　　1963: 306, 462
Loans, **1963:** 193
　Government, **1963:** 110, 134
　International, **1963:** 407
Lobbyists, foreign, **1962:** 279 [7]
Lobo, Fernando, **1961:** 122
Lockheed Aircraft Corp., **1962:** 38, 378 [20]
Lockheed Aircraft Corporation, equal employ-
　　ment, **1961:** 204
Lockheed Air Force Base, **1963:** 448 [3]
Locomotives, **1963:** 110, 455
Locomotives, exports, **1962:** 170
Lodge, Henry Cabot, **1962:** 20 [5], 74, 199; **1963:**
　　76n., 340, 356 [11, 15], 399, 405 [16], 459
　　[5]

Lodovichetti, Arthur, **1962:** 158
Logelin, Edward, **1963:** 110
Lombardi, Vincent T. (Vince), **1962:** 186
London, **1961:** 133n., 139 [19], 231, 467, 518; **1962:** 203, 552, 553; **1963:** 27, 144 [2, 7], 169 [7], 476
  Development Assistance Group, meeting, **1961:** 91
  U.S. foreign trade center, **1961:** 23
  Visit to, **1961:** 227-230
London, Jack, **1962:** 527
London School of Economics, **1962:** 180
Long, Clarence, **1962:** 446
Long, Sen Edward V., **1961:** 318 [17]; **1962:** 375n., 378 [22]
Long, Sen. Russell B., **1961:** 287; **1962:** 75 [22], 170, 171
Long Beach, U.S.S., **1961:** 99
Longfellow, Henry Wadsworth, **1963:** 387
Longshoremen's Association, International, **1962:** 421; **1963:** 18
Longshoremen's strikes.
  See Maritime labor disputes.
Longworth, Mrs. Alice Roosevelt, **1961:** 464; **1962:** 274
Look magazine, **1962:** 188, 552n.; **1963:** 14, 325n.
Looking Outward, Adlai E. Stevenson, **1963:** 433
López Bermudez, José, **1962:** 189n.
López Mateos, Adolfo (President of Mexico), **1962:** 94, 139 [14], 263-265, 269, 271, 273, 411; **1963:** 307
López Mateos, Señora, **1962:** 263, 264, 271
Lord, Thorn, **1961:** 448
Los Alamos, N. Mex., **1962:** 514, 536-538, 546 [11]; **1963:** 328 [4]
Los Angeles, Calif., **1961:** 143n., 477; **1962:** 20 [16], 77, 385, 527n.; **1963:** 228, 230
  White House Regional Conference, meeting, **1961:** 454n.
Los Banos, Calif., **1962:** 337
Loser, Repr. J. Carlton, **1962:** 340 [24]
"Lost generation," **1961:** 268
Lothian, Lord, **1962:** 552
Louis XIV, **1962:** 527
Louisiana, **1962:** 170, 171
Louisiana, Gov. Jimmie H. Davis, **1963:** 108
Louisville, Ky., **1962:** 457, 458; **1963:** 248ftn. (p. 486)
Louvain University, **1963:** 342
Love, J. Spencer, **1961:** 40n.
Love, Malcolm A., **1963:** 226
Lovell, Sir Bernard, **1963:** 305 [6]
Lovett, Robert A., **1961:** 29; **1962:** 20 [2, 14], 316 [18], 549 [10]; **1963:** 44n., 118, 338, and p. 902
Lowell, A. Lawrence, **1961:** 162
Luang Prabang, Laos, **1961:** 92 [3]
Lubbock, Tex., **1963:** 478

Lübke, Heinrich, **1963:** 258, 259, 262
Luce, Henry, **1962:** 234
Lucey, Partick J., **1962:** 186
Lukens, Alan W., **1961:** 167
Lulli, Louis J., **1963:** 410n.
Lumber imports, **1962:** 307
Lumber industry, **1962:** 307, 410 [7]
Luxembourg
  Ambassador Georges Heisbourg, **1963:** 152
  Grand Duchess Charlotte, **1963:** 150, 152, 154, 156, 157
  Prince Jean, **1963:** 150, 152, 154, 156, 157
  Schaus, Eugene, **1963:** 152, 156
  Werner, Pierre, **1963:** 152, 156
Lyautey, Marshal Louis, **1962:** 109, 174, 186, 216; **1963:** 379, 427, 430, 462
Lydon, James, **1962:** 298n.
Lynch, John M., **1961:** 212
Lyon, Waldo K., **1962:** 323
Lyon, Mrs. Waldo K., **1962:** 323
Lyons, John H., Jr., **1963:** 206

Maas, Maj. Gen. Melvin J., **1962:** 49n.; **1963:** 174, 452
Macapagal, Diosdado, **1962:** 131, 191
Macaroni, White House pony, **1962:** 201
MacArthur, Gen. Douglas, **1961:** 496; **1963:** 7, 107 [8]
MacArthur, Douglas, II, **1961:** 174
Macaulay, Thomas Babington, **1961:** 192
MacDonald, Mr. and Mrs. J. Clifford, **1963:** p. 901
Mach 2 aircraft, **1963:** 221
Machinery, **1963:** 34
Machinists, International Association of, **1962:** 247, 298, 376, 390, 410 [6]; **1963:** 39, 162
Mack, Repr. Peter F., Jr., **1962:** 58n., 481
Mackenna, Luis, **1962:** 543n.
MacLeish, Archibald, **1963:** 439, 440
Macmillan, Harold, **1961:** 115, 227, 229, 481, 518n.; **1962:** 48, 62, 70, 71, 90, 158, 159n., 553; **1963:** 12 (p. 15), 36, 232, 284-286, 328 [6, 8], 316
  Joint message with, **1962:** 42
  Joint statements with, **1961:** 97, 112, 345, 357, 519; **1962:** 160, 348, 554; **1963:** 285
  News conference remarks on, **1961:** 15 [22], 119 [7], 258 [18], 318 [1], 488 [11]; **1962:** 50 [2], 89 [1], 152 [7], 546 [5]; **1963:** 65 [9], 144 [4], 320 [16], 328 [6, 8]
  Visits of, **1961:** 97, 112, 345, 357; **1962:** 157, 160
Macmillan, Lady Dorothy, **1961:** 227; **1963:** 286
Macy, John W., Jr. (Chairman, Civil Service Commission), **1962:** 163, 304, 323; **1963:** 4, 76, 129, 130, 148, 174, 238, 357, 452
Madden, Repr. Ray J., **1962:** 456; **1963:** 107 [24]
Maddy, Dr. Joseph E., **1962:** 322n.
Madison, James, **1961:** 397; **1962:** 542; **1963:** 2, 245, 271, 387
Madison, Wis., **1962:** 186

Madison, Wis., White House Regional Conference, meeting, **1961**: 454n.

Magazine articles, based on interview with the President, **1963**: 319a note

Magglio, Walter A., **1962**: 390

Maglic, B.C., **1961**: 342

Magnesium, ocean resources, **1961**: 100, 248

Magnin, Cyril, **1963**: 49

Magnus, Albertus, **1963**: 254

Magnuson, Repr. Don, **1961**: 474

Magnuson, Sen. Warren G., **1961**: 23, 415 [12]; **1962**: 155, 320; **1963**: 41, 384, 386, 387, 388
    25th anniversary as Member of Congress, **1961**: 472, 474, 476

Magruder, Judge Calvert, **1961**: 152

Magsaysay (Ramón) Memorial School of Arts and Trades, **1963**: 239n.

Mahan, Rear Adm. Alfred Thayer, **1961**: 232; **1963**: 225, 330

Mahgreb, **1963**: 455

Mail
    Distribution of pornography, **1962**: 352 [8]
    Fraud statutes, enforcement, **1962**: 93 (p. 237)
    From Communist bloc, distribution, **1962**: 20 [13]
    The President's, **1962**: 210 [4]; **1963**: 52
    Transportation, **1962**: 129; **1963**: 310, 453

Mailliard, Repr. William S., **1963**: 98, 105, 359n.

Maine, **1962**: 326; **1963**: 248ftn. (p. 486), 301
    Gov. John H. Reed, **1963**: 108, 426

Makarios, Archbishop
    Joint statement with, **1962**: 227
    Message, **1962**: 249
    Visit of, **1962**: 224, 225, 227, 249

Malaccorto, Ernesto, **1962**: 86n.

Malagasy and African Organization for Economic Cooperation, 1961: 107n.

Malagasy and African states, conferences, **1961**: 107, 175, 304, 430

Malagasy and African States, Union of, **1962**: 105, 212
    Conference, **1962**: 368

Malaria, **1963**: 455

Malaya, **1962**: 226, 316 [7]; **1963**: 65 [19], 144 [16], 349

Malayan Federation, **1963**: 65 [19]

Malaysia, **1963**: 366, 385, 455, 459 [13]

Mali, Modibo Keita, **1961**: 359, 363, 364, 365

Malikyar, Abdullah, **1963**: 347

Mallory, George, **1962**: 373

Malraux, André, **1962**: 184, 280n., 284, 546 [1]; **1963**: 5, 112

Malraux, Madame, **1962**: 184

Malthus, Thomas Robert, **1963**: 430

Management, **1962**: 280; **1963**: 110
    See also Labor-management relations.

Management, President's Advisory Committee on, **1961**: 29

Management-labor panel, **1961**: 171 [6]

Management-Labor Textile Advisory Committee, **1961**: 428

Management improvement, Government, **1963**: 21 (p. 41)

Manatos, Mike N., **1961**: 25 [12]

Manganese, ocean deposits, **1961**: 49, 100

Mang'enya, Erasto A.M., **1963**: 302n.

Manhattan project, **1961**: 318 [12]

Manila Pact (Southeast Asia Collective Defense Treaty), **1962**: 192

Mann, J. Keith, **1961**: 425

Mann, Thomas C., **1961**: 15 [34], 25 [24], 258 [17]; **1962**: 270n., 271, 272

Mann, Rabbi Louis L., **1963**: 110

Mann Creek Federal Reclamation Project, approval, **1962**: 333

Manned space flights, **1962**: 56, 57, 60, 96, 226, 323, 373; **1963**: 221
    See also Astronauts Space research and exploration.
    Gemini project, **1963**: 175 [4], 202 [4]
    Mariner project, **1963**: 21 (p. 34)
    Mercury project, **1962**: 61, 426, 463; **1963**: 199, 202 [4], 472
    Moon exploration, **1962**: 13 (p. 30), 40 [16], 59 [18], 77, 340 [5], 372-375, 516 [11]
    Moon probes, **1961**: 139 [12], 205, 415 [17], 477
    News conference remarks, **1961**: 25 [11, 15], 119 [5], 171 [5, 13, 22, 23], 291 [13], 318 [17], 415 [17]; **1962**: 50 [19], 59 [1, 2], 340 [5, 8], 546 [11]
    Project Mercury, **1961**: 117, 415 [17]
    Soviet, **1961**: 25 [11, 15], 117, 118, 119 [5], 171 [13, 22], 318 [17]; **1962**: 59 [2], 68, 340 [5, 8]
    U.S. press coverage, **1961**: 171 [23]

Manned Spacecraft Center, Houston, Tex., **1962**: 323, 372-374; **1963**: 478

Manning, Bayless, **1961**: 152

Manning, Robert J., **1962**: 515 [14, 19]

Manpower Development and Training, National Advisory Committee, **1962**: 412

Manpower Development and Training Act of 1962, **1962**: 7 (p. 6), 16 (p. 56), 129, 412; **1963**: 21 (p. 38), 30 (p. 70), 43, 50, 64, 74, 92, 127, 185, 310, 393, 423, 462
    Approval, **1962**: 91

Manpower report of the President, **1963**: 30 (p. 70), 92

Manpower resources, **1963**: 92, 119, 336, 364, 376, 378, 383, 401, 423
    Development, **1962**: 547; **1963**: 30 (pp. 69, 70, 71), 43, 92, 110, 127, 248, 294, 310, 315, 336, 378, 385, 387, 393, 423, 445, 458, 478
    Executive branch, **1962**: 448
    Latin America, **1963**: 72
    Western Europe, **1963**: 72

Mansfield, Sen. Mike, **1961:** 476n., 488 [6]; **1962:** 27 [18], 107 [19], 179 [17], 205, 231, 245 [8, 9], 265, 270-272, 378 [18]; **1963:** 89 [20], 138, 203, 228, 354, 356 [1], 378, 379, 381, 382, 383

Mansfield, Mrs. Mike, **1962:** 272

Mansfield Committee, **1963:** 89 [20]

Mantelpiece, White House, restoration, **1962:** 274

Manuti, Alfred, **1961:** 330

Mao Tse-tung, **1962:** 184, 414n.

Maps and charts, ocean, **1961:** 100

Marble Industry Board of New York, **1962:** 274

March, Fredric, **1962:** 161n., 527n.

Marie Antoinette, **1961:** 226

Marietta, Ga., **1963:** 330, 448 [3]

Marine Air Station, Cherry Point, N.C., **1962:** 149

Marine Barracks, inspection, **1962:** 287

Marine Corps, **1961:** 92 [3], 99; **1962:** 149, 287, 423; **1963:** 21 (p. 33), 109, 227, 256, 312

  Increase in strength, **1961:** 99, 205, 302; **1962:** 7 (p. 10), 343

  Unit citations, **1962:** 521

Marine Exploration Company, Global, **1961:** 110

Mariner space project, **1962:** 373; **1963:** 21 (p. 34)

Maritime Administration, **1963:** 306

Maritime Administration, Reorganization Plan, **1961:** 238

Maritime Board, Federal, **1961:** 238

Maritime Commission, Federal, **1961:** 238

Maritime Commission, United States, **1961:** 238

Maritime Engineers Beneficial Association, National, **1962:** 21

Maritime labor dispute, **1961:** 256, 258 [11], 269, 270; **1962:** 139 [3]; **1963:** 18, 54 [9], 411

  Statements, **1962:** 421, 428

  Strike of 1961, settlement, **1962:** 21

Maritime safety, **1963:** 471

Mark Antony, **1961:** 222 [13]

Marker sharing, **1963:** 30 (p. 68)

Marketing programs, agricultural, **1962:** 25; **1963:** 169 [13], 197, 201, 202 [2, 12, 15, 18]

Marketing programs, agricultural commodities, **1961:** 85

Marks, Leonard, **1962:** 476n.

Mars, probe of planet, **1961:** 11; **1962:** 59 [1], 96, 546 [11]; **1963:** 21 (p. 34)

Marshall, Burke, **1963:** 169 [1, 4, 19], 181, 360

Marshall, Repr. Fred, **1962:** 440

Marshall, Gen. George C., **1962:** 161n.; **1963:** 124n., 271, 477

Marshall, George C., Space Flight Center, **1963:** 194n.

Marshall, George Preston, **1961:** 496

Marshall, Henry, murder of, **1962:** 210 [6]

Marshall, John, **1963:** 169 [8]

Marshall, John Ross, **1962:** 248

Marshall, Thurgood, **1962:** 340 [6]

Marshall, Walter P., **1961:** 433

Marshall plan, **1961:** 11, 90, 222, 388, 491, 497, 499; **1962:** 15, 22, 74, 89 [17], 178n., 229 [3, 5], 549 [6]; **1963:** 72, 118, 124, 266, 268, 271, 328 [1], 338, 362, 391, 442, 455, 459 [6], 466, 468

Marshals, Federal, at University of Mississippi, **1962:** 420

Marshals, Federal use in civil rights enforcement, **1963:** 202 [1]

Marti, Jose, **1962:** 86, 556

Martin, Edwin M., **1961:** 123; **1963:** 405 [7]

Martin, Repr. Joseph W., Jr., **1961:** 128

Martin, William McC., Jr. (Chairman, Board of Governors, Federal Reserve System), **1962:** 151, 549 [3]; **1963:** 54 [1], 62, 94n.

  See also Federal Reserve System, Board of governors, Chairman.

Martin Company, **1961:** 281n.

Martinez Sotomayor, Carlos, **1962:** 543n.

Martino, Gaetano, **1961:** 84

Marx, Karl, **1961:** 153, 455 [12], 497; **1963:** 12 (pp. 15, 18)

Marxism-Leninism, **1963:** 144 [8], 271

Marxist system.

  See Communism.

Maryland, **1961:** 26, 58; **1962:** 446; **1963:** 208, 248ftn. (p. 486), 448 [21], 461

  Development compact, National Capital Region, **1963:** 208

  Gov. J. Millard Tawes, **1962:** 446; **1963:** 461

Marzotto, Count Giannino, **1963:** 191

Masefield, John, **1963:** 232

Masferrer Rojas, Rolando, **1961:** 119 [4]

Masland, Richard L., **1963:** 435

Mason, Edward S., **1962:** 549ftn. (p. 887); **1963:** 118

Mason, George, **1963:** 387

Massachusetts, **1961:** 422, 441, 491, 499; **1962:** 77, 150, 216, 224, 326; **1963:** 178, 179, 223, 228, 248ftn. (p. 486), 308, 369, 417, 427, 451, 463, 466, 474

  Gov. Endicott Peabody, **1963:** 108, 136, 178, 427

  Gov. John A. Volpe, **1961:** 212

  News conference remarks, **1962:** 50 [15], 89 [2], 115 [12], 198 [19], 245 [17], 259 [10], 279 [26], 340 [18], 352 [10]

  Reapportionment, **1962:** 115 [12]

  Senatorial election, **1962:** 89 [2], 198 [19], 259 [10], 279 [26], 340 [18], 352 [10]

Massachusetts Bay Colony, **1961:** 71 [17]; **1962:** 504; **1963:** 226, 387

Massachusetts General Hospital, 150th anniversary, **1961:** 14

Massachusetts Historical Society, **1961:** 397; **1963:** 2, 245

Massachusetts Institute of Technology, **1961:** 460n.; **1962:** 375; **1963:** 477

Mass Transportation Bill, **1963:** 310

Masters, Mates and Pilots, International Organization of, **1962:** 21

Material and child health, research, **1961:** 289

Materials research, **1961:** 417

Maternal and Child Health and Mental Retardation Planning Amendments of 1963, **1963:** 364, 434

Maternal death rate, **1962:** 132

Maternal health services, **1962:** 65; **1963:** 50, 51, 53, 435, 447

Mathematicians, shortage of, **1962:** 546 [8], 547, 549

Matka Bosca, **1962:** 461

MATS.
    See Military Air Transport Service.

Matsu, **1962:** 259 [1, 7]

Mauritania, U.N. membership, **1961:** 309

Mauthe, J.L., **1961:** 254n.

Maximilian, Emperor, **1963:** 99

May, Elaine, **1962:** 201

Mayo, Leonard, **1961:** 413n.
    Telegram on urban renewal, **1961:** 20

Mayo Clinic, **1961:** 203

Maylove, Jose Antonio, **1961:** 272n.

Mayors, Conference of, **1962:** 190; **1963:** 229, 230

Mayors of U.S. cities.
    See specific cities.

Mazey, Emil, **1962:** 174

Mazzini, Guiseppe, **1963:** 291

McCall's Magazine, **1963:** 319a note

McCarran-Walter Act, **1963:** 107 [17]

McCarthy, Sen. Eugene J., **1962:** 284, 439; **1963:** 378

McCarthyism, **1963:** 305 [25]

McClellan, Sen. John L., **1961:** 171 [6], 361, 440; **1962:** 198 [1, 7], 361n.; **1963:** 400, 401, 405 [10]

McClellan (Sen. John L.) committee, **1963:** 107 [23], 448 [24]

McClellan, Mrs. John L., **1962:** 361

McClelland, Dr. William D., **1962:** 452

McClendon, Sarah, **1961:** 83 [15]; **1962:** 20 [15], 152 [15]

McCloskey, Matthew, **1961:** 3n.; **1962:** 15, 233; **1963:** 24, 275

McCloskey, Mrs. Matthew H., **1962:** 233

McCloy, John J., **1961:** 262, 388, 408, 483; **1962:** 515 [6], 546 [3]; **1963:** 439, 440
    Medal of Freedom, **1963:** p. 902
    Negotiations with Cuba, **1963:** 11
    News conference remarks on, **1961:** 8 [1, 7], 62 [19, 21], 83 [6]

McCollum, L. F., **1962:** 549 [10]; **1963:** 118

McConaughy, Walter P., **1963:** 120 [16]

McCone, John A., **1961:** 392, 485; **1962:** 27 [13], 109; **1963:** 54 [5], 89 [9], 144 [12], 349, 354, 405 [2, 12]
    See also Central Intelligence Agency, Director (John A. McCone).

McConnell, Joseph, **1963:** 470

McCormack, Repr. John W., **1961:** 212, 441
    See Speaker of the House of Representatives.

McCulloch, Repr. William M., **1963:** 444

McDermott, Edward A. (Director, Office of Emergency Planning), **1962:** 40 [17], 445

McDermott, Walsh, **1963:** 38

McDonald, David J., **1961:** 40n., 274, 366; **1962:** 8 [7], 89 [5], 115 [4], 121, 139 [7], 385

McDonald, Rt. Rev. William J., **1963:** 342

McDonnell, James S., **1962:** 375

McDonnell Aircraft Corp., **1962:** 375, 378 [22]; **1963:** 174

McDonough, Robert P., **1963:** 249

McDowell, Repr. Harris B., Jr., **1963:** 461

McEachen, Allan J., **1963:** 179

McEwen, John, **1962:** 88

McGee, Sen. Gale W., **1961:** 476n.; **1963:** 380-382

McGee, Capt. Richard, **1963:** 278

McGhee, George C., **1962:** 259 [21]; **1963:** 256, 272

McGill, Ralph, **1961:** 40n.

McGlon, Jesse, **1962:** 298n.; **1963:** 206

McGovern, George, **1962:** 335.
    See also Food for Peace, Director.

McGovern, W.C., **1963:** 95n.

McGowan, Maj. Gen. D.W., **1962:** 407

McGraw-Hill Book Co., **1962:** 113n.

McGrory, Mary, **1963:** 76n.

McGuire, Marie C., **1961:** 264, 371

McIntosh, A.D., **1961:** 66

McIntire, Repr. Clifford G., **1962:** 326; **1963:** 426

McKay, David O., **1963:** 385

McKeesport, Pa., **1962:** 453

McKelway, Benjamin M., **1962:** 497

McKim, Mead & White, **1962:** 274

McKinley, William, **1962:** 482

McKone, Capt. John R., **1961:** 8 [3]

McLintock, Rear Adm. Gordon, **1961:** 156n.

McMahon Act, **1963:** 54 [8], 320 [15]

McMahon Act on control of atomic energy, **1961:** 222 [3]

McMorrow, Maj. Gen. Francis, **1962:** 371n.

McMurray, Joseph P. (Chairman, Federal Home Loan Bank Board), **1962:** 279 [9]; **1963:** 49, 62.
    See also Federal Home Loan Bank Board Chairman.

McNamara, Sen. Pat, **1962:** 433, 437; **1963:** 74

McNamara, Robert S.
    See Defense, Secretary of.

McNaughton, Gen. Andrew G.L., **1962:** 123

McNichols, Gov. Steve L.R., **1962:** 216, 336

McSween, Repr. Harold B., **1962:** 170

McTyeire, Bishop Holland N., **1963:** 192

Meader, Vaughn, **1962:** 546 [19]

Meagher, Brig. Gen. Thomas F., **1963:** 278

Meany, George, **1961:** 40n., 169, 414, 499; **1962:** 200, 202, 204, 324, 405, 449, 509, 549ftn.

Meany, George — *continued*
(p. 887); **1963:** 44n., 85, 118, 139, 162, 179, 268, 270, 275, 299, 362, 462, and p. 901

Meat
Inspection, **1962:** 93 (p. 240)
Withholding from market, **1962:** 352 [4]

Meat cutters and Butcher Workers of North America, Amalgamated, **1963:** 187

Meat Inspection Act, **1962:** 93 (p. 240)

Mechanics and laborers employed by Government, workweek, **1962:** 327

Medals
Presentation or acceptance.
See also Awards and citations; Addresses or remarks at presentation ceremonies.
Sam Rayburn commemorative medal, approval, **1962:** 409

Medal of Freedom, Presidential, **1963:** 76 and p. 899

Medal of Honor, Congressional, **1963:** 109, 159

Medals, presentation
Distinguished Service Medal
Burke, Adm. Arleigh A., **1961:** 303
White, Gen. Thomas D., **1961:** 260
Medal of Freedom, Paul Henri Spaak, **1961:** 47
NASA Distinguished Service Medal, Comdr. Alan B. Shepard, Jr., **1961:** 177
National Geographic Society Medal, Capt. Jacques-Yves Cousteau, **1961:** 134
National Security Medal, Allen W. Dulles, **1961:** 485

Mediation Board, National, **1963:** 92, 95n., 244, 310, 414

Mediation and Conciliation Service, Federal, **1963:** 18, 92, 202 [20], 206

Medical Association, American, **1962:** 174, 202, 210 [4], 222, 229 [13], 279 [24]

Medical care, **1961:** 27, 52, 339, 406; **1962:** 16 (p. 46), 65; **1963:** 21 (pp. 37, 39), 22, 134, 458
See also Hospitals and medical care facilities.
Expenses, tax deduction, **1963:** 34, 74
Mental patients.
See Mental health and mental health programs.
Older persons, **1961:** 52, 71 [12], 83 [14], 94, 119 [11], 133, 139 [13], 341, 455 [7], 477, 499; **1962:** 7 (p. 8), 65, 359, 385; **1963:** 12 (p. 14), 74, 75 [1, 6], 138, 459 [11, 12], 460, 461
Under social security.
See Social security.
Sick pay, tax deduction, **1963:** 34
United Kingdom, **1962:** 202

Medical Librarianship, Second International Congress on, **1963:** 247

Medical and dental education, **1961:** 27, 52, 94; **1962:** 7 (p. 8), 8 [24], 13 (p. 31), 37, 65, 288; **1963:** 12 (p. 14), 21 (p. 38), 50, 53,

Medical and dental education — *continued*
64, 74, 89 [1], 92, 107 [21], 120 [8], 134, 144 [15], 146, 228, 336, 374, 400, 427

Medical research, **1961:** 11, 14, 27, 94, 488 [8]; **1962:** 13 (p. 31), 65, 163, 234, 323, 470; **1963:** 12 (p. 14), 30 (p. 69), 43, 50, 53, 64, 74, 202 [17], 247, 313, 366, 374, 435, 447, 472

Medical Sciences, Institute of General, **1963:** 53

Medicine, National Library of, **1963:** 247

Mediterranean Sea, **1962:** 216; **1963:** 266

Meiklejohn, Alexander, **1963:** p. 901

Mekong River, **1963:** 144 [16]

Melekh (Igor Y.) spy case, **1961:** 139 [20]

Melen, James, **1961:** 212

Memorandums of Disapproval.
See Veto Messages and Memorandums of Disapproval.

Memorandums to Federal agencies
Civil supersonic transport, **1963:** 29
Conflicts of interest and ethical standards, **1963:** 31
Credit programs, **1963:** 62
Employment of mentally retarded, **1963:** 357
Equal opportunity for women, **1962:** 304
Federal employers
Discrimination in recreational associations, **1961:** 137
Employee-management relations, **1961:** 250
Minimum wage, **1961:** 251
Federal office space, **1962:** 221
Federal salary reform, **1963:** 4
Food-for-peace program, **1961:** 6
Former Peace Corpsmen, Government employment, **1963:** 129
Government field activities, **1961:** 465
International Development Agency, Administrator, **1963:** 6
Manpower control and utilization, **1962:** 448
National Capital Region, redevelopment, **1962:** 525
Older workers, utilization in Federal service, **1963:** 96
Pennsylvania Avenue redevelopment, **1962:** 221
Puerto Rico, status, **1961:** 301n.
Red Cross campaign, **1961:** 60
Scientific and technical personnel, **1962:** 187
United Givers Fund campaign, **1961:** 259

Memphis, Tenn., **1963:** 82

Menshikov, Mikhail A., **1961:** 291 [19]

Mental health, **1961:** 492

Mental health and mental health programs, **1963:** 22, 30 (p. 65), 50, 51, 53, 66, 74, 89 [1], 130, 134, 174, 175, 230, 357, 393, 400, 434, **447, 459 [11]**

Mental Health, National Institute of, 1961: 413; 1963: 50, 66

Mental illness and Health, Joint Commission on, report, **1961:** 492; **1962:** 65

Mental illness and mental retardation, **1963:** 12 (p. 14), 21 (p. 37), 22, 43, 51, 64, 66, 89 [1], 134, 174, 228, 305 [19], 311, 313, 357, 364, 368, 374, 400, 427, 435, 455, 478

Message to Congress, **1963:** 50

Mental retardation, **1961:** 14, 25 [3], 413, 415 [2], 427, 444; **1962:** 3, 37, 65, 132, 396, 480, 534

Mental Retardation, Panel on, **1961:** 413, 415 [2], 427, 444; **1962:** 65, 534n.; **1963:** 50, 66

Mental Retardation, State-Federal Conference on, **1963:** 313

Mental Retardation, White House Conference on, **1963:** 364

Mental retardation bill, **1963:** 434

Mental retardation facilities and community mental health centers, construction of, **1963:** 447

Menzies, Robert G., **1961:** 51; **1962:** 251; **1963:** 297

Merchant, Livingston T., **1961:** 45, 191, 490; **1963:** 36

News conference remarks on, **1963:** 65 [6], 89 [14], 107 [11]

Merchant marine, U.S., **1961:** 121, 156, 238

Wages, **1961:** 258 [11]

Merchant Marine Academy, U.S., Inter-Faith Chapel, dedication, **1961:** 156

Merchant Marine Achievement Award, **1961:** 459

Merchant Marine Act of 1936, **1962:** 129

Merchant seamen, medical care, **1962:** 65

Mercury project, **1961:** 117, 415 [17]; **1962:** 61, 426, 463; **1963:** 199, 202 [4], 472

Meredith, James H., **1962:** 420, 551 [10]; **1963:** 35 [23]

Meriwether, Charles M., **1961:** 62 [14, 28], 71 [22]

Merrill Foundation, **1961:** 245

Merrow, Repr. Chester E., **1962:** 30n.

Messages to the American people

Berlin crisis, **1961:** 302

European trip, **1963:** 295

Flight of Astronaut L. Gordon Cooper, **1963:** 190

Inaugural address, **1961:** 1

National economy, **1962:** 328

Nuclear test ban treaty, **1963:** 316, 363

Response to, **1963:** 319a

Nuclear tests and disarmament, **1962:** 71

Soviet missile and bomber bases in Cuba, **1962:** 485

Removal, **1962:** 501

United Community Campaigns of America,**1963:** 369

University of Alabama, integration crisis, **1963:** 237

Messages to the American people — *continued*

University of Mississippi, integration crisis, **1962:** 420

Visit to Europe, **1961:** 231

Voting in Congressional election, **1962:** 502

Messages to Congress.

See Congress, messages to.

African and Malagasy States, conference, **1962:** 368

African States, conference, **1963:** 200

Argentina, President Frondizi, **1961:** 149

Austria, Chancellor Raab, **1961:** 109

Belgium, Prime Minister Lefevre, **1961:** 174

Bolivia, President Paz Estenssoro, **1961:** 184, 275, 409

Brazil, President Goulart, **1962:** 146, 490

President Kubitschek, **1961:** 13

President Quadros, **1961:** 12

British West Indies, Prime Minister Adams, **1961:** 36

Burma, Prime Minister U Nu, **1961:** 367

Burundi

King Mwami Mwambutsa, **1962:** 266

Prime Minister Muhirwa, **1962:** 415

Canada, Prime Minister Diefenbaker, **1962:** 477

Central African Republic, President Dacko, **1961:** 167

Ceylon, Governor General Gopallawa, **1962:** 106

China, Republic of, President Chiang Kai-shek, **1961:** 412

Cyprus, Archbishop Makarios, **1962:** 249

Finland, President Kekkonen, **1961:** 451

France, President de Gaulle, **1961:** 140

Germany

Chancellor Adenauer, **1962:** 2, 511; **1963:** 413

Chancellor Erhard, **1963:** 454

Ghana, President Nkrumah, **1961:** 273

Greece, Prime Minister Caramanlis, **1961:** 457

Indonesia, President Sukarno, **1962:** 334

Iran, Shah Mohammad Reza Pahlavi, **1962:** 364; **1963:** 60

Ireland

President de Valera, **1963:** 283

Prime Minister Lemass, **1963:** 283

Japan, Prime Minister Ikeda, **1961:** 444

Liberia, President Tubman, **1961:** 175

Pakistan, President Ayub Khan, **1962:** 404

Panama, President Chiari, **1961:** 469

Rwanda, President Kayibanda, **1962:** 267

Soviet Union

Chairman, Presidium of the Supreme Soviet, Leonid Brezhnev, **1961:** 2, 271, 453, 522; **1963:** 1

Premier Khrushchev, **1961:** 2, 118, 132, 271, 522; **1962:** 42, 48, 60, 62, 73, 96, 239, 435, 492, 493; **1963:** 1, 27

Syrian Arab Republic, President al-Qudsi, **1962:** 1

Tanganyika, President Nyerere, **1962:** 539

Messages to Congress — *continued*
  Togo, President Olympio, **1961:** 124
  Turkey, President Gursel, **1961:** 439; **1963:** 443
  Uganda, Prime Minister Obote, **1962:** 441
  Vatican, Pope John XXIII, **1962:** 430
  Viet-Nam, President Diem, **1961:** 435, 505; **1963:** 438
Metal extrusion plant, Adrian, Mich., **1961:** 83 [25], 171 [4]
Metal resources, **1963:** 179
Metcalf, Sen. Lee, **1963:** 379, 381, 382, 383
Meteorological Organization, World, **1963:** 430
Meteorological Satellites.
  See Weather satellites.
Methodists, **1961:** 26
Metropolitan areas, development, **1961:** 17, 76
Metropolitan Club, **1961:** 415 [14]; **1962:** 8 [23]
Metropolitan Opera Association, **1961:** 330
Mexican Revolution, **1962:** 264, 265, 268, 271, 273
Mexico, **1962:** 270; **1963:** 107 [1], 232, 311, 344, 382, 432, 462, 478
  Agriculture credit agreement, **1962:** 268
  Agricultural workers from, **1962:** 345
  Ambassador Antonio Carrillo Flores, **1962:** 265n., 269n., 270n., 406
  Amistad Dam and Reservoir, **1962:** 273
  Assistance, **1963:** 118
  Ballet Folklorico, **1962:** 406
  Chamizal zone, **1963:** 89 [13], 307
  Chamizal Zone controversy, **1962:** 279 [21]
  Economic and social development, **1962:** 273, 276
  International Boundary and Water Commission, **1962:** 94
  Lopez Mateos, Adolfo, **1962:** 94, 139 [14], 263-265, 269, 271, 273, 411; **1963:** 307
  News conference remarks, **1962:** 89 [3], 229 [14], 259 [17], 279 [10, 21]
  Parliamentarians, visit to U.S., **1962:** 189
  Salinity of waters delivered to, **1962:** 94
  Tax reforms, **1963:** 118
  Tello, Manuel, **1962:** 265n., 271n.
  Travel to Cuba via, **1963:** 107 [17]
  U.S. Ambassador Thomas C. Mann, **1962:** 270n., 271, 272
  U.S. relations with, **1963:** 232, 307
  Visit to, **1962:** 263-265, 268-273
Mexico, agricultural workers from, **1961:** 400
Mexico, Gulf of, **1963:** 382, 383
Mexico City, **1962:** 40, 529; **1963:** 164, 478
  Visit to, **1962:** 263-265, 268-273
Mexican-Americans in high Government positions, **1961:** 25 [14]
Meyer, Albert Cardinal, **1963:** 110
Meyer, Gov. Robert B., **1961:** 448
Miami, Fla., **1961:** 183; **1962:** 556; **1963:** 356 [16], 465

Miami, Florida — *continued*
  AFL-CIO, convention, **1961:** 499
  Cuban exiles in, **1963:** 134 [1]
  Cuban refugees, **1961:** 19
  Mayor Robert King High, **1961:** 498; **1963:** 467
  Young Democrats Convention, **1961:** 498
Miami Beach, Fla., **1962:** 77, 190, 385
Micey, L.E., **1961:** 222 [12]
Michener, Roland, **1961:** 192
Michigan, **1962:** 458; **1963:** 241, 248ftn. (p. 486), 400
  Candidates for public office, **1962:** 433, 436-438
  Gov. George Romney, **1963:** 202 [9]
  Gov. John B. Swainson, **1962:** 433, 436-438
  News conference remarks, **1962:** 89 [13], 279 [15]
Mićunović Veljko, **1963:** 421
Midas earth satellite, **1961:** 99; **1962:** 115 [24]
Middle East and Near East, **1961:** 192, 205, 244, 476; **1962:** 7 (p. 12), 70, 147; **1963:** 14, 232, 285, 330, 334, 366, 382, 426, 465 [1], 476
  See also specific countries.
  Assistance, **1963:** 12 (p. 17), 169 [2], 338, 459 [13]
  Communist expansion, **1963:** 118, 169 [2], 477
  Drug control, **1962:** 411
  Military assistance and defense support, **1963:** 89 [20], 464
  News conference operations, **1962:** 107 [5], 515 [15]; **1963:** 89 [20], 120 [10], 169 [2], 356 [25], 459 [6]
  United Nations operations, **1962:** 24, 107 [5], 319, 424; **1963:** 169 [2], 471
  Visit of Vice President Johnson, **1962:** 339
Middle Level Manpower, International Conference on, **1963:** 294
Middle West, **1962:** 410 [3]
Middleton, Drew, **1962:** 179 [16]
Midwestern Democratic Conference, **1962:** 346
Mies van der Rohe, Ledwig, **1963:** p. 901
MIG aircraft, Cuban, attacks on U.S. vessels, **1963:** 75 [3, 5, 8, 20]
Migrants, assistance, **1961:** 297
Migrant Health Act, **1963:** 53
Migrant workers, **1962:** 37, 65, 395; **1963:** 74, 130
Migration and Refugee Assistance Act of 1962, approval, **1962:** 261
Mikhaievsky, Capt. Nicholas, **1962:** 384n.
Milan, **1963:** 291
Milford, Pa., **1963:** 389
Military Academy, United States, **1962:** 226, 234; **1963:** 223, 321, 335
Military Air Transport Service, **1961:** 99; **1962:** 309
Military Assistance Advisory Groups, **1963:** 256
Military assistance and defense support, **1961:** 90, 99, 205, 207, 376, 436, 497, 505; **1962:** 13 (p. 29), 22, 83, 147, 232, 237, 280, 314, 375, 519, 521; **1963:** 12 (p. 16), 21 (p. 34), 54 [3, 8], 65 [3, 13, 15, 17, 19], 75 [10], 78, 89

Military assistance — *continued*
[20], 111, 112, 118, 134 [1], 179, 183 n.,
194, 219, 221, 225, 227, 253, 255, 257, 262,
263, 266, 271, 272, 285, 290, 291, 303, 306,
330, 333, 338, 340, 399, 422, 441, 443, 448,
455, 462, 464
See also Economic assistance; Foreign assistance; Mutual security program.
Asia, **1963:** 105 [5], 202 [10], 349, 464
India, **1963:** 202 [3]
Joint statements with foreign leaders, **1961:** 283,
309, 468
News conference remarks, **1961:** 171 [15], 334
[16], 488 [3]; **1962:** 40 [4], 50 [9], 279 [1],
515 [3, 5]; **1963:** 54 [3, 8], 65 [3, 13, 15, 17,
19], 75 [10], 89 [7, 14, 20], 120 [10], 169
[2], 202 [3, 10]
Military Assistance Program, U.S., **1963:** 183 n.
Military budgets, freezing of, Soviet proposal,
1961: 483
Military coups, **1963:** 405 [7], 448 [11], 459 [5, 18]
Military installations, **1961:** 436
Closing of, **1961:** 119 [8]
Overseas, **1961:** 99
Military Institute of Engineering, Brazilian, **1963:**
335
Military officers, foreign, remarks, **1963:** 183
Military personnel, **1961:** 99; **1963:** 183, 227,
251, 321, 476
See also Armed forces, U.S.
Allied, at U.S. Army missile school, **1962:** 371
Dependents overseas, **1961:** 8 [19], 15 [2, 18], 23,
171 [16], 497; **1962:** 59 [12, 17], 139 [5],
152 [11], 194, 203, 259 [6], 340 [25]; **1963:**
65 [15]
Equal opportunity, **1963:** 251
Expenditures abroad, **1961:** 15 ftn. (p. 31), 23,
497
Families of, **1963:** 159
Housing, **1963:** 169 [20]
Pay, **1962:** 13 (pp. 37, 38), 549 [9]; **1963:** 21
(p. 34), 169 [20], 175 [4], 194, 396
Political and diplomatic functions, **1963:** 221
Public statements of officers, **1961:** 15 [8]; **1962:**
20 [2, 14], 40 [5], 50 [8, 23]
Role of officers in educating public on commu-
nism, **1961:** 318 [9]
Schools for children, **1963:** 82
Military preparedness, **1961:** 477
Military procurement.
See Defense procurement.
Military rejects, **1963:** 393
Military Strategy, Soviet text, quoted, **1963:** 232
Military strength, U.S., **1961:** 34, 99, 302, 436, 442,
446; **1962:** 7 (p. 10), 13 (p. 28), 140, 179
.[5, 8], 243 [1], 309, 343, 346, 366, 395, 407,

Military strength, U.S. — *continued*
456, 458, 473; **1963:** 12 (p. 18), 120 [11],
144 [17], 169 [20], 183, 225, 232, 291,
319a, 321, 330, 335, 384, 385, 390, 426,
459 [10], 462, 472, 475, 476, 477
News conference remarks, **1961:** 8 [23], 15 [24],
25 [2], 62 [6, 29, 30], 455 [4, 18], 488 [10]
Milk
Price supports, **1961:** 94; **1962:** 20 [11], 25, 115
[20], 186
Radioactive fallout in, **1962:** 19, 20 [11, 18], 316
[22]
School programs, **1961:** 85, 94; **1962:** 7 (p. 8), 19,
25; **1963:** 89 [5], 135, 193, 423, 458
Milk and Nutrition, National Conference on, **1962:**
19
Milk Producers Federation, National, **1963:** 149 n.
Millay, Edna St. Vincent, **1963:** 425
Miller, Repr. George P., **1962:** 372, 373
Miller, Israel, **1963:** 203 n.
Miller, J. Clayton, **1962:** 20 [15]
Miller, Marvin J., **1963:** 206
Miller, Mitch, **1963:** 204
Miller, Patricia A., **1962:** 182 n.
Miller, Paul A., **1963:** 249
Miller, Repr. William E. (Chairman, Republican
National Committee), **1961:** 334 [11];
1962: 8 [16], 152 [12], 229 [6], 439, 481;
1963: 151
Millers Ferry, Ala., **1963:** 193
Millikan, Max F., **1961:** 119 [2]
Milliken, Frank R., **1963:** 450
Mills, Repr. Wilbur D., **1962:** 170, 199, 328, 449,
549; **1963:** 35 [14], 329, 351, 363, 400, 401,
434, 459 [11]
Letters, **1962:** 98, 108
News conference remarks on, **1962:** 302 [5], 546
[6, 13]
Mills-Ribicoff Bill, **1963:** 434
Millsop, Thomas E., **1961:** 254 n.
Milton, John, **1961:** 162, 418; **1963:** 118, 271
Milwaukee, Wis., **1962:** 186
Mineral industry, tax treatment, **1963:** 34
Mineral resources, **1961:** 17, 49, 100, 248; **1962:**
27 [3], 69, 410 [7]; **1963:** 37, 127, 179, 266
Minimum wage, **1961:** 477, 499; **1962:** 20 [26], 202,
324; **1963:** 85, 162, 187, 228, 248, 305 [18],
427, 445, 462
Approval of bill, **1961:** 69
Campaign remarks, **1962:** 396, 414, 431, 432,
436-439, 446, 451, 452, 454-456, 458, 472,
473, 481, 483
Exclusion of certain workers, **1961:** 171 [20], 251
Expansion of coverage, **1961:** 17, 24, 92 [5], 169;
1962: 16 (p. 44); **1963:** 30 (p. 67), 92
Government employees, **1961:** 251

Minimum wage — *continued*
 Increase, **1961:** 17, 24, 83 [14], 92 [5], 169, 344,
  448; **1962:** 16 (p. 44), 174, 396, 414, 431,
  432, 436-439, 446, 451, 452, 454-456, 458,
  459, 472, 473, 481; 483
 News conference remarks, **1961:** 35 [3], 83 [14],
  92 [5], 139 [16], 171 [20]
Mining, **1963:** 202 [13], 455
 Mathilde Mine disaster, **1963:** 454
 Safety, **1963:** 155
Mining depletion allowance, **1961:** 391
Mining industry, Bolivia, rehabilitation, **1961:** 184
Ministers of Labor, Inter-American Conference,
  message, **1963:** 163
Minneapolis, Minn., **1962:** 179 [2]
Minnesota, **1962:** 198 [1], 425, 439, 440; **1963:** 241,
  248 ftn (p. 486), 378
 Food for needy, **1961:** 17
 Gov. Karl F. Rolvaag, **1963:** 378
Minnesota River, **1963:** 377
Minority groups, **1963:** 134
 Education, **1963:** 10
 Equal employment opportunity, **1963:** 210
 Housing, **1962:** 545
 Unemployment, **1962:** 549
Minow, Newton N. (Chairman, Federal Communi-
  cations Commission), **1962:** 27 [16], 302
  [20], 515 [16], 532
Minuteman missile, **1961:** 415 [7], 436, 455 [4];
  1962: 7 (p. 10), 13 (p. 28), 75 [20], 107 [22],
  198 [9], 343, 376, 456, 549 [9], 551 [13];
  1963: 21 (p. 32), 35 [12], 89 [14], 462, 476,
  477, 478
Mirando, Secundo, **1962:** 556
Miro Cardona, José, **1961:** 138; **1962:** 556 n.;
  1963: 134 [1]
Miscegenation laws, **1963:** 320 [6]
"Missileer" fleet defense aircraft, **1961:** 99
Missiles, **1961:** 11, 302; **1962:** 71, 173, 554; **1963:**
  168, 221, 223, 385, 476
 Air Force program, **1961:** 62 [18]
 Antimissile, **1961:** 15 [35]; **1962:** 71, 89 [8], 551
  [13]; **1963:** 21 (p. 32), 320 [17], 328 [17],
  459 [17]
 Defense systems, **1963:** 12 (p. 18)
 Eagle, **1961:** 99
 Hound Dog, **1961:** 99; **1962:** 554, 557
 ICBM, **1961:** 99, 222
 Industry, labor negotiations, **1962:** 174
 IRBM, **1962:** 485, 489
 Jupiter, **1963:** 35 [18]
 Labor dispute, Huntsville, Ala., **1962:** 340 [17]
 Minuteman, **1961:** 415 [7], 436, 455 [4]; **1962:**
  7 (p. 10), 13 (p. 28), 75 [20], 107 [22], 198
  [9], 343, 376, 456, 549 [9], 551 [13]; **1963:**
  21 (p. 32), 35 [12], 89 [14], 462, 476,
  477, 478

Missiles — *continued*
 Missile gap, comments on, **1961:** 25 [4], 33, 71 [9]
 Multilateral force.
  See Multilateral nuclear force.
 News conference remarks, **1961:** 15 [35], 25 [4],
  35 [3], 62 [18], 71 [9], 92 [11], 171 [6], 222,
  415 [7], 455 [4]; **1962:** 75 [20], 89 [8], 107
  [22], 198 [9], 316 [6], 340 [5, 8], 378 [14],
  546 [5]; **1963:** 35 [1, 12, 18, 20], 54 [8], 75
  [20], 89 [5, 14], 107 [12], 120 [10, 11], 169
  [20], 320 [17], 328 [17], 459 [17]
 Nike-X, **1963:** 21 (p. 32)
 Nike-Zeus, **1961:** 15 [35]; **1962:** 89 [8], 551 [13];
  1963: 21 (p. 32), 89 [5], 169 [20]
 Polaris, **1961:** 11, 16, 35 [3], 99, 192, 205, 243,
  415 [7], 436, 455 [4], 477; **1962:** 7 (p. 10),
  13 (p. 28), 75 [20], 107 [22], 140, 343, 395,
  456, 458, 551 [13, 4], 554, 557; **1963:** 21
  (p. 32), 35 [12, 18], 54 [8], 89 [14], 120
  [11], 147, 175 [4], 203, 320 [2, 15], 462,
  476-478
 Production in Egypt, **1963:** 120 [10]
 Skybolt, **1961:** 99, 415 [7]; **1962:** 75 [20], 546 [5],
  551 [13, 22], 554, 557; **1963:** 35 [12], 54 [8],
  89 [5], 169 [20]
 Snark, **1961:** 99
 Soviet, **1962:** 71; **1963:** 107 [12], 320 [17], 459 [17]
 Bases in Cuba.
  See Cuba.
  Underground sites, report of, **1963:** 75 [20]
 Thor, **1962:** 316 [6]; **1963:** 35 [18]
 Titan, **1961:** 99; **1962:** 75 [20], 340 [5], 378 [14],
  551 [13]; **1963:** 35 [12], 400
 Transportation of, **1961:** 92 [11]
 Versus airplanes, **1962:** 551 [14]
 Warning system, **1962:** 198 [9]
Missile Range, White Sands, **1963:** 222
Missile Sites Labor Commission, **1962:** 244; **1963:**
  446
Missile and space sites, no-strike pledge, **1961:** 499
Mississippi, **1962:** 170, 378 [6], 420; **1963:** 202 [1],
  226, 356 [22], 381
 Chlorine barge disaster, **1962:** 445
 Civil Rights Commission, question of hearings
  in, **1963:** 107 [18]
 Federal funds, proposed withdrawal to enforce
  civil rights, **1963:** 134 [5], 135, 144 [13]
 Gov. Ross Barnett, **1962:** 420 n., 445; **1963:** 305
  [25]
 Integration at University of Mississippi, **1962:**
  420, 459, 551 [10]; **1963:** 35 [23], 82.
 National Guard, **1962:** 420, 445; **1963:** 426
 Voting rights, **1963:** 120 [22]
Mississippi River, **1962:** 170; **1963:** 109, 377, 425
 Sunken chlorine barge, **1962:** 445
Missouri, **1961:** 462 n.; **1962:** 378 [22]
 Gov. John M. Dalton, **1962:** 375 n.; **1963:** 108

[References are to items except as otherwise indicated]

Missouri River, **1963:** 301, 379
Missouri River Basin project, **1962:** 335, 336
Mitchell, James P., **1961:** 448; **1963:** 85
Mitchell, John E., **1962:** 456
Mitchell, Brig. Gen. William (Billy), **1963:** 221, 353
Mobile, Ala., **1963:** 350
Mobilization for Youth, **1962:** 220
Mobley, M.D., **1962:** 412 n.
Modern Language Association, **1961:** 144
Mohamed V, King, **1963:** 114, 115 n., 116
Mohammed Ali, **1963:** 347
Mohammed Zaher, King, **1963:** 343, 344, 347
Mohole, oceanographic project, **1961:** 100, 110
Molasses imported from Cuba, **1961:** 35 [8]
Molotov, Vyacheslav M., **1962:** 141
Mona Lisa, exhibition in U.S., **1962:** 546 [1]; **1963:** 5, 16, 112
Monessen, Pa., **1962:** 454
Monetary policy, **1961:** 17, 23, 62 [4].
   See also Fiscal policy.
Monetary reform, **1961:** 245
Monetary systems, **1963:** 305 [12], 306
Money and Credit, Commission on, **1962:** 16 (p. 51), 151, 229 [1, 15]; **1963:** 30 (p. 67)
Monogan, Repr. John S., **1962:** 472, 474
"Money and Credit: Their Influence on Jobs, Prices, and Growth," report, **1961:** 245
Monge Alfaro, Carlos, **1963:** 105
Monnet, Jean, **1962:** 302 [9]; **1963:** 32, 902
Monopoly, prohibition of, **1962:** 93 (p. 241)
Monroe, James, **1962:** 252, 352 [21]; **1963:** 387
Monroe, Marilyn, **1962:** 201, 233
Monroe Doctrine, **1961:** 171 [17]; **1962:** 50 [18], 352 [21], 378 [1]; **1963:** 107 [22], 477
Monroney, Sen. A. S. Mike, **1961:** 441
Monrovia, Conference of African and Malagasy States, **1961:** 175, 304, 430
Montana, **1963:** 248 ftn. (p. 486), 382, 383, 390, 425
   Gov. Tim M. Babcock, **1963:** 382, 383
Monterey, Mexico, **1962:** 264
Montevideo conference.
   See Punta del Este conference.
Montgomery, Ala., **1961:** 198
Monticello, Va., **1962:** 201; **1963:** 204, 297
Montoya, Repr. Joseph M., **1962:** 536-538; **1963:** 222
Monuments, national, **1962:** 69; **1963:** 63, 412
Moon exploration, **1962:** 13 (p. 30), 40 [16], 59 [18], 77, 340 [5], 372-375, 546 [11]; **1963:** 21 (p. 34), 120 [18], 144 [20], 175 [4], 305 [6], 328 [19], 405 [3], 406, 426, 448, 478
Moon probes and exploration, **1961:** 139 [12], 205, 415 [17], 477
Moore, John L.
   See General Services Administrator.
Moore, Sean (Mayor of Dublin), **1963:** 279
Moorehead,Repr. William S., **1962:** 452
Moos, Malcolm, **1961:** 403

Mora, Jose A., **1961:** 122 n., 491
Mora, Juan Rafael, **1963:** 99
Moreno Sanchez, Manuel, **1962:** 189 n.
Morgan, Arthur E., **1961:** 71 [15], 320
Morgan, Edward P., **1961:** 15 [8]; **1962:** 115 [7]; **1963:** 107 [9]
Morgan, Kenneth, **1963:** 455
Morgan, Repr. Thomas E., **1962:** 455
Morgenthau, Robert, **1962:** 340 [12], 461
Morias, Mascarenhas de, **1962:** 175
Morison, Rear Adm. Samuel E., **1962:** 260; **1963:** 410
Mormons, achievements of, **1963:** 385-387
Morocco
   Assistance, **1963:** 116
   Bases U.S., evacuation, **1963:** 115, 116
   Casablanca agreement with (1959), **1963:** 116 n.
   Hassan II, King, visit of, **1963:** 114, 115, 116
   Lalla Nezha, Princess, **1963:** 115
   Mohammed V, King, **1963:** 114, 115n., 116
   Sidi Mohammed Ben Abdullah, Sultan, **1963:** 115
Morrill Act, **1961:** 462, 473
Morrill Act of 1862, **1962:** 37, 109, 166; **1963:** 82, 226, 279, 469
Morris, Robert, **1963:** 226, 259
Morris, Repr. Thomas G., **1962:** 536-538; **1963:** 222
Morrison, deLesseps, **1961:** 240, 287; **1962:** 170, 171
Morrison, Gov. Frank B., **1963:** 108
Morrison, Repr. James H., **1962:** 170
Morse, Gerry E., **1963:** 206
Morse, Otis B., IV, **1962:** 394
Morse, Sen. Wayne, **1961:** 71 [13, 22], 83 [9], 291 [8], 334 [7]; **1962:** 30 n., 459; **1963:** 18, 98, 105, 387, 388
Mortgages, **1963:** 193
   Farm, **1963:** 193
   40-year mortages, proposed, **1961:** 76
   Government held, **1963:** 305 [2]
   Insurance, **1962:** 23, 545; **1963:** 21 (p. 37), 74, 445, 466
   Interest rates, **1961:** 15 [5], 17, 62 [4], 76; **1962:** 16 (p. 44), 93 (p. 238); **1963:** 74, 305 [22], 306
Mortgage Association, Federal National.
   See Federal National Mortgage Association.
Mortgage bankers, **1961:** 258 [22]
Mortimer, Charles G., **1962:** 549 n.; **1963:** 355
Morton, Sen. Thruston, **1963:** 448 [22]
Moscoso, Teodoro, **1961:** 491, 506, 508, 517; **1962:** 17, 86, 177, 265, 316 [23], 546 [20]; **1963:** 61, 72
   Assistant Administrator for Latin America, AID, **1961:** 466
   U.S. Ambassador to Venezuela, **1961:** 160
Moscow, **1961:** 302, 467; **1962:** 20 [4]; **1963:** 232, 316
   Cultural Center, **1962:** 233

Moscow — *continued*
Meeting on Laos, **1963:** 144 [2, 5]
Meetings on nuclear test ban, **1963:** 232, 314, 324
News conference remarks, **1963:** 144 [2, 4], 169 [9]
Telecommunications, direct link with Washington, **1963:** 232, 250, 319a
Moses, Robert, **1961:** 407; **1962:** 548; **1963:** 461
Mosk, Stanley, **1961:** 477
Moss, Sen. Frank E., **1963:** 384-388
Moss, Repr. John E., **1963:** 75 [4]
Mossbauer, Rudolf, **1962:** 161 n.
Motion Picture Arts and Sciences, Academy of, **1962:** 161 n.
Mount Everest, **1962:** 373
Mt. Everest Expedition, **1963:** 158, 296
Mount McKinley Italian Expedition, **1961:** 305
Mt. Olympia, **1963:** 325
Mt. Rainier, **1963:** 387
Mount Suribachi, **1962:** 61
Mt. Vernon, **1963:** 425
Mount Vernon, state dinner, **1961:** 280
Mountbatten, Vice Adm. Louis, **1961:** 115
Mountjoy, Lord, **1963:** 278
Moving expenses, tax deduction, **1963:** 34
Mueller, Frederick H., **1961:** 58
Muhirwa, André, **1962:** 415
Mukwonago, Wis., **1962:** 186
Muller, Walter, **1962:** 542 n.
Mullowny, John, **1963:** 115
Multilateral nuclear force, NATO, proposed, **1963:** 36, 65 [6, 8, 14], 89 [14], 107 [11], 144 [19], 262, 285, 320 [15, 16]
Mundt, Sen. Karl E., **1961:** 57n., 307
Municipal ordinances, public accomodation, **1963:** 248
Municipalities, Federal aid, **1961:** 49
Muñoz Marín, Gov. Luis, **1961:** 301, 464, 506; **1962:** 305; **1963:** 169 [3], 198, and p. 902
Muñoz Marín, Mrs. Luis, **1961:** 464
Murphy, Charles S., **1962:** 8 [22], 127n., 248
Murphy, Franklin G., **1961:** 57n.
Murphy, John J., **1962:** 456
Murphy, Robert D., **1961:** 168n.; **1963:** 405 [12]
Murray, Repr. Tom, **1963:** 192
Murrow, Edward R. (Director, U.S. Information Agency), **1961:** 42, 92 [14]; **1962:** 532
Muscle Shoals, Ala., **1963:** 193
Muscle Shoals power project, **1963:** 193
Muse, Benjamin, **1962:** 257n.
Music
Contest, Arezzo, Italy, **1962:** 352 [3], 361
National High School Symphony Orchestra, **1962:** 322
White House youth program, **1962:** 150; **1963:** 137
Music Camp, National, **1962:** 322n.
Muskegon, Mich., **1962:** 438

Muskie, Sen. Edmund S., **1961:** 212, 474, 476n.; **1962:** 326; **1963:** 301n., 426
Muskogee, Okla., **1961:** 496
Mussmano, Judge Michael A., **1963:** 410n.
Muto, Alfonso A., **1962:** 158
Muto, Anthony, **1962:** 158
Mutual Assistance Act, **1961:** 318 [2]
Mutual assistance program, **1963:** 12 (p. 17)
Mutual defense agreement, U.S.-British West Indies, **1961:** 36
Mutual defense and assistance bill of 1964, **1963:** 328 [1]
Mutual Defense Assistance Control Act, **1961:** 11
Mutual Defense Treaty, U.S.-Korea, **1961:** 468
Mutual Educational and Cultural Exchange Act, **1961:** 379
Mutual Educational and Cultural Exchange Act of 1961, **1963:** 332n.
Mutual Security Act, **1961:** 6, 63
Mutual Security Act of 1960, **1963:** 231n.
Mutual security authorization bill, **1963:** 333
Mutual security bill.
See Foreign Assistance Act.
Mutual security program, **1961:** 171 [6], 415 [15]; **1962:** 147, 192; **1963:** 118
See also Economic assistance and development; Foreign assistance; Military assistance and defense support; Technical assistance to less- developed and new countries.
Report, **1962:** 237
Mutual Security Treaty, U.S.- China (1954), **1962:** 259 [13]
Mutuc, Amelito R., **1963:** 239
Mwami Mwambutsa, King, **1962:** 266
Myrdal, Gunnar, **1962:** 302 [18]

Nabuco, Joaquin, **1961:** 122
Nagasaki, **1963:** 107 [20], 328 [17]
Nairobi, Kenya, **1963:** 361
NAM.
See National Association of Manufacturers.
Naples, Italy, **1963:** 291, 293
Napoleon Bonaparte, **1961:** 291 [5]; **1962:** 551 [22]
Narcotics, Bureau of, **1962:** 7 (p. 7), 411
Narcotic addicts, hospitals for, **1962:** 115 [27]
Narcotic and Drug Abuse, President's Advisory Commission on, report, **1963:** 121
Narcotic and Drug Abuse, White House Conference on, **1962:** 218, 411
NASA.
See National Aeronautics and Space Administration.
Nash, Philleo, **1962:** 317; **1963:** 113
Nashville, Tenn. **1963:** 192, 230
Mayor Beverly Briley, **1963:** 192
White House Regional Conference, meeting, **1961:** 454n.
Nassau, Bahamas, **1962:** 546 [5]; **1963:** 285
Visit to, **1962:** 553, 554

Nassau agreement, U.S.-U.K., **1962:** 557; **1963:** 12
  (p. 16), 36, 54 [8], 75 [19], 202 [3], 320 [2,
  15, 16]
  Text, **1962:** 554
Nasser, Gamal Abdel, **1961:** 108; **1962:** 229 [10],
  557; **1963:** 448 [5]
Nast, Cyril, **1963:** 172
Nast, Thomas, **1963:** 172
Natcher, Repr. William H., **1962:** 458
Natchez, Miss., **1962:** 445
Nation, Bill, **1963:** 380
National Academy of Foreign Affairs, President's
  Committee on, **1963:** 57n.
National Academy of Foreign Affairs, proposed,
  1963: 57
National Academy of Sciences, **1961:** 49, 110, 145;
  1962: 8 [1], 69, 100; **1963:** 144 [6], 252, 430
National Academy of Sciences, President (Detlev
  W. Bronk), **1961:** 110, 145
National Advisory Committee on Manpower De-
  velopment and Training, **1962:** 412
National Advisory Committee on Radiation, **1962:**
  229 [19], 259 [19]
National Advisory Council, Peace Corps., **1961:**
  199
National Advisory Council on International Monetary and Financial Problems, **1961:** 23,
  437; **1962:** 31
National Advisory Council, Small Business Admin-
  istration, **1963:** 188
National Aeronautic Association, **1962:** 294; **1963:**
  406
National Aeronautics and Space Administration,
  1961: 8 [26], 171 [23], 206; **1962:** 13 (pp.
  30, 32), 163, 323, 370, 373, 374, **1963:** 21
  (pp. 34, 40), 29, 30 (p. 69), 135, 194, 202
  [4], 405 [3]
  Distinguished Service Medal, **1961:** 177; **1962:**
    61; **1963:** 199
  News conference remarks, **1962:** 107 [1], 245 [15],
    340 [5, 8], 378 [14]
  Space program authorization, **1961:** 296
National Aeronautics and Space Administrator
  (James E. Webb), **1961:** 177, 178, 291 [13];
  1962: 61, 74, 163, 294, 323n., 370, 372-
  374, 463; **1963:** 29, 202 [14], 406, 414n.
  On industry's part in communications satellite
    program, **1961:** 139 [21]
National Aeronautics and Space Council, **1961:**
  139 [12], 147, 205, 254; **1962:** 39
  Communications satellites, policy coordination,
    1961: 299
National Air Lines, **1961:** 50
National Archives and Records Service, **1962:** 278,
  546; **1963:** 94
National Association of Broadcasters, **1961:** 178;
  1962: 49, 515 [7]
National Association of Home Builders, **1962:** 545

National Association of Manufacturers, **1961:** 497;
  1963: 75 [14]
National Association for Retarded Children, **1962:**
  534; **1963:** 435
National Audubon Society, **1963:** 196
National Automobile Show, **1962:** 378 [10]
National Banking System, **1963:** 77
National Broadcasting Co., **1962:** 551n.
National Capital Affairs, President's Advisor for
  (Charles A. Horsky), **1963:** 35 [15]
National Capital Park System, **1962:** 362
National Capital Planning Commission, **1962:** 221,
  525; **1963:** 208
National Capital Region, **1963:** 22, 456
  Redevelopment, **1962:** 525
  Report on transportation, **1963:** 208
National Capital Regional Planning Council, **1962:**
  525; **1963:** 208
National Capital Transportation Act of 1960, **1963:**
  208
National Capital Transportation Agency, **1963:** 22,
  208
National Cemetery, Arlington, **1963:** 173
National Citizens' Host Committee for the World
  Food Congress, **1963:** 33
National Civil Service League, **1962:** 167
National Collegiate Athletic Association, **1963:** 7
National Committee for an Effective Congress,
  1962: 340 [18]
National Committee on Health Care for the Aged,
  1963: 459 [12], 460
National Community Christmas Tree, **1962:** 550
National Conference of the Business Committee for
  Tax Reduction, **1963:** 351
National Conference of Christians and Jews, **1961:**
  479
National Conference of Commissioners on Uni-
  form State Laws, **1962:** 129
National Conference on Cooperatives, **1963:** 149
National Conference on International Economic
  and Social Development, **1961:** 244
National Conference on Milk and Nutrition, **1962:**
  19
National Conference of State Legislative Leaders,
  1963: 368
National Congress of American Indians, **1963:** 86
National Cotton Advisory Committee, **1962:** 198
  [17]
National Council of Farmer Cooperatives, **1963:**
  149n.
National Council of Negro Women, **1962:** 27 [11]
National Council of Senior Citizens, **1962:** 202n.,
  217
National Cultural Center, **1961:** 77, 467; **1962:**
  152 [5], 361, 527, 552
  See also John F. Kennedy Center for the
    Performing Arts.
National Cultural Center Act, **1963:** 327

National Cultural Center Week, **1962:** 527n.
National debt.
  See Debt, national.
National defense.
  See National security.
National Defense, Council of, **1963:** 133
National Defense, French Institute of High Studies for, **1963:** 112
National Defense Education Act, **1961:** 71 [13], 144, 291 [18], 318 [17], 398; **1963:** 43, 82, 92, 248, 378
National Defense Education Act of 1958, **1962:** 37, 469
National Democratic Committee, Chairman (John M. Bailey), **1961:** 498
National economy.
  See Economy, national.
National Education Association, **1961:** 255; **1963:** 469
National Education Improvement Act of 1963, **1963:** 43, 185
National Emergency Broadcasting System, **1961:** 154
National emergency, question of, **1962:** 378 [19]
National Environmental Health Center, proposed, **1962:** 65
National Environmental Health Research Center, **1963:** 448 [21]
National Farmers Organization, **1962:** 352 [4]
National Farmers Union, **1963:** 404n.
National Federation of Grain Cooperatives, **1963:** 149n.
National Football Foundation, **1961:** 496
National forests.
  See Forests, national.
National 4-H Club, **1961:** 67
National Gallery of Art, **1962:** 546 [1], 552; **1963:** 5, 16
National Geographic Society, **1962:** 262; **1963:** 296n.
National Geographic Society Medal, **1961:** 134
National groups.
  See Address or remarks to national groups.
National Guard, **1961:** 477; **1962:** 13 (p. 29), 309, 407
  Alabama, **1963:** 181, 234, 236n., 237, 242, 350n.
  Call to active duty, **1961:** 291 [4]; **1962:** 7 (p. 10)
  Cambridge, Md., **1963:** 305 [20]
  Mississippi, **1962:** 420, 445; **1963:** 426
  New York, **1962:** 416
  News conference remarks, **1962:** 20 [17], 139 [2, 16], 378 [19]
  Release of units from active duty, **1962:** 139 [2], 140
  Scholarships for mobilized members, proposed, **1962:** 20 [17]
  Wisconsin, **1962:** 186
National Guard Air, **1961:** 302
National Health Survey, **1963:** 64

National High School Symphony Orchestra, **1962:** 322
National Historical Publications Commission, **1963:** 26, 245
National Housing Act (1949), **1962:** 142; **1963:** 74
National Housing Agency, **1961:** 130
National Housing Conference, **1963:** 77
National Industrial Conference Board, **1961:** 33
National Institute of Child Health and Human Development, **1962:** 65, 470; **1963:** 53, 74, 447
National Institute of Child Health and Human Development, proposed, **1961:** 27
National Institutes of Health, **1961:** 27, 488 [8]; **1962:** 7 (p. 8), 65, 174, 209, 470; **1963:** 21 (p. 37), 50, 144 [6], 435
National Institute of Mental Health, **1961:** 413; **1962:** 65; **1963:** 50, 66
National Institute of Neurological Diseases and Blindness, **1961:** 413; **1963:** 435
National Labor-Management Panel, **1963:** 206
National Labor Relations Board, **1961:** 121; **1962:** 340 [17]; **1963:** 82
  Reorganization Plan 5 of 1961, **1961:** 200
National Library of Medicine, **1962:** 65; **1963:** 247
National Library Week, **1961:** 126
National Maritime Engineers' Beneficial Association, **1961:** 270; **1962:** 21
National Maritime Union of America, **1961:** 270
National Medal of Science, presentation, **1963:** 68
National Mediation Board, **1962:** 66, 245 [1], 253, 256; **1963:** 92, 95n., 244, 310, 414
National Mental Health, **1962:** 65
National Milk Producers Federation, **1963:** 149n.
National Music Camp, **1962:** 322n.
National Oceanographic Data Center, **1961:** 100
National Organizations, Annual Conference of, **1963:** 101
National parks.
  See also Parks.
National Parks Association, **1963:** 196
National Park Service, **1961:** 17; **1962:** 128
National Press Club, **1961:** 488 [5]
National Press Club, Women's, **1963:** 448 [2]
National product, **1961:** 11, 17, 90, 99, 258 [4], 291 [2], 436, 455 [7, 17], 499; **1962:** 13 (pp. 26, 32), 16 (pp. 43, 45), 40 [9], 111, 115 [16], 174, 203, 229 [16], 234, 316 [13], 328, 395, 473, 549; **1963:** 12 (p. 19), 21 (p. 30), 30 (pp. 57, 59, 62, 63), 34, 77, 92, 94, 110, 118, 120 [11], 134, 144 [14], 175, 305 [18], 328 [1], 329, 351, 361, 459 [6], 465, 466, 477
National Recreation Association, **1962:** 128
National Research Council, **1962:** 19
National Rural Electric Cooperative Association, **1962:** 499; **1963:** 149n.
National Science Board, **1962:** 118

National Science Foundation, **1961:** 94, 100, 110;
    1962: 8 [1], 13 (p. 32), 37, 118, 469; **1963:**
    21 (p. 38), 43, 82, 248
National Science Foundation, Director (Alan T.
    Waterman), **1961:** 110; **1962:** 163
National Science Foundation Act, **1963:** 92
National Science Youth Month, **1961:** 378
National security, **1961:** 17, 23, 33, 90, 94, 153, 161,
    168, 497; **1962:** 13 (pp. 26, 28), 16 (p. 44),
    140, 162, 163, 170, 174, 199, 226, 230, 247,
    250, 275, 280, 282, 314, 326, 328, 343, 369,
    375, 389, 395, 396, 398, 428, 432, 458, 485,
    486, 521, 530, 531, 535, 549, 551 [13, 17];
    1963: 12 (pp. 15, 18), 21 (pp. 31, 32, 34, 37,
    43), 30 (pp. 61, 70), 32, 34, 39, 43, 52, 58,
    64, 76, 77 [1, 4], 87, 92, 94, 102, 111, 112,
    118, 134, 136, 146, 147, 159, 166, 175, 179,
    195, 203, 216, 221, 222, 225, 227, 242, 244,
    251, 256, 257, 259, 287, 290, 303, 306, 310,
    316, 319a, 321, 324, 330, 333, 334, 338,
    339, 344, 349, 351, 354, 359, 361, 366, 378,
    383, 385, 389, 391, 396, 399, 414, 422, 426,
    427, 441, 445, 450, 451, 455, 462, 464, 465,
    472, 475-477
    News conference remarks, **1961:** 8 [23], 15 [8, 30,
        37], 25 [7, 22], 35 [7], 62 [24, 25], 171 [6],
        415 [7], 455 [4, 18]; **1962:** 20 [15], 40 [1],
        50 [25], 75 [3], 89 [4], 107 [7], 139 [1], 152
        [12, 17, 18], 179 [8], 198 [3], 259 [14], 279
        [1], 302 [3], 340 [8], 352 [22], 378 [1, 7],
        515 [7]; **1963:** 35 [12, 20], 65 [15], 89 [5,
        20], 107 [11, 21], 120 [11], 260 [5, 6, 13],
        305 [6], 320 [2, 10, 17], 328 [1, 2, 4, 16, 17],
        356 [1], 405 [4, 18], 448 [18], 459 [6]
National Security Council, **1961:** 171 [7, 12], 262,
    291 [9], 318 [9, 14], 258 [3, 21], 340; **1962:**
    71, 75 [21], 259 [21], 316 [18], 546 [4, 23],
    551 [4]; **1963:** 324, 328 [4], 349, 399, 405
    [1, 2], 407
National Security Medal, **1961:** 485
National Service Corps, proposed, **1963:** 21 (p. 38),
    50, 64, 74, 113, 130, 232, 458
National Service Life Insurance, **1962:** 16 (p. 44),
    517
National Trust for Historic Preservation, **1963:** 425
National University (Ireland), **1963:** 279
National Vocational Education Arts, **1961:** 46
National War College, **1963:** 120 [16]
National Wildlife Federation, **1963:** 196
    Dedication of new building, **1961:** 65
National Young President's Conference, **1963:** 436
Nationalism, **1963:** 12 (pp. 15, 18), 271, 291
NATO.
    See North Atlantic Treaty Organization.
Natural gas prices, **1962:** 93 (p. 237)
Natural gas rate increase cases, FPC backlog, **1961:**
    121

Natural resources, **1961:** 65, 445; **1962:** 13 (p. 28),
    22, 458; **1963:** 128, 378
    Appalachian region, **1963:** 127
    Columbia River Basin development, **1961:** 49,
        83 [2], 474
    Conservation, **1961:** 17, 49, 85, 94, 100
    Conservation and development, **1962:** 7 (p. 7), 13
        (p. 30), 25, 75 [23], 128, 216, 240, 332, 333,
        336, 410 [7], 413, 425, 495, 549; **1963:** 12
        (p. 14), 21 (p. 36), 34, 37, 41, 45, 47, 63, 70,
        127, 179, 193, 196, 252, 305 [14], 366, 376,
        377, 379, 380, 381, 383-385, 387, 388, 400,
        405 [5], 430, 474, 478
        Message to Congress, **1962:** 69
    Latin America, **1963:** 72
    Presidential advisory commission, proposed,
        1961: 49
    Research, **1961:** 49, 100; **1963:** 70, 127, 252
    Timber damage, Pacific Northwest, **1962:** 495
    Western Europe, **1963:** 72
Natural Resouces, Citizens Committee on, **1963:**
    196n.
Natural Resources, Committee on, **1963:** 252
Navajo Indians, **1962:** 240
Navajo Irrigation Project, approval, **1962:** 240
Naval Academy, United States, **1962:** 226; **1963:**
    222, 223, 321
Naval and Airspace Reservation, Guam, **1962:** 342
Naval Operations, Chief of (Adm. George W.
    Anderson, Jr.), **1963:** 169 [5], 318
Naval Ordnance Plant, U.S., South Charleston,
    W. Va., **1961:** 119 [13]
Naval prints, Franklin D. Roosevelt's, exhibit,
    1962: 260
Naval Research, Office of, **1961:** 100
Naval War College, **1961:** 392
Navigation, **1961:** 17, 49, 94; **1962:** 69; **1963:** 21 (p.
    36), 193
    Satellites, **1962:** 373; **1963:** 470
    Sub-Artic, **1962:** 323, 451
Navy, **1962:** 119, 148, 149, 260, 287, 326, 330, 384,
    402, 423; **1963:** 21 (p. 33), 147, 225, 227,
    263, 312, 321, 396, 448 [6, 15, 22], 476
    Bases abroad, **1963:** 202 [8]
    Construction program, **1961:** 99
    Fighter aircraft, **1961:** 99
    Guantanamo naval base in Cuba, **1961:** 71 [8]
    Increase in strength, **1961:** 99, 302; **1962:** 7 (p.
        10), 343; **1963:** 21 (p. 33), 120 [11]
    "Missileer" fleet defense aircraft, **1961:** 99
    News conference remarks, **1961:** 8 [16], 35 [7], 71
        [8], 92 [3]
    Reserve forces, release from active duty, **1962:**
        140, 309
    Santa Maria incident, **1961:** 8 [16]
    Unit citations, **1962:** 521
Navy, Chief of Operations (Adm. Goerge W.
    Anderson, Jr.), **1963:** 169 [5], 225, 312,
    318, 356 [24]

Navy, Secretary of the (John B. Connally, Jr.),
1961: 16, 232
Navy, Secretary of the (Fred Korth), **1962:** 294,
309, 323n.; **1963:** 318, 328 [20], 448 [6, 22],
459 [16]
Navy Electronics Laboratory, San Diego, Calif.,
1962: 323
Navy Relief Fund, **1962:** 326
Navy Summer Festival, **1962:** 326
Nazism, **1962:** 551 [23]
NDEA.
See National Defense Education Act.
Near East.
See Middle East and Near East.
Nebraska
Civil rights, **1963:** 248ftn. (p. 486)
Gov. Frank B. Morrison, **1963:** 108
SAC base, **1963:** 112
Neches River Basin, **1962:** 313
Nedzi, Repr. Lucien N., **1962:** 433, 436
Negro College Fund, United, **1963:** 355
Negro Women, National Council of, **1962:** 27 [11]
Negroes.
See also Civil rights; Voting rights.
Admission to University of Alabama, **1963:** 169
[4], 202 [1], 234, 236, 237, 243
Armed forces, **1963:** 82, 251
Birmingham, Ala., **1963:** 169 [1, 4, 14, 19], 181,
182, 202 [20], 228, 230, 248, 372
Century of Progress Exposition, **1963:** 153
Churches, bombing of, **1963:** 360, 365
Churches, burning of, **1962:** 378 [6]
Civil rights movement.
See Civil rights.
Conference of leaders on foreign policy, **1962:**
546 [9]
District of Columbia, **1963:** 22, 35 [15], 230, 305
[20], 328 [3, 9], 336, 356 [22]
Education, **1963:** 10, 237, 248, 328 [12], 339, 355,
444
Employment, **1963:** 10, 110, 220, 328 [12], 356 [8],
444, 462
Employment opportunities, **1962:** 302 [18]
Equal rights, **1962:** 399; **1963:** 59, 82, 89 [8], 107
[18], 135, 169 [1, 4, 14, 19], 181, 182, 202 [1,
20], 228, 230, 248, 251, 271
Housing, **1963:** 134
In Albany, Ga., **1962:** 316 [8]
In Peace Corps, **1962:** 243 [5]
Mississippi, **1963:** 107 [18], 135
Movements to northern States, **1962:** 179 [11]
News conference remarks, **1962:** 179 [11], 302
[18], 316 [8], 340 [11], 378 [6], 546 [9];
1963: 35 [15], 75 [7], 89 [9], 107 [18], 169
[1, 4, 14, 19], 202 [1, 20], 320 [9], 328 [12],
356 [22]
Occupational training, **1963:** 220, 248
Property, bombing of, **1963:** 181

Negroes — *continued*
Repr. Adam. C. Powell, role as leader, **1963:** 75
[7]
U.S. ambassadors, **1962:** 340 [11]
Veterans, **1963:** 135
Welfare programs, **1963:** 135
Nehemias, reference to, **1961:** 441
Nehru, B. K., **1963:** 296
Nehru, Jawaharlal, **1961:** 11, 35 [1], 455 [14], 460;
1962: 50 [10], 316 [14], 363, 554
Visit of, **1961:** 452, 456
Neri, Murillo, **1961:** 105
Neisch, Clarence, **1962:** 451n.
Nelson, Gov. Gaylord A., **1962:** 186; **1963:** 377,
392
Nepal, **1963:** 158, 296
Ambassador Matrika Prasad Koirala, **1963:** 296
Nepal, Peace Corps project, **1962:** 325
Nerva space project, **1962:** 546 [11]
Netherlands, **1962:** 230; **1963:** 254, 361
Crown Princess Beatrix, visit of, **1963:** 132
Dispute with Indonesia, **1961:** 119 [21]; **1962:**
8 [3, 19], 139 [10], 210 [22], 251, 316 [3, 7],
323, 334, 340 [14], 346; **1963:** 12 (p. 18),
232
Investment in capital goods, **1961:** 33
Prince Bernhard, visit of, **1963:** 132
Queen Juliana, **1963:** 132
Neuberger, Sen. Maurine B., **1963:** 387, 388, 409
Neuberger, Richard L., **1961:** 8 [31], 171 [11], 403
Neurological Diseases and Blindness, National
Institute of, **1961:** 413; **1963:** 435
Neustadt, Richard E., **1961:** 29
Neutral nations, **1962:** 50 [2]
See also Nonaligned nations.
Neutron bomb, **1961:** 318 [18]
Nevada, **1962:** 316 [22], 538
Gov. Grant Sawyer, **1963:** 390
Nuclear test site, **1961:** 349n.
Nuclear weapons tests, underground, postpone-
ment, **1963:** 40
New Brunswick, Canada, Louis J. Robinchaud,
1963: 180
New Deal, **1962:** 186, 439, 453; **1963:** 105, 268, 400
New Delhi, **1962:** 68, 515 [3]
New Dockside Terminal, New Orleans, dedication,
1962: 170
New England, **1961:** 26, 62 [13]; **1963:** 42, 459 [25]
New England's Salute to the President, **1963:** 427
New England-New York Inter-agency Committee
on the Passamaquoddy Tidal Power
Project, **1961:** 197
New Freedom, **1962:** 439
New Frontier, **1961:** 133, 497; **1962:** 77, 109, 186,
230, 439, 453
New Guinea, **1963:** 366, 471

New Guinea, West, **1961:** 119 [21]
  See also West New Guinea.
New Hampshire, **1962:** 326
  Civil rights, **1963:** 248ftn. (p. 486)
  Gov. John W. King, **1963:** 108, 427
  Gov. Wesley Powell, **1962:** 278
  Primary elections (1964), **1963:** 459 [7], 473
New Haven, Conn., **1962:** 234, 243 [2], 279 [19], 473
  Federal aid, **1963:** 423
  Mayor Richard C. Lee, **1962:** 473; **1963:** 230, 423
  Youth training demonstration project, **1963:** 423
New Haven Railroad, **1962:** 27 [7]
New Jersey, **1962:** 202, 450
  Candidates for public office, **1961:** 448, 455 [5]
New Jersey, civil rights, **1963:** 248ftn. (p. 486)
  Compact with Delaware, **1962:** 391
  Delaware River Basin compact, **1961:** 445
  Election, **1961:** 455 [5]
  Gov. Richard J. Hughes, **1962:** 174, 450
  Gov. Robert B. Meyner, **1961:** 448
New Mexico, **1962:** 240, 340 [22], 536-538; **1963:** 134 [5], 223
  Civil rights, **1963:** 248ftn. (p. 486)
  Gov. Jack M. Campbell, **1963:** 222
New Mexico, education of Indian children, **1961:** 94
New Orleans, La., **1962:** 170, 171, 179 [11]; **1963:** 82
  Integration of parochial schools, **1961:** 25 [8], 55; **1962:** 152 [13]
  Mayor Victor H. Schiro, **1962:** 170, 171
New Ross, Ireland, **1963:** 275, 276n.
New South Wales, **1962:** 383
New Year greetings to Soviet Union, **1961:** 522
New York, **1962:** 158, 183, 216, 335; **1963:** 228, 241, 381, 385, 436,
  Candidates for public office, **1962:** 460, 461
  Civil rights, **1963:** 248ftn. (p. 486)
  Delaware River Basin compact, **1961:** 455
  Democratic Party, divisions within, **1961:** 8 [20]
  District Courts, **1962:** 21, 247n.
  Gov. Nelson A. Rockefeller, **1961:** 83 [7], 448, 503; **1962:** 40 [8], 50 [6], 200, 229 [6], 439; **1963:** 65 [13], 89 [8], 202 [9, 19], 305 [24], 356 [12], 455, 459 [6]
  Gubernatorial election, **1962:** 340 [12]
  Housing laws, **1962:** 515 [10]
  Marble Industry Board, **1962:** 274
  National Guard, **1962:** 416
  Seneca Nation, opposition to Kinzua Dam project, **1961:** 71 [15], 320
  Taxes, **1963:** 356 [12]
New York City, **1961:** 15 [27], 467, 477; **1962:** 202, 527n.; **1963:** 16, 310, 474
  American Newspaper Publishers Association dinner, **1961:** 153
  Association of the Bar, **1961:** 152
  Birthday salute to the President, **1962:** 201; **1963:** 204

New York City — *continued*
  Candidates for public office, **1961:** 447, 455 [5]
  Ceremonies at signing of bill establishing U.S. Arms Control and Disarmament Agency, **1961:** 388
  Democratic primary, **1961:** 334 [24]
  Economic Club, **1962:** 546 [6], 549
  Election, **1961:** 455 [5]
  Foreign ministers meeting, **1962:** 352 [6]
  Hospital for narcotic addicts, **1962:** 115 [27]
  Juvenile delinquency, **1962:** 243 [4]
  Mayor Robert F. Wagner, **1961:** 215, 407, 447, 455 [5]; **1962:** 200, 201, 218, 220, 229 [23], 340 [12], 411, 548; **1963:** 107 [16], 203, 204, 455
  Meeting with President Arthruo Frondizi, **1961:** 389
  National Association of Manufacturers luncheon, **1961:** 497
  National Football Foundation banquet, **1961:** 496
  News conference remarks, **1962:** 115 [27], 352 [6], 546 [3, 8]
  Newspaper strike, **1963:** 35 [11], 75 [2, 13], 107 [16], 120 [9]
  Penn Station South Urban Renewal Project, **1962:** 200
  Port Authority, **1962:** 549 [2]
  Schools, lectures by scientists, **1962:** 546 [8]
  White House Regional Conference, meeting, **1961:** 454n.
  World's Fair, **1962:** 548
New York Herald Tribune, **1961:** 153
New York Herald-Tribune World Youth Forum, remarks, **1963:** 90
New York Shipping Association, **1963:** 18n.
New York Telephone Co., **1962:** 452
New York Times, **1962:** 260, 452; **1963:** 205, 245
New York World's Fair, **1961:** 407
New York Yacht Club, **1962:** 383
New Zealand, **1962:** 248; **1963:** 171, 296, 308
New Zealand, Keith Holyoake, **1961:** 66
Newark, N. J., **1962:** 450
Newhart, Bob, **1962:** 527n.
Newhouse, Samuel I., **1963:** 76n.
Newley, Anthony, *Stop the World-I Want to Get Off,* **1962:** 234
Newly independent nations.
  See Less developed countries and new nations.
Newport, R.I., **1962:** 383, 384, 403; **1963:** 216n., 368
  Meeting with Prime Minister Nehru, **1961:** 452n., 456
  Naval War College, **1961:** 392
  Releases from, **1961:** 388-391, 393, 394, 412, 430; **1962:** 348, 357, 358, 360, 381, 382, 386, 396, 404
  Summer White House, proposed, **1962:** 50 [20]
Newport Preservation Society, **1962:** 383n.

News briefings by government officials, comment on, **1961:** 25 [5]
News conferences, comments on, **1961:** 8 [12], 62 [12], 71 [10], 153, 455 [10]
News conferences, improvement, question of, **1963:** 356 [21]
News conferences, the President's
  January 15, **1962:** 8
  January 24, **1962:** 20
  January 24, **1963:** 35
  January 25 (no. 1), **1961:** 8
  January 31, **1962:** 27
  February 1 (No. 2), **1961:** 15
  February 7, **1962:** 40
  February 7, **1963:** 54
  February 8 (No. 3), **1961:** 25
  February 14, **1962:** 50
  February 14, **1963:** 65
  February 15 (No. 4), **1961:** 35
  February 21, **1962:** 59
  February 21, **1963:** 75
  March 1 (No. 5), **1961:** 62
  March 6, **1963:** 89
  March 7, **1962:** 75
  March 8 (No. 6), **1961:** 71
  March 14, **1962:** 89
  March 15 (no. 7), **1961:** 83
  March 21, **1962:** 107
  March 21, **1963:** 107
  March 23 (No. 8), **1961:** 92
  March 29, **1962:** 115
  April 3, **1963:** 120
  April 11, **1962:** 139
  April 12 (No. 9), **1961:** 119
  April 18, **1962:** 152
  April 21 (No. 10), **1961:** 139
  April 24, **1963:** 144
  May 5 (No. 11), **1961:** 171
  May 8, **1963:** 169
  May 9, **1962:** 179
  May 17, **1962:** 198
  May 22, **1963:** 202
  May 23, **1962:** 210
  June 2 (no. 12), Paris, **1961:** 222
  June 7, **1962:** 229
  June 14, **1962:** 245
  June 24, Bonn, Germany, **1963:** 260
  June 27, **1962:** 259
  June 28 (no. 13), **1961:** 258
  July 5, **1962:** 279
  July 17, **1963:** 305
  July 19 (No. 14), **1961:** 291
  July 23, **1962:** 302
  August 1, **1962:** 316
  August 1, **1963:** 320
  August 10 (No. 15), **1961:** 318
  August 20, **1963:** 328
  August 22, **1962:** 340

News conferences — *continued*
  August 29, **1962:** 352
  August 30 (No. 16), **1962:** 334
  August 30, Hyannis Port, Mass., **1963:** 338
  September 12, **1963:** 356
  September 13, **1962:** 378
  September 26, **1962:** 410
  October 9, **1963:** 405
  October 11 (No. 17), **1961:** 415
  October 31, **1963:** 448
  November 8 (No. 18), **1961:** 455
  November 14, **1963:** 459
  November 20, **1962:** 515
  November 29 (No. 19), **1961:** 488
  December 12, **1962:** 546
News management, question of, **1963:** 75 [9], 448 [2]
Newsmen.
  See Press.
Newspaper Editors, American Society of, **1961:** 138; **1963:** 134
Newspaper Publishers Association, American, **1961:** 153
Newspaper strikes, **1962:** 179 [2]; **1963:** 35 [11], 54 [6], 75 [2, 13], 107 [16], 120 [9]
Newspapers, intelligence data, publication, **1961:** 153, 185
Newsweek magazine, **1962:** 20 [2]
Newton, Isaac, **1962:** 373
Newton, Mass., **1963:** 136n.
Ngala, Ronald, **1962:** 18
Nhu, Ngo Dinh, **1963:** 202 [10], 356 [11], 459 [5]
Nhu, Madam, **1963:** 459 [5]
Niagara Falls, N.Y., **1962:** 460
Nicaragua, **1963:** 99, 100, 102, 106
Nicaragua, rural electrification, **1962:** 499
Nicholls, William H., **1962:** 412n.
Nichols, Mike, **1962:** 201
Nichols, Wade H., **1963:** 319a note
Nickel, ocean deposits, **1961:** 49, 100
Nickel, stockpile of, **1962:** 27 [3]
Nigeria, **1962:** 104; **1963:** 118
  Assistance, **1962:** 83
  Assistance and development, **1961:** 304
  Azikiwe, Nnamdi, **1961:** 188, 394
  Balewa, Abubakar Tafawa, **1961:** 304; **1963:** 331
  Peace Corps in, **1962:** 64, 325
Nike-X surface-to-air missile, **1963:** 21 (p. 32)
Nike-Zeus antimissile missile, **1963:** 21 (p. 32), 89 [5], 169 [20]
Nike-Zeus missile, **1961:** 15 [35]; **1962:** 89 [8], 551 [13]
Nikezic, Marko, **1961:** 363n.
Nile River, **1961:** 402
Nile Valley antiquities, preservation, **1961:** 108
Ninety-Nines, Inc., **1963:** 315
Nitze, Paul, **1961:** 25 [4], 218; **1962:** 515 [3]
Nix, Repr. Robert N.C., **1963:** 445

[References are to items except as otherwise indicated]

Nixon, Richard M., **1961:** 1, 8 [32], 139 [5, 10], 258
    [14], 318 [6], 319, 334 [8, 11], 448; **1962:** 89
    [19], 107 [6], 115 [6], 199, 201, 219, 229
    [20], 279 [26], 352 [25], 453, 515 [16];
    1963: 144 [8], 151, 320 [5], 455, 459 [6]
Nkrumah, Kwame, **1961:** 181, 273, 331
    Visit of, **1961:** 72, 73, 74
Noa, U.S.S., **1962:** 57
Nobel, Alfred, **1962:** 161
Nobel Prize, **1961:** 462; **1962:** 59 [15], 77, 109, 161,
    180; **1963:** 178
Nobel Prize winners, **1963:** 328 [17]
Nobel, Jeanne L., **1963:** 10n.
Noblitt, Harding, **1962:** 439, 440
Nolan, Monica, **1962:** 432
Nolan, Thomas B., **1961:** 490
Nolting, Frederick W., **1961:** 34n.
Nonaligned nations, **1961:** 497; **1962:** 50 [2]; **1963:** 12
    (p. 16)
    Belgrade conference, **1961:** 334 [4], 359, 363, 364,
        365, 387
Nondiscrimination.
    See Civil rights.
Noriega Morales, Manuel, **1962:** 86n.
Norris, George W., **1961:** 278; **1962:** 335, 336, 499;
    1963: 193
Norris Centennial Rate, TVA, **1961:** 278
Norstad, Gen. Lauris, **1961:** 15 [15], 25 [17], 115, 221
    1962: 40 [15], 295, 302 [16], 316 [20], 442;
    1963: 8, 65 [9], 221
North Africa, **1961:** 165, 173; **1962:** 464
North American Aviation, Inc. **1961:** 281n.; **1962:**
    390
North American continent, defense, **1962:** 13 (p. 28)
North American Wildlife Foundation, **1963:** 196
North Atlantic Alliance.
    See North Atlantic Treaty Organization.
North Atlantic Council, **1962:** 20 [5], 40 [15], 279
    [8], 302 [16], 340 [20]
    U.S. Permanent Representative (Thomas K.
        Finletter), **1961:** 25 [2, 17], 221
North Atlantic Treaty, **1961:** 355
    12th anniversary of signing, **1961:** 106
North Atlantic Treaty Organization, **1961:** 11, 41,
    47, 112, 115, 128n., 192, 220, 239, 302,
    376, 476; **1962:** 15, 22, 77-79, 129, 157,
    178, 492, 494, 531, 537, 551 [3, 21, 22];
    1963: 8, 15, 16, 36, 132, 147, 156, 179, 221,
    238, 262, 263, 266, 268, 285, 287, 288, 290,
    291, 292, 303, 314, 318, 362, 385, 442, 464,
    466
    Acting Secretary General (Alberico Casardi),
        1961: 106
    Advisory Group for Aeronautical Research and
        Development, **1963:** 68, 165
    Athens foreign ministers meeting, **1962:** 160, 179
        [16], 198 [14]
    Defense institute, **1963:** 303

North Atlantic Treaty Organization — *continued*
    Executive committee, proposed, **1963:** 65 [9]
    Foreign ministers meetings, **1961:** 25 [6], 171
        [14], 291 [5, 15], 318 [7], 334 [19], 481, 488
        [11, 12]
    French naval forces, withdrawal, question of,
        1963: 260 [15]
    German military forces, control of, **1961:** 483
    Heads of government meeting, question of, **1961:**
        25 [6]
    Italy, role of, **1963:** 290
    Joint statements, **1962:** 160, 183, 508, 554
    Joint statements with foreign leaders on, **1961:**
        120, 135, 193, 223, 242, 481
    Member countries, economic growth, **1963:** 291
    Military Committee meeting, **1961:** 115
    Military strength, **1961:** 239, 291 [5], 318 [7], 334
        [19]; **1962:** 7 (p. 13), 259 [6]; **1963:** 260 [15]
    Multilateral nuclear force, proposed, **1963:** 36, 65
        [6, 8, 14], 89 [14], 107 [11], 144 [19], 260
        [17], 262, 285, 320 [15, 16]
    NATO allies, wheat sales to Communist bloc
        countries, **1963:** 405 [1]
    NATO countries, shipments to Cuba, **1962:** 352
        [19], 378 [1], 546 [10]
    NATO journalists, visit to U.S., **1963:** 238
    Naval Headquarters at Norfolk, 10th anniver-
        sary, **1962:** 135
    News conference remarks, **1961:** 15 [15], 25 [2, 6,
        17], 62 [26], 171 [14], 222, 291 [5, 11, 15],
        318 [7], 334 [2, 19, 25], 415 [5, 13], 455
        [15], 488 [6, 11, 12]; **1962:** 65 [6, 9, 15],
        260 [4, 6, 17], 328 [11], 448 [1, 28]; **1963:**
        20 [5, 6, 10], 40 [15], 89 [4], 179 [16], 198
        [3, 6, 14, 16], 210 [11], 259 [6, 9], 279 [4, 8,
        25], 302 [6], 340 [20], 515 [6, 7], 546 [10]
    Non-aggression agreement, question of, **1963:**
        320 [4]
    Non-nuclear powers, **1963:** 320 [15, 16]
    Nuclear weapons for, **1961:** 25 [17], 115, 192,
        355; **1962:** 40 [15], 198 [3], 279 [25], 554,
        557; **1963:** 12 (p. 16), 20, 54 [8], 65 [6, 8,
        14], 89 [14], 107 [11], 262, 285
    Oil shipments to Cuba, U.S. efforts to halt, **1963:**
        89 [16]
    Ottawa foreign ministers meeting, **1963:** 65 [6],
        107 [11], 179
    Polaris submarines for, **1961:** 205
    Preparedness study, **1963:** 65 [18]
    Relations with Warsaw Pact countries, **1961:**
        483, 488 [6]
    Secretary General (Paul Henri Spaak), **1961:** 47
    Secretary General (Dirk Stikker), **1962:** 40 [15]
    Supreme Commanders
        Lemnitzer, Gen. Lyman L., **1962:** 422, 423
        Norstad, Gen. Lauris, **1961:** 15 [15], 25 [17],
            221; **1962:** 40 [15], 295, 302 [16], 316 [20]
    U.S. advisory group, **1961:** 25 [2, 17]

North Carolina, **1961:** 26; **1963:** 230, 448 [21]
 Gov. Terry Sanford, **1961:** 327, 416n., 418n.;
     1963: 108
 Trade Fair, **1961:** 416
North Dakota, **1962:** 178, 425; **1963:** 248ftn. (p.
     486), 379, 383, 390
 Gov. William L. Guy, **1963:** 379
North Pole, **1962:** 340 [1], 493
North-South highway project, **1962:** 414
Northern Great Lakes Region Land and People
     Conference, **1963:** 378
Northern Hemisphere, **1962:** 71
Northwest Ordinance (1787), **1961:** 71 [17], 473;
     1962: 37, 540; **1963:** 43, 92, 226, 228, 279,
     385, 469
Nortvedt, Robert, **1963:** 387
Norway, **1962:** 82
 Ambassador Paul Koht, **1962:** 161n.; **1963:** 133
 Gerhardsen, Einar, **1962:** 178, 182, 183
 Immigrants from, **1962:** 178
 Trade agreements with U.S., **1962:** 76
Notte, Gov. John A., Jr., **1961:** 212
Nova space project, **1961:** 139 [12]
Noyes, Crosby, **1961:** 222 [6]
Noyes, Mrs. Blanche, **1963:** 315
NSC.
 See National Security Council.
Nu (U), **1961:** 367
Nuccio, Nick, **1963:** 464
Nuclear age, **1962:** 226, 551 [14, 15]
Nuclear arms race, **1961:** 519
Nuclear attack on U.S., defense measures, **1962:** 13
     (p. 28), 320; **1963:** 21 (p. 33), 166, 390
Nuclear attack on U.S., retaliation in case of, **1961:**
     205
Nuclear pollution, **1963:** 366
Nuclear power projects, 1961: 49; **1962:** 100, 289,
     335, 382, 408; **1963:** 384
Nuclear-powered aircraft, **1961:** 99
Nuclear-power ships
 See Ships, nuclear-powered.
Nuclear reactors, **1961:** 99; **1962:** 289, 382, 408
Nuclear stockpiles, **1961:** 483
Nuclear test ban treaty, **1963:** 40, 314, 319a, 324,
     340, 344n., 349, 354, 366, 373, 375, 378,
     383, 390, 403, 421, 426, 430, 432, 471, 478
 Amendment, question of, **1963:** 356 [6]
 Cuban ratification, question of, **1963:** 356 [23]
 French signing, question of, **1963:** 35 [3]
 Messages to the American people, **1963:** 316, 363
 News conference remarks, **1963:** 35 [3], 320 [2, 8,
     10, 11, 13], 328 [2, 8, 17], 356 [1, 3, 6, 14,
     17, 23], 448 [18, 29]
 Ratification, **1963:** 320 [2], 356 [1, 23]
 Safeguards, **1963:** 328 [2]
 Signatories, **1963:** 320 [2]

Nuclear war, **1961:** 1, 302, 318 [2], 387, 410, 415 [5],
     446; **1962:** 8 [20], 13 (p. 28), 50 [25], 109,
     115 [18], 290, 310 [3], 485, 551 [2, 13];
     1963: 12 (p. 19), 14, 21 (p. 32), 221, 232,
     316, 319a, 324, 400, 421, 426, 449, 459 [17]
Nuclear weapons, **1961:** 1, 99, 115, 138, 387, 446,
     483; **1962:** 7 (p. 10), 71, 243 [1], 276, 310
     [3], 453, 549, 551 [13, 15], 557; **1963:** 14,
     20, 232, 316, 385, 445, 462, 476, 478
 See also Bombs, Missiles; Nuclear weapons tests.
 Chinese Communists, **1963:** 260 [9], 320 [11]
 Defense, **1963:** 12 (pp. 16, 18), 54 [8], 169 [20],
     260 [5], 319a, 320 [17], 328 [21]
 Defense systems, joint statement, **1962:** 554
 Development, **1963:** 320 [13]
 European, **1962:** 551 [22], 557; **1963:** 65 [6, 8, 15],
     89 [14]
 Expenditures for, **1961:** 99
 For NATO, **1961:** 25 [17], 115, 192, 355
 French, **1962:** 152 [8], 198 [3], 229 [9], 259 [9, 21],
     551 [21], 557; **1963:** 12 (p. 16), 35 [24], 54
     [3, 8], 65 [6, 17], 260 [9], 320 [2, 15]
 German, question of, **1961:** 455 [15], 483; **1963:**
     54 [8], 260 [7]
 In space, **1962:** 378 [14]
 Middle East, exclusion from, **1963:** 120 [10]
 NATO, **1962:** 40 [15], 198 [3], 279 [25], 554, 557
 News conference remarks, **1961:** 25 [17], 62 [30],
     222, 258 [3], 318 [2, 13], 334 [17], 415 [5,
     7], 455 [13, 15, 18], 488 [10]; **1962:** 40 [15],
     75 [9], 198 [3], 229 [9], 245 [4], 259 [6, 9,
     14, 21], 279 [17, 25], 316 [6, 20], 352 [26],
     378 [14], 515 [1, 15]; **1963:** 35 [7, 24], 54
     [2, 3, 8], 65 [6, 8, 14, 15, 17], 75 [12, 18,
     19], 89 [4, 14, 16], 107 [11, 12, 20], 120 [10]
     144 [4, 7, 19], 169 [18, 20], 202 [22], 260 [5,
     7, 9, 14], 305 [1], 320 [2, 11, 13, 15, 16, 17],
     328 [2, 4, 17, 18, 21], 356 [1, 3, 23], 405 [4],
     448 [2, 29]
 North Atlantic Treaty Organization, **1963:** 12 (p.
     16), 20, 54 [8], 65 [6, 8, 14], 89 [14], 107
     [11], 262, 285
 Multilateral force, proposed, **1963:** 36, 65 [6, 8,
     14], 89 [14], 107 [11], 144 [19], 260 [7],
     262, 285, 320 [15, 16]
 Nuclear free zones, proposed, **1962:** 75 [9]
 In Latin America, **1962:** 515 [15]
 Outer space, **1963:** 107 [12], 405 [4]
 Proliferation, danger of, **1963:** 75 [12, 19], 89
     [14], 107 [20], 144 [4], 319a
 Scientific and technical data, dissemination,
     1963: 54 [8]
 Soviet, **1961:** 222, 442, 446, 455 [13, 18]; **1962:**
     279 [25], 378 [14], 485, 515 [1]; **1963:** 30
     (p. 65), 35 [24], 54 [2], 107 [12], 305 [13],
     319a, 405 [4], 426
 In Cuba.
 See Cuba.

Nuclear weapons — *continued*
  Spread to other countries, **1962:** 352 [26], 557;
      1963: 12 (p. 16), 35 [24], 260 [7, 9, 14], 316,
      324, 356 [1]
  Submarine based, **1963:** 65 [15]
  United Kingdom, **1962:** 557
Nuclear weapons tests, **1961:** 8 [1, 7], 62 [19, 21], 83
      [6, 21], 139 [23], 171 [1], 214, 222, 258 [2,
      3, 12, 19], 318 [2, 8, 19], 415 [16], 446, 455
      [8, 18]
  See also Nuclear weapons.
  Advisory committee, **1961:** 8 [7]
  Atmospheric, **1961:** 365, 387, 415 [16], 455 [8,
      18], 519; **1962:** 8 [17], 316 [22], 348, 352
      [7, 12, 18], 378 [8], 503, 518; **1963:** 75 [18],
      107 [20], 319a, 320 [17], 328 [4, 17], 356
      [23]
    Resumption by U.S., **1962:** 40 [7, 10], 71, 89
        [8], 107 [22], 115 [3], 152 [7, 20], 179 [13],
        198 [13]
    Ban or suspension, **1961:** 83 [6, 21], 120, 132, 139
        [23], 225n., 231, 387, 483; **1962:** 7 (p. 11), 8
        [8], 27 [22], 40 [1, 6, 20], 50 [4, 16], 59 [14],
        62, 71, 75 [3, 7, 9, 19], 89 [1, 18], 116, 134,
        152 [7, 20], 179 [8], 198 [13], 245 [4], 302
        [3, 6], 310 [3], 316 [2, 18], 348, 352 [2, 7,
        12, 18, 22, 26], 419, 493, 503, 518, 544, 551
        [18], 554; **1963:** 3, 12 (p. 19), 20, 40, 58,
        179, 232, 262, 284, 292, 324, 382
  Geneva conference.
    See Geneva conferences.
  Joint statements with foreign leaders, **1961:**
      146, 230, 252, 345, 456, 519
    News conference remarks, **1963:** 75 [12, 18,
        19], 89 [4], 107 [20], 144 [4, 7, 19], 169
        [18], 202 [22], 260 [7, 9, 14], 305 [1], 320
        [2]
    Soviet proposals, **1961:** 139 [23], 171 [1]
    Treaty.
      See Nuclear test ban treaty.
    U.S.-U.K. proposals, **1961:** 171 [1], 318 [2],
        345, 357, 365; **1962:** 186; **1963:** 27, 232,
        285, 286
  Broadcast, **1962:** 71
  Christmas Island, **1962:** 41, 50 [2]
  Cuba, question of, **1963:** 320 [13]
  French, **1961:** 222 [3], 455 [8]; **1963:** 75 [19]
  Inspection and control, **1961:** 139 [23], 171 [1],
      318 [2, 8], 365, 446, 456; **1962:** 27 [22], 40
      [1, 24], 89 [10, 16], 107 [2, 16, 23], 115 [3,
      26], 152 [7], 160, 290, 302 [8], 316 [2, 5, 15,
      17, 18], 352 [7, 12]; **1963:** 27, 35 [7], 58, 89
      [4], 107 [20], 144 [4], 169 [18], 202 [8, 22],
      305 [1], 316, 319a, 324, 328 [21], 354, 448
      [29]
  Geneva conference.
    See Geneva conferences.

Nuclear weapons tests — *continued*
  Johnston Island, **1962:** 316 [9], 378 [8], 503; **1963:**
      328 [2]
  Joint statements with foreign leaders, **1961:** 193,
      225, 345, 357, 411
  Joint statements, U.S.-U.K., **1962:** 41, 134
      1962: 41, 134
  Moratorium (1958-61), **1962:** 71; **1963:** 328 [4]
  Outer space, **1962:** 348
  Panel report, **1961:** 318 [2, 19]
  Project Plowshare, **1961:** 349n.
  Project Vela, **1961:** 349n.
  Radioactive fallout, **1962:** 19, 20 [11, 18], 65, 71,
      229 [19], 259 [19], 316 [22], 320, 352 [7,
      18]; **1963:** 107 [20], 166, 320 [17], 328 [4,
      18], 356 [1], 385, 430, 472
  Soviet, **1961:** 225n., 258 [3, 19], 318 [19], 340,
      349, 357, 365, 387, 415 [16], 445 [8, 18],
      483, 519; **1962:** 8 [17], 40 [1, 6, 10, 24], 59
      [14], 62, 71, 89 [8], 134, 198 [13], 302 [3],
      352 [2, 7, 18, 22], 518; **1963:** 27, 35 [7], 58,
      59, 89 [4], 202 [22], 320 [17], 328 [17]
    Ban or suspension, proposals, **1961:** 139 [23],
        171 [1]
    50-megation bomb, **1961:** 426, 442, 446
    White House statement on resumption, **1961:**
        335
  Statement, **1962:** 116
  Underground, **1961:** 258 [19], 349, 365, 415 [16];
      1962: 8 [17], 71, 115 [26], 302 [8], 316 [2, 5,
      18], 348, 352 [2, 7, 12], 503; **1963:** 27, 40,
      75 [18], 89 [4], 319a, 320 [2, 13], 328 [2, 4],
      356 [3], 448 [29]
  Underwater, **1962:** 348
  United Kingdom, **1961:** 455 [8]; **1963:** 75 [19]
  U.S. 3-year moratorium, termination, **1961:** 387
Nueces River Basin, **1962:** 313
Nürnberg war crimes trials, **1963:** 298
Nurses, shortage of, **1962:** 65
Nurses, training of, **1961:** 27; **1963:** 53
Nursing homes, Federal aid for, **1961:** 27, 52, 406
Nutrition, **1961:** 85, 100
Nyasaland, Peace Corps projects in, **1963:** 294
Nyerere, Julius K., **1961:** 331, 500; **1962:** 539; **1963:**
      300, 302, 304
  Visit of, **1961:** 288

Oahe Dam project, **1962:** 335, 337
OAS.
  See Organization of American States.
Oats, prices, **1962:** 25
Obote, A. Milton, **1962:** 441
O'Brien, Comdr. J. C., **1963:** 203
O'Brien, Rev. Joseph E., **1963:** 203n.
O'Brien, Lawrence F., **1961:** 25 [12]; **1963:** 277
O'Brien, Repr. Thomas J., **1962:** 483
Ocasek, Oliver, **1962:** 480
Occupational Safety, President's Conference on,
      1963: 119

Occupational training, **1961:** 211, 233, 499; **1962:** 7 (p. 6), 16 (p. 46), 22, 25, 28, 37, 91, 186, 190, 205, 220, 255, 280, 317, 380, 385, 395, 396, 412, 551 [10]; **1963:** 21 (pp. 38, 39), 22, 30 (p. 61), 43, 50, 53, 64, 75 [14], 92, 110, 119, 134, 230, 248, 378, 423, 445, 458

Central America, **1963:** 99
Civil defense workers, **1963:** 82
Government employees, **1962:** 143
Handicapped workers, **1963:** 92
Indians, **1963:** 86, 113
Mentally retarded, **1963:** 357
Negroes, **1963:** 220, 248
News conference remarks, **1962:** 75 [18], 89 [5], 107 [19]
Older persons, **1962:** 205; **1963:** 74, 75 [1]
Physicians and dentists, **1962:** 288
Rural persons, **1963:** 45
Schools, **1963:** 469
Teachers, **1962:** 13 (p. 32)
Unemployed workers, **1962:** 6n., 13 (p. 32), 28, 91, 186, 202, 328, 414, 438, 446, 452, 453; **1963:** 30 (pp. 58, 71), 34, 85, 92, 127, 175 [2], 228, 310, 363, 448 [7]
Welfare personnel, **1962:** 28, 193, 306
Young people, **1962:** 7 (p. 6), 13 (p. 31), 16 (p. 56), 28, 201, 205, 220, 551 [10]; **1963:** 30 (p. 71), 43, 89 [1], 92, 120 [8], 142, 146, 217, 230, 248, 336, 358, 393, 458
Ocean freight forwarders, licensing, **1961:** 370
Ocean resources development, **1961:** 49, 100; **1963:** 384
Oceanographic Commission, Intergovernmental, UNESCO, **1961:** 100; **1963:** 430
Oceanographic Data Center, National, **1961:** 100
Oceanography, **1961:** 11, 49, 100, 110; **1962:** 69, 216
Interagency Committee on, **1963:** 430
Project Mohole, **1961:** 100, 110
O'Connell, Daniel, **1963:** 278
O'Connor, Frank, **1963:** 472
Octavius, **1961:** 222 [13]
Odegaard, Charles E., **1961:** 473
O'Donnell, Adm. Edward J., **1961:** 71 [8]
O'Donnell, Gen. Emmett, **1963:** 345
O'Donnell, P. Kenneth, **1963:** 24, 120 [13]
Oduber Quirós, Daniel, **1963:** 105
OECD.
See Organization for Economic Cooperation and Development.
OEEC.
See Organization for European Economic Cooperation.
Oettinger, Katherine B., **1962:** 132
O'Farrill, Romulo, **1963:** 468
Office of Naval Research, **1961:** 100
Office space, Federal, memorandum, **1962:** 221

Offutt Air Force Base, Nebr., **1962:** 535n.
Oglala Sioux Housing Authority, public housing loan, **1961:** 371
O'Hara, Repr. Barratt, **1962:** 483
O'Hara, Repr. James G., **1962:** 437
O'Hare, Lt. Comdr., Edward H. (Butch), **1963:** 109
O'Hare International Airport, Chicago, **1963:** 109, 110
O'Higgins, Bernardo, **1962:** 542, 556
Ohio, **1962:** 3, 89 [13], 102, 410 [1], 414; **1963:** 248ftn. (p. 486), 363, 378, 463, 465
Candidates for public office **1962:** 396, 432, 480
Gov. Michael V. DiSalle, **1962:** 3, 396, 431, 432, 480
Ohio State University, **1961:** 460n.
Ohira, Masayoshi, **1962:** 531n.
Oil, **1963:** 266, 381, 475, 478
Elk Hills Reserve, **1963:** 6
Embargo on shipments to Cuba, proposed, **1963:** 89 [16]
Imports, **1963:** 459 [14, 25]
Peru, U.S. imports, **1963:** 459 [14]
Resources, **1963:** 179
U.S. companies, agreement with Indonesia, **1963:** 212, 224
Venezuelan, U.S. imports, **1963:** 73
Oil and gas producers, tax treatment, **1963:** 34
Oil imports, **1961:** 62 [13]; **1962:** 8 [15], 27 [24], 410 [11]
Okinawa, U.S. base, **1962:** 75 [16]
Oklahoma, **1962:** 397
Gov. Henry Bellmon, **1963:** 108
Oklahoma City, Okla. **1962:** 397
Olah, Franz, **1962:** 12n.
Old-age and survivors insurance, **1961:** 17
Old-Age and Survivors Insurance, Bureau of, **1963:** 21 (p. 42)
Olden, Georg, **1963:** 153
Older persons, **1961:** 14, 454; **1962:** 205, 288; **1963:** 130, 177
Employment and training, **1962:** 205; **1963:** 74, 75 [1], 92, 96
Federal aid, **1962:** 28, 328
Health insurance, **1961:** 11, 27, 32, 94, 341
Housing, **1961:** 76, 448, 477; **1962:** 7 (p. 8), 13 (p. 31), 328, 395, 437, 452, 454, 456, 458, 545; **1963:** 21 (p. 37), 74, 75 [1], 77 [2], 455, 478
Medical care, **1961:** 52, 71 [12], 83 [14], 94, 119 [11], 133, 139 [13], 341, 455 [7], 477, 499; **1962:** 7 (p. 8), 65, 359, 385; **1963:** 12 (p. 14), 22, 74, 75 [1, 6], 138, 459 [11, 12], 460, 461
Under social security.
See Social security.
Medical care facilities, **1961:** 52, 406

Older persons — *continued*
  Medical care — *continued*
    Message to Congress, **1963:** 74
    National Council of Senior Citizens, **1962:** 202n.,
      217
    National Council of Senior Citizens, remarks,
      1963: 138 '
    Peace Corps, services in, **1963** 74
    Senior Citizens Act, proposed, **1962:** 193
    Senior Service Corps, proposed, **1962:** 245 [11]
    Social security.
      See main heading, Social Security.
    Tax treatment, **1963:** 34, 74, 75 [1]
    Unemployment, **1963:** 110
    Welfare measures, **1961:** 339; **1962:** 306
    Welfare measures, D.C., **1963:** 22
Oliva, Erneido, **1962:** 556n.
Olmstead, Capt. Freeman B., **1961:** 8 [3]
Olsen, Repr. Arnold, **1963:** 383
Olsen, Gilbert M., **1962:** 384
Olson, Alec G., **1962:** 439, 440
Olson, Edwin B., **1962:** 274n.
Olympic development program, **1961:** 496
Olympic Games, **1961:** 496
Olympic Games, ancient, **1962:** 291
Olympic Games (1964), **1962:** 546 [2]; **1963:** 7n.,
    107 [8]
Olympic Team of 1932, **1961:** 421, 422
Olympio, Sylvanus, **1961:** 124
Olympio, Sylvanus, death of, **1963:** 13
Olympio, Sylvanus, visit of, **1962:** 103-105
Omaha, Nebr., **1961:** 419; **1962:** 535; **1963:** 221, 266
O'Mahoney, Joseph C., **1963:** 380
Omar Mohallim Mohamed, **1962:** 523n.
O'Meara, Joseph, **1962:** 257n.
O'Neill, Francis A., **1962:** 253
O'Neill, Francis A., Jr., **1963:** 95n.
O'Neill, J. E., **1962:** 337
O'Neill, Mrs. J. E., **1962:** 337
Operation Big Lift, **1963:** 477
Operation Crossroads Africa, **1962:** 254
Operation Pan America, **1961:** 78, 81, 122, 285;
    1962: 124, 513; **1963:** 319
  Alliance for Progress.
  See main heading, Alliance for Progress.
Operations Coordinating Board, **1961:** 42
Oppenheimer, Robert, **1963:** 381
Order of Railroad Telegraphers, **1962:** 386
Oregon, **1962:** 495; **1963:** 248ftn. (p. 486),
    382, 390
O'Reilly, John Boyle, **1962:** 95; **1963:** 276, 278, 416
Organic Act of 1954, **1962:** 130
Organization of African States, **1962:** 105
Organization of African Unity, **1963:** 304, 398
Organization of American States, **1961:** ll, 78, 81,
    192, 376, 476, 488 [1], 491, 515; **1962:** 30,
    83, 86, 273, 432, 485, 493, 500, 501, 542,
    543, 551 [3]; **1963:** 73, 84, 99, 118, 147,
    217, 323, 412, 430, 465 [1], 468, 471

Organization of American States — *continued*
  Council of, remarks, **1961:** 122
  Cuban subversion, defense measures, **1963:** 144
    [17]
  Education ministers, meetings, **1963:** 323
  Expulsion of Cuba, **1962:** 50 [18], 89 [9]
  Foreign ministers meetings, **1962:** 485, 486,
    529
  Punta del Este Conference.
    See main heading, Punta del Este Conference.
  Inter-American economic and social conference.
    See Punta del Este conference.
  Joint statements, **1962:** 303, 529, 544
  News conference remarks, **1962:** 50 [18], 89 [9],
    107 [3], 229 [14], 340 [20], 352 [21], 378
    [1], 515 [4, 7], 546 [20]; **1963:** 65 [10],
    89 [10, 19], 144 [11, 17], 169 [12], 405
    [7], 459 [18]
  Report on Cuba, **1963:** 65 [10]
  Sanctions against Dominican Republic, **1961:**
    517
  Sanctions against Duvalier regime, question of,
    1963: 169 [12]
  Secretary General (Jose A. Mora), **1961:** 491
Organization of Economic Cooperation and
    Development, **1961:** 11, 34, 90, 123, 189,
    193, 222, 497; **1962:** 16 (p. 46), 22, 168n.,
    178, 297 [8], 340 [20], 549; **1963:** 15, 30
    (p. 68), 94, 175, 459ftn. (p. 849)
  Development Assistance Committee, **1961:** 91,
    481; **1962:** 16 (p. 50)
  Development Assistance Group, **1961:** 91, 192,
    193, 222 [2]
  Development center, proposed, **1961:** 192
  Growth target, **1961:** 497
  Joint statements with Chancellor Adenauer on,
    1961: 120, 481
  News conference remarks, **1961:** 62 [26], 222
  U.S. participation, **1961:** 23, 91
Organization for European Economic Coopera-
    tion, **1961:** 222
  Economic Policy Committee, **1961:** 123
Oriskany, U.S.S., **1963:** 225n.
Orlich, Francisco J., **1963:** 97, 99, 100, 102, 103,
    106
Ormsby Gore, David, **1962:** 383, 419; **1963:** 126, 457
Ormsby Gore, Lady, **1962:** 383
Osinski, Henry, **1962:** 461n.
Oslo, NATO foreign ministers meeting, **1961:** 25
    [6], 171 [14]
Otepka, Otto, **1963:** 405 [13], 448 [26]
Otis Air Force Base, **1963:** 178
Ottawa, **1961:** 218; **1962:** 40 [15]; **1963:** 179, 285
  Visit to, **1961:** 190-193
Ottoman Empire, **1962:** 141
Ouachita National Forest road, **1961:** 441
Outdoor recreation, 1962: 69, 337
  See also Recreation programs and facilities.

Outdoor Recreation Advisory Council, **1962:** 69

Outdoor Recreation, Bureau of, **1962:** 69; **1963:** 63, 209

"Outdoor Recreation for America", report, **1963:** 209

Outdoor recreation bill, approval, **1963:** 209

Outdoor Recreation Resources Review Commission, **1962:** 13 (p. 31), 69, 128, 377; **1963:** 63, 209

Outdoor Writers Association of America, **1963:** 196

Outer Mongolia, U.N. membership, **1961:** 309

Overpopulation in less developed countries, **1962:** 245 [5]

Owen, Bernis G., **1962:** 152 [3]

Oxford, Miss., **1962:** 281, 420n., 459, 551 [10]; **1963:** 144 [13], 169 [19], 202 [1], 426

Oxford University, **1963:** 426

Ozark Rivers National Monument, **1962:** 69

Paar, Emil N., **1961:** 463n.

Pace, Frank, **1961:** 215

Pacem in Terris, encyclical, **1963:** 136

Pacific islands, polio epidemic, **1963:** 465 [5]

Pacific Islands Trust Territory, **1962:** 297, 342

Pacific Northwest, **1963:** 21 (p. 36)

Pacific Northwest timber damage, conference, **1962:** 495

Pacific Ocean fisheries, **1963:** 352

Pacific Southwest, **1963:** 21 (p. 36)

Packages, labelling of, **1962:** 93 (p. 242)

Paderewski, Ignace Jan, dedication of grave marker, **1963:** 173

Padre Island, Tex., **1961:** 49

Padre Island National Seashore Park, **1962:** 69, 336, 337, 459; **1963:** 376, 474

Approval of bill, **1962:** 417

Pageant of Peace, 1962: 550

Pages, Capitol Page School, **1962:** 236

Pago-Pago, American Samoa, **1962:** 196

Pahlavi, Shah Mohammad Reza, **1963:** 60

Message, **1962:** 364

Visit of, **1962:** 138, 141, 147

Paine, Thomas, **1961:** 78, 125, 474; **1963:** 268

Painting of battle of Bunker Hill, acceptance, **1962:** 407

Pakistan, **1961:** 244; **1962:** 70, 354, 363; **1963:** 285, 361, 447, 455

Agricultural production, **1962:** 404

Alliance wth China, question of, **1963:** 356 [25]

Assistance, **1963:** 118, 285 328 [1], 338

Assistance and development, **1961:** 267, 283; **1962:** 50 [10], 83, 216

Ayub Khan, Mohammed, **1961:** 279, 280, 283, 291 [14]; **1962:** 402-404, 554; **1963:** 356 [25]

Detection stations, nuclear tests, proposed, **1963:** 27

Pakistan — *continued*

Dispute with India, **1962:** 8 [14], 20 [3], 50 [10], 551 [1], 554, 557; **1963:** 278, 349, 356 [25]

News conference remarks, **1962:** 8 [14], 20 [3], 50 [10], 352 [11], 515 [3]; **1963:** 120 [16], 260 [13], 328 [1], 356 [1, 25]

Peace Corps projects in, **1963:** 294

Soil problems, U.S. mission on, **1961:** 283

U.S. Ambassador Walter P. McConaughy, **1963:** 120 [6]

Palamenghi-Crispi, Francesco, **1962:** 523n.

Palestine

Refugees, **1961:** 297

Refugees, United Nations Relief and Works Agency for, **1963:** 471

United Nations operations, **1963:** 471

United Nations Truce Supervision Organization, **1963:** 471

Palestrina, Giovanni da, **1962:** 361n.

Palfrey, John G., **1962:** 356

Palm Beach, Fla., **1962:** 1n., 2n., 46, 89 [3], 155, 156n., 158, 316 [12], 555n., 557; **1963:** 1n., 3n.

Releases from, **1961:** 104, 106, 500, 517, 520, 521

Palmer, William I., **1963:** 386, 390

Palmerston (Henry J.), Viscount, **1963:** 385

Pan American Congress of Architects, **1963:** 412

Pan American Games, **1962:** 546 [2]

Pan American Health Organization, **1963:** 53

Pan American Highway Congress, **1963:** 164

Pan American Union, **1961:** 122

Pan American World Airways, **1961:** 50; **1962:** 204, 245 [1], 256; **1963:** 298

Panama, **1963:** 97, 103, 106, 107 [1]

Ambassador A. Guillermo Arango, **1962:** 238n.

Arias, Gilberto, **1962:** 238

Chiari, Roberto, **1961:** 469; **1962:** 235, 238, 242, 245 [14]; **1963:** 99, 100, 102, 106

Cooperatives in, **1963:** 149

First Inter-American Congress (1825), **1963:** 99

Solis, Galileo, **1962:** 235n., 238n.

Tax reforms, **1963:** 118

Panama Canal, **1961:** 104, 469; **1962:** 235, 238, 242, 378 [1]

Treaty on, **1962:** 245 [14]

Panama City, Panama, **1963:** 164

Panama Steamship Line, commercial services, discontinuance, **1961:** 104

Panel of Consultants on Vocational Education, **1963:** 92

Panel on Federal Salary Systems, **1963:** 44, 148

Panel on Federal Salary Systems, Advisory, **1962:** 55

Panel on Mental Retardation, President's, **1962:** 65, 534n.; **1963:** 50, 66

Papers, the President's storage of, **1962:** 546 [7]

Paramilitary operations, **1961:** 497; **1963:** 183

Parent-teacher associations, **1963:** 141, 449

Parents' magazine, **1963:** 319a note

[References are to items except as otherwise indicated]

Paris, **1961:** 34n., 215, 231, 467; **1962:** 180, 203;
 1963: 5, 144 [2], 199, 303n., 361
 NATO Council meeting, **1961:** 220, 318 [7[, 481,
  519
 OEEC Economic Policy Committee, meeting,
  1961: 123
 Visit to, **1961:** 216-223
Parity prices, agricultural, **1963:** 77 [1]
Park, Chung Hee, **1961:** 468
Parks
 State and local, **1963:** 193
Parks, national, **1961:** 49, 94; **1962:** 7 (p. 7), 13 (p.
 30), 69, 128, 336, 337; **1963:** 12 (p. 14), 63,
 134, 209, 301, 376, 390, 412, 445, 474, 478
 See also specific parks.
 Cape Cod National Seashore Park, **1961:** 49, 315
Parks Association, National, **1963:** 196
Parnell, Charles Stewart, **1963:** 278, 415
Parochial schools.
 See Private and parochial schools.
Parsons, J. Graham, **1961:** 51, 66, 318 [15]
Particle of matter, Omega, remarks, **1961:** 342
Parvin, Albert, **1961:** 487n.
Parvin Foundation awards, remarks, **1961:** 487
Passamaquoddy Tidal Power Project, **1961:** 197;
 1963: 301
Pasos, Phillipe, **1962:** 86n.
Passman, Repr. Otto E., **1962:** 170
Passport Office, **1962:** 448
Pasternak, Boris, **1962:** 527
Pastore, Sen. John O., **1961:** 15 [26], 84, 212; **1962:**
 50 [20]; **1963:** 374
Patents, **1962:** 93 (p. 242), 179 [15]; **1963:** 21 (p. 31)
Patent Office, **1962:** 137; **1963:** 21 (p. 42)
Pathet Lao, **1963:** 134 [2], 144 [5], 169 [9]
Patman, Repr. Wright, **1962:** 340 [13]; **1963:**
 228, 417
Patrol Bomber Squadron, **1963:** 110, 348
Patterson, Alicia, **1961:** 185
Patterson, Floyd, **1962:** 27 [19]
Patterson, Federick D., **1963:** 355
Patton, James G., **1963:** 33
Patton, Thomas F., **1961:** 254n.
Paul, Michael, **1962:** 155n.
Paul VI, Pope, **1963:** 260 [3, 10]
Pauley, Edwin, **1961:** 477; **1962:** 109
Pauling, Linus, **1961:** 455 [18]
Paulskirche, address, **1963:** 266
Pay
 See also Wages.
 Board of Governors, Federal Reserve System,
  1962: 151
 Equal pay for women, **1961:** 455 [19]
 Government employees, **1961:** 83 [15], 251, 396;
  1962: 7 (p. 7), 13 (p. 37), 163, 167, 187,
  210 [21], 229 [1], 448; **1963:** 4, 21 (pp. 32,
  40, 41, 43), 22, 44, 53, 134, 148, 175 [4]
  Approval of bill, **1962:** 447
  Message to Congress, **1962:** 55

Pay — *continued*
 Military personnel, **1962:** 13 (pp. 37, 38), 549 [9];
  1963: 21 (p. 34), 134, 169 [20], 175 [4],
  194, 396
 Postal employees, **1961:** 396; **1962:** 13 (p. 37), 50,
  [21], 447
 Railroad employees, **1962:** 179 [14]
 Teachers, **1961:** 46, 255; **1962:** 7 (p. 9), 13 (p. 32),
  16 (p. 46), 37; **1963:** 43, 226, 228, 469
Payne, Lt. Col. William R., **1962:** 475n.
Payroll Savings Committee, United States
 Industrial, campaign, **1963:** 450
Paz Estenssoro, Victor, **1961:** 184, 275, 409; **1963:**
 428-432, 448 [2]
Peabody, Gov. Endicott, **1963:** 108, 136, 178, 427
Peace, Women's League for, **1962:** 152 [15]
Peace Conference, World War I, **1963:** 173
Peace Corps, U.S., **1961:** 11, 48, 90, 185, 205, 207,
 506; **1962:** 7 (p. 12), 64, 133, 170, 232, 250,
 254, 258, 270, 358, 389, 437, 446, 452, 455,
 456, 458, 550; **1963:** 12 (pp. 13, 17), 21 (p.
 35), 48, 64, 74, 94, 176, 192, 217, 228, 232,
 258, 304n., 366, 431n., 445, 463
 African projects, Ghana and Tanganyika, **1961:**
  199, 213, 331
 Colombia project, **1961:** 187, 199, 213
 Cooperatives, training in organization of, **1963:**
  149
 Domestic, proposed, **1962:** 243 [4]; **1963:** 12 (p.
  13), 176, 305 [19], 465
 Establishment, **1961:** 61, 62 [5, 9]
  Bill, **1961:** 213, 380
  Message to Congress, **1961:** 63
 Ethiopia, **1963:** 294, 397n.
 Expansion, **1963:** 64, 120 [15], 294
 Movement, spread to other nations, **1963:** 294
  Inauguration of German Peace Corps., **1963:**
   258, 294
 News conference remarks, **1961:** 62 [5, 9], 71 [23],
  83 [15], 139 [4], 171 [16], 318 [3], 334 [9];
  1962: 245 [11], 340 [22], 546 [22]; **1963:**
  120 [15], 305 [19]
 Nyasaland, **1963:** 294
 Older persons in, **1963:** 74
 Philippines project, **1961:** 199, 213
 Pilot project, **1961:** 213
 Remarks to volunteers, **1962:** 325, 354
 Remarks to Washington staff, **1962:** 243
 Returning volunteers, Federal employment,
  1963: 129
 Training school in Puerto Rico, **1961:** 331n., 506
 Volunteer questionnaires, **1961:** 213
Peace Corps, Director (Robert Sargent
 Shriver, Jr.), 62 [9], 199, 334 [9], 380;
  1962: 243, 340 [22]; **1963:** 129, 304n.
Peace Corps, National Advisory Council, remarks,
 1961: 199

Peace Corps Secretariat, International, **1963**: 176, 294
Peaceful uses of atomic energy.
 See Atomic energy for peaceful uses.
Peanuts, **1962**: 25, 410 [3]
Peanuts, price supports, **1961**: 94
Pearce, Mrs. John N., **1962**: 262
Pearl Harbor, **1961**: 499
Pearl Harbor attack, **1962**: 61, 139 [15]
Pearl Harbor inquiry, **1963**: 298
Pearson, Drew, **1961**: 234
Pearson, Lester B., **1962**: 161; **1963**: 144 [1], 169 [6], 178-180, 411
Peary, Adm. Robert E., **1963**: 296
Peel, Robert, **1963**: 381
Pell, Sen. Claiborne, **1962**: 50 [20], 462; **1963**: 89ftn. (p. 243)
Peloponnesian War, **1963**: 266
Penn Station South Urban Renewal Project, dedication, **1962**: 200
Pendell, Sgt. Gerald, **1963**: 12 (p. 19)
Pennsylvania, **1962**: 89 [13], 328, 329, 410 [1], 414; **1963**: 241, 248ftn. (p. 486), 363, 390
 Candidates for public office, **1962**: 394, 395, 451-455
 Delaware River Basin compact, **1961**: 445
 Food distribution to needy, **1961**: 15 [3], 17
 Gov. David L. Lawrence, **1961**: 3, 179; **1962**: 89 [13], 278, 394, 395, 452-455
 Gov. William W. Scranton, **1963**: 108, 376
 Unemployment, **1961**: 83 [18]
Pennsylvania Avenue, Washington, D.C., redevelopment, **1962**: 221
Penobos, Manuel, **1963**: 35 [2]
Pension bill, self employed persons, **1962**: 410 [10]
Pension funds, **1963**: 30 (p. 67), 74, 134
Pentagon, reduction of waste in, **1963**: 351, 363
People-to-people program, **1961**: 146
 Appointment of President Eisenhower, **1961**: 455 [1]
Pepper, Repr. Claude, **1963**: 465-467
Pereira, Pedro T., **1962**: 383
Perez, J.M., **1961**: 509
Peréz San Ramón, José, **1962**: 556n.
Pericles, **1961**: 476; **1962**: 527
Perkins, Repr. Carl D., **1962**: 458
Perkins, Frances, **1963**: 85
Perkins, James A., **1963**: 57n.
Perloff, Harvey, **1962**: 86n.
Peron, Juan D., **1963**: 459 [14]
Persia, ancient, **1962**: 138, 141
Personal income, **1962**: 111
Personnel management in Federal Government, **1962**: 12
Peru, **1962**: 86, 302 [10], 316 [21], 341; **1963**: 405 [7]
 Ambassador Fernando Berckemeyer, **1962**: 383
 Assistance and development, **1961**: 318 [15], 376

Peru — *continued*
 Beltram, Pedro, **1963**: 468
 Cisneros, Manuel, **1963**: 468
 Election, **1962**: 238
 Military junta, **1963**: 459 [18]
 Oil, **1963**: 459 [14]
 Prado, Manuel, **1961**: 372, 373, 376; **1962**: 302 [10], 316 [21]
 Puno area, **1961**: 376
Pescadores Islands, **1962**: 259 [1, 7]
Pesticide regulation, **1962**: 93 (p. 236), 352 [24]
Peterson, Esther, **1961**: 504; **1962**: 43, 505n.; **1963**: 409
Petersen, Comdr. Forrest, **1962**: 294n.
Petersen, Howard C., **1962**: 8 [22], 449, 510n.
Pfohl, James Christian, **1961**: 327
Pheil, A. C., **1963**: 464
Philadelphia, Pa., **1962**: 270, 278, 279 [6], 340 [10]; **1963**: 35 [9], 230, 248, 445, 448 [4]
 Mayor Richardson Dilworth, **1961**: 264
 Mayor James H. J. Tate, **1962**: 278; **1963**: 445, 459 [15]
 Schuylkill expressway, **1961**: 58
 White House Regional Conference, **1961**: 454n.
Philae Island temples, preservation, **1961**: 108
Philip, Prince, **1961**: 231
Philippines, **1962**: 70, 226, 243, 279 [6]; **1963**: 77, 176
 Ambassador Amelito R. Mutuc, **1963**: 239
 Assistance, **1963**: 239
 Economic and social development, **1963**: 239
 Macapagal, Diosdado, **1962**: 131, 191
 Peace Corps project, **1961**: 199, 213; **1963**: 294
 War damages, statement, **1961**: 356
  War damage bill, **1962**: 191
  Approval, **1962**: 315
Philippine War Damage Commission, **1962**: 191n., 315n.
Philipps, Johnson, **1963**: 214
Phleger, Herman, **1962**: 549ftn. (p. 887); **1963**: 118
Phoenix, Ariz., **1961**: 475, 476
Photographers Association, White House, **1962**: 158, 254
Phoumi Nosavan, **1963**: 144 [5]
Physical fitness, **1961**: 14, 48, 293; **1962**: 552; **1963**: 64, 393
 American youth, **1961**: 27, 293, 348, 498
 Article on, **1963**: 325
 European youth, **1961**: 496
 Youth, **1962**: 37, 65, 132, 283, 291
Physical Fitness, President's Council on, **1963**: 64
Physicians, **1962**: 210 [1]
 Drug distribution, **1962**: 316 [24]
 Education.
  See Medical and dental education.
 Fees, exclusion from medical care bill, **1962**: 279 [24]
 Group practice, 1963: 53

[References are to items except as otherwise indicated]

Physicians — *continued*
   Health insurance under social security views
      respecting, **1962:** 112, 202
   Shortage of, **1963:** 43, 53, 134
   Training, **1961:** 27, 52; **1962:** 288
Physics, **1962:** 549
Physics research, **1961:** 94
Piccioni, Attilio, **1963:** 291-293, 373
Pierce, John R., **1962:** 398
Pierre, S. Dak., **1962:** 335, 337
Pierson, Warren Lee, **1961:** 277n.
Pilavachi, Aristide N., **1962:** 339n.
Pilgrims, **1961:** 26, 432, 482; **1962:** 504
Pinchot, Mrs. Amos, **1963:** 376
Pinchot, Gifford, **1961:** 49; **1962:** 216; **1963:** 376n.,
      385, 389, 390
Pinchot, Gifford B., 2d, **1963:** 376
Pindar, **1963:** 325
Pine Ridge Indian Reservation, **1963:** 113
Pipeline construction, FPC backlog of applica-
      tions, **1961:** 121
Pittman, Stewart, **1961:** 410; **1963:** 166n.
Pittsburgh, Pa., **1962:** 452
Pittsburgh, Pa., Golden Triangle, **1961:** 58
Pittsburgh, Pa., Mayor David L. Lawrence, **1963:**
      49, 445
Pitzer, K.S., **1962:** 373
Pival, Joseph, **1963:** 137n.
Plaine des Jarres, **1963:** 134 [2], 144 [5]
Planes for Progress, Government contractors.
   See Equal employment opporunity.
Plans for Progress program, **1962:** 7 (p. 8), 255, 344;
      1963: 19
Plant and equipment, industrial, **1961:** 33, 136
Plant reinvestment, **1961:** 499
Plato, **1962:** 527
Plazas Garcia, Agremil, **1963:** 118
Plazter, Wilfreid, **1962:** 168n.
Plimpton, Calvin H., **1963:** 439, 440
Plimpton, Francis T.P., **1961:** 358n.; **1962:** 107 [1];
      1963: 359n.
Plowshare project, **1961:** 349n.
Plumley H. Ladd, **1962:** 162
Plutonium, **1962:** 289
Plymouth Colony, **1961:** 375; **1962:** 373, 504
Poe, Edgar Allan, **1962:** 527
Poinsett, Joel, **1962:** 542
Point 4 program, **1961:** 90, 497; **1963:** 268, 362, 442,
      466
Point Reyes National Seashore Park, **1962:** 69, 336,
      377, 417, 459; **1963:** 376
Point Reyes Station, Calif., **1961:** 49
Poland, **1961:** 119 [17], 138, 483; **1962:** 461, 551
      [15]; **1963:** 54 [7], 271, 407
   Assistance, **1961:** 11; **1962:** 229 [3], 245 [9], 302
      [10]; **1963:** 35 [5]
   Cultural exchange with, **1962:** 461
   Exports to U.S., **1963:** 118
   Gomulka, Waldyslaw, **1961:** 119 [17]

Poland — *continued*
   News conference remarks, **1962:** 75 [4], 229 [3],
      245 [9], 302 [10]
   Paderewski, grave marker, dedication, **1963:** 173
   Poznan Boy's and Mens' Choir, **1963:** 93
   Trade with U.S., **1963:** 35 [5]
   U.S. Ambassador John M. Cabot, **1962:** 245 [9]
   U.S. trade with, **1962:** 75 [4], 461, 546 [22]
Polaris missile, **1961:** 11, 16, 35 [3], 99, 192, 205,
      243, 415 [7], 436, 455 [4], 477; **1962:** 7 (p.
      10), 13 (p. 28), 75 [20], 107 [22], 140, 343,
      395, 456, 458, 551 [13, 14], 554, 557; **1963:**
      21 (p. 32), 35 [12, 18], 54 [8], 89 [14], 120
      [11], 147, 175 [4], 203, 320 [2, 15], 462,
      476-478
Policemen, benefits veto, **1961:** 383
Policy Planning Council (State Department),
      Chairman (Walt W. Rostow), **1963:** 171,
      405 [13]
Poliomyelitis, reduction in, **1962:** 65
Poliomyelitis outbreak in Cuba, **1961:** 7 [8]
Poliomyelitis vaccine, anniversary of development,
      1961: 119 [1]
Political parties, responsibility of Presidents to
      head, **1961:** 448
Political philosophy, the President's, **1961:** 15 [21]
Political Rights of Women, Convention on the,
      1963: 309
Polk, Maj. Gen. James H., **1963:** 272
Polk, James K., President, **1963:** 478
Poll tax, **1962:** 340 [2], 396
Poll tax, abolition, proposed, **1963:** 82, 108
Pollaiuolo paintings, display in U.S., **1963:** 16
Polls, U.S. prestige abroad, **1963:** 65 [12], 75 [4]
Polygraph tests, **1963:** 120 [1]
Polyphonic Contest, International, **1962:** 352 [3],
      361
Pompey, **1961:** 222 [13]
Poor Richard's Almanac, **1961:** 217
Pope John XXIII, **1962:** 430; **1963:** 202 [7], 217
   Death of, **1963:** 213
   Medal of Freedom, **1963:** p. 903
   Meeting with Aleksei Adzhubei, **1963:** 107 [10]
Pope Paul VI, **1963:** 260 [3, 10]
Popovic, Koča, **1963:** 420n., 421
Popularity, the President's, **1962:** 302 [14]; **1963:**
      320 [7], 356 [22]
Population, **1963:** 21 (p. 31), 43
   Growth, **1963:** 30 (p. 65), 64, 110, 120 [11], 217,
      226
   Research, **1963:** 144 [6]
Pornography
   Distribution by mail, **1962:** 352 [8]
   District of Columbia, **1962:** 479
Porter, Paul, **1961:** 403
Port-of-Spain, Trinidad, West Indies, **1961:** 36n.
Portrait of President by William F. Draper, **1963:**
      160n.

[References are to items except as otherwise indicated]

Portugal, Ambassador Pedro T. Pereira, **1962:** 383
  Santa Maria cruise ship seized by rebels, **1961:** 8
    [16], 15 [29]
  U.S. Ambassador George W. Anderson, Jr.,
    1963: 312, 318
Post offices, construction, **1961:** 35 [3]
Post Office Department, **1961:** 35 [3], 94; **1962:** 20
    [13], 93 (p. 237), 129, 219, 352 [8]; **1963:** 21
    (p. 42), 125, 317, 363, 392
Postal deficit, **1962:** 15 [20], 94, 205, 29 [7], 302,
    396; **1962:** 7 (p. 7), 13 (p. 28), 280, 328, 549
Postal employees, **1961:** 291 [7]
  Longevity step increases, disapproval, **1961:** 396
  Pay, **1962:** 13 (p. 37), 50 [21], 447
  Postal Field Service, **1963:** 4n.
  Postal Field Service Compensation Act, **1962:** 55
Postal rates, **1961:** 94, 205, 415 [19]; **1962:** 7 (p. 7),
    13 (p. 31), 20 [13], 50 [21], 198 [12], 447;
    1963: 21 (p. 36)
  Increase, proposed, **1961:** 291 [7]
Postal service, **1962:** 55; **1962:** 6, 21 (pp. 32, 36),
    174 [4]
Postal Service and Federal Employees Salary Act
    of 1962, **1962:** 447, 448; **1963:** 44
Postal Union, Universal, **1963:** 453
Postman, shooting in Alabama, **1963:** 144 [13]
Postmaster General (J. Edward Day), **1961:** 244,
    339, 455 [11]; **1962:** 352 [8]; **1963:** 4, 107
    [6], 148, 153, 315, 317
Postmaster General (John A. Gronouski), **1963:**
    392, 408
Potassium, ocean resources, **1961:** 100
Potofsky, Jacob S., **1962:** 174
Potomac River, sewage disposal problem, **1963:**
    305 [14]
Potomac River Freeway, **1963:** 22, 208
Potsdam agreement, **1961:** 483
Potter, Dan, **1963:** 455
Poultry, **1963:** 45, 75 [17], 259
Powderly, Terence, **1963:** 85
Powell, Repr. Adam C., **1961:** 291 [16]; **1962:** 40
    [3]; **1963:** 75 [7], 320 [9]
Powell, Gov. Wesley, **1962:** 278
Power, Gen. Thomas S., **1962:** 139 [6], 535n.
Power projects, **1961:** 49; **1962:** 7 (p. 7), 69, 335,
    336; **1963:** 105
  Atomic, **1961:** 278
  Columbia River Basin development, **1961:** 474
  Hydroelectric, **1961:** 17, 49, 121, 445, 474; **1962:**
    69, 332; **1963:** 21 (p. 36), 175 [1], 179, 192,
    193, 301, 376, 379, 384, 386, 389, 400, 401,
    474, 478
  Nuclear, **1961:** 49; **1962:** 100, 289, 335, 382, 408
  Passamaquoddy Tidal Power Project, **1961:** 197
  Private vs. public, **1963:** 175 [1]
  St. John River, **1961:** 197
  Thermal, **1961:** 17
Power transmission lines, Upper Colorado and
    Trinity projects, **1961:** 360

Powers, David F., **1963:** 277
Powers, Francis Gary, **1961:** 8 [30], 119 [9]; **1962:**
    50 [1], 59 [10], 75 [6]
Powers, John E., **1963:** 368
Powers, John J., **1962:** 274n.
Poznan Boys' and Men's choir, **1963:** 93
Prado, Manuel, **1962:** 302 [10], 316 [21]
  Visit of, **1961:** 372, 373, 376
Prado, Senora Manuel, **1961:** 372, 373
Prairia National Park, **1962:** 69
Prather, Lt. Comdr. Victor A., Jr., **1962:** 475
Prather, Mrs. Victor A., Jr., **1962:** 475
Prayer breakfast, presidential, **1962:** 68; **1963:** 52
Prayers in public schools, Supreme Court decision,
    1962: 259 [3, 20]
Presbyterians, **1961:** 26
Presentation ceremonies.
  See Addresses or remarks at presentation
    ceremonies.
Presidency, **1961:** 8 [32], 15 [30], 133, 291 [20], 318
    [6]
  Advisers, comment on, **1963:** 169 [10], 448 [10],
    474
  Decision-Making in the White House (Theodore
    C. Sorensen), foreword by the President,
    1963: 370
  First anniversary, **1961:** 472, 476
  First 6 months, comments on, **1961:** 291 [20]
  Letters from citizens, **1963:** 52
  Powers, use in Birmingham, Ala., civil rights
    crisis, **1963:** 169 [4]
  Problems, comment on, **1961:** 15 [30]
  Secret Service protection for successors to,
    1961: 142
  Succession to, **1961:** 8 [32], 318 [6], 319
  Two-term limitation, **1963:** 35 [10]
Presidency, comments on, **1962:** 115 [19], 141, 226,
    551 [1, 3, 12, 23]
  First year in office, **1962:** 8 [8]
  Foreign affairs responsibilities, **1962:** 275, 551
    [11]
  Power of, **1962:** 198 [11]
  Role in consumer protection, **1962:** 296
  Two-term limitation, **1962:** 551 [9]
"President and the Press," **1961:** 153
President-elect, expenses of, **1962:** 219
President of Senate.
  See Vice President (Lyndon B. Johnson).
President's Advisory Commission on Narcotic and
    Drug Abuse, **1963:** 121
President's Advisory Committee on Government
    Organization, termination, **1961:** 29
President's Advisory Committee on Labor-
    Management policy, **1961:** 17, 23, 33, 87,
    205, 499; **1962:** 6, 203n., 164, 515 [17];
    1963: 30 (p. 67), 206, 299, 310
  Establishment, **1961:** 40
President's Advisory Committee on Management,
    1961: 29

President's Advisory Committee on a National
Academy of Foreign Affairs, **1963:** 57n.
President's Advisory Council on the Arts, **1963:**
240, 246
President's Award for Distinguished Federal
Civilian Service, **1963:** 238
President's Cabinet Textile Advisory Committee,
1961: 428
President's Club of New York, **1963:** 204
President's Commission on Campaign Costs, **1961:**
403; **1962:** 152 [4], 219; **1963:** 151
President's Commission on Registration and
Voting Participation, **1963:** 117, 167
President's Commission on the Status of Women,
1961: 504; **1962:** 43, 156, 304, 347, 505n.;
1963: 233, 409
President's Committee on Employment of the
Handicapped, **1962:** 49; **1963:** 174, 452
President's Committee on Equal Employment
Opportunity, **1961:** 116; **1962:** 7 (p. 8),
38n., 255n., 344, 509n; **1963:** 82, 220, 248
Establishment, **1961:** 68
Government contractors plans for progress,
1961: 204, 281
President's Committee on Equal Opportunity in
the Armed Services, report, **1963:** 251
President's Committee on Equal Opportunity in
Housing, **1962:** 515 [2]; **1963:** 49, 82
President's Committee on Government Contracts,
1961: 68
President's Committee on Government Employ-
ment Policy, **1961:** 68
President's Committee on Juvenile Delinquency
and Youth Crime, **1962:** 220; **1963:** 64
President's Committee for Traffic Safety, **1961:**
338; **1962:** 11; **1963:** 125
President's Committee on Youth Employment,
1962: 360; **1963:** 64, 141, 142, 248, 393
President's Committee on Youth Employment,
establishment, **1961:** 470
President's conference of Governors, proposed,
1963: 35 [21]
President's Conference on Heart Disease and
Cancer, **1961:** 83 [4]
President's Conference on Occupational Safety,
1963: 119
President's Council on Aging, **1962:** 193n., 245 [11];
1963: 74, 92
President's Council on Physical Fitness, **1963:**
64
President's Council on Youth Fitness, **1961:** 27,
48n., 293, 348, 496; **1962:** 65, 283, 291;
1963: 325
President's Cup Regatta trophy, **1961:** 317
President's Foreign Intelligence Advisory
Board (Killian committee), **1961:** 168, 258
[9], 291 [15]; **1963:** 405 [12]
President's Missile Sites Labor Commission, 1963:
446

President's Panel on Mental Retardation, **1962:** 65,
534n.; **1963:** 50, 66
President's Science Advisory Committee, **1961:** 15
[35], 49, 258 [3], 417; **1962:** 8 [1], 118, 411,
547; **1963:** 43, 53, 67, 92, 328 [17]
President's Task Force on Latin America, report,
1961: 276
President's Temporary Committee on the Im-
plementation of the Federal Employee-
Management Relations Program, **1962:**
215n.
Presidential appointees, oath of office ceremony,
1961: 10
Presidential Citation of Merit, **1963:** 133
Presidential coat of arms, **1961:** 11, 155
Presidential Commission on Automation, **1963:**
310
Presidential Commission on Federal Expenditures,
proposed, **1963:** 120 [6]
Presidential Contingency Fund, proposed, **1961:**
207
Presidential documents published in Federal
Register, **1961:** Appendix B, p. 839; **1962:**
Appendix B, p. 937; **1963:** Appendix B,
p. 211
Presidential Emergency Fund, **1963:** 320 [1]
Presidential inability, procedures, **1961:** 8 [32], 318
[6], 319
Presidential libraries, reorganization, **1963:** 207
Presidential Medal of Freedom, **1963:** 76 and p. 899
Presidential Panel of Consultants on Vocational
Education, **1963:** 92
Presidential prayer breakfast, **1962:** 68; **1963:** 52
Presidential Railroad Commission, **1962:** 66; **1963:**
310
Presidential reports to Congress
See also Congress, reports to, messages trans-
mitting.
List, **1961:** Appendix C, p. 844; **1962:** Appendix
C, p. 943; **1963:** Appendix C, p. 926
National forests development program, 1961:
377
Presidential Seal, **1963:** 426
Presidential standby authority, proposed, **1962:**
7 (p. 6), 13 (p. 35), 16 (pp. 51, 53), 27 [27],
245 [18], 259 [18]
Press
Availability of information to, **1962:** 410 [8], 515
[7, 14, 19], 546 [21]; **1963:** 54 [12], 75 [9]
Comments on, **1962:** 179 [3, 8], 515 [7, 19], 546
[4, 16, 21], 551 [6, 22]; **1963:** 134 [6], 245,
259
Conferences.
See News conferences.
Press, self-restraint in news publication, **1961:**
153, 185
Press Club, National, **1961:** 488 [5]
Prestige abroad, U.S., **1963:** 65 [12], 75 [4]

Prettyman, Judge E. Barrett, **1962:** 59 [10]; **1963:** 17, 121
Price, Don K., **1961:** 29; **1963:** 44n.
Price, Margaret, **1961:** 209
Price, Repr. Melvin, 1962: 58n., 481
Prices, **1961:** 17, 85, 136, 205, 302; **1962:** 25, 86, 162, 170, 174, 243 [2]; **1963:** 21 (p. 31), 30 (pp. 58, 61, 62, 64), 45, 77, 175, 189, 193, 197, 201, 266, 306, 326, 465
See also specific commodities.
Controls, **1962:** 139 [4], 410 [1]; **1963:** 131
Food, **1963:** 197, 202 [2, 12, 15, 18]
Increases, **1963:** 405 [14]
News conference remarks, **1961:** 15 [23], 83 [19], 119 [11], 171 [6], 334 [14, 20], 415 [21], 455 [17]; **1962:** 20 [19], 75 [5], 139 [1, 4, 7, 11], 152 [12, 17], 198 [15], 245 [2, 6, 9], 302 [19], 316 [19], 410 [1, 5]; **1963:** 65 [8], 75 [11], 175 [3], 202 [2], 260 [8], 405 [14]
Raw materials from less developed countries, **1963:** 65 [8]
Stability, **1961:** 23, 33, 350, 354, 366, 497, 499; **1962:** 7 (p. 6), 13 (p. 36), 14, 16 (pp. 43, 45), 20 [19], 121, 139 [7, 11], 152 [12, 17], 198 [15], 234, 280, 328, 410 [1, 5]; **1963:** 21 (pp. 27, 29, 41), 30 (pp. 57, 64), 34, 75 [11], 99, 110, 131, 134, 175, 306, 363, 391, 465, 477
Price Act, amendment proposed, **1962:** 99
Price supports, **1961:** 15 [28], 39, 85, 94, 436; **1962:** 8 [11], 16 (p. 44), 25, 89 [18], 115 [20], 245 [9], 410 [3], 440; **1963:** 12 (p. 14), 21 (pp. 32, 36, 40), 45, 77 [1], 189, 202 [2,, 12, 15]
See also specific commodities.
Priest, J. Percy, **1963:** 192
Príeto, Alejandro, 1962: 269n.
Primary election, **1962:** 279 [26]
Princess Anne County School Board, Virginia, relief of, approval, **1961:** 369
Prince Edward County, Va., opening of schools in, **1963:** 82
Princeton University, **1961:** 460n., 496; **1962:** 533
Pritchard, John, **1962:** 432, 456
Private clubs, racial discrimination, **1961:** 488 [5]
Private diplomacy, **1961:** 8 [24]
Private enterprise.
See Enterprise system.
Private and parochial schools, **1961:** 46, 62 [27], 71 [13], 83 [8, 9, 16, 21], 291 [18]
Federal aid for, question of, **1962:** 40 [3], 259 [4]
Integration in New Orleans, **1962:** 152 [13]
Privileged information, **1961:** 8 [23], 334 [7]; **1962:** 40 [5], 107 [15]
Emancipation Proclamation Centennial, **1962:** 555
Interdiction of delivery of offensive weapons to Cuba, **1962:** 486

Privileged information — *continued*
List, **1961:** Appendix B, p. 839; **1962:** Appendix B, p. 937; **1963:** Appendix B, p. 921
National Day of Mourning for President Kennedy, **1963:** p. 899
Sir Winston Churchill, honorary U.S. citizenship, **1963:** 126
Thanksgiving day, **1961:** 438; **1962:** 504; **1963:** 451
Procurement, Federal, **1961:** 71 [3]; **1962:** 16 (pp. 44, 50), 83; **1963:** 107 [4, 19, 23], 465
Acceleration to reduce unemployment, **1961:** 17
Foreign aid, **1961:** 497
Procurement, military.
See Defense procurement.
Production, **1962:** 7 (p. 6), 14, 16 (p. 42), 22, 111, 162, 174, 328, 395; **1963:** 12 (pp. 11, 12, 13), 21 (pp. 26, 28, 30, 39), 30 (pp. 57, 59, 61, 62), 34, 74, 92, 175, 197, 306, 351, 405 [5], 462, 465
Agricultural, **1962:** 8 [11], 25, 107 [10], 190, 197, 250, 440; **1963:** 21 (p. 35), 45, 110, 201, 445
U.S. vs. Communist countries, **1962:** 127
News conference remarks, **1962:** 8 [11], 20 [19, 21], 89 [5], 107 [10], 139 [1, 4], 152 [2], 179 [9]
Relation to wages, **1963:** 77
Soviet, **1962:** 549
Steel industry, **1962:** 139 [1, 4]
Production, increases in, **1961:** 17
Professions, manpower shortage in, **1963:** 92
Profits, **1962:** 7 (p. 6), 14, 16 (p. 44), 162, 174, 280, 328, 395, 473; **1963:** 12 (p. 12), 21 (p. 30), 30 (pp. 57-62, 64), 34, 77, 110, 131, 175, 177, 189, 305 [18], 306, 361, 363, 405 [14], 465, 477, 478
News conference remarks, **1962:** 75 [5], 139 [1], 152 [2, 14, 21], 179 [1], 302 [7], 316 [13], 340 [27], 410 [1]
Savings and loan association, **1962:** 179 [1]
Steel industry, **1962:** 139 [1], 152 [2, 14, 21]
Project Apollo, **1961:** 415 [17]
Project Mercury, **1961:** 415 [17]
Project Mohole, **1961:** 100, 110
Propaganda, U.S., in Latin America, **1961:** 276
Property abroad, U.S., expropriation by foreign governments, **1962:** 75 [22], 549 [4]
"Prospects of Mankind," TV series, 1962: 156n.
Protectionism, **1962:** 199
Protestant Council of the City of New York, **1963:** 455
Proving ground operations of missiles, **1961:** 99
Proxmire, Sen. William, **1962:** 186, 234
Pryor, Frederic L., **1962:** 50 [1]
Psychological Strategy Board, **1961:** 42
Public accommodations, equal access to, 1963: 21 (p. 37), 82, 144 [13], 230, 248, 462, 465 [3]

Public assistance, **1961:** 22; **1962:** 13 (p. 31), 288;
　　1963: 21 (p. 32), 74, 185
Public Assistance, Bureau of, change of name,
　　1962: 28
Public Debt.
　　See Debt, national.
Public facilities loans, **1961:** 76
Public health personnel, training of, **1961:** 52
Public Health Service, **1961:** 25 [3], 27, 49; **1962:**
　　13 (p. 31), 19, 65, 229 [18], 352 [24], 445;
　　1963: 50, 53, 74, 202 [17], 396
　　Child Health and Human Development, Institute
　　　　of, proposed, **1961:** 289, 290
　　General Medical Sciences, Institute of, proposed,
　　　　1961: 290
Public Health Service, Surgeon General (Dr.
　　Luther L. Terry), **1961:** 25 [3]
Public housing, **1961:** 17, 76; **1962:** 414; **1963:**
　　74, 240, 445
Public Housing Administration, **1962:** 23; **1963:** 113
Public Housing Administration, Commissioner
　　(Marie C. McGuire), **1961:** 264, 371
Public lands.
　　See Lands, public.
Public lands, highways, **1961:** 58
Public lands, management, **1961:** 49
Public opinion polls, **1961:** 83 [14], 415 [5]; **1963:**
　　65 [12], 75 [4], 77
Public Policy Conference, Brookings Institution,
　　1962: 230
Public roads, Bureau of, **1961:** 49, 58; **1962:** 11, 93
　　(p. 236); **1963:** 125
Public service, efficiency in, **1962:** 13 (pp. 37, 38)
Public utilities, **1962:** 129; **1963:** 175 [1], 444, 455,
　　462
　　Employment in industry, **1963:** 110
　　Industry, capital investment, **1963:** 175 [1]
Public Welfare, **1962:** 7 (p. 8), 16 (p. 46); **1963:** 21
　　(p. 32), 82, 92, 163, 230, 233, 248, 310,
　　358n., 423, 445, 478
　　Approval of bill, **1962:** 306
　　Message to Congress, **1962:** 28
Public Welfare Amendments Act of 1962,
　　approval, **1962:** 306; **1963:** 74
Public works, **1961:** 37, 171 [21], 499; **1962:** 6n.,
　　13 (pp. 35, 37), 128, 165, 174, 190, 328,
　　385, 395, 396, 411, 455, 545; **1963:** 21 (pp.
　　32, 37, 39, 40), 127, 248, 478
　　Acceleration, **1961:** 17, 37; **1963:** 30 (pp. 58, 66),
　　　　113, 123, 458, 478
　　Acceleration Act, **1963:** 30 (p. 66), 92, 185, 378,
　　　　448 [26], 462
　　Acceleration Act of 1962, **1962:** 53, 111, 380
　　Appropriation Act, **1962:** 487
　　Approval of bill, **1962:** 380
　　Capital improvements.
　　　　See Capital improvement program.

Public works — *continued*
　　Equal employment opportunity, **1963:** 220
　　Federal aid, **1962:** 16 (p. 52), 53, 229 [1]; **1963:** 92
　　Letter to Secretary Hodges, **1962:** 487
　　News conference remarks, **1962:** 89 [5], 115 [16],
　　　　229 [1], 279 [19]
　　Youth employment, **1961:** 233
Publications, historical, grants-in-aid for, **1963:** 245
Publications Commission, National Historical,
　　1963: 26, 245
Publishers and Editors, Business, White House
　　Conference of, **1962:** 410
Puccinelli, Robert L., **1962:** 337n.
Pucinski, Repr. Roman C., **1962:** 483; **1963:** 405
　　[11]
Pueblo, Colo., **1962:** 336
Puerto Rico, **1963:** 18, 72
　　Airports, Federal aids, **1961:** 141
　　Anniversary of commonwealth, **1961:** 301
　　Commission on future status, proposed, **1963:**
　　　　169 [3]
　　Commonwealth status, **1961:** 301n.
　　Decade of development, conference on, **1962:** 358
　　Economic Development Administration, **1961:**
　　　　160
　　Gov. Luis Muñoz Marín, **1961:** 301, 464, 506;
　　　　1962: 305; **1963:** 169 [3], 198, and p. 902
　　Immigrants to U.S., education, **1963:** 10
　　International Conference on Middle Level Man-
　　　　power (1962), **1963:** 294
　　Land-grant colleges, **1961:** 462
　　Naval base, strengthening, **1963:** 202 [8]
　　"Operation Bootstrap," **1961:** 160
　　Peace Corps training school, **1961:** 331n., 506
　　Presidential election, question of voting rights,
　　　　1963: 35 [6]
　　Self-determination, White House statement,
　　　　1963: 198
　　Small watershed projects, **1961:** 196
　　10th anniversary of Commonwealth, **1962:** 305
　　Visit to, **1961:** 506
Pugnetti, Don, **1963:** 384
Pugwash conference, nuclear inspection and
　　control, **1963:** 27
Puhak, John N., **1962:** 182n.
Pulaski, Casimir, **1962:** 460, 461
Punjab, India, **1963:** 294
Puno, Peru, **1962:** 86
Punta del Este Charter, **1961:** 324n., 376, 389, 491,
　　510; **1962:** 83, 86, 126, 242, 273, 303, 529,
　　544; **1963:** 99, 118, 163, 431, 459 [22], 468
　　See also Inter-American Economic and Social
　　　　Council.
Punta del Este conference, **1961:** 308, 313; **1963:**
　　323, 428, 432
　　Inter-American Economic and Social Con-
　　　　ference, **1962:** 83, 86, 273, 378 [4], 543n.;
　　　　1963: 107 [22]

Punta del Este conference — *continued*
  Mission of Secretary Dillon, **1961:** 324
  News conference remarks, **1961:** 171 [3], 258 [17], 291 [3, 15], 318 [11, 22, 24], 334 [7]
  OAS foreign ministers conference, **1962:** 8 [10], 20 [22], 27 [2, 6, 10, 15], 32, 50 [6], 89 [9], 238, 279 [10]; **1963:** 65 [10]
  Remarks to U.S. delegation, **1962:** 30
Punta del Este Declaration, **1963:** 134 [1]
Purdue University, **1961:** 460n.; **1962:** 410 [3]
Puritans, **1961:** 26
Pusey, Nathan N., **1963:** 136
Pushkin, Aleksander, *Boris Godunov,* **1961:** 387
Pyle, Ernie, **1962:** 226

Qaddafi, Wanis, **1962:** 467n.
Quadros, Janio da Silva, **1961:** 12, 105, 285
Quakers, **1961:** 26
Quality stabilization bill, **1963:** 448 [25]
Qudsi, Nazim al, **1962:** 1
Quebec, **1963:** 169 [17]
Queen Nefertari, **1961:** 108
Quemoy, **1962:** 259 [1, 7]
Quesada, Gen. E.R., **1962:** 512
Quincy, Mass., **1961:** 397
Quincy Irrigation District, Wash, **1963:** 41
Quinim Pholsena, **1962:** 308n.
Quonset Point, R.I., **1962:** 402

Raab, Julius, **1961:** 109
Rabin, Marvin, **1962:** 150n.
Rabinowitz, David, **1963:** 459 [23]
Raborn, Adm. William F., Jr., **1961:** 243
Rachal, William M.E., **1963:** 245
Racketeering, **1961:** 94, 362; **1962:** 7 (p. 7)
  In stock market, **1962:** 20 [24]
Radcliffe College, **1962:** 156
Radcliffe-Harvard Orchestra, **1962:** 271
Radford, Adm. Arthur W., **1961:** 455 [4]; **1962:** 259 [7], 422
Radhakrishnan, Sarvepalli, **1963:** 214, 215, 217, 218, 219
Radiation, National Advisory Committee on, **1962:** 229 [19], 259 [19]
Radiation Council, Federal, **1961:** 258 [12]; **1962:** 19, 71
Radicals in politics, **1963:** 169 [8]
Radio
  Role in Cuban crisis, **1962:** 532
  Use in election campaigns, **1962:** 219
Radio broadcasts, jamming of, **1963:** 232
Radio Conference on Space Communications, Geneva, **1963:** 470
Radio Corporation of America, **1961:** 281n.; **1962:** 317, 302 [7]
Radio Free Europe, **1961:** 71 [1]; **1963:** 437
Radio frequency allocations, international, **1963:** 471
Radio Officers Union, **1961:** 270

Radio and television Addresses.
  See Messages to the American people.
Radioactive fallout, **1961:** 49, 205, 410, 442, 446; **1962:** 65, 71, 320; **1963:** 21 (p. 33), 166, 314, 316, 324, 363, 366, 385, 430, 472
  Effect of food, **1962:** 19
    Milk, **1962:** 20 [11, 18], 316 [22]
  News conference remarks, **1961:** 258 [12], 455 [18], 488 [21]; **1962:** 20 [11, 18], 229 [19], 259 [19], 316 [22], 352 [7, 18]; **1963:** 107 [20], 320 [17], 328 [4, 18], 356 [1]
  Utah, **1963:** 328 [18]
Radiodifusion-Television Francaise, interview, **1961:** 214
Radziwill, Anna Christina, **1961:** 139 [19], 227, 229n.
Radziwill, Prince and Princess, **1961:** 229n.
Radziwill, Princess, **1962:** 259 [11]
Railroads, **1961:** 121; **1962:** 129; **1963:** 77, 85, 109, 244, 298, 402, 461
  Commuter, National Capital Region, **1963:** 208
  Decline, **1961:** 92 [11]
  Labor disputes, **1962:** 66, 198 [5], 378 [7], 386; **1963:** 95, 120 [17], 184, 244, 298, 299, 305 [5], 310, 328 [14], 337, 402, 414
  Pay increases, proposed, **1962:** 179 [14]
  Retirement system, **1961:** 27, 384, 385
  Tickets, tax on, **1962:** 229 [1]
  Unemployment, **1963:** 110
  Unemployment insurance, **1961:** 384, 385
Railroad Commission, Presidential, **1962:** 66
Railroad Eight Hour Law of 1916, **1963:** 310
Railroad Retirement Board, **1963:** 402
Railroad Retirement Board, Chairman (Howard W. Habermeyer), **1961:** 385
Railroad Telegraphers, Order of, **1962:** 386
Railway Labor Act, **1962:** 245 [1], 378 [7], 386; **1963:** 184, 244, 310
Rains, Repr. Albert, **1961:** 264; **1963:** 193, 194
Rameses II, **1961:** 108
Ramey, James T., **1962:** 356; **1963:** 439
Ramspeck, Robert, **1963:** 44
Randall, Clarence B., **1961:** 273n.; **1962:** 55; **1963:** 44, 148, and p. 901
Randolph, Sen. Jennings, **1961:** 474, 476n.; **1962:** 77, 414; **1963:** 35 [8], 249
Randolph, John, **1961:** 190
Range resources conservation, **1962:** 69
Rasor, Jerry, **1962:** 432
Ratti, Guido, **1962:** 274
Raushenbush, Stephen, **1961:** 15ftn. (p. 39)
Rawlings, Calvin W., **1963:** 385
Rayburn, Repr. Sam, **1961:** 128, 476; **1962:** 7 (p. 5), 15, 201, 211, 259 [8], 335, 397; **1963:** 478
  See also Speaker of the House of Representatives.
  Commemorative medal, approval, **1962:** 409
  Death, **1961:** 471

Rayburn House Office Building, cornerstone laying
    ceremony, **1962:** 211
Raytheon Company, **1963:** 239
RB-47 flier, **1961:** 8 [3, 4, 6, 8, 11, 17, 22, 30], 15
    [7], 25 [13], 71 [19], 139 [20]; **1962:** 50 [23]
R.E.A.
    See Rural Electrification Administration.
Reactors, nuclear, **1961:** 99; **1962:** 289, 382, 408
Reading, the President's, **1962:** 551 [6]
Ready reserve, **1961:** 302
Ready Reserve, mobilization, **1962:** 366, 486n.
Real estate taxes, **1963:** 22, 34
Reapportionment, Supreme Court decision on,
    1962: 115 [12, 22], 190
Reardon, Timoth J., Jr., (Special Assistant to the
    President), **1962:** 221
Recessions, **1962:** 7 (p. 6), 13 (p. 35), 16 (p. 43), 22,
    53, 111, 176, 203, 230, 243 [2], 328, 346,
    380, 395, 437, 439, 452, 458, 459, 549;
    1963: 12 (pp. 11, 12), 30 (pp. 57-60, 66,
    67), 34, 77, 94, 102, 110, 134, 146, 175,
    185, 187, 188, 228, 248, 310, 340, 349, 351,
    363, 378, 382, 427, 462, 465, 466, 478
    News conference remarks, **1962:** 27 [27], 59 [16],
        229 [1], 245 [6, 7, 17], 316 [13]; **1963:** 65
        [2, 4], 77 [2, 3, 5], 107 [9], 120 [11], 175 [4]
Recession of 1958, **1961:** 11, 499
Recession of 1960-61, **1961:** 11, 17, 22, 33, 58, 90,
    93, 94, 133, 205, 242, 302, 436, 497, 498,
    499
    News conference remarks, **1961:** 15 [9], 35 [6, 14],
        62 [7], 119 [14], 258 [16]
Recife University, **1962:** 310n.
Reciprocal trade.
    See Trade international.
Reclamation, bureau of, **1962:** 13 (p. 30); **1963:**
    21 (p. 36)
Reclamation programs, **1961:** 49
Reclamation projects, **1962:** 69; **1963:** 41, 465
Record album, *the First Family,* **1962:** 546 [19]
Records, U.S. diplomatic papers, **1961:** 353
Recreation Advisory Council, Outdoor, **1962:** 69
Recreation Association, National, **1962:** 128
Recreation programs and facilities, **1962:** 7 (p. 7),
    13 (p. 30), 25, 69, 128, 195, 337, 377, 417;
    1963: 12 (p. 14), 21 (p. 36), 22, 30 (p. 66),
    45, 47, 63, 74, 75 [1], 134, 193, 209, 240,
    248, 325, 366, 376, 377, 378, 379, 384, 386,
    387, 389, 405 [5], 423, 445, 474
Recreation Resources Review Commission,
    Outdoor, **1962:** 69, 128, 377
Recreational facilities, **1961:** 49, 94, 315, 445
    Federal employees associations, **1961:** 137
Red Crescent, **1962:** 351
Red Cross, **1961:** 71 [8]; **1962:** 36, 67, 107 [9], 351,
    501; **1963:** 83, 133
    Campaign, **1961:** 59, 60
Red Lion and Sun, **1962:** 351
Redbook Magazine, **1963:** 319a

Redstone Arsenal, Huntsville, Ala., **1963:** 194
Reece, Repr. Louise G., **1961:** 278
Reed, James A., **1963:** 439
Reed, Gov. John H., **1962:** 326; **1963:** 108, 426
Reed, Stanley F., **1963:** 44
Reedy, Adm. James R., **1963:** 348
Rees, Albert E., **1961:** 458n.
Reeves, Elizabeth, **1963:** 10n.
Refugees and escapees, **1963:** 217
    Assistance, proposed bill, **1961:** 297
    Chinese, in Hong Kong, **1962:** 210 [2, 5], 245 [10]
    Cuban, **1961:** 8 [15], 9, 19, 86, 132, 138, 139 [7],
        171 [9], 183, 297; **1962:** 378 [1], 556; **1963:**
        107 [13], 120 [5], 134 [1], 144 [8, 11], 202
        [11]
    East German, **1961:** 291 [1], 292, 302, 318 [10]
    European camps, **1961:** 297
    Migration and Refugee Assistance Act,
        approval, **1962:** 261
Regan, Edwin J., **1963:** 389
Regional activities, Federal, **1961:** 465
Registration and Voting Participation, President's
    Commission on, **1963:** 117, 167
Registry of Election Finance, proposed, **1962:** 219;
    1963: 151
Regulatory agencies, **1961:** 25 [9], 121; **1962:** 93, 129
    See also specific agencies.
Reid, Elliott, **1962:** 158
Reifman, Alfred, **1961:** 123n.
Reinhardt, G. Frederick, **1961:** 242
Reinhardt, Mrs. G. Frederick, **1963:** 289
Reischauer, Edwin O., **1962:** 275
Relay communications satellite, **1963:** 55, 126n.
Relief and Works Agency for Palestine Refugees,
    United Nations, **1963:** 471
Religion, comment on, **1962:** 68
Religious freedom, **1961:** 26
Religious prejudice, 1961: 83 [16]
Remick, Lee, **1962:** 15
Rental housing, **1962:** 93 (p. 238)
Reorganization Act of 1949, extension, **1961:** 111
Reorganization Plan No. 1, Franklin D. Roosevelt
    Library, **1963:** 207
Reorganization Plans, messages
    No. I, Department of Urban Affairs and Housing
        proposed, **1962:** 23
    No. I, Securities and Exchange Commission,
        1961: 150
    No. 2, Federal Communications Commission,
        1961: 151
    No. 2, Science and technology, **1962:** 118
    No. 3, Civil Aeronautics Board, **1961:** 163
    No. 4, Federal Trade Commission, **1961:** 180
    No. 5, National Labor Relations Board, **1961:**
        200
    No. 6, Federal Home Loan Bank Board, **1961:**
        237
    No. 7, Maritime functions, **1961:** 238

Report to Congress
 See also Congress, letters to Members of; Congress, messages to; Congress, reports to, messages transmitting.
 List, **1961**: Appendix C, P. 844; **1962**: p. 943; **1963**: p. 926
 National forests development program, **1961**: 377
Reporters.
 See Press.
Reports to the President
 Acting Secretary of State, test ban treaty, **1963**: 324
 Ad Hoc Committee on Federal Office Space, **1962**: 221
 Administrative Conference, U.S., **1963**: 17
 Advisory Panel on Federal Salary Systems, **1962**: 55; **1963**: 44, 148
 Advisory Panel on National Academy of Foreign Affairs, **1963**: 57n.
 Area redevelopment in souther Illinois, **1962**: 58
 Attorney General Kennedy, Civil rights in Albany, Ga., **1962**: 316 [8]
 Bi-partisan National Committee on Health Care of the Aged, **1963**: 460
 Civil Rights Commission, **1963**: 59, 135
 Civil Service Commission, training of Federal employees, **1962**: 143
 Commission on Civil Rights, housing in Washington, D.C., **1962**: 142
 Commission on Money and Credit, **1961**: 245; **1962**: 151
 Commission on Status of Women, **1963**: 409
 Committee on Federal Credit Programs, **1963**: 62
 Committee to Strengthen the Security of the Free World, **1963**: 111
 Committee for Traffic Safety, **1963**: 125
 Committee on Youth Employment, **1963**: 141, 142
 Council of Economic Advisers, **1963**: 30n.
 Federal Council for Science and Technology, **1962**: 187; **1963**: 70, 252
 Food-for-Peace Committee, **1961**: 6n.
 Indonesian oil negotiations, **1963**: 224
 Labor disputes
  Aerospace industry, **1962**: 369; **1963**: 39n.
  Aircraft industry, **1962**: 247
  Maritime industry, **1962**: 21, 139 [3]; **1963**: 18
  Railroad, **1963**: 184, 414
 McConnell, Joseph C., radio space Communications, **1963**: 470
 Missile Sites Labor Commission, **1962**: 244
 National Capital Transportation Agency, **1963**: 208
 Nuclear weapons tests, **1961**: 318 [2, 19]
 Outdoor Recreation Resources Review Commission, **1962**: 128; **1963**: 209
 Passamaquoddy Tidal Power Project, **1963**: 301
 Presidential Railroad Commission, **1962**: 66

Reports to the President — *continued*
 President's Advisory Commission on Narcotic and Drug Abuse, **1963**: 121
 President's Advisory Committee on Labor-Management Policy, **1962**: 6, 164; **1963**: 310
 President's Commission on Campaign Costs, **1962**: 152 [4]; **1963**: 151n.
 President's Commission on the Status of women, **1962**: 347
 President's Committee on Equal Employment Opportunity, **1962**: 344
 President's Committee on Equal Opportunity in the Armed Services, **1963**: 251
 President's Committee on Juvenile Delinquincy and Youth Crime, **1962**: 220
 President's Committee for Traffic Safety, **1962**: 11
 President's Council on Aging, **1963**: 74
 President's Council on Youth Fitness, **1962**: 283
 President's Missile Sites Labor Commission, **1963**: 446
 President's Science Advisory Committee, **1962**: 547
 Seaborg, Glenn T., civilian nuclear manpower, **1962**: 100n.
 Secretary Dillon, balance of payments, **1962**: 114
 Secretary Freeman, timber cutting in national forests, **1962**: 307n.
 Secretary Goldberg
  Federal employee-management relations, **1962**: 215
  Mexican farm labor program, **1962**: 345
 Secretary Hodges, urban transportation, **1962**: 153
 Secretary McNamara, cost reduction in Defense Department, **1962**: 282
 Secretary Ribicoff, University of Havana faculty, **1961**: 19n.
 Secretary Wirtz, manpower, **1963**: 92
 Science Advisory Committee, **1963**: 67
 Special Consultant on the Arts, **1963**: 246
 Task force reports
  Agricultural commodities, **1961**: 15 [27]
  Coal mine safety, **1963**: 155n.
  Distressed areas redevelopment, **1961**: 7, 35 [15]
  Federal employee-management relations, **1961**: 250, 494; **1962**: 154
  Interurban transportation, **1962**: 462n.
  Latin America, **1961**: 276
  Ryukyu Islands, **1962**: 99
  Space explorations, **1961**: 8 [26]
  Water resources, **1963**: 70
 Taylor, Gen. Maxwell D., Cuban invasion, **1961**: 258 [8]
 Tennessee Valley Authority, **1961**: 30

Reports to the President — *continued*
  United States Study commission — Texas, **1962:**
    313
  Vice President Johnson, crisis in Southeast Asia,
    1961: 205
  Weaver, Robert C., urban transportation, **1962:**
    153
Republic Aviation Corp., **1962:** 247
Republic National Committee, **1962:** 50 [9]; **1963:**
    305 [18]
Republican National Committee, Chairman (Repr.
    William E. Miller), **1961:** 334 [11]; **1962:**
    8 [16], 152 [12], 229 [6], 439, 481; **1963:**
    151
Republican Party, **1961:** 3, 35 [14], 498; **1962:**
    158, 459; **1963:** 94, 118, 204, 223, 228, 322,
    333, 340, 349, 445, 463, 472
  Campaign remarks, **1962:** 394-396, 414, 431, 432,
    436-440, 446, 451-456, 458, 473, 481, 483
  News conference remarks, **1962:** 27 [9], 40 [13],
    245 [7, 9], 259 [8, 15, 16], 279 [22], 302
    [4, 14, 19], 352 [11], 378 [11, 21], 515 [8];
    1963: 35 [22], 65 [12, 13], 75 [6], 89 [5, 8,
    9], 120 [6], 144 [8], 169 [3], 202 [8, 9, 12],
    305 [24], 328 [13], 356 [19, 22], 459 [12, 15,
    20]
Research, **1963:** 332
  Aeronautical, **1963:** 68, 165
  Agricultural, **1961:** 85; **1962:** 25; **1963:** 30
    (p. 69), 110
  Air pollution, **1962:** 65; **1963:** 53
  Archeological, **1961:** 108
  Children's Bureau functions, **1961:** 289
  Educational, **1962:** 37; **1963:** 43
  Employee productivity, **1962:** 448
  Engineering, **1963:** 68
  Equipment for, tax deduction, **1963:** 34
  Forestry, **1961:** 85
  Government contracts for, **1962:** 163
  Health, **1961:** 406
  Housing, **1962:** 93 (p. 238)
  Housing and urban problems, **1961:** 76
  Industrial, **1962:** 170; **1963:** 21 (p. 37), 30 (p. 69),
    34
  Juvenile delinquency, **1963:** 64
  Medical, **1961:** 11, 14, 27, 94, 413, 488 [8]; **1962:**
    13 (p. 31), 65, 163, 234, 323, 470; **1963:** 12
    (p. 14), 30 (p. 69), 43, 50, 53, 64, 74, 202
    [17], 247, 313, 366, 374, 435, 447, 472
  Natural resources, **1962:** 69; **1963:** 70, 127, 252
  Nuclear, **1963:** 21 (p. 39), 328 [2]
  Occupational, **1963:** 92
  Oceanographic, **1961:** 49, 94, 100, 110
  Older persons, problems of, **1962:** 193; **1963:** 74
  Population, **1963:** 144 [6]
  Scientific, **1962:** 13 (p. 32), 118, 187, 209, 234; **1963:**
    11, 49, 94, 99, 436
    See also Science.

Research — *continued*
  Space.
    See Space research and exploration.
  Urban transportation, **1962:** 129
  Water desalinization, **1961:** 49, 94
  Water pollution, **1961:** 49
  Water resources, **1963:** 21 (p. 36)
Research Council, National, **1962:** 19
Research Institute of America, **1962:** 259 [16]
Reserve forces, **1961:** 205, 302; **1962:** 13 (p. 29), 378
    [1, 19], 407; **1963:** 169 [20]
  Call to active duty, **1961:** 291 [4], 334 [19], 488
    [10]; **1962:** 7 (p. 10), 107 [17], 152 [3], 186,
    366, 486n.; **1963:** 181
  Desegregation, **1963:** 82
  National Guard.
    See main heading, National Guard.
  Release from active duty, **1962:** 50 [24], 139 [2],
    309
    Statement, **1962:** 140
Reserve Officers Training Corps., **1962:** 416
Reservoirs, **1962:** 69
Reservoir sites reservation, **1961:** 49
Resignations or retirements, letters
  Day, J. Edward, **1963:** 317
  Dean, Arthur H., **1963:** 3
  Frankfurter, Justice Felix, **1962:** 353
  Goldberg, Arthur J., **1962:** 393
  Heckscher, August, **1963:** 246
  McGovern, George, **1962:** 293
  Norstad, Gen. Lauris, **1962:** 295
  Ribicoff, Abraham A., **1962:** 288
  Troutman, Robert, Jr., **1962:** 344
Resources, national, allocation of, **1963:** 120 [21]
Rest, Rev. William L., **1962:** 483n.
Restaurant and hotel workers, **1961:** 171 [20]
Reston, James B., **1962:** 40 [8]
Retail Clerks International Associations, **1961:**
    203
Retail sales, **1962:** 328
Retardation, mental.
    See Mental health programs *and* mental illness
      and mental retardation.
Retarded Children, National Association for, **1962:**
    534; **1963:** 435
Retirement
  Government employees, **1962:** 447
  Insurance, **1963:** 74
  Military personnel, **1961:** 99
  Pension funds, **1963:** 30 (p. 67), 74, 134
  Policemen and firemen, **1961:** 383
  Private program, **1962:** 16 (p. 55)
  Railroad system, **1961:** 27, 384, 385
  Self-employed persons, **1962:** 410 [10]
  Tax treatment of retired persons, **1963:** 34, 74
  Under Social Security, age reduction, **1963:** 445
Reuss, Repr. Henry S., **1961:** 63; **1962:** 186
Reuter, Richard W., **1963:** 439

Reuther, Walter, **1961:** 40n., 201, 350; **1962:** 174, 179 [9], 298n.; **1963:** 139
Revelle, Roger, **1962:** 404
Revenue Act of 1962, **1963:** 34
Revenue Act of 1962, approval, **1962:** 468
Revere, Paul, **1961:** 212
Review Committee for Balance of Payments, Statistics, **1963:** 143
Revolutionary Council, Cuban, **1963:** 144 [11]
Revolutionary War, **1961:** 78, 212, 217, 218, 397
Reynolds, James J., **1963:** 141, 244
Reynolds, Gov. John W., **1963:** 108, 377, 378, 392
Reynolds, Richard, **1961:** 40n.
Rhode Island, **1962:** 326, 383; **1963:** 248ftn. (p. 486)
Gov. John A. Notte, Jr., **1961:** 212
Rhodes Scholarships, **1963:** 221
Ribicoff, Abraham A., **1962:** 472-474; **1963:** 423n., 434, 435
See also Health, Education, and Welfare, Secretary of.
Rice, **1962:** 25
Exports, **1962:** 22, 170
Price supports, **1961:** 94
Rice University, **1962:** 372-373
Richards, Richard, **1962:** 337
Richardson, Duane, **1962:** 252
Richardson, John, **1963:** 405 [2]
Richmond, Adm. Alfred C., **1961:** 311
Rickover, Adm. Hyman G., **1963:** 203, 448 [15]
Rifkind, Judge Simon H., **1962:** 66; **1963:** 310
Rift space project, **1962:** 546 [11]
Right-wing groups, **1961:** 488 [14]; **1962:** 20 [16], 50 [25], 546 [22]; **1963:** 169 [8], 328 [13]
Riley, Kenneth, **1962:** 407
Riley, Robert, **1962:** 432
Rio de Janeiro, **1961:** 119 [20], 122
Rio Grande Basin, **1962:** 240
Rio Pact (1947).
See Inter-American Treaty of Reciprocal Assistance.
Rio Treaty, **1961:** 515
Rishtiya, Sayyid Kasem, **1963:** 347
River Basin development, **1961:** 49, 83 [2], 445, 474
River and Harbor Act of 1960, **1962:** 313
River and harbor improvement, **1962:** 69, 128; **1963:** 41, 193
River pollution, **1962:** 69
Rivera, Julio A., **1963:** 99, 100, 102, 106
Rives, Judge Richard T., **1962:** 420
Roa, Gonzales, **1963:** 89 [18]
Roads.
See Highway system, interstate; Highways.
Robbins, Jerome, **1962:** 201
Roberts, Chalmers M., **1961:** 83 [22]; **1962:** 546 [16, 17]
Robertson, Sen. A. Willis, **1963:** 353

Robichaud, Louis J., **1963:** 180
Robinson, Rev. James H., **1962:** 254
Robinson, Ray, **1963:** 319a note
Robles, Gonzalo, **1962:** 86n.
Rock, John, **1963:** 144 [6]
Rockefeller, David, **1962:** 280, 549; **1963:** 77
Rockefeller, John D., **1962:** 533
Rockefeller, John D., 3d, **1962:** 533n.
Rockefeller, Mary (Mrs. William J. Strawbridge, Jr.), **1962:** 152 [11]
Rockefeller, Gov. Nelson A., **1961:** 83 [7], 448, 503; **1962:** 40 [8], 50 [6], 229 [6], 439; **1963:** 65 [13], 89 [8], 202 [9, 19], 305 [24], 356 [12], 455, 459 [6]
Rockefeller Foundation, **1961:** 490; **1962:** 340 [13]; **1963:** 430
Rockefeller Public Service Awards, **1961:** 490; **1962:** 533
Rockets, **1962:** 486; **1963:** 472
See also Satellites, earth; space research and exploration; Space vehicles.
News conference remarks, **1963:** 75 [10], 120 [18]
Rover, **1961:** 119 [15], 139 [12], 205; **1962:** 546 [11]
Saturn project, **1961:** 35 [9], 119 [15], 139 [12]; **1962:** 340 [5], 373, 378 [14]; **1963:** 472, 474, 475, 478
Soviet, **1962:** 340 [5]
Soviet, in Cuba, **1963:** 75 [20]
Rockville, Md., **1963:** 397
Rodino, Repr. Peter W., Jr., **1962:** 450
Rodriguez Quiros, Archbishop Carlos Humberto, **1963:** 99
Rogers, Repr. Byron G., **1962:** 336
Rohr Corp., **1963:** 39
Rojas, Fernando, **1963:** 103
Roland, Adm. Edwin J., **1962:** 330n.
Rolvaag, Karl F., **1962:** 439n., 440n.; **1963:** 378
Romagna, Jack, **1961:** 483n.
Rome, **1961:** 467; **1962:** 171, 201, 203; **1963:** 254, 266, 289, 292, 478
Ancient, **1962:** 141, 225; **1963:** 289, 325, 351
Mayor Glauco Della Porta, **1963:** 288
Meeting with Pope John XXIII, **1963:** 202 [7]
Visit to, **1963:** 287
Rome, treaty of, **1961:** 21, 189, 318 [1]; **1962:** 20 [20]; **1963:** 290
Romney, George, **1962:** 40 [12]; **1963:** 202 [9]
Roncalio, Teno, **1962:** 123
Rooney, Repr. Fred B., **1963:** 376
Rooney, Repr. John J., **1962:** 316 [12]; **1963:** 93
Roosa, Robert V., **1961:** 123; **1962:** 316 [19]
Roosevelt, Eleanor, Cancer Foundation, **1961:** 215, 414
Roosevelt, Eleanor, Foundation, **1963:** 139, 408
Roosevelt, Elliott, **1963:** 139n., 408n.

Roosevelt, Franklin D., **1961:** 11, 65, 112, 122, 161,
169, 209, 212, 313, 321, 372, 373, 452, 474,
498, 499, 500n., 509, 515; **1962:** 3, 15, 22,
46, 74, 86, 104n., 124, 170, 184, 186, 199,
201, 202, 205, 216, 233, 234, 250, 252, 263,
264, 324, 326, 328, 329, 335-337, 346, 436,
439, 446, 451-453, 455, 458, 459, 481-483,
550, 551 [11], 552; **1963:** 6, 23, 46, 72, 103,
105, 109, 152, 159, 160, 162, 173, 193, 217,
214n., 215n., 223, 228, 268, 297, 370, 376,
377, 383, 385, 389, 390, 400, 401, 426, 427,
439, 462, 466, 467, 473, 474, 478
  Campobello Island cottage, **1963:** 180
  Library, Hyde Park, N.Y., **1962:** 260, 546 [7];
1963: 207
  London statue of, **1963:** 169 [7]
  Meeting with Emperor Haile Selassie (1945),
1963: 395n.
  Naval prints exhibit, **1962:** 260
  News conference remarks, **1961:** 119 [1], 222 [11]
1962: 27 [24], 107 [8], 259 [17], 302 [10],
546 [7]; **1963:** 65 [5], 169 [7], 356 [22]
  Stamp collection, **1962:** 260
Roosevelt, Mrs. Franklin D., **1961:** 139 [14], 201,
215, 482n., 504n.; **1962:** 43, 200, 347;
1963: 101, 409
  Commemorative stamps, **1963:** 408
  Eleanor Roosevelt Foundation, **1963:** 139, 408
  Interview with, **1962:** 156
  Statement on death of, **1962:** 505
Roosevelt, Franklin D., Jr., **1962:** 185; **1963:** 65 [5],
139n.
Roosevelt, Franklin D., 3d, **1963:** 408n.
Roosevelt, Hall Delano, **1963:** 408n.
Roosevelt, Repr. James, **1963:** 408n.
Roosevelt, John, **1963:** 139n.
Roosevelt, Kermit Jr., **1963:** 408n.
Roosevelt, Mrs. Kermit, **1963:** 408n.
Roosevelt, Theodore, **1961:** 48, 49, 65, 122, 162,
403, 404, 464; **1962:** 203, 216, 235, 274,
275, 335-337, 551 [11]; **1963:** 23, 151, 159,
160, 296, 325 [22], 376, 377, 379, 381
160, 296, 325 [22], 376, 377, 379, 381,
383, 385, 387, 389, 390, 400, 408n., 427
  News conference remarks on, **1961:** 8 [31], 25
[22], 171 [11]
Rose, Alex, **1962:** 200
Rosellini, Gov. Albert D., **1961:** 472n., 474; **1963:**
384, 387
Rosenberg, Anna, **1962:** 201
Rosenberg, Ludwig, **1963:** 268
Rosenbloom, Carroll, **1962:** 15
Rosenblum, William F., **1963:** 445
Rosenfield, Arthur H., **1961:** 342
Rosenhaus, Matthew B., 1961: 215
Rosenman, Samuel I., 1961: 256; **1962:** 21, **1963:**
184, 310
Rosenstein-Rodan, Paul, **1962:** 86n.

Ross, Arthur, **1962:** 386
Ross, Comdr. Malcolm D., **1962:** 475n.
Ross, Ronald R., **1962:** 456
Rossides, Zenon, **1962:** 227, 339n.
Rostenkowdki, Repr. Dan, **1962:** 483
Rostow, Walt W., **1962:** 180n., 259 [21]; **1963:** 171,
405 [13]
ROTC.
  See Reserve Officers Training Corps.
Roth, Robert, **1962:** 158
Roush, Repr. J. Edward, **1962:** 456
Rover space project, **1961:** 119 [15], 139 [12], 205;
1962: 546 [11]
Rowley, James J., **1963:** 277
Royal Air Force, **1962:** 554
Royal Canadian Air Force, **1963:** 476
Royal Canadian Mounted Police, **1962:** 443
Royal Highland Regiment (Black Watch), **1963:**
457
Royall, Brig. Gen. Kenneth C., **1962:** 549; **1963:**
365, 372
Royster, Vermont C., **1963:** 134
Rozmarek, Charles, **1963:** 173
Rubber, tread, tax on, **1961:** 58
Rubin, Seymour J., **1961:** 71 [6]
Rubio Mane, Jorge Ignacio, **1961:** 432n.
Rules governing this publication, **1961:** Appendix
D, p. 845; **1962:** Appendix D, p. 944
Rumania, **1963:** 271
Rummel, Archbishop Joseph F., **1962:** 152 [13]
Rural area development program, **1962:** 25, 340 [2]
Rural areas, **1963:** 21 (pp. 36, 37), 43, 45, 74, 92,
149, 423, 468, 478
Rural education, **1962:** 25
Rural Electric Cooperative Association,
National, **1962:** 499; **1963:** 149n.
Rural electric cooperatives, **1961:** 136
Rural electrification, **1961:** 49, 85; **1962:** 7 (p. 7),
13 (p. 30), 25, 335, 336, 499; **1963:** 21 (p.
39), 45, 105, 149, 193
Rural Electrification Administration, **1961:** 94;
1962: 7 (p. 7), 13 (p. 30), 25, 335, 336, 440,
499; **1963:** 45, 379, 478
Rural housing, **1961:** 76; **1962:** 25, 93 (p. 238)
Rural transportation, **1962:** 25
Rusk, Dean.
  See State, Secretary of.
Rusk, Howard, **1963:** 118
Russell, D.J., **1963:** 95n.
Russell, Gov. Donald R., **1963:** 108
Russell, Sen. Richard B., **1961:** 62 [2]; **1962:** 320;
1963: 75 [3], 222, 330, 356 [23]
Russia.
  See Soviet Union.
Rutherford, Repr. J.T., **1962:** 189n., 362
Ruttenburg, Stanley H., **1961:** 458n.
Rwanda, Republic of, **1963:** 471
Rwanda, Republic of, Gregoire Kayibanda, **1962:**
267, 388

Ryan, Repr. Harold M., **1962:** 433, 436
Ryan, Mary Kennedy, **1963:** 276n.
Ryukyu Islands, **1961:** 252; **1962:** 99, 130

Saad, Ahmed Zaki, **1962:** 392n.
Saarinen, Mrs. Eero, **1962:** 512
SAC.
   See Strategic Air Command.
Saez, Paul, **1962:** 86n.
Safety hazards, **1963:** 51
Sagamore Hill National Historic Site, **1962:** 69
Sahara Desert, **1962:** 465
Saigon, **1961:** 218, 415 [1], 488 [3]; **1963:** 255, 312,
   334, 340, 349
St. Augustine, Fla., **1962:** 77
St. Cloud, Minn., **1962:** 440
Saint Elizabeths Hospital, D.C., **1962:** 65; **1963:** 22,
   66
St. John River power project, **1963:** 301
St. Lawrence River, **1963:** 179
St. Lawrence Seaway, **1963:** 422
St. Louis, Mo., **1961:** 454n.; **1962:** 375; **1963:**
   248ftn. (p. 486), 423
St. Louis Post-Dispatch, **1962:** 245 [7]
St. Patrick's Day, **1963:** 416
St. Patrick's Day, statement, **1962:** 95
St. Paul, Minn., **1962:** 439
St. Paul's Church (Paulskirche), Frankfurt,
   address, **1963:** 266
St. Petersburg, Fla., Mayor Herman Goldner,
   1963: 464
St. Sure, J. Paul, **1963:** 206
Salamanca University, **1963:** 342
Salaries.
   See Pay; Wages.
Salary Reform Act of 1962, Federal, **1963:** 148
Salem, Mass., **1961:** 143; **1963:** 361
Salerno, Joseph, **1962:** 483
Sales tax, national, question of, **1961:** 83 [17]
Salinger, Pierre E. G., **1961:** 8 [16], 217, 388, 483n.;
   1962: 20 [11], 27 [4, 26], 50 [18], 59 [17],
   89 [2, 3], 115 [10, 18], and ftn. (p. 273),
   378 [5]; **1963:** 75 [9], 120 [13], 221
   News conference remarks on, **1961:** 8 [1, 23], 25
   [4, 22], 35 [7], 92 [17], 258 [7, 22], 318 [6],
   455 [10], 488 [4]
Salk, Dr. Jonas E., **1963:** 353
Salk vaccine, **1961:** 119 [1]
Salt, ocean resources, **1961:** 100
Salt Lake City, Utah, **1963:** 385, 386, 405 [8]
Salt water convention, **1961:** 11, 17, 49, 94, 119 [13],
   248, 257; **1962:** 69, 337
   Approval of bill, **1961:** 381
Saltonstall, Sen. Leverett, **1961:** 476n.; **1963:** 245,
   427
Salvioli, Alex, **1962:** 274
Salzgitter, **1961:** 184
Sam Houston, U.S.S., **1961:** 16
Samoa, American, **1962:** 196

Samos earth satellite, **1962:** 115 [24]
Samuels, Howard J., **1963:** 204
San Angelo, Tex., project, **1963:** 474, 478
San Antonio, Tex., **1963:** 472
San Antonio River Basin, **1962:** 313
San Carlos Indian Reservation, **1963:** 113
San Diego, Calif., **1963:** 227
   Marine Recruit Depot, remarks, **1963:** 227
   State College, commencement address, **1963:** 226
San Francisco, Calif., **1961:** 454n., 501; **1963:** 366,
   387, 423, 433
San Jacinto River Basin, **1962:** 313
San Jose, Calif., **1963:** 478
San Jose, Costa Rica, Central American Presi-
   dents Conference, **1963:** 97-100, 102-106,
   118
   Declaration, **1963:** 107 [17], 134 [1]
   News conference remarks, **1963:** 89 [10], 107 [1,
   7, 17, 22], 120 [12], 134 [1]
   Stand on Cuba, **1963:** 107 [7]
San Juan, **1961:** 506
San Juan-Chama Reclamation Project, **1962:** 69,
   336
   Approval, **1962:** 240
San Leandro Chamber of Commerce, **1962:** 113n.
San Luis Dam, **1962:** 337
San Martin, Jose de, **1961:** 78, 515; **1962:** 86, 556
Sanchez, Alvaro, Jr., **1962:** 556
Sánchez, Mireles, Romulo, **1962:** 271n.
Sand, Harry, **1962:** 432
Sandburg, Carl, **1961:** 462
Sanders, Gov. Carl E., **1963:** 108
Sandys, Duncan, **1962:** 554; **1963:** 285
Sanford, Gov. Terry, **1961:** 327, 416n., 418n.; **1963:**
   108
Sanford, Mrs. Terry, **1961:** 327
Santa Fe, N. Mex., **1962:** 536
Santa Maria, **1961:** 8 [16], 15 [29]
Santander, Francisco de Paula, **1961:** 515
Santiago, Chile, **1963:** 323
Sao Paulo, Brazil, **1962:** 546 [2]; **1963:** 361, 459
   [22], 468
   University, **1962:** 310n.
Sarnoff, Brig. Gen. David, **1962:** 546 [8]
Satellite countries, Soviet, **1961:** 480; **1962:** 461
   See also Communist bloc; Sino-Soviet block;
      specific countries.
Satellites, earth, **1962:** 373
   See also Rockets; Space research and explora-
      tion; Space vehicles.
   Advent, **1961:** 99
   Communications, **1961:** 11, 99, 139 [21], 205,
      254, 299, 387
      See also main heading, Communications.
   Discoverer, **1961:** 99
   Midas, **1961:** 99; **1962:** 115 [24]
   Navigation, **1962:** 373; **1963:** 470
   News conference remarks, **1962:** 115 [24], 210
      [15], 340 [5, 8]

Satellites, earth — *continued*
Samos, **1962:** 115 [24]
Soviet, **1961:** 35 [9], 205
Sputnik, **1963:** 120 [11], 406
Tiros, **1962:** 373
Transit, **1962:** 373
Weather, **1961:** 139 [21], 205; **1962:** 7 (p. 11), 96, 109, 210 [15], 373; **1963:** 21 (p. 34), 470, 477, 478
Saturday Evening Post, **1962:** 534, 546 [23]
Saturn space project, **1961:** 35 [9], 119 [15], 139 [12]; **1962:** 340 [5], 373, 378 [14]; **1963:** 472, 474, 475, 478
Saud, King, **1962:** 50 [12]
Visit of, **1962:** 44-46
Saudek, Robert, **1962:** 527n.
Saudi Arabia, **1963:** 334
Crown Prince Faysal, **1962:** 429
Dhahran, U.S. base, **1962:** 50 [12]
King Saud, **1962:** 44-46, 50 [12]
U.S. Ambassador Parker T. Hart, **1963:** !20 [16]
Yemen dispute, **1963:** 448 [5], 459 [13], 471
Saunders, Stuart T., **1963:** 145n., 299, 351
Savang Vatthana, King, **1961:** 51, 60; **1962:** 50 [22], 308; **1963:** 78, 79, 81
Savannah, **1962:** 129
Savings, personal, **1962:** 93 (p. 237), 229 [16], 473
Savings bonds, **1962:** 14; **1963:** 94, 325
Federal, **1961:** 75
Savings and loan associations, **1962:** 179 [1]; **1963:** 118
Sawyer, Gov. Grant, **1963:** 390
Sawyer, Roland M., **1963:** 49n.
Sayre, Rev. Francis B., Jr., **1961:** 33
Scammon, Richard M., **1963:** 117n., 167
Scandinavia, **1962:** 534; **1963:** 191, 308, 434
Settlements in U.S., **1962:** 178
Scanlon, Tom, **1962:** 250
Shaff, Philip, **1963:** 294
Schärf, Adolf, **1961:** 224, 226
Schary, Dore, **1963:** 46
Schaus, Eugene, **1963:** 152, 156
Scheel, Walter, **1963:** 258
Schenck, David, **1963:** 230
Scherer, Raymond L., **1962:** 75 [12]
Schiro, Victor H., **1962:** 170, 171
Schirra, Comdr. Walter, **1962:** 426, 427, 435, 463; **1963:** 406
Schlesinger, Arthur, Jr., **1961:** 15ftn. (p. 39)
Schmerling, Anton Ritter von, **1963:** 264n.
Schoemann, Peter T., **1962:** 412n.
Schoenbrun, David, **1962:** 400
Schola Cantorum, University of Arkansas, **1962:** 352 [3], 361
Scholarships, **1961:** 27, 46, 57, 70, 144; **1962:** 3, 7 (p. 8), 13 (p. 32), 16 (p. 47), 37, 40 [2], 65, 259 [4]; **1963:** 10, 43, 221, 294, 400
News conference remarks, **1961:** 62 [27], 71 [13, 17], 318 [17]

Scholarships, Board of Foreign, remarks, **1961:** 57
Schomp, K. K., **1963:** 95n.
Schonbrunn, **1961:** 226
Schools, **1962:** 360; **1963:** 43, 74, 141, 290, 455, 461, 465
See also Education.
Choate School, message to alumni, **1963:** 160
Construction, **1963:** 21 (p. 38), 22, 226, 400, 478
Construction, Federal aid, **1962:** 7 (p. 9), 37
Corporal punishment in, **1963:** 202 [6]
Cuban refugees, **1961:** 19
District of Columbia, **1963:** 35 [15], 202 [6], 230
Dropouts, **1963:** 10, 12 (p. 13), 43, 64, 65 [1], 77 85, 110, 142, 226, 230, 248, 305 [19], 320 [1], 351, 358, 385, 387, 423, 445, 448 [7], 455, 462, 463
Fallout shelters in, **1962:** 320
Federal aid, **1963:** 82, 248, 358n., 423
Indians, **1962:** 331
Integration, **1962:** 152 [13], 198 [8]; **1963:** 82, 169 [4], 248, 350, 356 [2, 8, 22], 455, 462
Latin American, **1963:** 326
Lunch and milk programs, **1962:** 7 (p. 8), 19, 25, 413, 440; **1963:** 89 [5], 135, 193, 423, 458
New York City, **1962:** 546 [8]
Physical fitness program, **1961:** 496; **1962:** 283, 291; **1963:** 325
Prayers in, Supreme Court decision, **1962:** 259 [3, 20]
Private and parochial, **1962:** 40 [3], 152 [13], 259 [4]; **1963:** 160
U.S. abroad, **1963:** 118
Vocational training, **1963:** 469
Washington, D.C. area, **1962:** 59 [3]
School districts in Federally affected areas, aid to, **1961:** 37, 291 [16], 398
School integration.
See Integration.
School lunch program, **1961:** 17, 85, 94
School milk program, **1961:** 85
School Safety Patrol, awards, **1962:** 182
Schramek, William E., **1962:** 475n.
Schroeder, Gerhard, **1961:** 480n.; **1962:** 507n., 508; **1963:** 258, 262
Schultz, Henry E., **1963:** 46
Schuman, Robert, **1963:** 35 [17], 266, 341
Schurz, Carl, **1963:** 255
Schweitzer, Pierre-Paul, **1963:** 391
Schwulst, Earl B., **1963:** 49n.
Science, **1962:** 109, 181; **1963:** 21 (p. 32), 136, 179, 192, 215n., 225, 246, 271, 369, 378, 385, 474, 478
Education, **1961:** 94, 318 [17]; **1962:** 8 [1], 13 (p. 32), 37, 546 [8]; **1963:** 21 (p. 38), 30 (p. 69), 43, 64, 92, 136, 226, 366
Research, **1962:** 13 (pp. 32, 35), 118, 187, 209, 234; **1963:** 21 (p. 39), 30 (p. 69), 43, 67, 68, 77, 92, 144 [20], 202 [17], 240, 247, 252, 301, 342, 366, 378, 381, 430, 472

[References are to items except as otherwise indicated]

Science Advisory Committee, President's, **1961:** 49, 417; **1962:** 8 [1], 118, 411, 547; **1963:** 43, 53, 67, 92, 328 [17]
 Availability of information to, **1963:** 54 [12], 75 [9]
 Comments on, **1963:** 134 [6], 245, 259
 News conference remarks, **1961:** 15 [35], 258 [3]
Science Board, National, **1962:** 118
Science Foundation, National, **1963:** 21 (p. 38), 43, 82, 248
Science Information, Panel on, **1963:** 67n.
Science and Technology, Federal Council, for, **1961:** 49, 417; **1962:** 8 [1], 69, 118, 187, 547; **1963:** 53
 Report, **1963:** 70, 252
Science and Technology, Office of, **1963:** 45, 301
 Director (Jerome B. Wiesner), **1963:** 29, 70, 252, 301, 430
 Establishment, **1962:** 118
Science and Technology, U.N. Conference on, **1963:** 38
Science and World Affairs Conference, **1961:** 347
Science Youth Month, **1961:** 378
Sciences, National Academy of, **1963:** 144 [6], 252, 430
Scientific research, **1961:** 94, 99, 436
Scientific and technical work contracts, **1961:** 314
Scientific training, **1961:** 100
Scientific Unions, International Council of, **1961:** 100
Scientists
 In Federal Government, **1962:** 187
 Shortage of, **1962:** 8 [1], 546 [8], 547, 549; **1963:** 43
Scotland, **1963:** 297, 457
Scranton, Gov. William W., **1963:** 108, 376
Scranton, Pa., **1962:** 89 [13]
Screvane, Paul R., **1962:** 548
Sea Dragon, U.S.S., **1962:** 340 [1]
Sea exploration, **1961:** 100, 110
Sea power, U.S., **1963:** 225
Seaborg, Glenn T., **1962:** 100, 109, 163, 356n., 530n.; **1963:** 328 [4], 354, 448 [15]
 See also Atomic Energy Commission, Chairman
Seafarers International Union of North America, **1961:** 270
Seafood resources, **1961:** 100
Seals
 Presidential, **1961:** 11, 155; **1963:** 426
 United States, **1961:** 418
Seamen, war casualties, **1963:** 203
Seashores, national, **1962:** 69, 75 [23], 216, 336, 337, 377, 417, 459
Seashore recreational development, **1961:** 49, 94, 315
Seath, Mark, **1962:** 231
SEATO.
 See Southeast Asia Treaty Organization.

Seaton, Louis, **1961:** 350
Seattle, Wash., **1961:** 454n., 472, 473, 474, 476; **1962:** 20 [16], 376
 Mayor Gordon S. Clinton, **1961:** 472n.
 World's Fair, **1961:** 474; **1962:** 155
SEC.
 See Securities and Exchange Commission.
Second Vatican Council, **1962:** 430
Secret Service, **1963:** 204
Secret Service protection, letter, **1961:** 142
Securities and Exchange Commission, **1961:** 121, 150; **1962:** 93 (p. 237); **1963:** 120 [2], 466
Security of the Free World, Committee to Strengthen the, **1963:** 89 [20], 111, 118, 120 [6]
Segni, Antonio, **1961:** 239n., 242; **1962:** 352 [3]; **1963:** 16, 200 [10], 287, 290-293
Segregation.
 See Civil rights; Integration.
Seismology, use to detect underground nuclear explosions, **1963:** 27, 319a, 448 [29]
Seitz, Frederick, **1963:** 430
Selden, Repr. Armistead I., Jr., **1962:** 30n; **1963:** 98, 105
Selective Service, **1961:** 413, 496
Selective Service System, **1962:** 208; **1963:** 64, 310, 393
Selective Service System, Director (Gen. Lewis B. Hershey), **1961:** 348
 Rejectees, training and rehabilitation, **1963:** 393
Self-determination for nations, **1961:** 387; **1962:** 242, 273
 Eastern Europe, **1961:** 291 [17]
Self-employed pension bill, **1962:** 410 [10]
Selland, Arthur L., **1962:** 338n.
Sellers, Peter, **1962:** 158
Sen, B. R., **1963:** 217
Senate Youth Program, **1963:** 48
Seneca, **1963:** 217
Seneca Nation, opposition to Kinzua Dam project, **1961:** 71 [15], 320
Senegal, **1961:** 116; **1962:** 325
Senghor, Leopold Sedar, **1961:** 450
Sengstacke, John, **1962:** 257n.
Senior citizens.
 See Older persons.
Senior Citizens, Gold Ring Council of, **1962:** 202n.
Senior Citizens, National Council of, **1962:** 202n., 217; **1963:** 138
Senior Citizens Act, proposed, **1962:** 193
Senior Citizens Community Planning and Services Act, **1963:** 185
Senior Citizens Housing Act of 1962, **1963:** 74
Senior Citizens Month, **1963:** 138n.
Senior Service Corps, proposed, **1962:** 245 [11]
Separation of powers of Government, **1962:** 20 [7], 522
Serkin, Rudolf, **1963:** p. 901

Service Corps, National, proposed, **1963:** 64, 232
Sevilla-Sacasa, Guilermo, **1961:** 373n.
Sewage treatment works, **1961:** 49
Seward, Ralph T., **1962:** 298
Shamrock, Tex., **1963:** 277
Shanahan, Foss, **1962:** 248
Shannon, Ireland, **1963:** 282
Shapiro, Sam, **1961:** 155
Sharp, John G., **1962:** 247
Shaw, George Bernard, **1963:** 278
Shelley, Percy Bysshe, **1963:** 291
Shen Chang-Huan, **1961:** 306, 309
Shepard, Comdr. Alan B., Jr., **1961:** 170, 171 [13],
         178, 205; **1962:** 61, 63, 171, 323; **1963:** 199,
         406
    NASA Distinguished Service Medal, **1961:** 177
Shepard, Mrs. Alan B., Jr., **1961:** 177, 178
Sheppard, Repr. Harry R., **1961:** 62 [18]
Sherman Antitrust Act, **1962:** 93 (p. 241)
Sherpas, **1963:** 296
Shields, Murray, **1962:** 549n.
Shipley, Repr. George E., **1962:** 58n., 481
Shipping Act, amendment, **1961:** 370, 401
Ships, **1961:** 302; **1963:** 179, 221, 474
    Barbara Anne, **1961:** 25 [10]
    Construction, **1962:** 129; **1963:** 477
    Cuban air attacks on, **1963:** 75 [3, 5, 8, 20]
    Cuss I, **1961:** 110
    Dennison, **1962:** 129
    Eagle, **1962:** 330
    Foreign, use in intercoastal trade, **1962:** 307
    Gretel, **1962:** 383; **1963:** 216n.
    Hope, **1961:** 146
    Intrepid, **1962:** 213
    Joseph P. Kennedy, Jr., **1962:** 384
    Kearsarge, **1962:** 427n.; **1963:** 190n.
    Kitty Hawk, **1963:** 225, 228
    La Flore, gift model to President, **1963:** 112
    Maritime labor disputes.
       See Maritime labor disputes.
    NATO countries, shipments to Cuba, **1962:** 352
         [19], 378 [1], 546 [10]
    NATO nuclear surface fleet, proposed, **1963:** 75
         [19]
    Noa, **1962:** 57
    Nuclear powered, **1963:** 448 [15]
       Enterprise, **1962:** 148
       Long Beach, **1961:** 99
       Savannah, **1962:** 129
       Submarines. *See Submarines, nuclear
          powered.*
    Oceanographic, **1961:** 100, 110
    Oriskany, **1963:** 225n.
    Santa Maria, **1961:** 8 [16], 15 [29]
    Soviet, attack by Cuban exiles, **1963:** 107 [13],
         120 [5]
    Subsidies, **1961:** 238; **1962:** 129
    Sulphur Queen, disappearance, **1963:** 75 [20]

Ships — *continued*
    Surface, Polaris missile-equipped, **1963:** 89 [14]
    U.S., under foreign flags, **1961:** 258 [11]
    U.S. flag, grain shipments to Soviet Union, **1963:**
         405 [1], 448 [12]
    Weatherly, **1962:** 383; **1963:** 216n.
    Western, use in Soviet-Cuban trade, **1963:** 65 [11]
Shoemaker, A. Whitney, **1962:** 279 [8]
Shooshan, Harry, **1961:** 273n.
Shoup, Gen. David M., **1962:** 149n., 287, 416; **1963:**
         312, 448 [9]
Shriver, R. Sargent (Director, Peace Corps), **1962:**
         243, 340 [22]; **1963:** 129, 304n.
    See also Peace Corps, Director.
Shriver, Mrs. R. Sargent, **1962:** 243 [4], 534; **1963:**
         275
Shriver, Mrs. Sargent, Jr., **1961:** 413n.
Sickles, Carlton, **1962:** 446
Sick pay exclusion, tax treatment, **1963:** 34
Sidey, Hugh, *John F. Kennedy, President,* **1963:**
         356 [7]
Sidi Mohammed Ben Abdullah, Sultan, **1963:** 115
Sierra Club, **1963:** 196
Sierre Leone, **1962:** 325
Sierre Leone, independence, **1961:** 148
Sierre Leone, Peace Corps projects in, **1963:** 294
Sihanouk, Prince Norodom, **1962:** 352 [16]; **1963:**
         459 [1]
Sikes, Repr. Robert L. F., **1962:** 170
Sikorsky, Igor, **1961:** 486; **1962:** 475
Sikta, Abdullah, **1962:** 467n.
Silent Spring, Rachel Carson, **1962:** 352 [24]
Siler, Repr. Eugene, **1963:** 137
Silver, Cortland V., **1963:** 188n.
Silver, decontrol of, **1962:** 16 (p. 55)
Silver, free, **1961:** 484
Silver policy, **1963:** 30 (p. 67), 94
Simkin, William E., **1962:** 390; **1963:** 206
Sino-Soviet bloc, **1961:** 119 [6], 209, 214, 222, 497
    See also Communist bloc; Satellite countries,
         Soviet; Warsaw Pact countries; *specific
         countries.*
Sioux Indians, **1963:** 257
Sisk, Repr. B. F., **1962:** 337, 338
Sita, Lt. Albert, **1961:** 235
Sit-ins, Supreme Court decision on, **1963:** 202 [20]
Sitting Bull, Chief, **1963:** 257
Skaggs, Luther, Jr., **1962:** 159n.
Skate, U.S.S., **1962:** 340 [1]
Skoplje, Yugoslavia, earthquake, U.S. relief, **1963:**
         421
Skybolt missile, **1961:** 99, 415 [7]; **1962:** 75 [20], 546
         [5], 551 [13, 22], 554, 557; **1963:** 35 [12], 54
         [8], 89 [5], 169 [20]
Slack, Repr. John M., Jr., **1962:** 414; **1963:** 249
Slavery, abolition, **1962:** 362
Slavery, convention on abolition of, **1963:** 309
Slayton, Maj. Donald K., **1963:** 406

Sleeping Bear Dunes National Lakeshore, **1962:** 69
Slim, Mongi, **1961:** 387n.
Slum areas
  Educational needs, **1961:** 46
Slum clearance, **1961:** 76; **1962:** 50, 305 [19], 326,
    423, 445, 469, 478; **1963:** 23, 395
Small business, **1962:** 7 (p. 7), 72, 395, 414; **1963:** 21
    (pp. 30, 37, 39), 30 (pp. 58, 63), 34, 177,
    465, 478
Small Business Act, amendement proposed, **1962:**
    72
Small Business Administration, **1961:** 35 [3], 161;
    1962: 16 (p. 49), 72, 307; **1963:** 478
  National Advisory Council, **1963:** 188
Small business defense contracts, **1961:** 35 [3], 83
    [1]
Small Business, White House Committee on, **1961:**
    337
Smart, Gen. Jacob E., **1963:** 221
Smathers, Sen. George A., **1962:** 77, 89 [2], 107
    [19], 179 [4], 205; **1963:** 345, 353, 464-467
Smith, Benjamin A., II, **1963:** 89 (p. 243), 352
Smith, Bromley, **1961:** 42
Smith, C. R., **1963:** 110
Smith, Elizabeth R., **1961:** 75n.
Smith, George L., **1963:** 2d, 368
Smith, Gerard C., **1963:** 36
Smith, H. Alexander, **1961:** 307
Smith, Repr. Howard W., **1963:** 107 [24]
Smith, Sen. Margaret Chase, **1961:** 212; **1962:** 326;
    1963: 301n., 426, 459 [7]
Smith, Merriman, **1962:** 198 [21], 229 [23]
Smith, Stephen E., **1961:** 203
Smith, Mrs. Stephen E., **1961:** 203; **1963:** 275
Smith, Walter Bedell, **1962:** 50 [9]
Smith, Rear Adm. Willard J., **1962:** 330n.
Smith-Hughes Vocational Education Act of 1917,
    1963: 92
Smith-Mundt Act, **1961:** 307, 379
Smithies, Arthur, **1961:** 119 [2]
Smoking, cigarette, effect on health, **1963:** 202 [17]
Smoot-Hawley Tariff, **1962:** 199; **1963:** 9
Snake River, Idaho, power project, **1963:** 175 [1]
Snark missile, **1961:** 99
Snyder, John I., **1963:** 204n.
Sobieski, John, sword of, **1962:** 461
Social security, **1961:** 17, 43, 263, 339, 474; **1962:** 7
    (p. 8), 16 (p. 44), 20 [26], 28, 107 [8], 186,
    202, 210 [4], 222, 288, 324, 328, 437-439;
    1963: 21 (pp. 27, 32), 30 (p. 58), 34, 74,
    110, 134, 175 [4], 228, 427, 458, 464, 466,
    478
  Extension of benefits, **1963:** 75 [1]
  Health insurance under, proposed, **1961:** 11, 27,
    32, 83 [14], 94, 119 [11], 133, 341, 477;
    1962: 3, 7 (pp. 8, 9), 13 (p. 31), 16 (p. 46),
    65, 81, 174, 186, 201, 217, 222, 310 [2],
    395, 396, 431, 436-439, 451, 453, 454, 456,

Social security — *continued*
  Health insurance under — *continued*
    458, 459, 472, 473, 480, 481, 483; **1963:** 12
    (p. 14), 21 (p. 38), 53, 74, 138, 445, 460,
    467
  Address, **1962:** 202
  Defeat of bill, statement, **1962:** 292
  News conference remarks, **1962:** 8 [24], 20 [12],
    75 [18], 89 [20], 107 [8], 210 [1, 4, 8], 229
    [13], 259 [8, 12], 279 [2, 24], 302 [4, 19,
    21], 340 [24]
  Statement by physicians, **1962:** 112
  Increase in benefits, **1961:** 35 [3], 448
  News conference remarks, **1961:** 25 [25], 35 [3],
    83 [14], 119 [11]; **1963:** 75 [1, 6], 459 [12]
  Tax increase, **1961:** 27
Social Security Act, **1961:** 339; **1963:** 22
Social Security Act, amendment proposed, **1962:**
    28, 288
Social Security Amendments of 1961, **1961:** 263
Social Security Financing, Advisory Council on,
    proposed, **1963:** 74
Social workers, shortage of, **1962:** 28
Socialism, comment on, **1962:** 310 [1]
Sockman, Ralph W., **1963:** 455n.
Sohn, Louis, **1962:** 107 [16], 316 [18]
Soil bank, **1963:** 202 [12]
Soil conservation, **1961:** 49, 85, 278; **1962:** 25, 69;
    1963: 193, 376
Soil Conservation and Domestic Allotment Act,
    amendment proposed, **1962:** 25
Soil Conservation and Domestic Allotment Act of
    1936, **1961:** 85
  Approval, **1962:** 425
Soil Conservation Service, **1963:** 127
Solicitor General (Archibald Cox), **1962:** 115 [12],
    231, 245 [2]; **1963:** 320 [6]
Solis, Galileo, **1962:** 235n., 238n.
Solon, Athenian law-maker, **1961:** 153
Somalia, **1963:** 455
Somali Republic, **1962:** 549 [10]
  Abdirascid Ali Scermarche, **1962:** 522, 523, 526,
    551 [17]
  Abdullahi Issa Mohamud, **1962:** 523n.
  Ambassador Omar Mohallim Mohamed, **1962:**
    523n.
Somoza, Luis, **1963:** 99, 100, 102, 106
Sophocles, **1962:** 527
Sorensen, Theodore C., **1963:** 202 [6]
  Decision-Making in the White House, **1963:** 370
Sorkin, Martin, **1962:** 439, 481
Sosa Rodriguez, Carlos, **1963:** 366
South Africa, U.N. resolution on racial policies,
    1961: 488 [15]
South Africa
  Lead imports from, **1963:** 202 [13]
  Racial policy, **1963:** 305 [21]
  U.N. participation, **1963:** 305 [21]

South America.
  See Latin America.
South Carolina, **1962:** 241
  Gov. Donald R. Russell, **1963:** 108
  News conference remarks, **1963:** 356 [22]
South Charleston, W. Va., **1961:** 119 [3]
South Dakota, **1962:** 178, 293, 335, 337, 338, 425;
          1963: 113, 248ftn. (p. 486)
  Gov. Archie Gubbrud, **1962:** 335
South Korea.
  See Korea.
South Pacific Commission, **1962:** 196
Southeast Asia Collective Defense Treaty
          (Manila Pact), **1962:** 192
Southeast Asia Treaty Organization, **1961:** 92 [1, 6,
          9, 17], 205, 279, 476; **1962:** 50 [9], 157, 192,
          198 [17, 20], 210 [11], 250, 251, 340 [20],
          531; **1963:** 349, 356 [25], 378, 385, 390, 464
  Foreign ministers meeting, **1961:** 38, 92 [1], 97
  Joint statements, **1961:** 51, 66
Southern Pacific Railroad, **1963:** 95
Souvanna Phouma, Prince, **1961:** 83 [11]; **1962:** 50
          [20], 115 [8], 239; **1963:** 78, 81, 134 [2],
          144 [5]
  Visit of, **1962:** 308, 312, 160, 184n., 203, 205, 308,
          310 [3], 323, 395, 440, 483, 503, 531, 551
          [2, 10, 14-20], 554
Soviet Union, **1961:** 11, 97, 155, 205, 271, 302, 499,
          519; **1962:** 13 (p. 28), 25, 77, 140, 141;
          1963: 9, 12 (pp. 16, 18), 30 (p. 65), 79, 105,
          134, 253n., 262, 271, 284, 290, 301, 302n.,
          316, 382, 385, 400, 455, 464
  Agriculture, **1962:** 74
  Aid to less-developed countries, **1961:** 90, 244
  Air transport agreement with U.S., **1963:** 448 [20]
  Aircraft, sale to India, **1962:** 245 [3, 9], 316 [14]
  Airspace violation by U.S. aircraft, **1962:** 493
  Alliance for Progress, attitude toward, **1963:** 459
          [22]
  Ambassador Anatoly F. Dobrynin, **1962:** 160,
          179 [6], 279 [20], 302 [13]; **1963:** 75 [18]
  Armed forces in East Germany, **1961:** 483
  Assistance to foreign countries, **1962:** 107 [15],
          352 [11]
  Astronauts, **1961:** 117, 118, 119 [5]; **1962:** 340 [5,
          8]; **1963:** 366, 448 [18]
  Barghoorn, Frederick C., detention of, **1963:** 459
          [2, 8, 19, 24]
    Gagarin, Maj. Yuri, **1961:** 117n., 171 [13], 178,
          318 [17]; **1962:** 59 [2]
    Titov, Maj. Gherman, **1962:** 59 [2], 68
  Berlin crisis.
    See Berlin.
  Berlin question.
    See Berlin.
  Books, worldwide distribution, **1961:** 92 [14]
  Brezhnev, Leonid, **1961:** 2, 271, 453, 483, 522;
          1963: 1

Soviet Union — *continued*
  Changes in, since death of Stalin, **1963:** 89 [17]
  Communications with U.S., **1962:** 546 [17], 551
          [14]; **1963:** 232, 250, 320 [8], 319a
  Communist China, relations with, **1963:** 12 (p.
          17), 305 [13, 17], 319a, 459 [3]
  Cuban activities.
    See Cuba.
  Disarmament proposals, **1961:** 62 [19], 365, 483
  Downing of U.S. aircraft
    C-130, **1961:** 8 [30]
    RB-47. *See* RB-47 fliers.
    U-2, **1961:** 8 [4, 30], 119 [9]
  Economy, **1962:** 174, 186, 458; **1963:** 319a
  Education, **1963:** 43
  Fedorenko, N. T., **1963:** 27n.
  Foreign aid program, **1963:** 169 [17]
  Geneva conferences.
    See main heading, Geneva conferences.
  Grain purchases from U.S., **1963:** 405 [1, 15, 17],
          407, 448 [12]
  Gromyko, Andrei A., **1961:** 92 [16], 364, 365, 415
          [3, 9, 13, 18]; **1963:** 35 [3], 144 [2], 314,
          356 [4], 366, 405 [3]
    See also main heading, Gromyko, Andrei A.
  Indian Ocean expedition, **1961:** 100
  Izvestia, interview with editor, **1961:** 483, 488 [4,
          7]
  Khrushchev, Nikita S.
    See main heading, Khrushchev, Nikita S.
  Kuznetsov, V. V., **1963:** 27
  Laos, talks on, **1963:** 144 [2, 5]
  Laotian situation, **1961:** 92 [1], 119 [10], 139 [9],
          171 [8]
  Melekh spy case, **1961:** 139 [20]
  Military Strategy, **1963:** 232
  Military strength, **1961:** 222, 455 [4, 18], 483
  Military threat to Europe, **1963:** 112
  Missiles, **1962:** 71; **1963:** 107 [12], 320 [17], 459
          [17]
  In Cuba.
    See Cuba.
  Underground sites, report of, **1963:** 75 [20]
  Negotiations with, **1963:** 328 [11]
  News conference remarks, **1961:** 8 [3, 4, 6, 8, 11,
          17, 22, 29, 30], 15 [7, 15], 25 [11, 13, 15,
          22, 26], 35 [4, 7, 9, 13, 16], 62 [19, 20, 21,
          22, 24], 71 [11, 16, 18], 83 [6, 10, 21], 92 [1,
          6, 13, 14, 16], 119 [5, 9, 10, 15, 19], 139 [8,
          9, 12, 17, 20, 23], 171 [1, 8, 13, 22, 23], 222,
          258 [2, 3, 4, 15, 16, 19], 291 [1, 19], 318 [2,
          4, , 17, 18, 19, 20], 334 [2, 5, 11, 13, 15, 21,
          23, 26], 415 [3, 5, 7, 8, 16, 18, 22], 455 [4,
          8, 12, 13, 18], 488 [4, 7, 18]; **1962:** 8 [2, 16,
          17], 27 [4, 14, 17, 22, 23, 26], 40 [1, 6, 10,
          24], 50 [1, 4, 11, 17, 18, 24], 59 [1, 2, 5, 8,
          9, 14, 15, 18], 75 [4, 14], 89 [8, 12], 107 [1,
          2, 3, 13, 15, 16, 22, 23], 115 [3, 24], 152

Soviet Union — *continued*
  News conference remarks — *continued*
      [15, 16, 19], 179 [5, 6, 16], 198 [3, 9, 13],
      210 [9, 15], 229 [3], 245 [3, 9, 13], 259 [14],
      279 [5, 17, 25], 302 [2, 3, 8, 13], 316 [2, 14],
      340 [5, 8], 352 [2, 7, 9, 11, 18, 19, 22], 378
      [1, 11, 13-15, 17], 515 [1, 6, 7, 15, 18], 546
      [3, 17]
  1939 visit, **1961**: 483
  November Revolution, anniversary, **1961**: 453
  Nuclear test ban treaty, **1963**: 35 [3], 40, 260 [9],
      314, 316, 319a, 324, 354, 366, 448 [18, 29]
  Nuclear weapons, **1962**: 279 [25], 378 [14], 485,
      515 [1]; **1963**: 30 (p. 65), 35 [24], 54 [2],
      107 [12], 305 [13], 319a, 405 [4], 426
  See main heading; Nuclear weapons tests.
  Nuclear weapons tests, **1962**: 8 [17], 40 [1, 6, 10,
      24], 41, 59 [14], 62, 71, 89 [8], 134, 198
      [13], 302 [3], 352 [2, 7, 18, 22], 518; **1963**:
      27, 35 [7], 58, 89 [4], 202 [22], 320 [17],
      328 [17]
  Peace treaty with East Germany, question of,
      1961: 258 [2], 291 [1], 318 [4], 387, 483
  Production, **1962**: 549
  Production. U.S. vs Soviet, **1961**: 258 [4]
  Rift with Communist China, **1961**: 61 [20], 455
      [12]
  Relations with Yugoslavia, **1962**: 229 [3]
  Scientific and cultural exchange with U.S., **1963**:
      459 [2]
  Scientists, graduation of, **1961**: 318 [17]
  Ship, attack by Cuban exiles, **1963**: 107 [13], 120
      [5]
  Sino-Soviet threat to U.S., **1963**: 144 [3]
  Space exploration, **1961**: 11, 25 [11, 15], 35 [4, 9],
      62 [24], 117, 118, 119 [5, 15], 139 [12], 171
      [13, 22], 178, 205, 318 [17], 387, 477; **1962**:
      174, 243 [3], 328, 340 [5, 8], 370, 373, 378
      [14]; **1963**: 107 [12], 120 [18], 175 [4], 305
      [6], 448 [18], 475
    Cooperation with U.S., **1962**: 59 [1, 2, 9, 18],
      60, 75 [14], 96, 107 [11], 109, 210 [15], 378
      [17]; **1963**: 144 [19], 305 [6], 328 [19], 405
      [3], 448 [18]
  Stalin, Joseph V., **1963**: 89 [17], 118, 319a
  Supreme Soviet, proposed exchange visits with
      Congress, **1962**: 50 [17]
  Trade with, **1961**: 71 [18], 483; **1963**: 107 [15], 407
      426, 448 [8, 12, 14], 459 [9, 19, 24], 465 [2]
  Troika plan for U.N., **1962**: 319; **1963**: 12 (p. 11)
  Tsarapkin, S.K., **1963**: 27n.
  U-2 plane incident, **1962**: 59 [10], 75 [6]
    Release of Francis Gary Powers, **1962**: 50 [1]
  United Nations dues, **1962**: 24
  U.N. structure, disapproval, **1961**: 119 [19], 387
  U.S. Ambassador Foy D. Kohler, **1962**: 279 [5],
      302 [13]; **1963**: 144 [4], 169 [9], 459 [2]

Soviet Union — *continued*
  U.S. Ambassador Llewellyn E. Thompson, **1961**:
      8 [6, 8, 11, 17], 15 [15], 25 [13], 71 [16], 83
      [10], 334 [13], 415 [3]; **1962**: 8 [2], 27 [4,
      14, 23], 40 [19], 59 [5]
  U.S. flights over, suspension, **1961**: 8 [4, 30]
  U.S.-Soviet relations, **1961**: 25 [13, 22], 35 [4, 7,
      13], 62 [20], 92 [13], 112, 483, 522n.; **1962**:
      7 (p. 13), 50 [24], 109, 245 [13], 279 [5, 17],
      302 [13]; **1963**: 75 [18], 232, 390, 405 [3],
      426
  Visit of Secretary Udall, **1962**: 335
  Weather prediction and control, cooperation
      with U.S., **1963**: 144 [19]
  Western diplomats, restrictions on, **1963**: 459
      [10]
  Wheat sale to, **1963**: 405 [1], 407, 448 [8, 12, 14],
      459 [9, 19, 24], 465 [2]
  World War II losses, **1963**: 232
Soybeans, **1962**: 22, 25
Spaak, Paul Henri, **1961**: 47; **1962**: 554
Spaatz, Gen. Carl, **1962**: 173
Space Council, National Aeronautics and, **1961**: 139
      [12], 147
Space research and exploration, **1961**: 11, 99, 114,
      145, 147, 205, 387, 436, 456, 477; **1962**: 3, 7
      (p. 11), 13 (p. 29), 15, 16 (p. 44), 39, 77,
      163, 171, 174, 186, 216, 223, 226, 243 [3],
      280, 323, 328, 343, 369, 370, 372-375, 395
      426, 427, 432, 435, 439, 450, 456, 458, 463,
      473, 549; **1963**: 12 (p. 15), 21 (pp. 27, 31,
      32, 34, 39), 30 (pp. 58, 60), 37, 55, 77, 165,
      175, 190, 1974, 199, 222, 225, 351, 394n.,
      406, 414, 426, 430, 465, 470-472, 474, 475,
      477, 478
  See also Astronauts; Manned space flights; Sat-
      ellites, earth; Space vehicles.
  Address, **1962**: 373
  Conference on Peaceful Uses of Space, **1961**: 206
  Cooperation with Soviet Union, **1963**: 144 [19],
      305 [6], 328 [19], 405 [3], 448 [18]
  Expanded program, approval, **1961**: 296
  Expenditures, **1963**: 107 [21], 120 [11, 21], 134
  International cooperation, **1962**: 319
  Man-in-space.
    See Astronauts; Manned space flights.
  Message to Premier Khrushchev, **1962**: 96
  Military significance, **1962**: 245 [15], 340 [8], 378
      [14]
  Moon exploration, **1961**: 139 [12], 205, 415 [17],
      477; **1962**: 13 (p. 30), 40 [16], 59 [18], 77,
      340 [5], 372-375, 546 [11]; **1963**: 21 (p.34),
      120 [18], 144 [20], 175 [4], 305 [6], 328
      [19], 405 [3], 406, 426, 448, 478
    Mercury project, **1963**: 199, 202 [4], 472
    NATO Advisory Group for, **1963**: 68

Space research and exploration — *continued*
  News conference remarks, **1961:** 8 [26], 25 [11,
     15], 35 [4, 9], 62 [24], 119 [5, 15], 139 [12],
     171 [5, 6, 13, 22, 23], 291 [13], 318 [12,
     17], 415 [17], 488 [10]; **1962:** 40 [16], 59 [1,
     2, 9, 18], 107 [1, 7], 179 [8, 13], 245 [9, 15],
     279 [5], 340 [5, 8], 378 [14, 17], 546 [11];
     1963: 89 [5], 107 [21], 120 [11, 18, 21], 144
     [19, 20], 202 [4], 305 [6], 328 [4, 19], 405
     [3], 448 [18], 459 [6]
  Peaceful uses, **1962:** 26, 59 [1], 71, 107 [7], 179 [8,
     13], 279 [5], 373, 378 [14]
  Radio tracking stations, **1962:** 96
  Report, **1962:** 26
  Soviet, **1961:** 11, 25 [11, 15], 35 [4, 9], 62 [24], 117,
     118, 119 [5, 15], 139 [12], 171 [13, 22], 178,
     205, 318 [17], 387, 477
  See also Soviet Union.
  Task force report, **1961:** 8 [26]
  Weapons, **1961:** 199
Space vehicles.
  See also Rockets; Satellites, earth; Space
     research and exploration.
  Apollo, **1962:** 12 (p. 30), 378 [14]; **1963:** 21 (p.
     34), 328 [19]
  Gemini, **1962:** 378 [14]; **1963:** 175 [4], 202 [4]
  Industry, labor dispute, **1963:** 39, 446
  Mariner, **1962:** 373; **1963:** 21 (p. 34)
  Mercury, **1963:** 199, 202 [4], 472
  Nova, **1961:** 139 [12]
Spain, **1962:** 107 [21]; **1963:** 2, 77 [1], 99, 455
  Franco Francisco, **1962:** 229 [11]
Spaniards in North America, history of, **1961:** 373,
     432
Spanish American War, **1963:** 227
Sparkman, Sen. John J., **1961:** 264; **1962:** 189n.;
     1963: 193, 194, 417
Speaker of the House of Representatives (John W.
     McCormack), **1962:** 7 (p. 5), 15, 68, 107
     [19], 211; **1963:** 52, 75 [3], 138, 139, 276,
     427, 444
  Letters.
  See Congress, letters to Members of.
Speaker of the House of Representatives (Sam
     Rayburn), **1961:** 1, 11, 17, 84, 205, 209,
     441
  Letters.
  See Congress, letters to members of.
  News conference remarks on, **1961:** 8 [14], 15
     [19], 25 [27], 415 [11]
*Speeches of Senator John F. Kennedy, Presiden-
     tial Campaign of 1960,* **1961:** 371n.; **1963:**
     113n.
Spellman, Cardinal Francis J., **1961:** 83 [9]; **1962:**
     40 [3]
Spence, Repr. Brent, **1961:** 264; **1962:** 431

Spending by Government, **1961:** 11, 17, 23, 90, 94,
     99, 205, 302, 343, 440, 448, 497, 499; **1962:**
     13 (p. 25), 16 (pp. 44, 48, 49), 23, 234, 259
     [15], 279 [19], 280, 328, 549; **1963:** 12 (pp.
     12, 13), 21 (pp. 27, 28, 29, 31, 34, 36, 37,
     38, 39), 22, 30 (pp. 59, 66), 34, 35 [23], 45,
     63, 65 [2], 75 [14], 77 [2], 89 [5], 94, 107 [9,
     21], 118, 120 [6, 7, 11, 21], 134, 144 [14,
     20, 21], 175, 207, 208, 242, 248, 252, 305
     [2], 306, 328 [23], 329, 351, 363, 391, 407,
     465
  See also Budget; Defense spending.
  Measures to reduce, **1961:** 436
  News conference remarks, **1961:** 15 [10, 25], 35
     [10], 62 [16, 25], 119 [8], 171 [21], 291 [7]
  Waste in, **1961:** 62 [16], 244
Spengler, Oswald, **1961:** 219
Spivak, Alvin A., **1961:** 334 [12]
Spock, Dr. Benjamin, **1962:** 202; **1963:** 157
Sports, role in national life, **1961:** 496
Sports dispute, arbitration, **1963:** 7
Sports events, betting on, **1962:** 443
Sports Illustrated magazine, **1962:** 291n., 443
Sprague, Mansfield, **1963:** 239
Sprayberry, Mrs. Jack, **1961:** 328
Springfield, Ill., **1962:** 481
Springfield College, **1963:** 325
Sputnik earth satellites, **1961:** 35 [9], 205; **1963:**
     120 [11], 406
Staats, Elmer B., **1961:** 490
Staebler, Neil, **1961:** 403; **1962:** 433, 438
Staggers, Repr. Harley O., **1962:** 414; **1963:** 249
Stahr, Elvis J., Jr., **1962:** 128, 152 [3], 216, 226;
     1963: 173
  See also Army, Secretary of the.
Stalin, Joseph V., **1961:** 222 [11]; **1963:** 89 [17], 118,
     319a
Stalingrad, battle of, **1961:** 203
Stam, Colin F., **1961:** 490
Stamps, **1963:** 453
  Collection of Franklin D. Roosevelt, **1962:** 260
  Commemorative
     Amelia Earhart, **1963:** 315
     Eleanor Roosevelt, **1963:** 408
     Emancipation Proclamation, **1963:** 153
  Food stamp plan, **1961:** 15 [3], 85, 436
  Food stamp program, **1962:** 318, 328, 414, 440;
     1963: 21 (p. 36), 45, 74, 127, 445
  Hunting, **1961:** 49; **1962:** 69
Standard of living, U.S., **1962:** 93 (p. 235), 328;
     1963: 30 (pp. 58, 60), 34, 64, 77, 85, 98,
     103, 230, 260 [8], 268, 271, 339, 379, 384,
     386, 451
Standard and Poor index of stock prices, **1962:** 316
     [13]

Standards, Bureau of, **1963:** 430
Stanford University, **1962:** 109, 546 [7]
Stans, Maurice, **1963:** 120 [11]
Starcher, George W., **1963:** 379
Starkweather, Eugene, **1962:** 298n.
State, Department of, **1961:** 11, 38, 42, 63, 90, 353;
    1962: 13 (p. 38), 51n., 113, 129, 237,
    250, 275, 276, 358, 551 [5]; **1963:** 11, 36,
    57, 82, 88, 98, 134 [1], 140n., 231n., 238n.,
    256, 306, 307, 349, 354, 361, 433
    Administration of, **1961:** 291 [15]
    Censorship, **1962:** 50 [23]
    Commercial facilities abroad, **1961:** 23
    Export expansion program, **1962:** 114n.
    Foreign student programs, **1961:** 443
    Information availability, policy on, **1962:** 515 [7,
        14, 19]
    News conference remarks, **1961:** 25 [22], 35 [12],
        62 [21], 83 [6], 139 [17], 171 [2, 16, 19], 258
        [10, 17], 291 [15], 318 [14], 334 [22], 488 [9];
        1962: 20 [2], 15], 27 [17], 50 [23], 107 [15],
        179 [6], 259 [21], 302 [8], 316 [16], 340 [3],
        352 [17], 515 [3, 5, 7, 14, 19], 546 [22];
        1963: 54 [4], 120 [16], 320 [2], 405 [13, 16],
        448 [11, 27], 459 [2]
    Personnel changes, **1961:** 161
    Textile conference, **1961:** 161
State, Secretary of (Dean Rusk), **1961:** 23, 41, 42,
    45, 51, 57, 66, 84n., 90, 99, 112n., 120, 125,
    135, 146, 235n., 242, 262, 272n., 279n., 288,
    355, 428, 466, 468, 480, 497, 501; **1962:** 4,
    14n., 30, 62, 73, 96, 109, 116, 146n., 157n.,
    160, 180n., 192, 212, 227, 235, 248, 271, 312,
    323n., 419, 486, 508, 551 [3, 21]; **1963:** 3, 62,
    72, 97, 98, 148, 171, 173, 238n., 256, 262,
    270, 285, 289, 301, 311, 354, 359n., 373
    407n., 416, 421
    Letters, **1961:** 197, 353; **1962:** 89 [1], 90
    Memorandum to, **1963:** 4, 62
    News conference remarks on, **1961:** 8 [7, 24], 25
        [2, 23, 24], 92 [1, 13], 139 [7], 171 [17],
        291 [15], 318 [17], 334 [3, 22, 26], 415 [3, 7,
        13], 455 [3, 9]; **1962:** 20 [15], 27 [10], 40
        [17, 23], 50 [9], 75 [13], 89 [12], 107 [2, 5,
        18], 115 [3, 7, 9], 179 [5, 16], 198 [14], 259
        [9], 279 [20], 302 [2, 16], 378 [16], 515 [19];
        1963: 54 [4, 12], 75 [18], 328 [1], 405 [3, 7,
        13], 448 [1, 27]
    SEATO foreign ministers conference, **1961:** 38
State, Secretary of, foreign assistance duties, **1961:**
    207
State College of Washington, **1961:** 474
State School Officers, Chief, **1961:** 144
State of the Union message, **1961:** 11; **1962:** 7; **1963:**
    12
    Comments on, **1961:** 8 [19, 21], 15 [11, 13, 20,
        36], 18, 25 [7]; **1963:** 15, 16, 30 (p. 60), 34,
        65 [6]

State Universities and Land-Grant Colleges,
    Association of, **1961:** 462
State-Federal Conference on Mental Retardation,
    1963: 313
Statement of Agreed Principles, U.S.-U.S.S.R.,
    1962: 62
Statements by the President.
    See also Legislation, statements upon approval.
    Alabama
        Church bombing in Birmingham, **1963:** 360
        Desegregation in schools, **1963:** 350
        Meetings with leaders of Birmingham, **1963:**
            372
    Alliance for Progress
        Aid to Chile, **1963:** 61
        Second anniversary, **1963:** 326
    Area redevelopment bill, defeat of, **1963:** 241
    Arts, Advisory Council on the , establishment,
        1963: 240
    Business Committee for Tax Reduction in 1963,
        meeting with, **1963:** 145
    Chamizal border dispute with Mexico solution
        of, **1963:** 307
    Civil rights bill, **1963:** 444
    Congo, restoration of peace, **1963:** 28
    Connally, Tom, death of, **1963:** 442
    Credit Union Day, **1963:** 417
    Dryfoos, Orvil, death of, **1963:** 205
    Equal employment opportunity in Federal
        apprenticeship and construction
        programs, **1963:** 220
    Feed grain bill, **1963:** 189
    Frost, Robert, death of, **1963:** 42
    Gaitskell, Hugh, death of, **1963:** 25
    Geneva disarmament meetings, resumption,
        1963: 58
    Geneva Radio Conference on Space
        Communications, **1963:** 470
    Great Lakes Maritime Union Controversy, **1963:**
        411
    Jacobsson, Per, death of, **1963:** 161
    Kentucky, assistance for, **1963:** 458
    Labor-Management Panel, National, reactiva-
        tion, **1963:** 206
    Longshoremen's strike, **1963:** 18
    Manpower utilization program, Federal, **1963:**
        371
    March on Washington for jobs and freedom,
        1963: 336
    Medal of Freedom, order on, **1963:** 76
    Mount Everest, conquest by American climbers,
        1963: 158
    Mutual security authorization bill, **1963:** 333
    NATO multilateral nuclear force, proposed,
        1963: 36
    North Pacific fisheries, negotiations, **1963:** 352
    Nuclear Test Ban Treaty, Senate approval, **1963:**
        375

[References are to items except as otherwise indicated]

Statements by the President — *continued*
  Nuclear tests in Nevada, postponement, **1963:** 40
  Occupational Safety, Conference on, **1963:** 119
  Oil agreement between Indonesia and American
      companies, **1963:** 212
  Olympio, Sylvanus, death of, **1963:** 13
      Pan American Congress of Architects, 1965
          meeting, **1963:** 412
  Pope John XXIII, death of, **1963:** 213
  Radio Free Europe, **1963:** 437
  Railroad labor dispute, **1963:** 184, 244, 298
  Red Cross centenary, **1963:** 83
  Registration and Voting Participation,
      Commission on, establishment, **1963:** 117
  Reports to the President
      Health Care of the Aged, National Committee
          on, **1963:** 460
      Railway labor dispute, emergency board, **1963:**
          184
      Science Advisory Committee, **1963:** 67
      Traffic Safety, Committee for, **1963:** 125
      Youth Employment, Committee on, **1963:** 142
  Schuman, Robert, death of, **1963:** 341
  Selective Service rejectees, training and rehabil-
      itation, **1963:** 393
  Steel industry, price and wage stability, **1963:** 131
  United Nations conference on science and
      technology for less developed areas, **1963:**
      38
  Von Karman, Theodore, death of, **1963:** 165
  Walter, Francis E., death of, **1963:** 211
  Wheat referendum, **1963:** 189, 201
  Women, role in securing world peace, **1963:** 449
  Youth training demonstration project, New
      Haven, **1963:** 423
States.
  See also Federal-State-local governmental re-
      sponsibilities; specific States.
  Agricultural stabilization and conservation
      committees, **1962:** 127
  Alliance for Progress, participation, **1963:** 61,
      118
  Appalachian, economic development, **1963:** 127
  Atomic industrial development, safety standards,
      1961: 25 [18]
  Civil defense, **1961:** 410
  Civil defense directors, message, **1963:** 166
  Congressional districts, **1961:** 25 [27]
  Debt, **1963:** 30 (p. 64)
  Defense contracts, distribution in, **1963:** 107
      [19]
  Democratic chairmen, **1963:** 23
  Education, **1963:** 43, 92, 141, 469
  Emergency measures in labor disputes, **1963:** 120
      [9]
  Employment responsibilities, **1963:** 21 (p. 38),
      174, 464

States — *continued*
  Expenditures, **1963:** 351
  Federal aid.
      See Federal aid to States.
  Foreign aid participation, **1963:** 118
  Governors
      Comment on, **1963:** 322
      Governors Committee on Employment of the
          Handicapped, **1963:** 452
      Letters from citizens, **1963:** 52
      Telegrams on anti-poll tax amendment and
          mental health programs, **1963:** 108, 313
  Health and welfare programs, **1962:** 28, 65
  Highway systems, **1963:** 21 (pp. 27, 32, 36, 39),
      30 (p. 67), 127, 461
  Land-grant colleges, **1961:** 462
  Legislatures, reapportionment, **1962:** 115 [12,
      22], 190
  Mental health programs, **1963:** 50, 434, 452
  Mental retardation projects, **1961:** 413
  National Conference of State Legislative
      Leaders, **1963:** 368
  News conference remarks, **1963:** 107 [19], 120 [9],
      144 [13], 202 [1], 210 [9]
  Poll tax, abolition, proposed, **1963:** 82, 108
  Recreational programs and facilities.
      See Recreational programs and facilities.
  Selective Service Directors, **1962:** 208
  Spending, **1963:** 175, 465
  Tax systems, **1962:** 16 (p. 57)
  Unemployment insurance, **1963:** 185
  Urban renewal problems, **1962:** 23
  Vocational training programs, **1962:** 412
  Welfare programs.
      See main heading, Welfare programs.
States' rights, **1963:** 134 [5]
Statistics, Balance of Payments, Review
      Committee, **1963:** 143
Statistics, employment, **1961:** 458
Statue of Liberty, **1963:** 5, 203
Steamship and Railway Clerks, Brotherhood of,
      1963: 95n., 298
Steed, Repr. Tom, **1961:** 441
Steel industry, **1961:** 25 [25], 133, 274; **1962:** 174;
      1963: 204, 378, 455
  Capacity, **1962:** 139 [1], 152 [21], 410 [1]; **1963:**
      175 [3]
  Employment, **1963:** 110, 131
  European, **1963:** 175 [3]
  Grand jury investigation of monopoly, **1962:**
      152 [6, 12]
  Labor contract, **1962:** 40 [22], 115 [4, 15], 139
      [1, 4, 9, 11]
  Labor dispute, **1962:** 75 [1, 17], 121, 410 [6];
      1963: 134
  Letter to leaders, **1961:** 354

Steel industry — *continued*
  News conference remarks, **1962:** 8 [7], 40 [22],
    50 [3], 75 [17], 115 [4, 15], 139 [1, 4, 7, 9,
    11, 13], 152 [2, 6, 12, 14, 21]. 179 [10], 378
    [20], 410 [1, 6]; **1963:** 54 [9], 134 [3], 175
    [2, 3], 405 [14], 448 [16]
  Plant and equipment modernization, **1963:** 175
    [3]
  Prices, **1963:** 131, 134 [3], 175 [3], 405 [14]
  Profits, **1962:** 139 [1], 152 [2, 14, 21]
  Telegram to leaders, **1962:** 75 [1]
  Unemployment, **1962:** 50 [3], 139 [1], 410 [1];
    1963: 110, 175 [2]
  Wages, **1963:** 54 [9], 131, 134 [3], 175 [3]
Steel Magazine, **1962:** 113n.
Steel mill, construction in India, **1963:** 169 [17]
Steel prices, **1961:** 334 [14, 20], 415 [20]; **1962:**
    115 [15], 139 [1, 4, 7, 9, 11, 13], 152 [2, 9,
    12, 14], 162, 551 [12]
  Unemployment, **1961:** 25 [25], 35 [3]
Steelworkers
  Unemployment, **1961:** 25 [25], 35 [3]
  Wage increase, **1961:** 334 [14]
Steelworkers of America, United, **1961:** 274, 336;
    1962: 20 [19], 75 [1], 115 [4], 121 139 [1, 9,
    11], 152 [12, 14], 162; **1963:** 131, 466
  Convention, remarks, **1962:** 385
Steeves, John M., **1961:** 146
Steichen, Edward, **1963:** p. 901
Stein, Robert, **1963:** 319a.
Stein, Sydney, Jr., **1961:** 29; **1963:** 44n.
Steinbeck, John, **1962:** 527
Steiner, Ludwig, **1962:** 168n.
Steinkraus, Herman W., **1962:** 82n.
Steinmann, Cain & White, **1962:** 274
Steinmann, Milton B., **1962:** 274n.
Stelle, Charles, **1963:** 359n.
Stennis, Sen. John, **1962:** 20 [2], 68
Stephan, Frederick F., **1961:** 458n.
Stephansky, Ben S., **1961:** 275
Stern, Issac, **1961:** 467
Stevens, Roger L., **1961:** 467; **1962:** 527; **1963:** 327
Stevenson, Adlai E.
  See also United Nations, U.S. Representative.
  Looking Outward, **1963:** 433
Stevenson, Frederick J., **1963:** 463
Stevenson, M. L., **1961:** 342
Stewart, C. Allan, **1961:** 508
Stewart, Potter, **1963:** 171
Stikker, Dirk, **1962:** 40 [15]
Stillman, John S., **1961:** 156n.
Stock market, **1963:** 94
  Decline, **1962:** 198 [10], 203, 210 [10], 243 [2], 245
    [7], 259 [18], 328; **1963:** 30 (p. 59)
  Dividends, **1962:** 210 [10]
  News conference remarks, **1962:** 20 [24], 198 [10],
    210 [10], 229 [1], 245 [7], 259 [18]; **1963:**
    120 [2], 134 [3], 356 [12]

Stock market — *continued*
  Racketeering in, **1962:** 20 [24]
  Regulation, **1963:** 120 [2]
  Stock options, tax treatment, **1963:** 34
Stockdale, Grant, **1962:** 233
Stockpiles of strategic and critical materials, **1962:**
    27 [3, 5, 20], 40 [17], 210 [18], 340 [15, 27]
Stop the World-I Want to Get Off. Anthony
    Newley, **1962:** 234
Storey, Robert G., **1961:** 57n.
Story, Joseph, **1962:** 393n.
Strategic Air Command, **1961:** 9, 265, 455 [4], 477;
    1962: 139 [6], 395, 398, 538; **1963:** 112, 441
  Flight safety plaque, presentation, **1962:** 535
Strategic and critical materials, **1963:** 168, 476, 477
  Europe-Soviet trade in, **1963:** 107 [15]
  Imports, **1962:** 22
  Stockpiles, **1962:** 27 [3, 5, 20], 40 [17], 210 [18],
    340 [15, 27]; **1963:** 12 (p. 14), 45, 324, 426
Strategic weapons **1961:** 25 [4]
Strategy, military, Soviet text. **1963:** 232
Stratford, Conn., **1962:** 472
Stratton, Richard J., **1963:** 312
Strauss, Franz Josef, **1961:** 480n.
Strawbridge, Mrs. William J., Jr. (Mary
    Rockefeller), **1962:** 152 [11]
Strikes.
  See Labor disputes.
Strong, Edward W., **1962:** 109n.
Stubblefield, Repr. Frank A., **1962:** 458
Students, **1962:** 171; **1963:** 21 (p. 38), 378
  Allied, at Army Guided Missile School, **1962:**
    371
  American Field Service, **1962:** 284; **1963:** 308
  College, summer intern program, **1962:** 250, 349;
    1963: 334
  Exchange programs, **1963:** 65 [14], 128, 140, 231,
    308, 332
  Federal aid, **1963:** 439
  Foreign, **1961:** 181, 205, 282, 443; **1962:** 59 [15],
    75 [21], 180, 284, 310, 324, 371, 496, 546
    [22]; **1963:** 128, 140, 171, 294, 303, 308,
    319, 332, 335
  Latin America, **1963:** 65 [14], 104, 140
  Loan program, **1961:** 46, 144; **1962:** 40 [2], 288;
    1963: 43, 378, 478
  Elimination of anti-Communist affidavit,
    1962: 469
  Medical and dental, Federal aid, **1961:** 27, 94
  Negro, admission to University of Alabama,
    1963: 169 [4], 202 [1], 234, 236, 237, 243
  News conference remarks, **1963:** 65 [14], 169 [4],
    202 [1, 21]
  Operation Crossroads Africa, participants, **1962:**
    254
  Work-study program, **1963:** 43
Stutz, Robert L., **1962:** 421

Subandrio, Dr., **1961:** 146
Submarines, nuclear-powered
   Andrew Jackson, **1963:** 203
   For NATO, **1961:** 192
   Polaris missile-based, **1961:** 11, 35 [3], 99, 205,
      415 [7], 436, 455 [4], 477; **1962:** 7 (p. 10),
      13 (p. 28), 140, 395, 456, 458, 551 [14],
      554; **1963:**21 (p. 32), 35 [18], 89 [14], 147,
      476, 477, 478
   Sam Houston, **1961:** 16
   Sea Dragon, **1962:** 340 [1]
   Skate, **1962:** 340 [1]
   Sub-Arctic navigation, **1962:** 323, 451
Subsidies, Federal, **1961:** 121; **1962:** 129; **1963:** 21
   (pp. 36, 37)
   Ships, **1961:** 238
Suburban expansion, **1961:** 76
Subversive Activities Control Act, **1962:** 469
Sudan
   Abboud, Ibrahim, **1961:** 108, 402, 404, 411
   Assistance and development, **1961:** 411
   Mahdist revolt, **1961:** 404
   Nubian monuments, preservation, **1961:** 108
SUDENE.
   See Development Agency for Northeast Brazil.
Suez conference (1945), **1963:** 395n.
Suez crisis (1956), **1962:** 557
Suffrage.
   See Voting rights.
Suffragettes, World War I era, **1963:** 228
Suffridge, James A., **1961:** 203
Sugar Act, **1962:** 279 [7]
Sugar quota, Dominican Republic, **1961:** 517
Sugar quotas, **1962:** 179 [7]
Sukarno, Achmed, **1961:** 119 [21], 365; **1962:** 334,
      340 [29]; **1963:** 212, 224, 459 [13]
   Visits of, **1961:** 143, 146, 359, 363, 364
Sukarnoputri, Megawati, **1961:** 363n.
Sukarnoputri, Mohammed Guntar, **1961:** 363n.
Sullivan, Leonor K., **1962:** 238
Sulphur Queen, **1963:** 75 [20]
Summer intern program for college students, **1962:**
   250, 349
Summit meetings.
   See Heads of state and government, meetings.
Sun Yat-Sen, **1961:** 412
Sundlun, Bruce G., **1962:** 476n.
Supersonic air transport, **1963:** 21 (p. 37), 29, 221,
   242
Supreme Commander of Allied Forces in Europe
   (Gen. Lyman L. Lemnitzer), **1962:** 422,
   423
Supreme Commander of Allied Forces in Europe
   (Gen. Lauris Norstad), **1961:** 115, 221,
   393; **1962:** 40 [15], 302 [16], 316 [20]
   Resignation, **1962:** 295

Supreme Court of the United States, **1961:** 121,
   395, 418; **1962:** 420; **1963:** 46, 52, 82, 171,
   237, 310
   See also Courts, Federal.
   Appointment of Arthur J. Goldberg, **1962:** 352
      [1, 13], 393
   Appointment of Byron R. White, **1962:** 119
   Chief Justice.
      See Chief Justice of the United States.
   Decisions
      Antitrust case, **1962:** 33
      Building of Kinzua Dam, **1961:** 71 [15]
      Cannelton case, **1961:** 391
      Everson case, **1961:** 62 [27], 71 [13]
      Integration, **1963:** 230, 237, 248
      Pornography, distribution by mail, **1962:** 352
         [8], 479
      Prayers in public schools, **1962:** 259 [3, 20]
      Public school integration, **1962:** 198 [8]
      Reapportionment, **1962:** 115 [12, 22], 190
      Sit-ins protesting segregation, **1963:** 202 [20]
   Justices, special duties, **1963:** 298
   News conference remarks, **1961:** 62 [27], 71 [13,
      15]; **1962:** 40 [3], 115 [1, 12, 13, 22], 198
      [8], 259 [3, 20], 352 [1, 8, 13]; **1963:** 169
      [1, 8], 202 [1, 20], 320 [6], 459 [6]
   Retirement of Justice Frankfurter, **1962:** 352 [1,
      13], 353
Supreme Headquarters of Allied Powers in Europe,
   remarks, **1961:** 221
Surgeon General, Public Health Service (Dr. Luther
   L. Terry), **1961:** 25 [3]; **1962:** 229 [18]; **1963:**
   53
Surplus agricultural commodities.
   See agricultural surpluses.
Surplus Federal lands, transfer to States, **1962:** 195
Surrey, Stanley S., **1961:** 157
Swainson, Gov. John B., **1962:** 433, 436-438
Swan Island, **1962:** 529
Sweden, **1961:** 368; **1962:** 75 [9], 480
   Ambassador Gunnar Jarring, **1962:** 161n.
   Erlander, Tage, **1961:** 71 [4]
   Exports, volume of, **1963:** 361
   Investment in capital goods, **1961:** 33
   Jacobson, Per, death of, **1963:** 77, 161, 391
   Mental health in, **1963:** 12 (p. 14), 134, 174, 228
      230, 305 [19], 435
   Trade agreements with U.S., **1962:** 76
   U.S. Ambassador Graham Parsons, **1961:** 318
      [15]
   Vice President Johnson, visit of, **1961:** 393
Sweeney, Gen. Walter C., Jr., **1962:** 172
Swing, Gen. J. M., **1961:** 312
Switzer, Dr. Mary E., **1962:** 329
Switzerland, **1963:** 296, 361, 391
   Geneva
      See also Geneva conferences.
   Interhandel Co., **1963:** 89 [12]

Switzerland — *continued*
  Geneva — *continued*
    Mount Everest expedition, **1963:** 158, 296
    News conference remarks, **1961:** 15 [32], 71 [4], 318 [15]
    Tax haven for U.S. citizens, **1961:** 136
Sword of John Sobieski, **1962:** 461
Sylvester, Arthur, **1962:** 410 [8], 515 [14, 19]; **1963:** 54 [12], 169 [10]
Symington, James, **1961:** 15ftn. (p. 30)
Symington, Sen. Stuart, **1962:** 27 [3, 5, 20], 210 [18]; **1963:** 107 [4], 353
Symphony Orchestra, National High School, **1962:** 322
Synchrotron, dedication, **1961:** 361
Syncom II, communications satellite, **1963:** 331n.
Syrett, Harold, **1963:** 245
Syrian Arab Republic, **1962:** 515 [15]
  Al-Qudsi, Nazim, **1962:** 1

Tabouis, Genevieve, **1961:** 222 [7]
Tacoma, Wash., **1963:** 387
  Mayor Harold M. Tollefson, **1963:** 387
Tactical Air Command, **1962:** 309
Taft, Charles P., **1961:** 244; **1962:** 199
Taft, William Howard, **1961:** 162; **1962:** 234, 482
Taft-Hartley Act, **1961:** 258 [11]; **1962:** 21, 139 [3], 230, 247, 378 [7], 421, 428, 453; **1963:** 18, 35 [11], 39, 54 [6], 134 [3], 206, 310
Taiwan, **1963:** 361
  See also China, Republic of; Formosa.
Tales of Vienna Woods, **1961:** 226
Talmadge, Sen. Herman E., **1963:** 330
Tampa, Fla., **1963:** 466
  Address and remarks at, **1963:** 464-466
  Mayor Nick Nuccio, **1963:** 464
Tampa Air Force Fuel Annex, **1963:** 465
Tanganyika, **1962:** 83, 243 [1]; **1963:** 85
  Assistance, **1961:** 139 [4], 299
  Economic and social development, **1963:** 304
  Independence, **1961:** 500
  Kambona, Oscar, **1963:** 300
  Nyerere, Julius K., **1961:** 288, 331, 500; **1962:** 539; **1963:** 300, 302, 304
  Peace Corps project, **1961:** 199, 213, 331; **1963:** 294
  U.S. relations with, **1963:** 304
Tangiers, **1963:** 115
Tannenwald, Theodore, Jr., **1961:** 119 [2]
Tape, Gerald F., **1963:** 384
Tardieu, Julien, **1961:** 219
Tariffs, **1961:** 23; **1962:** 199; **1963:** 35 [5], 292, 381
  See also Trade, international.
  Bicycles, **1962:** 484
  Carpets, **1963:** 9
  Carpets, tile and glass, **1962:** 98, 115 [23], 245 [16]
  Cotton textile imports, **1961:** 488 [19]
  Geneva conference, **1962:** 76; **1963:** 9, 169 [21], 179, 202 [5, 18], 292, 361

Tariffs — *continued*
  Glass, **1963:** 9
  Lamps, discharge, **1963:** 9
  News conference remarks, **1962:** 20 [21], 75 [2], 115 [23], 245 [16], 410 [4], **1963:** 35 [5], 54 [11], 75 [17], 202 [5, 18]
  Polish and Yugoslav imports, **1963:** 118
  Reduction, **1962:** 7 (p. 15), 16 (p. 49), 22, 75 [2], 76, 170, 449; **1963:** 306, 361, 400
    Approval of bill, **1962:** 214
  Softwood lumber, **1962:** 307
  Textiles, **1962:** 20 [21], 365
  Wool, **1963:** 75 [17]
Tariff Act (1930), **1962:** 214; **1963:** 9
Tariff Classification Act, **1962:** 410 [4]
Tariff Commission, United States, **1961:** 71 [20], 478; **1962:** 22, 76, 98, 115 [23], 245 [16], 307, 365; **1963:** 9
Tariff conference, 1960-61, **1963:** 9
Tariffs and Trade, General Agreement on, **1962:** 303, 477, 484; **1963:** 9, 169 [21], 202 [5, 18], 292
Tarjan, Dr. George, **1961:** 413n.
Tashkent, Uzbec SSR, **1963:** 27
Task force reports
  Agricultural commodities, **1961:** 15 [27]
  Area redevelopment, **1961:** 7, 35 [15]
  Federal employee-management relations, **1961:** 250, 494; **1962:** 154
  Interurban transportation, **1962:** 462n.
  Latin America, **1961:** 276
  Ryukyu Islands, **1962:** 99
  Space exploration, **1961:** 8 [26]
Tate, James H. J., **1962:** 278; **1963:** 445, 459 [15]
Tawes, Gov. J. Millard, **1962:** 446; **1963:** 461
Taxes, **1961:** 17, 33, 157, 185, 205, 436, 484, 497, 499; **1962:** 16 (pp. 44, 47), 230, 234, 396, 459; **1963:** 21 (pp. 27, 29, 43), 30 (pp. 60-63, 67), 50, 89 [7], 188, 361, 436, 445, 462, 465

  Capital gains, **1963:** 34
  Corporate, **1961:** 17, 23, 33, 136; **1962:** 7 (p. 7), 13 (p. 3), 16 (p. 57), 229 [1], 328, 549; **1963:** 12 (p. 12), 21 (pp. 29, 30), 30 (pp. 61-63), 34, 175 [2]
  Deductions, **1963:** 34
  Deductions for political campaign contributions, proposed, **1962:** 219
  Depletion allowances, **1963:** 34
  Depreciation allowances, **1963:** 12 (p. 12), 30 (p. 62), 34, 92, 131
    See also main heading, Depreciation allowances.
  District of Columbia, **1963:** 22, 56, 122
  Dividends and interest.
    See income taxes.
  Enforcement, **1961:** 94, 136
  Estate, **1961:** 136

Taxes — *continued*
  Excise, **1961:** 58, 136; **1962:** 7 (p. 7), 13 (p. 34),
    16 (p. 57), 128, 129, 328, 395, 549 [5];
    1963: 21 (p. 30)
  Farm cooperatives, **1962:** 440
  Foreign central banks, **1961:** 23, 54, 497
  Foreign investment companies, **1961:** 136; **1962:**
    13 (p. 34)
  Foreign tax credit, **1963:** 34
  Fuel, **1963:** 34, 63
  Gift, **1963:** 34
  Holding companies, personal, **1963:** 34
  Income, **1961:** 15 [10], 17, 23, 54, 136
    See also Income taxes.
  Increase, **1961:** 302
  Interest equalization, proposed, **1963:** 306
  Investment incentive plan, **1962:** 7 (p. 6), 13 (p.
    33), 16 (p. 48), 108, 114n., 115 [2, 15], 152
    [2, 9, 14], 162, 174, 229 [1], 259 [16, 18],
    279 [19], 280, 286, 328, 395, 410 [2], 468,
    549 [6]; **1963:** 12 (p. 12), 30 (p. 62), 34, 92,
    110, 118, 131, 465
  Legislation, proposed, **1963:** 422, 427
  Letter to Representative Mills, **1962:** 108
  Medical expense deductions, **1963:** 34, 74
  Message to Congress, **1961:** 136
  News conference remarks, **1961:** 15 [9, 10], 25
    [25], 35 [3], 83 [17], 139 [18], 171 [6], 291
    [7], 415 [19], 455 [17]; **1962:** 27 [27], 59
    [16], 75 [18], 115 [2, 15], 152 [2, 9, 11, 14],
    179 [1], 210 [4, 16], 229 [1, 4, 17], 245 [7, 9,
    18], 259 [16, 18], 279 [3, 19], 302 [5, 17],
    316 [10, 19], 340 [2, 13, 16], 378 [12, 21],
    410 [1, 2, 12], 515 [17], 546 [6, 13]; **1963:**
    35 [14], 65 [2, 4, 18], 75 [1, 14], 89 [2, 7],
    107 [9, 21], 120 [8, 11], 144 [14, 21], 169
    [15], 175 [1, 3], 305 [2, 4, 18], 328 [7, 15,
    23], 405 [18], 459 [4, 11]
  Older persons, **1963:** 34, 74, 75 [1]
  Panama Canal Zone, **1962:** 242
  Poll, **1962:** 340 [2], 396
  Poll, abolition, proposed, **1963:** 82, 108
  Real estate, **1963:** 22, 34
  Receipts, **1963:** 305 [2]
  Reduction, **1961:** 15 [9], 25 [25], 136; **1962:** 6n.,
    16 (p. 43), 59 [16], 111, 174, 229 [1, 17],
    279 [3, 19], 286, 302 [5, 17], 316 [10], 328,
    432, 515 [17], 546 [6, 13], 549
    Presidential standby authority, proposed,
      1962: 7 (p. 6), 13 (p. 35), 16 (p. 51), 27 [27],
      176, 245 [18], 259 [18]
  Reduction and reform, **1961:** 15 [9], 25 [25], 136;
    1962: 6n., 16 (p. 43), 59 [16], 111, 174, 229
    [1, 17], 279 [3, 19], 286, 302 [5, 17], 316
    [10], 328, 432, 515 [17], 546 [6, 13], 549;
    1963: 12 (pp. 12, 13), 21 (pp. 27, 29, 30),
    30 (pp. 57, 59-64, 66, 68, 69), 35 [14], 65
    [2, 4, 18], 74, 75 [14], 77, 89 [2], 92, 94, 107

Taxes — *continued*
  Reduction and reform — *continued*
    [9, 21], 110, 120 [11], 134, 144 [21], 145,
    169 [15], 175, 177, 187, 197, 228, 305 [2,
    4], 306, 310, 329, 340, 349, 351, 361, 363,
    378, 391, 400, 458, 462, 465, 466, 477, 478
    Message to Congress, **1963:** 34
    News conference remarks, **1963:** 35 [14], 65 [2,
      4, 18], 89 [2], 134 [4], 305 [2, 18], 459 [4,
      11]
    Presidential standby authority, proposed, **1962:**
      7 (p. 6), 13 (p. 35), 16 (p. 51), 27 [27], 176,
      245 [18], 259 [18]; **1963:** 30 (p. 66)
  Retired persons, **1963:** 34, 74
  Refunds, **1961:** 35 [3]
  Revisions, **1961:** 17, 136, 139 [18]; **1962:** 7 (p. 7),
    13 (p. 33), 16 (p. 57), 210 [16], 229 [1, 4],
    279 [3], 328, 378 [12], 385, 452, 468, 549
  Social security, **1961:** 27
  State and local, **1962:** 16 (p. 57)
  Tax bill, **1962:** 108, 378 [12, 21], 410 [12]; **1963:**
    35 [14], 65 [2, 4, 18], 89 [2], 107 [9, 21],
    120 [8], 127, 144 [21], 145, 175 [1, 3], 233,
    305 [4, 18], 328 [7, 15], 405 [18]
    Approval, **1962:** 468
  Tax credit incentive plan, **1961:** 17, 136, 139 [18],
    161
  "Tax havens," **1961:** 136, 497
  Tax havens abroad, **1962:** 7 (p. 14), 108, 114n.,
    115 [2], 152 [11], 162, 203, 229 [4], 280;
    1963: 34
  Transfer, **1963:** 34
  Transportation, **1962:** 13 (p. 34), 129, 229 [1],
    328, 395; **1963:** 21 (p. 31)
  Working mothers, tax treatment, **1963:** 233
Tax Reduction in 1963, Business Committee for ,
  1963: 145, 169 [15], 351
Tax Reduction and Revision in 1963, Citizens
  Committee for, **1963:** 177
Taylor, Francis H., **1962:** 552
Taylor, George W., **1961:** 40n., **1962:** 204, 298, 378
  [20], 410 [6]; **1963:** p. 901
Taylor, Gen. Maxwell D., **1961:** 168n., 435; **1962:**
  27 [13], 226, 276, 423; **1963:** 35 [2], 399,
  405 [16], 448 [3]
  Investigation of Cuban situation, **1961:** 258 [8]
  News conference remarks, **1961:** 258 [8], 291 [15],
    415 [1, 10], 455 [2]
  Visit to Viet-Nam, **1961:** 415 [1, 10], 455
    [2]
Teachers, **1961:** 255, 462; **1962:** 288; **1963:**
  43, 74, 462
  Corporal punishment of school children,
    1963: 202 [6]
  Exchange program, **1961:** 48; **1962:** 341
  For mentally retarded, **1961:** 413
  Fulbright exchange program, **1963:** 140,
    332

Teachers — *continued*

Induction into armed forces, **1961:** 455 [20]

Pay, **1961:** 46; **1962:** 7 (p. 9), 13 (p. 32), 16 (p. 46), 37; **1963:** 43, 226, 228, 469

Peace Corps assignments, **1962:** 325; **1963:** 294, 304n.

Shortage, **1961:** 144

Training, **1962:** 13 (p. 32), 37; **1963:** 21 (p. 38), 22, 43, 82, 193, 226, 228, 447

Teacher of the Year award, presentation, **1962:** 188

Technical assistance to less-developed and new countries, **1961:** 63, 90, 285, 299, 491, 510; **1962:** 7 (p. 12), 212, 245 [5]; **1963:** 118, 163, 217, 239

See also Economic assistance and development Foreign assistance; Mutual security program.

U.N. conference, **1963:** 38

Technological changes, **1961:** 211, 332, 499; **1962:** 373; **1963:** 30 (p. 68, 69), 43, 67, 119, 179, 215n., 225, 226, 310, 342, 376, 378, 384, 385, 423, 430, 448 [7, 29], 465, 472

Technological research, **1961:** 99

Technological training, **1963:** 134

Latin America, **1963:** 163

Technology, Federal Council for Science and, **1963:** 53, 70, 252

Technology, Office of Science and, **1963:** 45, 301

Techo, Colombia, housing project, **1961:** 513, 515, 516

Teixeira Martini, Adm. Luis, **1963:** 335n.

Telecommunications Management, Director of, **1962:** 39

Telecommunications Union, International, **1963:** 470

Telegraph, centennial of transcontinental line, **1961:** 433

Telegraph key, historic, presentation to President, **1962:** 155

Telephone service tax, **1961:** 136

Television

Debates, **1962:** 352 [25]

By presidential candidates, **1961:** 15 [26], 403

Presidential campaign (64), question of, **1963:** 448 [24]

With President Eisenhower, question of, **1962:** 210 [20]

Educational, **1962:** 20 [23], 37, 93 (p. 237), 156, 166; **1963:** 137, 445

Federal regulation, **1962:** 27 [16]

International, **1963:** 126n.

International, censorship of, **1962:** 352 [23]

Television — *continued*

Interviews.

See Interviews of the President.

Military programs, **1962:** 310 [3]

Operation on UHF channels, **1962:** 93 (p. 241)

Quality of programs, **1962:** 302 [20]

Use in election campaigns. **1962:** 219

Television and radio addresses.

See Messages to the American people.

Teller, Dr. Edward, **1962:** 530; **1963:** 328 [4, 17], 334

Telles, Raymond, **1963:** 98, 102, 103, 105, 223

Tello, Manuel, **1962:** 265n., 271n.

Telstar communications satellite, **1962:** 302 [1, 2, 6, 20], 398; **1963:** 55, 416n.

Statement, **1962:** 285

Temporary Extended Unemployment Compensation Act, **1961:** 93

Tenant farming, **1963:** 82, 105

Tennessee, **1962:** 115 [12], 340 [24], 352 [5]; **1963:** 192

Gov. Frank G. Clement, **1963:** 192

Tennessee, school integration, **1961:** 405

Tennessee River, **1963:** 301

Tennessee River development, **1961:** 278

Tennessee Valley, **1963:** 105, 192, 385

Tennessee Valley Authority, **1961:** 30, 49, 278; **1962:** 13 (p. 30), 55, 69; **1963:** 21 (pp. 36, 42), 192, 193, 376, 448 [2], 462

Tennessee Valley Authority, Chairman (Herbert D. Vogel), **1961:** 98, 278

Tennessee Valley Authority, Chairman (Aubrey J. Wagner), **1963:** 193, 194

Tennessee Valley development, **1962:** 336

Terry, Dr. Luther L. (Surgeon General, Public Health Service), **1961:** 25 [3]; **1962:** 229 [18]; **1963:** 53

Tetanus, eradication, **1962:** 65

Texarkana, Tex., **1963:** 478

Texas, **1961:** 119 [12, 22], 455 [5]; **1962:** 77, 150, 170, 171, 409, 417, 538; **1963:** 223, 226, 228, 472, 474, 477, 478

Chamizal zone, transfer to Mexico, **1963:** 89 [14]

Gov. John B. Connally, **1963:** 108, 223, 472, 474, 475, 476, 478

Gov. Price Daniel, **1962:** 68, 373n.

News conference remarks, **1962:** 115 [27], 139 [16], 179 [4], 198 [7], 210 [6], 378 [19, 22]

SAC base, **1963:** 112

United States Study Commission, report, **1962:** 313

Textile Administrative Committee, Inter-agency, **1961:** 428

Textile Advisory Committee, Management-Labor, **1961:** 428

Textile Advisory Committee, President's Cabinet, **1961:** 428

Textile Agreement, International, **1961:** 428
Textile machinery, **1961:** 161; **1963:** 407
Textile workers, unemployment, **1961:** 161
Textiles
    Conference on, **1961:** 161, 258 [10], 428
    Cotton, **1961:** 258 [10], 428, 488 [19]; **1962:** 365;
        1963: 21 (p. 36), 45, 75 [17], 169 [13], 306,
        478
    Imports, **1961:** 161, 258 [10], 488 [19]; **1962:** 8
        [15], 20 [21], 410 [9]; **1963:** 45, 75 [17]
    Industry, **1961:** 161, 258 [10]; **1962:** 8 [15], 229
        [1], 365, 410 [9]
    Wool, **1963:** 75 [17], 459 [25]
TFX aircraft contract, **1963:** 107 [4, 19, 23], 120 [7],
    169 [5], 328 [20], 448 [23], 475, 476
Thailand, **1961:** 26, 92 [6], 205; **1962:** 70, 226, 287;
    1963: 77, 333, 349, 477
    Assistance, **1963:** 89 [20], 338
    Communist threat to, **1963:** 144 [16]
    News conference remarks, **1962:** 198 [4, 17, 20],
        210 [3, 11], 245 [8], 352 [11]
    U.S. armed forces in, **1962:** 192, 198 [4, 17], 210
        [3, 11], 250
Thalidomide, harmful effects of, **1962:** 316 [1, 4,
    24], 442
Thanksgiving Day, proclamation, **1961:** 438; **1962:**
    504; **1963:** 451
Thant (U), **1961:** 449
    See also United Nations Secretary General.
Thayer, Robert H., **1961:** 57n.
Thayer, Walter, **1961:** 403
Theodore Roosevelt Island, **1963:** 456n.
Thermal power projects, **1961:** 17
Thermopylae, **1961:** 162, 418; **1962:** 349
Thiam, Doudou, **1961:** 450n.
Third Armored Division, **1963:** 263
Thirty-five hour workweek, proposed, **1963:** 75
    [11], 77 [2]
Thomas, Repr. Albert, **1962:** 320, 372, 373, 378
    [22]; **1963:** 474
Thomas, Mrs. Albert, **1963:** 474
Thomas, Danny, **1962:** 15
Thomas, David D., **1963:** 238
Thompson, Charles, Sr., **1961:** 317
Thompson, Repr. Frank, Jr., **1961:** 255, 291 [8],
    448; **1962:** 363n.
Thompson, R. Franklin, **1963:** 387
Thompson, Llewellyn E., Jr., **1961:** 8 [6, 8, 11, 17],
    15 [15], 25 [13], 71 [16], 83 [10], 334 [13], 415
    [3]; **1962:** 8 [2], 27 [4, 14, 23], 40 [19], 59 [5],
    323, 533n.
Thompson, Repr. T. A., 1962: 170
Thor missile, 1962: 316 [6]; **1963:** 35 [18]
Thoreau, Henry, 1961: 192; **1963:** 382, 387
Thorlin, Maj. Gen. John F., **1963:** 222
Thorneycroft, Peter, **1962:** 316 [6], 554; **1963:** 285
Thorpe, Willard, **1961:** 71 [6]
Thrasher, Wilkes, **1962:** 352 [5]

Three Sisters Bridge, proposed, **1963:** 22, 208
Threthowan, Ian, **1961:** 133
Thucydides, **1963:** 266
Thurmond, Sen. Strom, **1962:** 50 [8], 459
Ticknor, George, **1963:** 140
Ticonderoga, **1963:** 457
Tiger, Dick, **1963:** 331
Tighe, Eileen, **1963:** 319a. note
Tile, tariffs on, **1962:** 98
Tillett, Gladys A., **1961:** 358n.
Timber
    Conservation, **1963:** 45
    Damage in Pacific Northwest, conference, **1962:**
        495
    Production, **1962:** 69
Timberlake, Clare H., **1961:** 15 [15]
Time magazine, **1961:** 334 [26]; **1963:** 245
Tin, sale of, **1961:** 409
Tin Agreement, International, **1961:** 409
Tin prices, **1962:** 86
Tipton, Elden C., **1962:** 456
Tires, tax on, **1961:** 58
Tiros weather satellite, **1962:** 373
Titan missile, **1961:** 99; **1962:** 75 [20], 340 [5],
    378 [14], 551 [13]; **1963:** 35 [12], 400
Tito, Marshal Josip Broz, **1963:** 328 [8], 349, 419,
    420, 421
Tito, Mrs. Josip Broz, **1963:** 419, 420
Titov, Maj. Gherman, **1962:** 59 [2], 68
Tjio, Joe Hin, **1962:** 543n.
Tobacco, **1962:** 25
    Exports, **1962:** 170
    Price supports, **1962:** 198 [11], 245 [9], 410 [3]
Tobago, **1963:** 311
Tobin, James, **1961:** 123n.
Tobriner, Walter N. (President, Board of D.C.
    Commissioners), **1963:** 66, 122n., 456
Tocks Island National Recreation Area, **1963:** 376
Tocqueville, Alexis de, **1962:** 552
Todorovic, Mijalko, **1963:** 421
Togo, Republic of, **1962:** 325
    Olympio, Sylvanus, **1962:** 103-105
        Death of, **1963:** 13
        Message to, **1961:** 124
Togo, Republic of, message to President Olympio,
    1961: 124
Togo, Republic of, Sylvanus Olympio, death of,
    1963: 13
Tokyo, **1962:** 122, 546 [2]; **1963:** 476
Tollefson, Harold M., **1963:** 387
Tollefson, Repr. Thor C., **1963:** 387
Tolstoy, Leo, **1962:** 527
Tomsic, Albert, **1962:** 336
Tongue Point, Oreg., **1963:** 388
Tools for freedom program, **1963:** 239
Tootell, R. B. (Governor, Farm Credit Adminis-
    tration), **1963:** 62'
Topeka, Kans., **1962:** 188n.

Toplow, Leo, **1963:** 119

Torres, Ary, **1962:** 86n.

Touré, Sékou, **1962:** 444

Tourists.
  See Travel.

Toynbee, Arnold, **1963:** 74

Track and Field Federation, U.S., **1963:** 7

Tractors-for-freedom movement, **1961:** 201, 258 [6]

Trade, international, **1961:** 23, 85, 161, 189, 207,
  497; **1962:** 13 (p. 36), 83, 170, 174, 199,
  214, 359, 392, 413, 436, 449, 456, 484, 510,
  549; **1963:** 12 (pp. 15, 16, 17), 21 (pp. 29,
  35, 36), 45, 77 [4], 80, 94, 118, 175, 192,
  217, 228, 242, 253, 262, 266, 291, 306, 361,
  391, 400, 407, 465
  See also Tariffs.
  Australia-Soviet Union, **1963:** 407, 459 [19]
  Canada-Soviet Union, **1963:** 407, 459 [19]
  Cuba, reduction, **1963:** 144 [8]
  Europe-Latin America, **1962:** 86, 126, 144, 279
    [6], 302 [9], 378 [4]
  Europe-Soviet Union, **1963:** 107 [15]
  Geneva conference, **1963:** 9, 169 [21], 179, 202 [5,
    18], 292, 361
  Japan, **1963:** 9, 266
  Joint statements, **1961:** 66, 112, 193, 252; **1962:**
    144, 160, 248, 251, 273, 303
  Latin American, **1963:** 35 [17], 77, 118
  Letter to Prime Minister Diefenbaker, **1962:** 477
  Message to Congress, **1962:** 22
  News conference remarks, **1961:** 8 [18], 71 [18,
    20], 171 [12], 258 [10], 318 [1], 455 [9, 16],
    488 [17]; **1962:** 8 [4, 15, 22], 20 [5, 21], 27
    [10], 72 [2], 75 [2], 89 [9], 115 [23], 152 [2],
    229 [1], 245 [9], 259 [2], 279 [6], 302 [6, 9],
    340 [2, 16], 378 [1, 4, 21], 410 [1, 2], 546
    [22]; **1963:** 35 [5], 54 [11], 65 [11], 75 [17],
    107 [15], 144 [8], 169 [21], 202 [5, 18], 260
    [5, 8, 13], 448 [8, 12, 14], 459 [3, 9, 19, 24]
  Soviet-Cuban, use of western ships for, **1963:** 65
    [11]
  Textiles, conference on, **1961:** 161, 258 [10], 428
  Trade agreements, **1962:** 22, 75 [2], 76; **1963:** 9
  TV remarks, **1962:** 400
  U.S.-Argentina, **1961:** 389
  U.S. balance of trade, **1961:** 8 [18], 455 [16], 488
    [17], 499; **1962:** 7 (p. 14), 8 [4], 16 (p. 47),
    162; **1963:** 175 [3]
  U.S.-Belgium, **1963:** 80
  U.S.-Canada, **1962:** 22, 307; **1963:** 179
  U.S.-Common Market, **1963:** 175 [3], 202 [5]
  U.S.-Communist bloc, **1961:** 71 [18]; **1962:** 546
    [22]
  U.S.-Communist China, question of, **1963:** 459
    [3]
  U.S.-Cuba, **1962:** 27 [10]
  U.S.-Cuba, decline, **1963:** 134 [1]

Trade, international — *continued*
  U.S.-Cuba, embargo, **1961:** 171 [12], 455 [9];
    1962: 32, 89 [9], 378 [1]
  U.S.-Europe, **1963:** 75 [17], 102, 259, 292, 407,
    426
  U.S.-Japan, **1961:** 258 [10], 455 [16]; **1962:** 8 [4],
    22, 199, 531
  U.S.-Latin America, **1962:** 22
  U.S.-Norway and Sweden, **1962:** 76
  U.S.-Poland, **1962:** 461; **1963:** 35 [5]
  U.S.-Soviet, **1961:** 483; **1963:** 448 [8, 12, 14], 459
    [9, 19, 24]
  U.S.-United Kingdom, **1962:** 75 [2], 76
  U.S.-Venezuela, **1963:** 73
  U.S.-Western Europe, **1961:** 455 [16]; **1962:** 7 (p.
    14), 8 [22], 75 [2], 76, 259 [2], 279 [6],
    410 [1]
  U.S.-Yugoslavia, **1963:** 35 [5], 421

Trade, United Nations Conference on, **1963:** 366

Trade Agreements Act, **1961:** 8 [18], 161, 497; **1962:**
  7 (p. 14), 22, 76, 170, 199

Trade Agreements Extension Act of 1951, **1963:** 9

Trade and Economic Affairs, Joint U.S.-Japan
  Committee on, **1961:** 252, 444n., 455 [3];
  1962: 531n.

Trade and Economic Affairs, U.S.-Canada Committee on, **1961:** 45

Trade Expansion Act of 1962, **1962:** 458, 459, 461,
  473, 477, 484, 510, 549; **1963:** 9, 21 (pp. 35,
  37), 30 (pp. 65, 70), 35 [5], 45, 54 [11], 92,
  118, 202 [5], 306, 310, 361, 462
  Approval, **1962:** 449
  Proposed, **1962:** 7 (p. 14), 16 (p. 49), 20 [21], 22,
    76, 83, 109, 114n., 115 [23], 144, 152 [2],
    162, 170, 185, 199, 205, 248, 251, 259 [2, 6,
    16], 302 [4, 19], 316 [10], 328, 340 [2, 16],
    378 [21], 393, 395, 396, 400, 410 [1, 2],
    437, 446

Trade Mission to Europe, Illinois, **1963:** 422

Trade Negotiations, Special Representative for
  (Christian A. Herter), **1962:** 510, 541, 549
  [2]; **1963:** 75 [17], 76, 179, 306

Trade Policy, Conference on, **1962:** 199

Trade Policy Committee, **1962:** 98

Trade practices, unfair, **1963:** 30 (p. 68)

Trade union movement, **1963:** 85, 139, 162, 163,
  270, 339
  Costa Rica, **1963:** 104
  Destruction in Communist bloc, **1963:** 268
  Germany, **1963:** 268

Trademarks, **1962:** 93 (p. 242)

Trading With the Enemy Act, **1961:** 455 [9]

Traffic accidents, **1961:** 58, 338; **1962:** 11, 93
  (p. 237)

Traffic Safety, President's Committee for, **1961:**
  338; **1962:** 11; **1963:** 125

Train tickets, tax on, **1962:** 229 [1]

Training.

  See also Occupational training.

  Nurses, **1961:** 27

  Occupational skills, **1961:** 205, 211, 233, 499

  Oceanographers, **1961:** 100

  Physicians and dentists, **1961:** 27, 52

  Public health personnel, **1961:** 52

  Young people, **1961:** 233, 499

Training Program, Manpower Development and, **1963:** 248

Trans World Airlines, **1961:** 50; **1962:** 245 [1], 253, 256, 516

Transcontinental Telegraph Centennial, **1961:** 432

Transit navigator, satellite, **1962:** 373

Transportation, **1961:** 92 [11], 121; **1962:** 13 (p. 31), 93 (p. 236), 359, 410 [1, 2, 3]; **1963:** 12 (p. 14), 21 (pp. 32, 36, 37), 30 (pp. 65-67), 63, 110, 127, 146, 230, 238, 242, 310, 366, 378, 381, 401, 445, 461, 462, 465, 478

  Air, **1963:** 109, 179, 186, 298

  Appalachian region, **1963:** 127

  Eastern seaboard, **1962:** 391

  Federal aid, **1963:** 30 (p. 65), 69

  Great Lakes, U.S.-Canada discussions, **1963:** 179, 411

  Industry, **1961:** 310

  Intercity, **1962:** 129, 462

  Interstate, Freedom Riders, **1961:** 291 [10]

  Message to Congress, **1962:** 129; **1963:** 208

  National Capital Region, **1962:** 525; **1963:** 208

  National policy, letter, **1963:** 87

  Progress, **1963:** 385

  Racial discrimination, **1963:** 82, 144 [13], 230

  Railroad.

    See main heading, Railroads.

  Rural, **1962:** 25

  Taxes, **1962:** 13 (p. 34), 129, 229 [1], 328, 395; **1963:** 21 (p. 31)

  Technological progress, **1963:** 215n.

  Urban, **1961:** 76, 246; **1962:** 7 (p. 7), 13 (p. 31), 23, 129, 153, 190, 200, 395, 458; **1963:** 12 (p. 14), 22, 69, 120 [8], 144 [15], 162, 208, 228, 310

Transportation Act of 1960, National Capital, **1963:** 208

Transportation Agency, National Capital, **1963:** 22, 208

Trapnell, Gen. Thomas J.H., **1961:** 419n.

Travel

  Agents, subversive, in Latin America, **1963:** 107 [1, 7], 144 [17]

  Duty-free allowance, **1961:** 23, 53

  Foreign, in U.S., **1961:** 23, 497; **1962:** 7 (p. 14), 16 (p. 49), 279 [12], 280, 410 [12]; **1963:** 82, 193, 306, 422

  Interstate, Freedom Riders, **1961:** 291 [10]

  President's plans for, **1963:** 107 [3], 196, 202 [7], 235

Travel — *continued*

  U.S. citizens to Cuba, **1963:** 107 [17]

  U.S. tourists abroad, **1962:** 203, 280, 340 [25], 410 [12]; **1963:** 77 [1], 134 [3], 306, 361, 397, 422

  Visa requirements, simplification, **1963:** 311

Travel Service, United States, **1963:** 306

Treasurer of the United States (Elizabeth R. Smith), **1961:** 75n.

Treasury, Department of the, **1961:** 17, 23, 152, 161; **1962:** 13 (p. 35), 16 (pp. 44, 55), 33, 115 [2], 128, 129, 152 [2], 252, 275; **1963:** 21 (pp. 41, 42), 22, 30 (pp. 3, 65, 67), 41, 45, 54 [1, 4], 56, 151, 305 [2, 22], 306

  Foreign currency transactions, **1961:** 497

  News conference remarks, **1961:** 25 [16], 139 [18]

  Silver, actions re, **1961:** 484

  Tax review, **1961:** 136, 139 [18]

Treasury, Secretary of the (C. Douglas Dillon), **1961:** 23, 54, 82, 136, 157, 242, 244n., 302, 322, 353n., 484, 497; **1962:** 14, 16, 168, 203, 330, 411n. 549 [1]; **1963:** 30 (pp. 67, 68), 34, 49, 62, 94n., 160, 278, 306, 329, 351, 361, 391, 450, 465

  Export credit study, **1961:** 437

  News conference remarks, **1961:** 8 [19], 92 [18], 119 [20], 139 [18], 291 [3, 15]; **1962:** 115 [15], 139 [13], 152 [11], 279 [3]

  Punta del Este conference, **1961:** 291 [3, 15], 308, 313, 324

  Report, **1962:** 114

  Rio de Janeiro conference, **1961:** 119 [20]

Treaties.

  See International agreements.

Treaty banning nuclear weapons tests.

  See Nuclear test ban treaty.

Treaty of Friendship, establishment, and Navigation, U.S.-Luxembourg, **1963:** 156

Treaty of Geneva, **1963:** 78

Tree diseases control, **1961:** 49, 85

Trenton, N.J., **1961:** 448

Trieste, **1962:** 323

Triffin, Robert, **1961:** 123n.

Trimble, Repr. James W., **1961:** 440; **1963:** 400, 401

Trinidad, **1961:** 36n.; **1962:** 352 [5]; **1963:** 311

Trinity (Calif.) Project, **1961:** 360

Trinity River, **1963:** 389

Trinity River Basin, **1962:** 313

Trinity University (Ireland), **1963:** 279

Tripoli, **1962:** 243

Trippe, Juan, **1962:** 549

Troutman, Robert, **1962:** 255, 344

Truce Supervision Organization in Palestine, United Nations, **1963:** 471

Trucks, highway use tax, **1961:** 58

Trujillo y Molina, Hector, **1961:** 483

Truman, Harry S., President, **1961:** 1, 90, 112, 121, 128, 133, 139 [14], 208, 209, 212, 237, 392, 480, 482n., 499; **1962:** 3, 15, 78, 79, 174, 186, 199, 202, 205, 219, 232-234, 252, 314, 346, 349, 352 [11], 439, 446, 452, 453, 482, 506n., 507n., 546 [7], 549 [10], 550, 551 [9]; **1963:** 6, 23, 33n., 82, 94, 146, 147, 151, 159, 206, 228, 245, 251, 257, 268, 297, 338, 349, 420, 426, 427, 459 [6], 462, 467, 478

    Birthday greetings, **1961:** 179

    Birthday telephone call to, **1963:** 170

    Committee on Civil Rights, **1963:** 248

    Library, **1961:** 448

    Library, Independence, Mo., **1962:** 546 [7]; **1963:** 207

Truman doctrine, **1961:** 128, 222; **1963:** 118, 442, 443

Truman Doctrine, 15th anniversary, **1962:** 78, 79

Trust funds, **1962:** 245 [6]; **1963:** 21 (pp. 27, 32, 38, 39, 40)

    Highway program, **1962:** 13 (p. 31); **1963:** 21 (pp. 27, 32, 36)

    Interstate highway system, **1961:** 58

    Social security, **1963:** 21 (pp. 27, 32), 74

Trust Territory, Pacific Islands, **1962:** 297, 342

Tsarapkin, Semyon, **1962:** 152 [15]; **1963:** 27n.

Tshombe, Moise, **1961:** 519, **1962:** 8 [19], 302 [11], 316 [7], 340 [14]

Tubman, William V.S., **1961:** 175, 429, 430

Tucker, Raymond, **1962:** 375n.

Tucker, Gen. Reuben, **1962:** 226

Tucson, Ariz., **1961:** 476

Tulane University, **1962:** 416

Tulsa, Okla., **1961:** 206

Tunisia, Habib Bourguiba, **1961:** 164, 165, 171 [15], 172, 173

Tunnell, Byron, **1963:** 476

Tupper, Repr. Stanley R., **1962:** 326; **1963:** 426

Turk, Joseph, **1961:** 455 [20]

Turkey, **1962:** 70, 352 [11], 491n., 549 [4]; **1963:** 77, 477

    Assistance, **1961:** 222; **1963:** 118, 328 [1], 338, 443

    Gursel, Cemal, **1961:** 439; **1963:** 443

    Independence anniversary, **1963:** 443

    Message to people, **1962:** 79

    Missile bases in, **1963:** 35 [18]

    Visit of Vice President Johnson, **1962:** 339

Turkmen, Ilter, **1962:** 339n.

Turman, Solon B., **1961:** 459

Tuscaloosa, Ala., **1963:** 236, 243

Tuthill, John W., **1961:** 123

Tuttle, Judge Elbert Parr, **1962:** 420

TVA.

    See Tennessee Valley Authority.

Twain, Mark, **1962:** 527

Tweedsmuir, Baron, **1963:** 294

Twentieth Century Fund, **1963:** 246

Twining, Gen. Nathan F., **1962:** 422

Tyler, John, **1963:** 478

Tyler, William R., **1963:** 421

Typewriter of Woodrow Wilson, presentation to White House, **1962:** 36

Typographical Union, International, **1963:** 75 [2, 13], 107 [16]

U.A.R.

    See United Arab Republic.

U'Nu, **1961:** 367

U Thant, **1961:** 499

    See also United Nations Secretary.

U-2 aircraft

    Export policy, **1962:** 378 [2]

    Incident over Soviet Union, **1962:** 50 [1], 59 [10], 75 [6]

U-2 plane incident, **1961:** 8 [4, 30]

Udall, Stewart L.

    See Interior, Secretary of the.

Uffizi Gallery, Florence, **1963:** 5

Uganda, message to Prime Minister Obote, **1962:** 441

Ulbricht, Walter, **1961:** 291 [1], 292, 483

Ullman, Repr. Al, **1962:** 231; **1963:** 384, 388

Unemployment, **1961:** 7, 11, 17, 20, 22, 33, 44, 87, 96, 133, 136, 205, 211, 241, 274, 354, 448, 458, 470; **1962:** 7 (p. 6), 13 (p. 35), 16 (pp. 43, 45), 22, 53, 80, 111, 165, 174, 190, 201, 205, 328, 359, 380, 395, 414, 549; **1963:** 12 (p. 12), 21 (pp. 27, 30, 37), 30 (pp. 57, 58, 59, 61, 62, 66, 67, 70), 43, 77 [2], 85, 92, 94, 134, 145, 146, 162, 175, 185, 187, 188, 220, 226, 230, 237, 241, 248, 306, 310, 339, 340, 351, 362, 363, 368, 378, 402, 436, 439, 462, 465, 478

    Aircraft industry, **1962:** 50 [14]

    American Indians, **1963:** 86

    Appalachian region, **1963:** 127

    Automation, effect of, **1962:** 89 [5]; **1963:** 228

    Budget effect, **1963:** 349

    Campaign remarks, **1962:** 395, 431, 432, 436-439, 446, 451-456, 458, 472-474, 480

    Coal industry, **1962:** 50 [3], 410 [1]; **1963:** 110, 175 [2], 228

    Construction industry, **1962:** 115 [16]

    Construction workers, **1961:** 76

    Depressed areas.

        See main heading, Depressed areas.

    Food distribution to unemployed, **1961:** 8 [10], 11, 15 [3], 17, 35 [3]

    Imports, effect of, **1962:** 22

    Negroes, **1963:** 110

    News conference remarks, **1961:** 8 [10, 21], 15 [13, 23], 15 [25], 35 [3, 6, 14], 62 [7], 83 [18], 92 [2], 119 [8, 18], 139 [8], 171 [2], 291 [2, 20], 334 [10], 415 [20], 455 [7]; **1962:** 27 [27], 50 [3, 13, 14], 75 [5], 89 [5,

Unemployment
  News conference remarks — *continued*
        13, 19], 115 [16, 23], 139 [1], 210 [10], 229
        [1, 12], 245 [18], 279 [12], 316 [10], 410 [1];
        1963: 65 [1, 2, 4], 89 [1, 7], 120 [11], 144
        [21], 169 [15], 305 [2, 18], 328 [15], 405
        [11], 448 [7, 26]
  Older persons, **1963:** 110
  Railroad industry, 1963: 110
  Reduction, **1963:** 349, 445
  Rural, **1963:** 21 (p. 36)
  Steel industry, **1962:** 50 [3], 139 [1], 410 [1];
        1963: 110, 175 [2]
  Steel workers, **1961:** 25 [25], 35 [3]
  Textile workers, **1961:** 161
  Unemployed workers
    Aid for children of, **1962:** 132, 288, 328, 414,
        446, 456; **1963:** 162, 462
    Food for, **1963:** 74, 455
    Occupational training, **1962:** 6n., 13 (p. 31), 28,
        91, 186, 202, 328, 414, 438, 446, 452, 453;
        1963: 30 (pp. 58, 71), 34, 85, 92, 127, 175,
        [2], 228, 310, 363, 448 [7]
  Women, **1963:** 110
  Young people, **1963:** 64, 65 [1], 89 [1], 110, 141,
        142, 162, 248, 393, 423
Unemployment Compensation Act, Temporary
        Extended, **1961:** 93
Unemployment insurance, **1961:** 17, 241, 339, 499;
        1962: 7 (p. 6), 13 (p. 28), 111, 174, 205,
        324, 328, 359, 385, 414, 432, 451, 455;
        1963: 21 (p. 38), 30 (p. 67), 92, 185, 402
  Anniversary, letter, **1961:** 323
  Approval of bill, **1961:** 93
  Extension of benefits, **1961:** 11, 17, 22, 35 [3], 93,
        436; **1962:** 16 (p. 43), 176, 431, 436, 439,
        453, 455, 458
  Government employees, **1961:** 94
  Letter, **1962:** 80
  News conference remarks, **1961:** 15 [17], 25 [25],
        35 [3, 14], 62 [7]; **1962:** 89 [5], 229 [1]
  Railroad employees, **1961:** 384, 385
  Temporary, extension proposed, **1962:** 120, 136
  Veterans, **1961:** 94
UNESCO.
  See United Nations Educational, Scientific and
        Cultural Organization.
Unger, Leonard, **1963:** 120 [16]
UNICEF.
  See United Nations International Children's
        Emergency Fund.
Unidad Independencia Housing Project, Mexico
        City, **1962:** 269
Union of African and Malagasy States, **1962:** 105,
        212
  Conference, **1962:** 368
Union of American Hebrew Congregations
        Trustees, remarks, **1961:** 463

Union Miniere du Haut Katanga, **1962:** 302 [11]
Union shop, **1962:** 378 [20]
  Aerospace industry, **1962:** 410 [6]
Unions.
  See Labor organizations.
United Aerospace Workers, **1962:** 390
United Aircraft Corporation, **1961:** 281n.
United Arab Republic, **1962:** 229 [10], 515 [15]
  See also Egypt.
  Assistance, **1963:** 459 [13]
  German missile technicians in, **1963:** 120 [10]
  Nasser, Gamal Abdel, **1961:** 108; **1962:** 229 [10],
        557
  Yemen dispute, **1963:** 448 [5], 459 [13], 471
United Association of Journeymen and Ap-
        prentices of the Plumbing and Pipe Fit-
        ting Industry, **1962:** 247
United Automobile, Aerospace, and Agriculture
        Implement Workers of America, **1963:** 39
United Automobile Workers, **1961:** 334 [12], 350;
        1962: 174, 179 [9], 298
United Brotherhood of Carpenters and Joiners of
        America, **1962:** 247
United Community campaigns, **1961:** 375; **1963:**
        369
United Givers Fund campaign, **1961:** 259; **1963:**
        457n.
United Kingdom, **1961:** 148, 205, 231, 292, 302, 387,
        483; **1962:** 14, 31, 48, 71, 116, 157, 158,
        383, 506, 551 [5, 15]; **1963:** 144 [4], 150,
        254, 260 [1], 267, 295, 296, 306, 455, 477
  Ambassador David Ormsby Gore, **1962:** 383,
        419; **1963:** 126, 457
  Armed forces, **1963:** 15
  Armed forces, recall, **1961:** 497
  Assistance, **1963:** 118
  Balance of payments, **1963:** 175, 228
  Berlin crisis.
    See main heading, Berlin crisis.
  Bicycles, exports, **1962:** 484
  Business, **1963:** 175
  Christmas Island, use for U.S. nuclear tests,
        1962: 40 [7, 21], 41, 50 [2]
  Commonwealth, **1961:** 36
  Economy, **1963:** 349, 351
  Elizabeth, Queen Mother, **1963:** 457
  Elizabeth II, **1961:** 227, 231
  European Economic Community, membership,
        question of, **1961:** 222 [8], 318 [1], 519;
        1962: 7 (p. 14), 20 [20], 22, 160, 198 [16],
        210 [19], 229 [9], 248, 251, 279 [4], 549 [2],
        554; **1963:** 20, 35 [17], 54 [3, 11], 65 [8],
        75 [17], 260 [8]
  Gaitskell, Hugh, statment on death of, **1963:** 25
  General elections in, **1963:** 120 [19]
  Geneva conferences.
    See main heading, Geneva conferences.

United Kingdom — *continued*
George I, King, **1963:** 426
Hailsham, Lord, **1963:** 260 [14], 285, 286, 314, 320 [8], 328 [6]
Health and welfare programs, **1962:** 174, 202
Home, Lord, **1961:** 112, 258 [18], 318 [7]; **1962:** 73, 89 [12], 419, 554; **1963:** 52, 144 [2], 285, 305 [17], 328 [6]
Indian-U.K. relations, **1961:** 452n.
Labor Party, **1962:** 310 [1]; **1963:** 120 [19]
Laotian situtation, **1961:** 92 [1], 97, 139 [9]
Macmillan, Harold.
    See main heading, Macmillan, Harold.
Military aid to India, **1963:** 202 [3]
Military survey team, U.S.-U.K., in India, **1963:** 107 [14]
Mount Everest expedition, **1963:** 158
Nassau agreement with U.S., **1962:** 554, 557; **1963:** 12 (p. 16), 36, 54 [8], 75 [19], 202 [3], 320 [2, 15, 16]
News conference remarks, **1961:** 8 [29], 25 [19], 92 [1], 119 [7], 139 [19], 171 [1], 222, 258 [2, 18], 318 [1, 2], 334 [2], 455 [8], 488 [17]; **1962:** 8 [16], 20 [20], 27 [12], 40 [7, 21], 50 [2], 59 [5], 75 [2], 89 [12], 107 [2], 198 [16], 210 [2, 5, 19], 229 [9, 10], 245 [10], 259 [14], 279 [4], 316 [6], 340 [3, 4], 546 [5]; **1963:** 35 [3, 17, 18], 54 [3, 8, 11], 65 [8, 19], 75 [17, 19], 107 [14], 120 [19], 202 [3], 260 [1, 8, 9, 14], 305 [17], 320 [8], 328 [6]
Nuclear test ban treaty, **1963:** 35 [3], 40, 232, 260 [9], 314, 316, 324, 366
Nuclear weapons, **1962:** 557
Nuclear weapons tests, **1961:** 455 [8]; **1963:** 75 [19]
    Ban or suspension, proposals, **1961:** 171 [1], 318 [2], 335, 357
    Joint statements, U.S.-U.K., **1962:** 41, 134
    U.K. proposals, **1962:** 107 [2], 186
Polaris missile agreement, **1962:** 554, 557; **1963:** 35 [18], 54 [8]
Prince Philip, **1961:** 231
Queen Elizabeth II, **1963:** 297
Royal Air Forces, **1962:** 554
Skybolt missile dispute, **1962:** 546 [5], 551 [13, 22], 554, 557; **1963:** 54 [8]
Students from, **1962:** 284
Tanganyika trusteeship, **1961:** 500
Taxes, **1963:** 175
Trade agreements with, **1962:** 75 [2], 76; **1963:** 9
Troops in Germany, **1963:** 272
U.S. Ambassador David K.E. Bruce, **1961:** 228; **1962:** 419; **1963:** 126
U.S. expenditures in, **1963:** 77 [1]
U.S. exports, **1963:** 118
U.S. forces and missile bases, **1962:** 259 [14], 316 [6]

United Kingdom — *continued*
U.S. relations with, **1963:** 120 [19]
Visit to, **1961:** 227-230; **1963:** 284-286
Wilson, Harold, **1963:** 120 [19]
Withdrawal from Malaya, **1963:** 65 [19]
United Nations, **1961:** 72, 146, 192, 193, 205, 299, 376, 447; **1962:** 7 (pp. 10, 11), 15, 29, 35, 63, 71, 82, 83, 85, 103, 109, 116, 133, 157, 168n., 178n., 418, 461, 485, 492-494, 500, 523; **1963:** 12 (p. 16), 14, 15, 27, 139, 192, 217, 232, 278, 285, 290, 300n., 309, 314, 316, 347, 349, 359, 367, 381, 385, 390, 394, 398, 418, 421, 426, 432, 433, 455
Address, **1961:** 387
Air for less developed countries, **1962:** 82, 319; **1963:** 101
Bonds, purchase by U.S., **1962:** 7 (p. 11), 8 [9], 24, 27 [12], 40 [14, 23], 75 [12], 82, 107 [5, 11], 302, [4], 316 [3], 340 [2, 14], 352 [11, 20], 381
    Approval, **1962:** 424
China, Republic of, membership, **1961:** 119 [7], 309
Communist China, admission, question of, **1961:** 119 [7, 8], 222 [12], 309
Communist efforts to undermine, **1962:** 24
Conference on Science and Technology, **1963:** 38
Congo operations, **1961:** 8 [2], 11, 15 [14], 35 [1, 13, 16], 62 [8], 132, 173, 456; **1962:** 7 (p. 11), 24, 40 [14, 23], 107 [5], 302 [11], 316 [3], 319, 340 [14], 352 [20], 424, 557; **1963:** 12 (pp. 16, 18), 28, 278, 366, 416, 418, 471
Cuba, negotiations on, **1963:** 11
Decade of Development, **1963:** 38, 101, 118, 366, 430, 471
Disarmament proposals, **1962:** 82
Farm aid to Cuba, **1963:** 65 [16]
Financial support of, **1962:** 24, 82, 319
General Assembly.
    See United Nations General Assembly.
Joint statements, **1961:** 45, 51, 74, 112, 135, 304, 430, 456, 468; **1962:** 105, 183, 273, 446, 544
Korean operations, **1961:** 468
Middle East operations, **1962:** 24, 107 [5], 319, 424; **1963:** 169 [2], 471
Military force, question of, **1962:** 152 [15]
News conference remarks, **1961:** 8 [2, 5, 25], 15 [6, 14], 35 [1, 4, 5, 13, 16], 71 [23], 62 [8], 83 [6], 92 [1], 119 [7, 8, 19], 139 [2], 222 [12], 318 [17], 488 [7]; **1962:** 8 [3, 9, 14, 19], 27 [12], 40 [14, 23], 59 [1], 75 [9, 12], 107 [1, 3, 5, 7, 11], 152 [15], 179 [8], 210 [22], 302 [4, 11], 316 [3, 7], 340 [2, 9, 14, 20], 352 [6, 11, 20], 515 [1, 6, 13, 15], 546 [23]; **1963:** 35 [2], 54 [5], 65 [16], 169 [2], 305 [21], 328 [8], 356 [10], 448 [29], 459 [13]

United Nations — *continued*
Population study, U.S. participation, **1963:** 144
[6]
Secretary General.
See United Nations Secretary General.
Security Council, **1963:** 471
See also United Nations Security Council.
South African participation, **1963:** 305 [21]
Soviet troika plan, **1962:** 319; **1963:** 12 (p. 11)
Space activities, **1962:** 60, 82, 96, 107 [1, 7], 319
U.S. delegation, oath-of-office ceremony, **1961:**
358
U.S. participation and support, **1962:** 7 (p. 11),
24, 40 [14, 23], 107 [5], 186, 254; **1963:** 12
(pp. 16, 18), 169 [2], 179, 232, 292, 356
[10], 471
Reports, **1962:** 92, 319
U.S. support, **1961:** 1, 11, 35 [1], 112
West New Guinea negotiations, **1962:** 316 [3, 7]
Women delegates, remarks, **1961:** 501
Women in U.S. delegation, **1962:** 156
United Nations, American Association for the,
1962: 82; **1963:** 101
United Nations , U.S. Representative
Adlai E. Stevenson, **1961:** 210, 215, 239n., 358n.,
449, 482n.; **1962:** 40 [14], 201, 219, 418,
424, 488, 505n., 515 [6, 19], 532n., 534n.,
546 [3, 4, 23]; **1963:** 11, 27, 35 [2], 139,
151, 160, 204, 223, 359, 367, 408, 433, 439,
455n., 459 [6]
Arthur H. Dean, resignation, **1963:** 3
News conference remarks on, **1961:** 15 [6], 35 [1],
83 [6], 119 [19], 258 [17]
United Nations Charter, **1961:** 128n., 135, 292, 302,
387, 424, 449, 481; **1962:** 7 (p. 11), 24, 82,
92, 192, 266, 267, 273, 303, 319, 441, 485,
515 [13]; **1963:** 219, 344n., 366, 419, 471
News conference remarks, **1961:** 35 [1], 291 [1],
334 [4]
United Nations Commission on Narcotic Drugs,
1962: 411
United Nations Committee on Peaceful Uses of
Outer Space, **1962:** 96, 107 [1, 7], 319
United Nations Conference on Science and Tech-
nology, **1963:** 38
United Nations Conference on Trade, **1963:** 366
United Nations Decade of Development, **1963:** 101
United Nations Disarmament Commission, **1961:**
365
United Nations Economic Commission for Latin
America, **1961:** 81
United Nations Economic and Social Council,
1962: 210 [15]; **1963:** 455
United Nations Educational, Scientific and
Cultural Organization, **1961:** 100, 108;
1962: 122
United Nations Emergency Force, **1963:** 471

United Nations Food and Agricultural Organization, **1961:** 139 [2], 482; **1962:** 478; **1963:**
33, 217, 455
United Nations General Assembly, **1961:** 442, 473;
1962: 24, 29, 35n., 48, 63, 82, 89 [1], 90,
96, 107 [5], 319, 352 [6], 378 [16]; **1963:**
359, 430, 471
Address, **1961:** 387; **1963:** 366
Joint statements, **1961:** 468, 519
News conference remarks, **1961:** 8 [5], 35 [1, 16],
83 [5], 318 [8, 17], 415 [1], 488 [15]; **1963:**
356 [4, 10], 405 [3, 4]
President (Mongi Slim), **1961:** 387n.
Resolution on South Africa, **1961:** 488 [15]
United Nations High Commissioner for Refugees,
1961: 297
United Nations International Children's
Emergency Fund, **1961:** 420
United Nations Participation Act, **1963:** 471
United Nations Relief and Works Agency for Pal-
estine Refugees, **1963:** 471
United Nations Secretary General (Dag Hammer-
skjold), 1961: 51
Death of, **1961:** 368, 387
News conference remarks on, **1961:** 35 [16], 62 [8]
United Nations Secretary General (U Thant), **1962:**
192, 251, 419n., 491n., 492-494; **1963:** 28,
54 [5], 89 [18], 285, 366, 448 [5], 471
United Nations Secretary General, Acting
(U Thant), **1961:** 449
Message, **1962:** 488
News conference remarks, **1962:** 8 [3, 19], 139
[10], 302 [11], 316 [7], 340 [14], 515 [19]
United Nations Secretary General, vacancy in
office, **1961:** 387
United Nations Security Council, 1961: 35 [1], 119
[19]; **1962:** 35n., 485, 488, 498; **1963:** 471
United Nations Truce Supervision Organization in
Palestine, **1963:** 471
United Negro College Fund, **1963:** 355
United Service Organizations, **1962:** 27 [21]
United States Advisory Commission on Education-
al Exchange, **1961:** 57
United States Air Force Academy, **1962:** 226; **1963:**
221, 222, 223, 321
United States Arms Control and Disarmament
Agency, **1961:** 205, 262, 388, 408; **1962:** 29,
40 [9], 186, 302 [8], 316 [18], 346, 452, 455,
456; **1963:** 228, 449
United States Arms Control and Disarmament
Agency, Director (William Foster), **1961:**
388; **1962:** 107 [2], 316 [18], 352 [18];
1963: 3, 27, 35 [7], 75 [12], 124n.
United States attorneys, **1962:** 443
United States-Canada Committee on Trade and
Economic Affairs, **1961:** 45
United States Chamber of Commerce.
See Chamber of Commerce of the United States.

United States Civil Service Commission, **1961:** 121, 504

United States Communications Satellite Corporation, **1963:** 470

United States Conference of Mayors, **1963:** 229, 230

United States Courts of Appeals, **1961:** 28

United States District Courts, **1961:** 28

United States Economic Assistance Mission, **1961:** 517

United States Employment Service, **1961:** 17, 136; **1962:** 13 (p. 31), 16 (p. 56), 28, 91; **1963:** 21 (p. 38), 92, 305 [15]

United States of Europe, Action Committee for, President (Jean Monnet), **1963:** 32

United States Industrial Payroll Savings Committee, campaign, **1963:** 450

United States Information Agency, **1961:** 8 [23], 92 [14], 205; **1963:** 54 [10], 238n., 256

   Director (Edward R. Murrow), **1961:** 42, 92 [14]; **1962:** 532

   News broadcasts to armed forces, **1963:** 144 [9]

   Polls on U.S. prestige, **1963:** 65 [12], 75 [4]

   Transmitter at Greenville, N.C., **1963:** 55

United States-Japan Committee on Trade and Economic Affairs, **1961:** 252, 444n., 455 [3]; **1962:** 531n.

United States Maritime Commission, **1961:** 238

United States Merchant Marine Academy, 1961: 156

United States Military Academy, **1962:** 226, 234; **1963:** 223, 321, 335

United States Naval Academy, **1961:** 232; **1962:** 226; **1963:** 222, 223, 321

United States Office of Education, **1963:** 21 (p. 38), 43, 50, 82, 258, 447

United States Steel Corp., **1962:** 121n., 152 [21], 139 [1, 4, 11], 158; **1963:** 448 [16]

United States Study Commission - Texas, report, **1962:** 313

United States Supreme Court.

   See Supreme Court of the United States.

United States Tariff Commission, **1961:** 71 [20], 478; **1962:** 22, 76, 98, 115 [23], 245 [16], 307, 365; **1963:** 9

United States Track and Field Federation, **1963:** 7

United States Travel Service, **1963:** 306

United Steelworkers of America, **1961:** 274, 366; **1962:** 121, 162; **1963:** 131, 466

   Convention, remarks, **1962:** 385

   News conference remarks, **1962:** 20 [19], 75 [1], 115 [4], 139 [1, 9, 11], 152 [12, 14]

Universal Postal Union, **1963:** 453

Universities, role in public affairs, **1963:** 136, 192

University of Alabama, integration, **1963:** 169 [4], 202 [1], 234, 236, 237, 243

University of Arkansas, Schola Cantorum, **1962:** 352 [3], 361

University of California, **1961:** 342, 460n.; **1962:** 59 [15], 77, 109, 122

University of Costa Rica, remarks, **1963:** 105

University of Havana, **1961:** 19, 86

University of Hawaii, **1963:** 231n.

University of Maine, address, **1963:** 426

University of Maryland, **1961:** 417; **1962:** 325

University of Massachusetts, **1962:** 224

University of Miami, **1961:** 86n.

University of Michigan, **1961:** 460n.

University of Minnesota, **1962:** 198 [1]

   Address, **1963:** 378

University of Mississippi, **1963:** 35 [23], 82

   Integration, **1962:** 420, 459, 551 [10]

University of North Carolina, **1961:** 417, 418

University of North Dakota, address, **1963:** 379

University of Oklahoma, **1963:** 325

University of Pittsburgh, **1962:** 452

University of Washington, **1961:** 415 [12], 472, 473

University of Wyoming, address, **1963:** 381

Unsoeld, William, **1963:** 158n.

Upper Colorado Project, **1961:** 360

Upper Missouri River Basin, Garrison Diversion project, **1961:** 247

Uranium-235, **1961:** 390

Urban affairs and housing department, proposed, **1961:** 130, 246; **1962:** 7 (p. 7), 13 (p. 38), 20 [1, 7, 8], 23, 27 [7, 25], 40 [8], 59 [7], 100, 437, 458, 459; **1963:** 21 (p. 37)

Urban areas, **1963:** 22, 130, 134, 162, 472

   Civil rights enforcement in, **1963:** 230

Urban growth, **1961:** 76; **1962:** 23, **1963:** 423

   Housing, **1962:** 23, 190; **1963:** 21 (p. 37), 423, 445

   Recreational needs, **1962:** 69; **1963:** 423

   Slums, clearance, **1963:** 50, 305 [19], 326, 423, 445, 469, 478

   Transportation, **1961:** 76, 246; **1962:** 7 (p. 7), 13 (p. 31), 23, 129, 153, 190, 200, 395, 458; **1963:** 12 (p. 14), 22, 69, 120 [8], 144 [15], 162, 208, 228

Urban Mass Transportation Act of 1963, **1963:** 69

Urban planning, **1963:** 412

Urban renewal, **1961:** 15 [36], 17, 58, 76, 94, 101, 436; **1962:** 7 (p. 7), 13 (p. 31), 23, 190, 200, 205, 328, 340 [10], 438, 452, 454, 456, 458, 480, 545; **1963:** 21 (p. 32, 37), 22, 30 (p. 58), 77, 92, 162, 175, 230, 240, 423, 445, 462

   Federal aid, **1961:** 76, 130

   Telegram to U.S. mayors, **1961:** 20

Urban Renewal Administration, **1962:** 545

Uruchurtu, Ernesto P., **1962:** 265n.

Uruguay, **1963:** 118

Uruguay, Punta del Estate conference.

   See Punta del Este conference.

USO.

   See United Service Organization.

[References are to items except as otherwise indicated]

U.S. diplomatic missions, **1961:** 207
U.S. Information and Educational Exchange Act
of 1948, **1963:** 231n.
U.S. News and World Report, **1963:** 35 [2]
USIA.
See United States Information Agency.
U.S.S. *Long Beach,* **1961:** 99
U.S.S. *Sam Houston,* **1961:** 16
U.S.S.R.
See Soviet Union.
Usumbura, Burundi, **1962:** 415
Utah, **1962:** 316 [22]; **1963:** 328 [18], 383, 386
Gov. George D. Clyde, **1963:** 385

Vaccination Assistance Act, **1963:** 53
Vaccinations, **1963:** 247, 294
Valachi, Joseph, hearings, **1963:** 405 [10]
Valencia, Guillermo Leon, **1962:** 258
Valley Forge, **1961:** 402n.
Van Allen, James A., radiation belt, **1962:** 179 [13];
1963: 328 [4]
Vance, Cyrus R. (Secretary of the Army), **1962:**
309, 323n., 335, 416; **1963:** 173
Vanderbilt, Cornelius, **1962:** 383n.; **1963:** 192
Vanderbilt University, 90th anniversary, **1963:** 192
Vandiver, Gov. S. Ernest, **1961:** 334 [1]
Vanier, George P., **1961:** 190
Vanik, Repr. Charles A., **1962:** 480
Vanocur, Sander, **1961:** 139 [17]; **1962:** 551
Vargas, Getulio, **1962:** 124, 175
Vatican, communications with U.S., **1963:** 305 [3]
Vatican Council, Second, **1962:** 430
V-E Day, 17th anniversary, **1962:** 175
Vela, nuclear test control system, **1961:** 349n.
Venezuela, **1961:** 272, 466; **1962:** 8 [15], 325, 341,
546 [20]; **1963:** 71, 107 [1], 118, 120 [12],
459 [25], 478
Betancourt, Romulo, **1961:** 272, 507, 509, 510,
511; **1963:** 71-73, 89 [19]
Oil exports to U.S., **1963:** 73
U.S. Ambassador Teodoro Moscoso, **1961:** 160,
466, 491, 506, 508, 517
U.S. support, **1963:** 89 [19]
Visit to, **1961:** 507-511
Venice, Italy, **1962:** 450
Venus, probe of planet, **1961:** 11, 35 [9]; **1962:** 59
[1], 96; **1963:** 21 (p. 34)
Verdon, Gwen, **1962:** 158
Vereide, Abraham, **1963:** 52n.
Vermont, **1961:** 467; **1962:** 243 [1], 326
Civil rights, **1963:** 248ftn. (p. 486)
Gov. Philip H. Hoff, **1963:** 427
Verne, Jules, **1962:** 77
Versailles, **1961:** 226
Versailles Peace Conference, **1963:** 173
Vessels.
See Ships.
Veterans Administration, **1961:** 76; **1962:** 55, 65,
480, 517; **1963:** 4n., 21 (p. 42)

Veterans Administration, Administrator (John S.
Gleason, Jr.), **1961:** 461, 492; **1963:** 4,
49n., 62, 130, 148, 174
Insurance dividend, **1961:** 15 [4], 17, 139 [3]
News conference remarks, **1961:** 15 [4], 139 [3]
Veterans benefits, **1961:** 94, 159; **1962:** 13 (p. 32),
245 [9], 280, 549; **1963:** 21 (p. 38), 74, 77
Disability compensation, **1962:** 367
Insurance dividend, **1961:** 15 [4], 17, 35 [3], 139
[3]
Life insurance dividend, **1962:** 16 (p. 44), 517
Negroes, **1963:** 135
Veterans Day ceremony, **1961:** 461
Veterans housing, **1961:** 76, 94
Veterans of World War II, American, **1962:** 343
Veto Messages and Memorandums of Disapproval.
1961: *For citations to private bills (not in-
cluded in this volume), see Appendix A,*
p. 821. **1962:** p. 917. **1963:** p. 920.
Bicycles, tariff classification, disapproval, **1962:**
484
District of Columbia, amendment of indecent
publications law, disapproval, **1962:** 479
Policemen and firemen, benefits, **1961:** 383
Postal employees longevity pay increases, disapproval, **1961:** 396
Vice President
Chairman, Aeronautics and Space Council,
1961: 147
Secret Service protection, **1961:** 142
Vice President (Lyndon B. Johnson), **1961:** 1, 10,
11, 17, 26, 68, 78, 84, 115, 116, 177, 178,
179, 205, 209, 215, 234, 248, 319, 339,
434, 476; **1962:** 7 (p. 5), 15, 38, 61, 68, 86,
149n., 158, 172, 201, 205, 219, 231, 233,
255, 287, 370, 372-374, 396, 409, 509, 527,
534, 536-538, 550; **1963:** 19, 24, 46, 52, 82,
85, 91, 204, 221-223, 230, 248, 406, 448
[22], 472-476, 478
Letters to President of the Senate.
See Congress, letters to Members of.
Letters, **1961:** 254, 393
News conference remarks, **1961:** 8 [32], 62 [15],
139 [22], 171 [2, 7], 455 [7]; **1962:** 59 [1],
179 [12]
Visit to Berlin, **1961:** 325
Visit to Europe and Far East, **1962:** 339
Visit to Iran, **1963:** 60
Visit to Southeast Asia, **1961:** 116, 139 [22], 171
[2], 203, 218
Report, **1961:** 205
Visit to Sweden, **1961:** 393
Vice President-elect, Secret Service protection,
1961: 142
Victoria, Queen, **1961:** 464; **1963:** 381
Vienna, **1961:** 205, 212, 215, 231, 483, 522n.; **1962:**
11, 203, 239, 245 [8], 461, 551 [5, 16, 18];
1963: 65 [19], 81, 382

Vienna — *continued*
  Meeting with Premier Khrushchev (1961), **1963:**
    65 [19], 79, 144 [3], 169 [9]
  News conference remarks, **1961:** 222 [13], 258
    [13]
  Visit to, **1961:** 224, 225, 226
Vienna Choir Boys, **1962:** 5
Vientiane, Laos, **1961:** 92 [3]; **1963:** 256
Viet-Nam, **1961:** 11, 112, 138, 155, 205, 309, 387;
    1962: 7 (pp. 12, 13), 70, 170, 171, 226, 250,
    251, 278, 389, 395, 396, 400, 439, 456, 521,
    549 [9, 10], 551 [21, 22]; **1963:** 12 (pp. 11,
    15, 16, 18, 19), 14, 159, 168, 194, 227, 237,
    285, 340, 381, 382, 383, 385, 455, 464, 476,
    477
  Anniversary message, **1961:** 435; **1962:** 438
  Assistance, **1961:** 488 [3], 505; **1963:** 89 [20], 118,
    305 [10], 338, 349, 356 [18], 399
  CIA activities, **1963:** 405 [2, 16]
  Communist aggression, **1963:** 21 (p. 34), 118, 144
    [16], 356 [5], 399, 438
  Defense of, **1963:** 194, 202 [10]
  Diem, Ngo Dinh, **1961:** 435, 505; **1963:** 340, 438,
    459 [5]
  Military coup, **1963:** 459 [5]
  New Year celebration, message, **1962:** 34
  News conference remarks, **1961:** 92 [6, 17], 139
    [14], 171 [7, 8], 415 [1, 10], 455 [2], 488 [3,
    10]; **1962:** 8 [5], 27 [8], 40 [4, 14], 50 [9], 59
    [4, 11], 75 [11], 89 [7], 139 [1, 16], 210 [11],
    245 [8], 316 [7], 352 [11], 410 [12], 546
    [14]; **1963:** 169 [11], 305 [10], 356 [5, 11,
    15, 19], 405 [6], 459 [5, 6]
  Nhu, Ngo Dinh, **1963:** 202 [10], 356 [11], 459 [5]
  Religious disputes, **1963:** 305 [10], 340, 349
  U.S. Ambassador Henry Cabot Lodge, **1963:**
    340, 356 [11, 15], 399, 405 [16], 459 [5]
  U.S. dependents in, **1963:** 356 [20]
  U.S. mission to, **1963:** 399
  U.S. relations with, **1963:** 349
  U.S. troops in, **1963:** 12 (p. 19), 202 [10], 356 [5],
    459 [21]
  Visit of General Taylor, **1961:** 415 [1, 10], 455 [2]
  Visit of Vice President Johnson, **1961:** 218
Viet-Nam, North, **1961:** 92 [1, 3], 138; **1962:** 50 [9],
    549 [10]
Viet-Nam, North, agreement on Laos, **1963:** 144 [5]
"Viet-Nam and Southeast Asia", report, **1963:** 89ftn.
    (p. 243)
"Vigor We Need", article, **1962:** 291
Villeda Morales, Ramón (President of Honduras),
    1962: 546 [20]; **1963:** 99, 100, 102, 106
  Visit of, **1962:** 528, 529
Villeda Morales, Senora, **1962:** 528
Vinci, Leonardo da, **1962:** 546 [1]
Vinson, Repr. Carl, **1961:** 62 [2]; **1962:** 75 [6], 320,
    378 [18]; **1963:** 330, 356 [24]
Vinson, Fred M., **1962:** 119

Virgin Islands, **1961:** 141; **1962:** 130
Virgin Islands Corporation, **1962:** 130
Virginia, **1962:** 340 [28]; **1963:** 174 [4], 208, 369,
    425, 451
  Development compact, National Capital region,
    1963: 208
  Gov. Albertis S. Harrison, Jr., **1963:** 108
  Prince Edward county, opening of schools in,
    1963: 82
Virginia House of Burgesses, **1961:** 418
Visa requirements for foreign visitors, simplifica-
    tion, **1962:** 114n.
Visitors, foreign leaders, **1963:** 16
  Abboud, Ibrahim, **1961:** 402, 404, 411
  Abdirascid Ali Scermarche, **1962:** 522, 523, 526
  Adenauer, Konrad, **1961:** 120, 480, 481; **1962:**
    506-508
  Adoula, Cyrille, **1962:** 35
  Ahidjo, Ahmadou, **1962:** 84, 85, 87
  Albert, Prince, **1963:** 80
  Alessandri Rodriguez, Jorge, **1962:** 542-544
  Arosemena Monroy, Carlos, **1962:** 299, 300, 303
  Ayub Khan, Mohammed, **1961:** 279, 280, 283;
    1962: 402-404
  Balewa, Abubakar Tafawa, **1961:** 304
  Ben Bella, Ahmed, **1962:** 464-466
  Betencourt, Rómulo, **1963:** 71-73
  Bourguiba, Habib, **1961:** 164, 165, 171 [15], 172,
    173
  Caramanlis, Constantine, **1961:** 128, 135
  Charlotte, Grand Duchess, **1963:** 150, 152, 154,
    156
  Chen Cheng, **1961:** 306, 309
  Chiari, Roberto, **1962:** 235, 238, 242
  Diefenbaker, John G., **1961:** 45
  Fanfani, Amintore, **1961:** 239, 242; **1963:** 15, 16,
    20
  Faysal, Crown Prince, **1962:** 429
  Franco Montoro, André, **1962:** 54
  Frondizi, Arturo, **1961:** 389
  Gerhardsen, Einar, **1962:** 178, 182, 183
  Gorbach, Alfons, **1962:** 168, 169
  Goulard, João, **1962:** 124-126
  Haile Selassie I, **1963:** 394, 395, 397, 398
  Hallstein, Walter, **1961:** 189
  Hasan al-Rida al-Sanusi, Crown Prince, **1962:**
    467, 471
  Hassan II, King, **1963:** 114-116
  Holyoake, Keith, **1961:** 66
  Houphouet-Boigny, Felix, **1962:** 206, 207, 212
  Ikeda, Hayato, **1961:** 249, 252
  Jean, Prince, **1963:** 150, 152, 154, 156
  Kayibanda, Grégoire, **1962:** 388
  Keita, Modibo, **1961:** 359, 363, 364
  Kekkonen, Urho K., **1961:** 421, 422, 424, 451
  Lemass, Sean F., **1963:** 415, 416, 418
  Macmillan, Harold, **1961:** 97, 112, 345, 357;
    1962: 157, 160

Visitors, foreign leaders — *continued*
  Makarios, Archbishop, **1962:** 224, 225, 227, 249
  Malraux, André, **1962:** 184
  Marshall, John Ross, **1962:** 248
  McEwen, John, **1962:** 88
  Menzies, Robert G., **1961:** 51; **1962:** 251; **1963:** 297
  Mexican parliamentarians, **1962:** 189
  Mohammed Zaher, King, **1963:** 343, 344, 347
  Nehru, Jawaharlal, **1961:** 452, 456
  Nkruman, Kwame, **1961:** 72, 73, 74
  Nyerere, Julius K., **1961:** 288; **1963:** 300, 302, 304
  Olympio, Sylvanus, **1962:** 103-105
  Pahlavi, Mohammad Reza, **1962:** 138, 141, 147
  Park, Chung Hee, **1961:** 468
  Paz Estenssoro, Victor, **1963:** 428-432
  Pearson, Lester B., **1963:** 178-180
  Prado, Manuel, **1961:** 372, 373, 376
  Radhakrishnan, Sarvepalli, **1963:** 214, 215, 217-219
  Saud, King, **1962:** 44-46
  Savang Vatthana, King, **1963:** 78, 79, 81
  Senghor, Leopold Sedar, **1961:** 450
  Souvanna Phouma, Prince, **1962:** 308, 312
  Spaak, Paul Henri, **1961:** 47
  Sukarno, Achmed, **1961:** 143, 146, 359, 363, 364
  Tito, Josip Broz, **1963:** 419-421
  Touré, Sékou, **1962:** 444
  Tubman, William V. S., **1961:** 429, 430
  Valencia, Guillermo Leon, **1962:** 258
  Villeda Morales, Ramón, **1962:** 528, 529
  Von Brentano, Heinrich, **1961:** 41, 120
  Youlou, Fulbert, **1961:** 235, 236
Visits to foreign countries
  Austria, **1961:** 224, 225, 226
  Bahamas, **1962:** 553, 554
  Bermuda, **1961:** 518, 519
  Broadcast on return from Europe, **1961:** 231
  Canada, **1961:** 190-193
  Colombia, **1961:** 512-516
  Costa Rica, **1963:** 97-100, 102-106
  France, **1961:** 216-223
  Germany, **1963:** 253-259, 261-273
  Ireland, **1963:** 274-282
  Italy, **1963:** 287-293
  Mexico, **1962:** 263-265, 268-273
  United Kingdom, **1961:** 227-230; **1963:** 284, 286
  Venezuela, **1961:** 507-511
Vocational education, **1961:** 46, 144
  Mentally retarded, **1961:** 413
Vocational Education, Panel of Consultants on, **1963:** 92
Vocational Education Act of 1946, **1963:** 43
Vocational Education Acts, National, **1961:** 46
Vocational education and training.
  See Occupational training.
Vocational rehabilitation, **1961:** 27; **1962:** 16 (pp. 46, 56), 28, 329

Vocational Rehabilitation, Office of, **1962:** 13 (p. 31)
Voice of America, **1962:** 34n.; **1963:** 326n., 356 [15], 405 [17], 477
  Broadcasts on Cuban crisis, **1962:** 532
  Transmitter at Greenville, N.C., **1963:** 55
  20th anniversary, **1962:** 63
Vogel, Herbert D., **1961:** 98, 278
Volpe, Gov. John A., **1961:** 212
Volta River project, **1961:** 273, 415 [15]
Voluntary Overseas Aid Week, **1962:** 133
Von Bekesy, George, **1962:** 161n.
Von Braun, Wernher, **1963:** 194
Von Brentano, Heinrich, **1961:** 41, 120
  News conference remarks on, **1961:** 25 [19], 62 [23, 26]
Von Eckhart, Felix, **1962:** 152 [19]
Von Karman, Theodore, **1963:** 68, 165
Voorhees, Tracy, **1961:** 8 [15]
Vorys, John, **1961:** 403
Voting Participation and Registration, President's Commission on, **1963:** 117, 167
Voting rights, **1962:** 7 (p. 8), 350, 399, 436; **1963:** 12 (p. 14), 82, 135, 167, 233, 237, 248, 339, 444, 445, 462, 478
  District of Columbia, **1961:** 103, 186, 286; **1963:** 122
  Duty to exercise, **1963:** 167
  Greenwood, Miss., **1963:** 120 [22]
  Literacy tests, **1962:** 27 [18], 179 [17]; **1963:** 82
  News conference remarks, **1961:** 8 [9], 92 [12], 455 [7]; **1962:** 8 [18], 27 [18], 115 [12, 22], 179 [17], 340 [2], 378 [6]; **1963:** 35 [6], 120 [22], 169 [1, 4], 202 [20]
  Poll tax, proposed abolition, **1963:** 82, 108
  Puerto Rico, in Presidential elections, **1963:** 35 [6]
  Reapportionment, Supreme Court decision on, **1962:** 115 [12, 22], 190
  Statement, **1963:** 117

Wade, Robert H. B., **1962:** 122n.
Wade, Gen. Sidney, **1963:** 227
Wage Policy Committee, International, **1962:** 121
Wages, **1961:** 33, 87, 136, 205; **1962:** 7 (p. 6), 14, 16, (p. 44), 80, 162, 174, 328, 359, 395; **1963:** 12 (p. 12), 21 (pp. 27, 31, 34), 30 (pp. 57, 58, 60-62, 64), 34, 43, 75 [11], 77, 85, 134 163, 185, 290, 306, 310, 465
  See also Pay.
  Aerospace industry, **1962:** 410 [6]
  Dockworkers, **1963:** 54 [9]
  Flight engineers, **1962:** 245 [1]
  Laundry workers, **1961:** 171 [20], 251
  Minimum, **1961:** 17, 24, 35 [3], 83 [14], 92 [5], 139 [16], 169, 171 [20], 251, 258 [11], 448, 477
  See also Minimum wage.

Wages — *continued*
  News conference remarks, **1961:** 35 [3], 83 [14],
      92 [5], 139 [16], 171 [6, 20], 258 [11], 334
      [14]; **1962:** 20 [26], 115 [16], 139 [1, 4, 9],
      152 [2, 18, 21], 179 [9], 198 [15], 245 [1, 2],
      316 [19], 410 [1, 5, 6]
  Stabilization, **1963:** 30 (p. 64), 134 [3], 175
  Steel industry, **1962:** 139 [9]; **1963:** 54 [9], 131, 134
      [3], 175 [3]
  U.S. merchant marine, **1961:** 258 [11]
  U.S. vs. foreign, **1962:** 22
  Wage base, social security, **1963:** 74
  Women, **1963:** 233
  Youth, **1963:** 64
Waggonner, Repr. Joe D., Jr., **1962:** 170
Wagner, Aubrey J., **1961:** 30
Wagner, Richard, **1962:** 162, 179 [7]
Wagner, Robert F., **1961:** 215, 407, 447, 455 [5];
      1962: 200, 201, 218, 220, 229 [23], 340
      [12], 411, 548; **1963:** 107 [16], 203, 204
      455
Walgren, Margaret, **1962:** 452
Walker, Maj. Gen. Edwin A., **1961:** 139 [11]; **1962:**
      40 [13]
Walker, Joseph A., **1961:** 486n.; **1962:** 294n.
Walker, William, **1963:** 99
Wall, Charles C., **1961:** 280
Wall Street Journal, **1962:** 152 [12]; **1963:** 144 [15],
      465, 478
Wallace, Gov. George C., **1963:** 108, 169 [4], 182,
      193, 194, 202 [1], 234, 236, 243, 305 [25],
      350
Wallen, Saul, **1962:** 376
Wallingford, Conn., **1963:** 160
Walrath, Laurence K. (Chairman, Interstate Com-
      merce Commissin), **1963:** 62
Walsh, Rev. Michael P., **1963:** 136
Walter, Repr. Francis E., **1961:** 318 [21]; **1962:** 261
  Death of, **1963:** 211
Walter Reed Army Institute of Research, **1962:** 323
War.
  See also specific wars.
  Limited, **1961:** 15 [24], 99; **1962:** 13 (p. 28)
  Nuclear, **1961:** 1, 302, 318 [2], 387, 410, 415 [5], 446;
      1962: 8 [20], 13 (p. 38), 50 [25], 109, 115
      [18], 290, 310 [3], 485, 551 [2, 13]
War College, Brazilian National, **1963:** 335
War College, French National, **1963:** 112
War College, National, **1963:** 120 [16]
War crimes trials, Nürnberg, **1963:** 298
War damage bill, Philippines, **1962:** 191
  Approval, **1962:** 315
War of 1812, **1961:** 397
War of Independence, French alliance in, **1963:** 112
Ward, Artemus, **1961:** 498; **1962:** 482; **1963:** 379
Warheads, nuclear, joint control of, **1963:** 75 [19]

Warning systems for missile and aircraft detection,
      1961: 99, 302; **1962:** 7 (p. 10)
Warren, Earl (Chief Justice), **1961:** 1, 4, 10; **1962:** 20
      [16], 68n., 158, 211, 512, 527; **1963:** 52, 157,
      260 [3], 416, and pp. 899, 900
Warren, Maj. Gen. Robert H., **1962:** 172; **1963:** 221
Warren, Stafford L., **1963:** 313, 364
"Wars of liberation," Communist, **1961:** 212, 231,
      244, 387; **1962:** 226, 276, 551 [16, 17]
Warsaw conferences, U.S.-Communist China,
      1961: 15 [32, 33], 71 [21], 415 [6]; **1962:**
      243 [6]
Warsaw Pact, **1962:** 229 [3], 492, 494, 515 [6]; **1963:**
      314, 320 [4]
Warsaw Pact countries, **1961:** 483, 488 [6]
Warschaw, Mrs. Carmen H., **1963:** 228
Washington, D.C.
  See District of Columbia.
Washington, George, **1961:** 26, 71 [15], 78, 84, 162,
      165, 217, 280, 402n., 467; **1962:** 86, 170,
      270, 275, 278, 452, 465, 495; **1963:** 72, 73,
      86, 114, 115, 278, 383, 385, 451
  Farewell Address, **1961:** 125
Washington, Gov. Albert D. Rosellini, 1961: 472n.,
      474; 1963: 384, 387
Washington, Pa., 1962: 455
Washington, State of, **1963:** 47, 248ftn. (p. 486),
      316, 383, 385, 390
  Columbia River Basin, reclamation, **1963:** 41
Washington International Center, **1963:** 140n.
Washington and Lee University, **1961:** 162
Washington Monument, **1963:** 300, 301 [20]
Washington Post, **1961:** 397n.; **1963:** 24, 77, 245,
      459 [22]
Waste in Government spending, **1961:** 62 [16], 244
Waste treatment plants, **1961:** 37; **1962:** 65
Water carriers, rate regulation, **1962:** 129
Water conservation, **1961:** 49, 85; **1962:** 25, 69, 128;
      1963: 45, 376, 378, 382, 386, 430, 461, 474
Water Conservation Fund, **1963:** 209
Water desalinization, **1961:** 11, 17, 49, 94, 119 [13],
      248, 257; **1962:** 69, 337, 404; **1963:** 381,
      461, 474
  Approval of bill, **1961:** 381
Water pollution, **1961:** 11, 17, 49, 284, 294, 445;
      1962: 7 (p. 7), 69, 190, 288, 336, 395, 453,
      480; **1963:** 53, 134, 193, 366, 376, 377, 478
Water Pollution Control Act, **1962:** 69
Water Pollution Control Act, amendments, **1961:**
      294
Water Resources Council, proposed, **1961:** 284;
      1962: 69
Water resources development, **1961:** 17, 49, 284,
      445; **1962:** 7 (p. 7), 13 (p. 30), 25, 69, 216,
      240, 313, 332, 333, 335-338; **1963:** 12 (p.
      14), 21 (p. 36), 41, 45, 70, 127, 144 [15],

Water resources development — *continued*
146, 179, 209, 252, 301, 383, 385, 386, 389, 390, 474

Water Resources Planning Act, proposed, **1962:** 69, 313

Waterbury, Conn., **1962:** 474

Waterloo, **1963:** 457

Waterman, Alan T., (Director, National Science Foundation), **1961:** 110; **1962:** 163; **1963:** p. 902

Waters delivered to Mexico, salinity of, **1962:** 94

Watershed development, **1961:** 17, 49, 85, 196, 445, 477; **1962:** 69, 440

Watershed Protection and Flood Prevention Act, **1963:** 45

Watershed Protection and Flood Prevention Act, amendment proposed, **1962:** 25, 69, 129

Waterways, **1963:** 461

Waterways, inland, **1962:** 13 (p. 34)

Watkinson, Harold, **1962:** 316 [6]

Watson, Maj. Gen. Albert E., **1961:** 334 [3]

Watson, Mark S., **1963:** p. 902

Watson, Thomas, **1961:** 40n.; **1962:** 203

Watts, Repr. John C., **1962:** 458; **1963:** 137

Wauneka, Annie D., **1963:** p. 902

Weapons, **1961:** 302; **1963:** 12 (p. 18), 21 (pp. 32, 34), 35 [12]
　　See also Missiles; Nuclear weapons; Nuclear weapons tests.
　　Cancellation of obsolete systems, **1962:** 549
　　Hydrogen bomb, **1962:** 179 [13]
　　New and improved, **1961:** 23, 99, 222; **1962:** 551 [13]; **1963:** 183, 221
　　Soviet, in Cuba.
　　　See Cuba.
　　Space, **1961:** 99
　　Strategic, **1961:** 25 [4]
　　Technicians, German, in Egypt, **1963:** 120 [10]

Weather Bureau, **1961:** 205; **1962:** 210 [15]; **1963:** 430

Weather prediction and control, **1961:** 11, 387; **1962:** 59 [1], 210 [15]; **1963:** 21 (p. 37), 144 [19]

Weather satellites, **1961:** 139 [21], 205; **1962:** 7 (p. 11), 96, 109, 210 [15], 373; **1963:** 21 (p. 34), 470, 477, 478

Weather Watch, World, **1963:** 430, 471

Weatherly (yacht), **1962:** 383; **1963:** 216n.

Weaver, George, **1961:** 36n.

Weaver, Robert C., **1961:** 31, 58, 70, 264, 371
　　See also Housing and Home Finance Agency, Administrator.

Weaver, Mrs. Robert C., **1961:** 31

Webb, James E., **1961:** 139 [21], 177, 178, 291 [13]
　　See also National Aeronautics and Space Administrator.

Weber, Sonya, **1961:** 496

Weber-Kraus survey on youth fitness, **1962:** 291

Webster, Daniel, **1961:** 418; **1962:** 109; **1963:** 334, 381, 474

Weinberg, Alvin M., **1963:** 67n.

Weinberg, Sidney J., **1962:** 476n.

Weinstein, Lewis H., **1963:** 49

Welfare Administration, **1963:** 64

Welfare and pension plans, **1963:** 119

Welfare and Pension Plans Disclosure Act, **1961:** 194; **1962:** 16 (p. 56), 75 [18], 107 [19]
　　Amendments, approval, **1962:** 101

Welfare personnel, training of, **1962:** 28

Welfare programs, **1962:** 7 (p. 8), 13 (p. 31), 229 [1]; **1963:** 21 (pp. 32, 37), 22, 51, 64, 74, 92, 230, 423
　　Approval of bill, **1962:** 306
　　Children, **1962:** 132
　　Family, **1963:** 64
　　Indians, **1963:** 86, 113
　　Mental health, **1963:** 50
　　Message to Congress, **1962:** 28
　　Negroes, **1963:** 135
　　Veterans, **1963:** 21 (p. 39)
　　Youth, **1963:** 12 (p. 13)

Wells, H. G., **1962:** 7 (p. 9)

Welsh, Gov. Matthew E., **1962:** 279 [14], 346n., 456

Wemyss, Scotland, **1963:** 297

Werhahn, Libeth, **1962:** 511

Werner, Pierre, **1963:** 152, 156

West Branch, Iowa, **1963:** 207

West Indies, British, **1961:** 36

West Irian.
　　See West New Guinea.

West New Guinea, **1961:** 119 [21]

West New Guinea, Dutch-Indonesian dispute, **1962:** 8 [3, 19], 139 [10], 210 [22], 251, 316 [3, 7], 323, 334, 340 [14], 346; **1963:** 12 (p. 18), 232

West Point, **1962:** 226, 234; **1963:** 223, 321, 335

West Virginia, **1962:** 77, 102, 328, 395, 410 [1], 414, 453; **1963:** 162, 175 [2], 228, 241, 249, 363, 378, 463
　　Centennial celebration, **1963:** 195, 249
　　Food distribution, **1961:** 15 [3], 17
　　Gov. William W. Barron, **1962:** 414; **1963:** 195, 249
　　Unemployment, **1961:** 83 [18]

Western Aerospace magazine, **1962:** 410 [8]

Western Airlines, **1961:** 50

Western Electric Company, **1961:** 281n.

Western Hemisphere, **1961:** 208; **1962:** 3, 7 (p. 10), 86, 117, 124, 126, 160, 189, 235, 242, 263–265, 269, 273, 303, 444, 492, 496, 532, 542–544, 556; **1963:** 14, 53, 73, 84, 97, 98, 99, 105, 106, 118, 134, 164, 168, 319, 323, 326, 331, 404, 412, 426, 429, 431, 462, 464, 471, 473
　　See also Latin America.

Western Hemisphere — *continued*
  Communism in, **1963:** 14, 65 [14], 71, 89 [10, 18], 107 [1, 7], 144 [8, 17], 328 [1], 333, 477
  Communist expansion in, **1961:** 19, 171 [14], 373, 376; **1962:** 50 [6], 77, 89 [9], 529
  Defense, **1963:** 89 [7], 100, 179
  Disease prevention, **1963:** 53
  Economic and Social Development, **1963:** 103, 107 [1, 7]
  Highways, **1963:** 164
  News conference remarks, **1961:** 171 [14], 318 [11]; **1962:** 50 [6], 89 [9], 279 [1, 10], 302 [10], 352 [21], 378 [1], 410 [3], 515 [1, 4]; **1963:** 65 [14], 89 [7], 107 [1, 7], 144 [8, 17], 328 [1], 459 [18]
  Nobel Prize winners, **1962:** 161
  Nuclear threat to, **1962:** 485, 486, 491
Westlands Water District, Calif., **1963:** 41
Westmoreland, Maj. Gen. William C., **1962:** 226
Westover Air Force Base, Mass., **1963:** 441
Wetzel, Walter, **1963:** 86
Wexford, Ireland, **1963:** 276, 297
Wexler, Harry, **1962:** 210 [15], 378 [17]
Weygandt, Judge Carl V., **1962:** 3n.
Wharton, Clifton R., **1961:** 358n
Wheat, **1961:** 15 [27], 85, 300, 316, 436; **1962:** 13 (p. 30), 22, 25, 89 [14], 340 [2], 410 [3], 413; **1963:** 21 (p. 35), 407, 426
  Exports, **1963:** 45, 89 [11], 202 [18]
  For overseas relief, **1963:** 45
  Marketing referendum, **1963:** 45, 169 [13], 189, 197, 201, 202 [2, 12, 15, 18]
  Prices, **1963:** 197, 202 [2, 12, 15]
  Soviet Union, sale to, **1963:** 107 [15], 405 [1, 15, 17], 407, 426, 448 [8, 12, 14], 459 [9, 19, 24], 465 [2]
  Surpluses, **1963:** 197
Wheeler, Gen. Earle G., **1962:** 423; **1963:** 312, 330
Wheeler, Mrs. George Y., **1961:** 2d, 209
Wheeling, W. Va., **1962:** 414
"Where We Stand," article, **1963:** 14
Whig Party, **1961:** 498
Whipple, Fred L., **1963:** 238
Whiskeytown Dam and Reservoir, **1963:** 389
White, Justice Byron R., **1961:** 496; **1963:** 392n.
  Appointment to Supreme Court, **1962:** 119
White, Charles M., **1961:** 33
White, E. B., **1963:** p. 902
White, E. R., **1962:** 298n.
White, Col. J. R., **1961:** 298
White, Lee C., **1961:** 278
White, O. D. L., **1961:** 66
White, Maj. Robert M., **1961:** 486n.; **1962:** 294
White, Gen. Thomas D., **1961:** 260; **1962:** 20 [2, 14], 422, 423
White, Tom, **1963:** 427
White House, **1963:** 195, 259n., 275, 300, 425
  Destruction (1814), **1962:** 70

White House — *continued*
  Guide book, **1962:** 262
  Picketing by suffragettes, World War I era, **1963:** 228
  Restored mantelpiece, dedication, **1962:** 274
  Trees, **1963:** 312, 322
White House Committee on Small Business, **1961:** 337
White House Conference of Business Editors and Publishers, **1962:** 410
White House Conference on Conservation, **1962:** 69, 216
White House Conference on Export Expansion, **1963:** 306, 361
White House Conference on Mental Retardation, **1963:** 364
White House Conference on Narcotic and Drug Abuse, **1962:** 218, 411
White House Conference on National Economic Issues, **1962:** 164, 203, 210 [13]
White House Correspondents Association, **1962:** 158
White House millionth visitor, **1961:** 328
White House News Photographers Association, **1961:** 119 [16]; **1962:** 158, 254
White House Regional Conference, **1961:** 454
White House releases, list, Appendix A, **1961:** p. 821; **1962:** p. 917; **1963:** p. 905
White House statements
  Assistance to lumber industry, **1962:** 307
  Congo, end of secession in, **1963:** 28
  Free access to Berlin, **1961:** 329
  Long-term development programs, **1961:** 333
  National Capital Region, redevelopment, **1962:** 525
  Nuclear weapons tests, **1961:** 349n.
    Soviet resumption, **1961:** 335, 340
  Puerto Rico, self-determination, **1963:** 198
  South Viet-Nam mission, **1963:** 399
  Soviet missile bases in Cuba, **1962:** 489, 491
White River, **1963:** 401
White Sands, N. Mex., **1963:** 222, 328 [19]
White Sands Missile Range, **1963:** 222
Whitman, Walt, **1962:** 527, 552; **1963:** 46
Whitney, John Hay, **1961:** 25 [14], 36n.; **1962:** 234
Whittaker, Justice Charles E., **1961:** 395
  Retirement, **1962:** 115 [1]
  115 [1]
Whittaker, James W., **1963:** 158n.
Whitton, Rex M., **1963:** 164
Wholesale Price Index, **1961:** 354
Whooping cough, eradication, **1962:** 65
Wichita, Kans. **1962:** 376
Wichita Falls, Kans., **1963:** 478
Widener Library, **1963:** 440
Widows of certain policemen and firemen, annuities, **1961:** 383
Wieland, William A., **1962:** 20 [15]; **1963:** 405 [13]

Wiesbaden, visit to, **1963:** 266a
Wiesner, Jerome B., **1961:** 15 [35], 145; **1962:** 404, 411, 546 [8], 547n.; **1963:** 29, 70, 252, 301, 430
Wiggins, J. R., **1961:** 397
Wiggins, Warren W., **1962:** 325n.
"Wild Geese," **1963:** 278
Wilde, Frazar B., **1963:** 351
Wilder, Thornton, **1963:** p. 902
Wilderness areas, preservation, **1962:** 7 (p. 7), 69, 216, 336, 337, 410 [7]
Wilderness bill, **1963:** 196
Wilderness protection, **1961:** 49
Wilderness Society, **1963:** 196
Wildlife conservation, **1961:** 49, 65, 100; **1962:** 25, 69, 128, 425; **1963:** 12 (p. 14), 21 (p. 36), 63, 209
Wildlife Federation, National, **1961:** 65; **1963:** 196
Wildlife Foundation, North American, **1963:** 196
Wildlife Management Institute, **1963:** 196
Wiley, Sen. Alexander, **1962:** 373
Wilkins, Fraser, **1962:** 227
Wilkinson, Charles B. (Bud), **1961:** 496; **1962:** 291; **1963:** 325
Williams, Basil, **1961:** 320
Williams, G. Mennen, **1961:** 62 [17]; **1962:** 433, 437
Williams, Sen. Harrison A., Jr., **1961:** 399, 448; **1962:** 450; **1963:** 173
Williams, Sen. John J., **1963:** 75 [7]
Williams, Judson, **1963:** 223n.
Williams, Walter, **1961:** 177
Williams, Walter C., **1962:** 223, 294
Williamsburg, Va., **1962:** 528n.
Williamson, Francis T., **1963:** 289
Willis, Repr. Edwin E., **1962:** 170
Willis, George H., **1961:** 123n.
Willkie, Wendell, **1963:** 455
Wilson, Repr. Bob, **1962:** 439, 481
Wilson, Edmund, **1963:** p. 902
Wilson, Harold, **1963:** 120 [19]
Wilson, Henry H., Jr., **1961:** 25 [12]
Wilson, James, **1963:** 226
Wilson, Woodrow, **1961:** 162, 209, 222, 232, 392, 399, 418, 448, 482, 498, 499; **1962:** 3, 7 (p. 9), 15, 77, 104n., 109, 186, 202, 203, 243 [1], 250, 252, 329, 346, 349, 439, 446, 452, 482, 483; **1963:** 2, 23, 43, 136, 159, 173, 192, 228, 232, 310, 319a, 427, 439, 467, 478
　Birthday, statement, **1961:** 520
　Typewriter owned by, presentation to White House, **1962:** 36
Wilson, Mrs. Woodrow, **1961:** 399, 482
Wilson, Woodrow, Foundation.
　See Woodrow Wilson Foundation.
Wilson, Woodrow, Memorial Commission.
　See Woodrow Wilson Memorial Commission.
Wingate Gray, Maj. W. M., **1963:** 457
Winston, Norman, **1962:** 548

Wirtz, W. Willard, **1962:** 253
　See also Labor, Secretary of.
Wisconsin, **1962:** 139 [16], 178, 186, 378 [19]; **1963:** 77, 248ftn. (p. 486), 356 [13], 378, 379, 390, 459 [23]
　First workmen's compensation law, **1961:** 339
　Gov. Gaylord Nelson, **1961:** 339; **1962:** 186
　Gov. John W. Reynolds, **1963:** 108, 377, 378, 392
Wisdom, Judge John Minor, **1962:** 420
Wise, Rabbi Isaac Mayer, **1961:** 463n.
Wolffer, William A., **1962:** 122n.
Woman's Day magazine, **1963:** 319a note
Women
　Aviation, **1963:** 315
　Congressional wives, remarks, **1963:** 157
　Democratic committeewomen, remarks, **1963:** 228
　Demonstrators for disarmament and peace, **1962:** 8 [20]
　Education, **1962:** 156
　Employment and training, **1963:** 92, 409
　Equal opportunity, **1962:** 43, 156, 304, 347; **1963:** 233, 409
　Equal rights, **1961:** 455 [19], 504
　In Government, **1962:** 156, 304
　In politics, **1963:** 157, 309
　Newspaper reporters, **1961:** 488 [5]
　Role in search for world peace, **1963:** 319a, 499
　Role in work force, **1961:** 166
　U.N. delegates, **1961:** 501; **1962:** 156
　Unemployment, **1963:** 110
　Working mothers, aid for, **1962:** 28; **1963:** 34, 233
Women, Commission on Equal Rights for, **1963:** 315
Women, Convention on Political Rights of, **1963:** 309
Women, President's Committee on Status of, **1961:** 504; **1962:** 43, 156, 304, 347, 505n.; **1963:** 233, 409
Women Voters, League of, **1962:** 156
Women's League for Peace, **1962:** 152 [15]
Women's National Press Club, **1962:** 158; **1963:** 448 [2]
Wood, Barry, **1961:** 496
Woodcock, Leonard, **1962:** 174, 298n., 476n.; **1963:** 206
Woodrow Wilson Foundation, **1961:** 520
Woodrow Wilson Memorial Commission, **1961:** 399
Woods, George, **1963:** 391
Woodward, Robert F., **1961:** 258 [17], 287, 466
Wool, **1963:** 75 [17], 459 [25]
Wool imports, **1962:** 8 [4]
Worcester, Mass., **1961:** 219; **1963:** 270
Work Hours Act of 1962, approval, **1962:** 327
Workmen's compensation, **1963:** 119
Workmen's compensation law, anniversary, **1961:** 339

[References are to items except as otherwise indicated]

Workweek, **1962:** 6n., 20 [19], 198 [15], 549; **1963:**
    12 (p. 11), 30 (p. 58), 34, 405 [5]
  Flight engineers, **1962:** 245 [1]
  Laborers and mechanics employed by Govern-
    ment, **1962:** 327
  Reduction, **1961:** 83 [12]; **1963:** 65 [4], 85, 162
  35-hour, proposed, **1963:** 75 [11], 77 [2]
World Bank.
  See International Bank for Reconstruction and
    Development.
World Council of Churches, **1961:** 35 [11]; **1962:** 68;
    1963: 136
World Court.
  See International Court of Justice.
World Food Bank, **1962:** 293
World Food Congress, **1962:** 478; **1963:** 33, 217,
    218
World Food Forum, **1962:** 197
World Food Program, **1962:** 319; **1963:** 471
World Health Organization, **1963:** 53, 366
World health program, **1961:** 27
World Meteorological Organization, **1962:** 96;
    1963: 430
World Refugee Year, **1961:** 297
World War I, **1961:** 212, 222, 419, 450n., 461; **1962:**
    70, 139 [16], 168, 398, 407, 440, 551 [15];
    1963: 2, 88, 227, 228, 351, 379, 416, 419,
    430, 457, 462, 468, 472, 476
  Seamen lost in, **1963:** 203
  Versailles Peace Conference, **1963:** 173
World War II, **1961:** 90, 212, 302, 373, 397, 419,
    429, 450n., 461, 512; **1962:** 25, 46, 70, 175,
    178, 226, 243, 284, 330, 384, 398, 402, 407,
    416, 461, 530, 537, 543, 551 [15], 552, 557;
    1963: 51, 52, 53, 57, 64, 72, 88, 92, 98, 100,
    110, 134, 154, 168, 178, 214, 221, 227, 228,
    232, 256, 257, 297, 325, 333, 335, 345, 349,
    351, 362, 379, 382, 384, 393, 395, 401, 416,
    420n., 423, 430, 457, 462, 465, 466, 472,
    475, 476
  Alien enemy property, distribution, **1963:** 89 [12]
  American Field Service, **1963:** 308
  Australians in, **1962:** 383
  Brazilians in, **1962:** 496
  Congressional Medal of Honor winners, **1963:**
    109
  Luxembourg in, **1963:** 105, 152
  News conference remarks, **1961:** 258 [2], 291 [1];
    1962: 139 [16], 302 [13]
  Philippine war damages, **1961:** 356
  Philippines war damage bill, **1962:** 191, 315
  President's service, **1961:** 483
  Red Cross Women's Motor Corps, France, **1963:**
    133
  Seaman lost in, **1963:** 203
  Soviet losses in, **1961:** 483; **1963:** 232
World's Fairs
  New York, **1961:** 407; **1962:** 548
  Seattle, **1961:** 474; **1962:** 155

World series, **1962:** 452
World Weather Watch, **1963:** 430, 471
World Youth Forum, remarks, **1963:** 90
Worthy, James, **1961:** 403
Wright, Repr. Jim, **1963:** 475, 476
Wyatt, Robert, **1963:** 469
    224
Wyatt, Wilson, **1962:** 431, 457, 458; **1963:** 212n.,
    224
Wyeth, Andrew, **1963:** p. 902
Wynne, Bedford S., **1963:** 24
Wyoming, **1963:** 248ftn. (p. 486), 380-383, 390;
  Gov. Cliff Hansen, **1963:** 381
  Jackson Hole, **1963:** 383, 387, 388, 390

X-15 rocket plane pilots, award, **1962:** 294

Yacht racing, U.S.-Australia competition, **1963:**
    216
Yachts, the President's, **1961:** 25 [10]
Yacimientos Petroliseros Fiscales Bolivianos, **1961:**
    184
Yale University, **1962:** 245 [2, 6], 473; **1963:** 175,
    325
  Commencement address, **1962:** 234
Yale University Law School, **1961:** 496
Yalta conference (1945), **1961:** 477, 483
Yaounde, Cameroun, **1961:** 107
Yarborough, Sen. Ralph, **1961:** 476n.; **1962:** 20
    [17], 179 [4], 378 [22], 409; **1963:** 223, 472,
    474, 475, 476, 478
Yarbrough, R. A., **1962:** 499n.
Yates, Sidney R., **1962:** 58n., 482, 483; **1963:** 359n.
Ydigoras, Miguel, **1963:** 99, 100, 102
Year 2000 Plan, National Capital Region, **1962:**
    525; **1963:** 208
Yeats, William Butler, **1963:** 278
Yeh, George K. C., **1961:** 306, 309
Yellow fever, eradication, **1963:** 53
Yellowstone National Park, **1963:** 383
Yemen, **1963:** 285, 334, 455, 471
  News conference remarks, **1963:** 120 [16], 448 [5],
    459 [13]
  U.S. Ambassador Parker T. Hart, **1963:** 120 [16]
Yosemite National Park, **1962:** 337
Yost, Charles W., **1961:** 358n.; **1963:** 359n.
Youlou, Fulbert, **1961:** 235, 236
Young, Brigham, **1963:** 385, 386
Young, Dr. Francis A., **1963:** 140n.
Young, Ralph A., **1961:** 123n.
Young, Sen. Stephen M., **1961:** 476n; **1962:** 3, 396,
    432, 480; **1963:** 35 [8]
Young, Whitney, **1962:** 257n.
Young American Medals, presentation, **1962:** 231
Young Australian League, **1963:** 216
Young Democrats, **1963:** 146, 356 [19]
Young Democrats Convention, **1961:** 498
Young Presidents' Conference, National, **1963:** 436
Young Republicans, **1963:** 356 [19]

Youngdahl, Luther W., **1961:** 234
Youth, **1962:** 16 (p. 47),; **1963:** 175, 320 [1]
    See also Children.
    "Boys Nation," **1963:** 312, 322
    Costa Rican Christian Democrats, **1963:** 104
    Delinquency, **1961:** 11, 15 [36], 182, 382; **1962:** 7
        (p. 7), 132, 220, 243 [4], 395; **1963:** 22, 30
        (p. 65), 43, 64, 74, 230, 248, 351, 363, 423
    District of Columbia, **1962:** 546 [24]; **1963:** 35
        [15], 305 [19]
    Education, **1963:** 12 (p. 13), 43, 64, 110
    Employment and training, **1961:** 233, 234, 470,
        477, 499; **1962:** 7 (p. 6), 13 (p. 31), 16 (p.
        56), 28, 89 [5], 174, 186, 201, 205, 220, 288,
        328, 336, 337, 360, 551 [10]; **1963:** 12 (p.
        13), 21 (pp. 32, 38), 30 (p. 71), 43, 50, 64,
        65 [1], 75 [14], 89 [1], 92, 120 [8], 130, 134,
        141, 142, 146, 162, 226, 228, 230, 248,
        336, 358, 363, 393, 458, 462
    Government, positions, **1963:** 171
    Income tax, reduction, **1963:** 34
    Labor Day message, **1962:** 360
    Mental fitness, **1963:** 393
    Message to Congress, **1963:** 64
    National CYO convention, **1963:** 463
    National High School Symphony Orchestra,
        1962: 322
    News conference remarks, **1962:** 89 [5], 229 [1],
        302 [4], 546 [24]
    Physical fitness, **1961:** 27, 48, 293, 348, 496; **1962:**
        37, 65, 132, 283, 291; **1963:** 64, 325, 393
    Preparation for war, question of, **1962:** 310 [3]
    School dropouts, **1963:** 10, 12 (p. 13), 43, 64, 65
        [1], 77, 85, 110, 142, 226, 230, 248, 305
        [19], 320 [1], 351, 358, 385, 387, 423, 445,
        448 [7], 455, 462, 463
    School Safety Patrol, awards, **1962:** 182
    Unemployment, **1963:** 64, 65 [1], 89 [1], 110, 141,
        142, 162, 248, 383, 423
    Wages, **1963:** 64
    Welfare programs, **1963:** 12 (p. 13)
    White House musical program, **1962:** 150; **1963:**
        137
Youth, Mobilization for, **1962:** 220
Youth Conservation Corps, **1961:** 233; **1963:** 64,
    113, 134, 339, 378

Youth Conservation Corps, proposed, **1962:** 69,
    336, 337
Youth Employment Act, **1963:** 92, 113, 185, 336,
    423
Youth Employment Opportunities Act, **1963:** 30 (p.
    71), 43, 75 [14], 89 [1], 110, 120 [8], 127,
    142
Youth Employment Opportunities Act, proposed,
    1961: 499; **1962:** 7 (p. 6), 16 (p. 56)
Youth Employment, President's Committee, **1961:**
    470; **1962:** 360; **1963:** 64, 92, 141, 142, 248,
    393
Youth Fitness, President's Council on, **1961:** 217,
    48n., 293, 348, 496; **1962:** 65, 283, 291;
    1963: 325
Youth Fitness Conference, **1961:** 48
Youth Forum, World, remarks, **1963:** 90
Youth Service Corps, proposed, **1963:** 107 [24]
YPFB.
    See Yacimientos Petroliseros Fiscales Boli-
        vianos.
Yugoslavia, **1961:** 222 [13]
    Ambassador Veljko Mićunović, **1963:** 421
    Assistance, **1962:** 3, 75 [4], 77, 229 [3], 245 [9],
        302 [10]; **1963:** 35 [5], 420n.
    Earthquake, U.S. relief, **1963:** 421
    Exports to U.S., **1963:** 118
    Marshal Josip Broz Tito, **1963:** 328 [8], 349, 419,
        420, 421
    Trade with U.S., **1963:** 35 [5], 421
    U.S. Ambassador George F. Kennan, **1962:** 245
        [9], 551 [15]

Zablocki, Repr. Clement J., **1962:** 186
Zain, Zairin, **1961:** 146
Zanzibar, **1963:** 77
Zenger, Peter, **1963:** 259
Zinn, Georg August, **1963:** 265, 266, 266a
Zollverein, **1963:** 266
Zoning laws, **1963:** 248
Zorin, Valerian, **1961:** 408, 483; **1962:** 134
Zuckert, Eugene M. (Secretary of the Air Force),
    1962: 172, 294, 309, 398
    See also Air Force, Secretary of the.

ue